Inside/Out

Contemporary
Critical Perspectives
in Education

Inside/Out

Contemporary
Critical Perspectives
in Education

Rebecca A. Martusewicz
Eastern Michigan University

William M. Reynolds
Oklahoma State University

Editors

St. Martin's Press, New York

Editor: Naomi Silverman
Manager, publishing services: Emily Berleth
Publishing services associate: Kalea Chapman
Project management: Omega Publishing Services, Inc.
Art director: Sheree Goodman
Text design: Gene Crofts
Cover design: Marek Antoniak

For information, write:
St. Martin's Press, Inc.
175 Fifth Avenue
New York, NY 10010

ISBN: 0-312-08067-0

Acknowledgments
Acknowledgments and copyrights are continued at the back of the book on page 294, which constitutes an extension of the copyright page.

It is a violation of the law to reproduce these selections by any means whatsoever without the written permission of the copyright holder.

Angeline Martel and Linda Peterat, "Margins of Exclusion, Margins of Transformation: The Place of Women in Education." An adaptation of Angeline Martel and Linda Peterat, "A Hope for Hopelessness: Womanness at the Margin in Schools," from the *Journal of Curriculum Theorizing*, 8(1), 103–135, 1988. Reprinted with permission of *Journal of Curriculum Theorizing*.

"I CAN'T DANCE" (Tony Banks, Phil Collins, Mike Rutherford) © 1991 ANTHONY BANKS LTD. (PRS)/PHILIP COLLINS LTD. (PRS)/MIKE RUTHERFORD LTD. (PRS)/HIT & RUN MUSIC (PUBLISHING) LTD. (PRS) All rights administered by HIT & RUN MUSIC PUBLISHING, INC. (ASCAP) in the United States and Canada. All Rights Reserved. Used By Permission.

"WORKING CLASS HERO," Words and Music by JOHN LENNON © Copyright 1970 by YOKO ONO, SEAN LENNON and JULIAN LENNON. All Rights Controlled and Administered by MCA Music Publishing, A Division of MCA Inc., New York, NY 10019. Under License of ATV Music. USED BY PERMISSION. ALL RIGHTS RESERVED.

"SUBTERRANEAN HOMESICK BLUES," Words and Music by Bob Dylan © 1965 by Warner Brothers Inc., Copyright renewed 1993 by Special Rider Music. Reprinted with permission of Special Rider Music.

p r e f a c e
//

This book is a collection of essays chosen as representative of contemporary critical perspectives on education. The word "critical" indicates the editors' and contributing authors' commitment to a process of questioning and problematizing all aspects of educational relations and practices as a way to create better ways of living in the world. Readers are encouraged to look at education from the "inside" (the complex processes, relations, and methods that operate within schools) and from the "outside" (the larger social, political, economic, and historical forces that influence what goes on in schools). As such, this book is organized to encourage as much questioning, interaction, thinking, and decision making as possible from its readers.

The Introduction to the book indicates our basic philosophy that any organizational structure is necessarily imposed, and as most of these essays are interdisciplinary in nature, they do not fit easily into any traditional or even topical organizational frame. Hence, rather than place them in a limited and limiting schema, we decided simply to arrange them alphabetically by the author's last name. The introductory essay explains the major contemporary critical perspectives in education (critical theory, reproductive theory, resistance theory, critical pedagogy, multiculturalism, phenomenology, post-structuralism, and feminist theory) and invites the reader to use these theories as "lenses" through which to view and respond to the ideas in the essays that follow. To aid users in topical selection and course coordination, we have included a chart (at the end of this preface, p. vii) of what topics, theoretical perspectives, and discipline areas each essay addresses.

Prefacing each essay are general Guiding Questions. We hope the reader will use these questions as tools for thinking through the ideas and questions that each essay presents, especially as they affect the readers' own experiences in classrooms. With each chapter, Glossary Notes appear at the bottom of the page on which the term defined is first used. At the end of each essay are specific Questions for Discussion, which may be used for classroom dialogue or outside class assignments. In addition to these sets of questions, the authors provide suggestions for further research into some aspect of the problematics their essays address. These sections are entitled Teachers as Researchers. *Inside/ Out* concludes with an Epilogue in the form of a dialogue between the editors of this text, discussing the meaning and the implications for practice of the contemporary critical perspectives explored in this book.

We believe the organization of this anthology will allow flexibility in use and diversity of perspective for both the teachers and students reading it. We are committed to the tension between necessary structure and flux of boundaries. There is no one critical perspective, only interdisciplinary problematics, infinite questions, and nomadic searches for different and better ways of educating ourselves and our children.

Acknowledgments

Putting this book together has been an adventure in friendship. We have called on old friends, made new friends, and nurtured the friendship that we, the editors, have shared during these past ten years. These friendships have made it possible to put together a book that we believe expresses our commitment to teaching for a better world. As such, there are many who deserve special acknowledgment for their efforts.

Together we would like to thank first Kathleen Keller for getting us started and staying excited about the project. We also thank the reviewers for St. Martin's Press who read the manuscript at various points during its development and provided us with many excellent suggestions: William Armaline, University of Toledo; Alden Carlson, State University of New York, State University College at Cortland; Kathleen Bennett deMarrais, University of Tennessee, Knoxville; Lloyd Duck, George Mason University; Maxine Greene, Teachers College; Lawrence Klein, Central Connecticut State University; David Labaree, Michigan State University; John Laska, University of Texas, Austin; Susan Martin, Indiana State University; Carolyn Panofsky, Rhode Island College; and Jeanne Pietig, Eastern Michigan University.

Rebecca would like to thank the following students for reading particular essays, offering excellent editorial advice and generally keeping me sane throughout the process of putting this book together: Noreen Hanlon, Ben McMurray, Barbara Tarockoff, Julie Walsh, and Jill Watson. Thanks also to Maureen Mc-Cormack and Carol Baier for their help getting loose ends tied up when time was running out.

Bill would like to express appreciation to Kathryn Castle, Russell Dobson, and Carolyn Bauer for their continual support and advice. Thanks also to Mark Bernu and Stacy Sawyer for their efforts transcribing, typing, and reviewing pieces of this manuscript.

Finally, we extend our gratitude to the contributing authors and to our editor, Naomi Silverman, whose commitment to critical inquiry in education made this project possible. Thank you.

	Philosophical Analysis	Socio-Cultural Analysis	Historical Analysis	Gender Analysis	Post-Structural Analysis	Phenome-nological Analysis	Reproduction Theory	Resistance Theory	Multicultural Theory	Curriculum Concerns	School Reform Concerns	Professional Development Concerns
Chapter 1 Introduction: Turning the Study of Education Inside/Out	X	X	X	X	X	X	X	X	X	X		
Chapter 2 Deconstruction and Nothingness: Some Cross-Cultural Lessons on Teaching Comparative World Civilization	X		X		X					X		
Chapter 3 Antiracist Pedagogy in a College Classroom: Mutual Recognition and a Logic of Paradox				X	X			X	X	X		
Chapter 4 Marxism and Education	X	X					X			X		
Chapter 5 School Routines and the Failure of Curriculum Reform		X					X	X		X	X	X
Chapter 6 Representation, Self-Representation, and the Meanings of Difference: Questions for Educators		X		X	X				X	X		
Chapter 7 Enticing Challenges: An Introduction to Foucault and Educational Discourses	X	X			X					X		
Chapter 8 From the Margin to the Center: Teachers' Emerging Voices through Inquiry						X			X	X		X

	Philosophical Analysis	Socio-Cultural Analysis	Historical Analysis	Gender Analysis	Post-Structural Analysis	Phenome-nological Analysis	Reproduction Theory	Resistance Theory	Multicultural Theory	Curriculum Concerns	School Reform Concerns	Professional Development Concerns
Chapter 9 The Social Construction of "The Problem of Teenage Pregnancy"		X		X	X					X		
Chapter 10 Margins of Exclusion, Margins of Transformation: The Place of Women in Education	X	X		X		X				X		
Chapter 11 Guardians of Childhood		X	X	X	X							
Chapter 12 Margaret A. Haley, 1861–1939: A Timeless Mentor for Teachers as Leaders			X	X							X	X
Chapter 13 Solitary Spaces: Women, Teaching, and Curriculum	X			X		X				X		
Chapter 14 Curriculum as Making Do		X					X	X		X		
Chapter 15 The Practice of Freedom: A Historical Analysis of Critical Perspectives in the Social Foundations		X	X	X						X		
Chapter 16 Resisting Racial Awareness: How Teachers Understand the Social Order from Their Racial, Gender, and Social Class Locations	X	X		X			X	X	X	X		X
Chapter 17 The Foundations of Social Education in Historical Context		X	X						X	X	X	

contents

//

Inside/Out

Contemporary
Critical Perspectives
in Education

Introduction

Turning the Study of Education Inside/Out

Rebecca A. Martusewicz &
William M. Reynolds

In her journal for a social aspects of teaching class, a student wrote that she felt she had been "turned inside out" by the reading she had been doing (several of the essays she read are included in this book). The phrase she used—"inside out"—strikes us as a particularly apt way of describing the kind of learning we envision taking place in our classes in curriculum and social foundations of education. "Inside/out" generally means that an inside surface has been turned to the outside: Things are no longer seen "as they usually are"; that some other aspect or new way of looking is brought to our attention; what was once the boundary, frontier, or surface is gone, replaced by another. In this book, subtitled "Contemporary Critical Perspectives in Education," we introduce students of education to perspectives that indeed turn our "normal" understandings of schooling, curriculum, pedagogy, students, and teachers thoroughly inside/out.

The authors contributing to this book have things to say about our field and about our work that shift, challenge, even shake up our everyday, commonsense understandings about what goes on in the lives of students and teachers. These authors are part of what could be referred to as a "critical educational community." This community is made up of teachers, teacher educators, educational scholars, curriculum theorists, administrators, and students who, though they may take different theoretical and/or methodological tacks, are generally interested in education as a means toward social and personal transformation. They are interested in finding ways, through education, of making the world a more just, equitable place to live. They believe that freedom is a matter of constant action on and thought about the complex social, political, and ideological processes that weave together in our day-to-day lives. Freedom is a matter of a certain caring about ourselves and for the world, a caring that entails a willingness to change our beliefs and our practices, to shift the boundaries of our thought through education in order to alleviate the suffering of others. In this sense, education is critical and ethical. It means asking tough, often disruptive questions, and changing the way we live our lives.

Indeed, this is the job of social foundations of education as a general area of study within education: to raise questions and offer points of view that ask us to see what we do as teachers or as students in new or at least unfamiliar ways, from another side, perhaps from the inside, or perhaps from both inside and outside. It is an invitation to look at education both socially and historically as well as practically, that is, from the inside (the complex processes, methods, and relations that affect individuals in schools, for example) within the context of the outside (the larger social, economic, and political forces that have affected those processes over time).

It is also an invitation to imagine that there is no solid boundary between this inside and outside, or perhaps better, no fixed boundary, nothing to dictate or guarantee an outcome, or to ensure that we will know precisely what to do in our classrooms. This is an uncomfortable place to be, especially for those just beginning to learn to teach, but difficult as well for those of us who are veterans. Our visions and versions of what is inside and what is outside of what we do are in constant flux, shifting with political tides, with economic conditions, and with our own personal interpretations or readings of what matters. And yet, we do frame what we do with our words, our metaphors. We use expressions of all kinds to create meaning. We explain, discuss, interpret, argue, plead, read, write.

In short, as teachers and as students, we are constantly engaged in making sense of what we do, how we live, and what matters. And we do this within a larger cultural system made up of institutions (families, media, schools, churches, government) and woven through with discourses (daily conversations, practices, policies, sense making, knowledges) that help to form certain (though unstable) boundaries on what is possible to say, think, teach, live, and so on. We have a culture, a society, an educational "system" precisely and only because we use discourse to make distinctions, to put boundaries around certain activities in our lives. We could say that these organizing practices, discourses, and institutions help us to decide or create what is inside and what is outside, what is true and what is false, what exists and what does not exist, what is good and what is bad, and on and on. There are boundaries, but only to the extent that we have created them as such, through our conversations, our arguments, our metaphors, our struggles, and thus to the extent that they are always in question, they are always subject to change. Thus, the inside can quickly become the outside and vice versa because there is no essential foundation that exists outside our attempts to name the world, to read and to write about it, to define it.

Turning the "Foundations" Inside/Out
//

This book takes seriously this flux of boundaries, this INSIDE/OUT. Contrary to the way most texts in the social foundations of education are organized, this book questions the notion of "foundations" as a stable set of knowledges, concepts, or principles to be discovered, defined, and then presented in a unilinear way. It questions that there is one way of organizing our understanding of what happens in education or in the world, while paying particular attention to perspectives that maintain a critical stance, a willingness to put existing assumptions and interpretations into question. As contributor Edward Berggren writes in this volume, "there are indefinitely many possible worlds. . . . Whichever world we choose, it becomes in turn subject to indefinitely many possible interpretations because we can always create another interpretation of that world, in addition to the ones in play now. In any case, our interpretations hinge upon metaphors, rules, initial enframing assumptions and countless other choices. . . ."

INSIDE/OUT: We use a slash in Inside/Out to indicate this necessary though unstable boundary between what gets included and excluded in our visions and versions of education and cultural definitions of all kinds.

The most traditional way of organizing knowledge in the social foundations follows a familiar liberal arts scheme found in most universities. Thus we have philosophy of education, history of education, sociology of education, and so forth. And in each of these areas of study specific questions and methods are used to guide the study of education. These disciplines, with their attending theories and methods, are commonly seen as the fundamental knowledge bases, while education, always seen as a secondary area of study, becomes their object, or even their servant. This is indicative of a specific POLITICS OF KNOWLEDGE whereby certain areas of study are bestowed with more value than others within university settings and other institutions, as well as by the public more generally. Such a politics functions to maintain particular categorical boundaries that are manifested institutionally in departments and colleges and that are given more or less resources, respect, and power depending on their position on the "knowledge hierarchy." The traditional disciplines have historically functioned as "border guards," protecting their territory and thus keeping in place a certain order and hierarchy of power.

We want to reemphasize that the boundaries between these disciplines are not simply a matter of a natural order of knowledge. Rather, the drawing of boundaries around what is to be included and excluded, inside and outside our interpretations and explanations, is always a matter of politics, human struggle, and human decision making. Thus, such disciplines as history, philosophy, sociology, economics, and anthropology are constructions that serve particular functions and particular interests, and should be treated as such. While we may use or even depend on them to give shape to our world, we need not leave their assumptions unquestioned.

Most traditional foundations texts present an organizational scheme that reflects this ordering of the world according to separate disciplines; traditional "bodies of knowledge" that claim to "ground" or anchor the field to essential metaphysical principles, historical events, or social functions. In this way, these disciplines determine the questions that might be asked of our experience and practice. We prefer to see and present knowledge of the social "foundations" of education as constructed discursively and thus multidimensionally, framed only by the limits on our ability to ask questions, to read and write, to think, and to imagine possible frameworks. We prefer to take seriously that any understanding of education is always a matter of the questions that get asked of it and the metaphors used to frame it. The authors contributing to this text push at the boundaries offered by the traditional disciplines to ask questions that often deconstruct those distinctions holding together certain privileged knowledges. Given our historically MARGINALIZED position as educators and,

POLITICS OF KNOWLEDGE: Sociologists of knowledge introduced this term to indicate that knowledge—the processes and practices and organization of meaning that we use to make sense of the world—is never neutral. Rather, it is a result of struggle and conflict over diverse interests. Knowledge gets produced in the context of shifting struggles for control over meaning.

MARGINALIZED: To be marginalized means that one is not in the mainstream or that one is excluded from the center of power. The term is used here to describe the position that education as a field of study and as a practice has held in the politics of knowledge and university life.

moreover, as members of a critical community, it is not surprising that challenges to such ordering would come from the contributors to this book. As editors, we have decided to honor those challenges.

Organization of This Book

We came to this understanding of our text after a long struggle over just how to organize it. We started this project with the intention to organize the book along traditional lines. The essays, however, refused to stay in any category. If we did find a place within this traditional organizational scheme for a particular essay, it would soon slip across the border into another place, turning such boundaries inside/out.

As you will notice, the authors represented in this book draw on material from across disciplinary, methodological, and theoretical boundaries to make their analyses. Their work is clearly part of what Clifford Geertz (1973) called a "blurring of genres" in the social sciences. Shoving them into one category or another finally seemed completely contrived and, frankly, quite counter to our own ways of thinking about knowledge and about education. This does not mean that there is no way to make sense of the work being done in the critical study of education. Rather, it means that we are committed to presenting this material in a way that does not try to put it in any boxes. The thinking/writing simply refuses to stay put.

The plural form *perspectives* in our subtitle for this book is important. Against current accusations waged against those who would challenge traditional notions of knowledge, society, or education, this book emphasizes a variety of critical views of the relation and conceptualization of education and social life.

While the essays are presented in alphabetical order according to the author's last name, there are several major theoretical perspectives that have influenced and given shape to the work represented in them. Far from pressing for a "politically correct" position, this book emphasizes multiple readings from a wide range of theoretical positions: critical theory, phenomenology, post-structuralism, feminist theories, and the intersection of many of these theoretical positions. To help the reader get a sense of this broad field we offer here the theoretical landscape cultivated by these thinkers. What follows is a summary of these perspectives and the questions that they address.

The Theoretical Landscape

A theory is a worldview, a way of looking at and explaining a set of phenomena. In this section we will introduce you to the main theories and perspectives that have shaped the work done by critical scholars and teachers of education in the last twenty years. Again, as you read the essays you will see boundary crossing, as many of these scholars draw on two or more of these broad theoretical categories to make their analyses. We offer you here a broad overview of these theoretical perspectives in the hope that it will give you some context within which to understand the work represented in this book. Throughout the text, you will notice questions that ask you to think about this context and to try to trace the theoretical threads woven together by each of the authors. We hope that you will become proficient in recognizing these points of view and even in using some of them as tools to help you ask your own questions and shape your own educational practice.

Critical Theory

One broad perspective that has had a major influence, perhaps *the* major influence on the critical educational community, is referred to as critical theory. Several of the more specific theories discussed below, reproduction theory, resistance theory and critical pedagogy, for example, can be seen as branches of this broader theoretical category. And though there are major disagreements, it is probably safe to argue that the others have been influenced by the general principles held by critical theorists.

Critical theorists are generally concerned with issues of social justice and believe that many of the institutions and structures that organize our lives, especially our economic system, the STATE and its institutions, operate to keep in place fundamentally unequal and unjust social and political relations. As such, critical theorists believe that democratic struggle is necessary to the historical accomplishment of social and economic justice. People ought to have the right to determine through democratic processes the quality of their day-to-day lives. This can only happen if we become aware of the ways in which our lives are exploited by the economic and political system in which we work and live. According to critical theorists, collective struggle is the key to overcoming oppressive conditions and relations, and education is the key to collective empowerment. As Joel Spring points out, this "simply means giving students the knowledge and skills they need to struggle for a continued expansion of political, economic, and social rights. Of utmost importance is making students aware that they have power to affect the course of history and that history is the struggle for human rights" (Spring, 1991, p. 30).

Thus, critical theorists are interested in the processes and practices, policies and structures on both the micro level of everyday life in schools and the macro level of our economic, political, and social system. They analyze the ways that inequality and oppression are created at the intersection of these macro and micro relations, within institutions such as schools. They begin from a willingness to question our taken-for-granted assumptions about our government and therefore our schools' ability to guarantee equality of opportunity. They

---

STATE: By "state" we mean local, state, and federal governments as they operate to produce policies and frame our daily lives legally.

ask that students become active participants in ask⸍
all the aspects of their lives in order to become
makers.

8

Reproduction Theory

One effort to use critical theory in the study of educ.
corresponding unequal and stratified social relations foun.
and the larger society. This perspective has been referred to as ι.
theory. Drawing on Marx's concepts of base and superstructure (see ᴅ.
essay in this volume), Bowles and Gintis argued in *Schooling in Capitalisι
America* (1976) that schools prepare students to enter the current economic
system via a correspondence between school structure and the structure of
production in the larger economic sphere. In other words, the schools comply
in relations of domination, assisting those in power to maintain the status quo.

> The structure of social relations in education not only inures the student
> to the question of the discipline of the workplace, but develops the types
> of personal demeanor, modes of self-presentation, self image, and social
> class identifications which are the crucial ingredients of job adequacy.
> Specifically, the social relationships of education—the relationships be-
> tween administrators and teachers, teachers and students, and students
> and students, and students and their work—replicate the hierarchical
> division of labor (Bowles & Gintis, p. 131).

Relying on this concept of correspondence, Apple (1979) and Giroux (1981)
argued that schools function to reproduce the class structure of the workplace.
Simply put, the concept of reproduction states that the schools serve to maintain (through both the overt and hidden curriculum, school structure, and
its emphasis on control) the current economic system and the perpetuation
of uneven social class divisions. For example, working-class students receive
an education that would assure that they remain working class and, likewise,
upper-class students receive an education that would assure their position of
privilege in the social hierarchy.

Reproduction theory challenged traditional views of schooling by raising
questions about whose interests were actually being served by these institutions, often taken for granted as guarantors of equal opportunity. Still, this theory is not without its shortcomings. Reproduction theory has been criticized
for being overly deterministic. It allows for no sense of agency amongst human
beings. Taken alone, it views people as if they were incapable of directing their
destiny. It treats them instead as robots on the stage called life, robots pro-
grammed to simply carry out the desires of those in power. In this sense, reproduction theory functions as a "discourse of despair" (Giroux, 1988).

Not long after Bowles and Gintis published their ground-breaking book,
critical theorists of education began to ask tough questions about the actual
lives of those in schools. Even Bowles and Gintis themselves said that their

nal notion of correspondence left little room for the notion of contesta-
n. The idea that the processes of reproduction could be resisted came to the
re as a new critical perspective on life in schools.

Resistance Theory

In his widely read *Learning to Labour: How Working Class Kids Get Working
Class Jobs,* Paul Willis (1977) demonstrated the importance of the concept
of resistance for a more complete understanding of the contradictions and
complexities of the relationship between schools and broader social and economic structures. Willis observed that working-class boys he studied resisted
both the official and the hidden curriculum of their English secondary school.
The roots of resistance, he wrote, "are in the shopfloor cultures occupied by
their family members and other members of their class" (p. 45). Willis's concept of resistance demonstrated that the process of reproduction was contest-
able, thereby correcting the determinism of reproduction theory.

What is resistance? How does it operate? Let's take one example. We are
sure that you can think of many more from your own experience of being in
school. Take a college-bound class, the "smart kids." These are the students
who know how to "play the game" in education—and they know it is a game.
They know all the rules, and they play by the rules. They know how to get an
"A," the equivalent of the paycheck in school. They know how to please the
teachers and administrators. They usually win the game. Do most of these
students buy into the game? Not for a minute. Their resistance to the game is
to form their own subculture of importance. This subculture might center on
rock and roll music or athletics, for example. But, their resistance allows them
to be successful at the game and to "get ahead," to maintain their position in
the social hierarchy and receive the privileges that come with it.

On the other hand, working-class students' resistance appears more overt.
They too may recognize the game, but they either refuse to play or attempt to
disrupt or defy it. Their resistance manifests itself as open resistance to classroom work and open oppositional behavior to school rules and procedures.
The irony of this resistance is that it assures their place in the social structure.

For example, in the case of Willis's young men, their rejection of mental labor and other expectations of the school hearkens back to the manual labor of
their fathers. Rather than leading to any real critique of the unequal hierarchy
in the school or larger society, the boys' contesting of the school expectations
leads to a contradictory reproduction of the status quo. Thus, the question was
raised about lived outcomes of resistant behaviors for students of different
class backgrounds.

Resistance theory remains a very popular concept within the political analysis of education. Indeed, since 1985 it has been used as a point of departure
in the analysis of the day-to-day experiences of teachers and students in schools.
How do both teachers and students resist the oppressive structures, policies,
and practices in schools, and what are the outcomes of those daily contests? It
has been a short leap from questions such as these to questions concerning the

development of alternative forms of pedagogical practice that could emancipate teachers and students, leading to a transformation of these social and educational structures. Thus, the discussion of radical or critical pedagogy gained in popularity and importance in the critical educational community.

Critical Pedagogy

Henry Giroux, relying on the earlier work of Paulo Freire and his text, *Pedagogy of the Oppressed* (1971), called for the development of critical pedagogy. "At the core of radical pedagogy," insists Giroux, "must be the aim of empowering people to work for change in the social, political, and economic structure that constitutes the ultimate source of class-based power and domination (Giroux in Olson, 1981, p. 24).

Critical pedagogy continues to be a primary point of departure for those involved in critical perspectives on teaching. What is critical pedagogy? How is it different from current educational practice? Critical pedagogy emphasizes a different relationship between students and teachers. Freire calls the major type of pedagogy in existence, "banking education" (Freire, 1971). Students are considered to be empty banks and the teacher's job is to fill those empty banks with as many deposits of knowledge as possible. The main goal of teaching in this system is transmission. The information and authority flows in one direction. The teacher, as the source of knowledge, teaches and the students listen, passively. Learning is a process of consumption. This pedagogical process, of course, helps to reproduce a social and economic system that requires consumption and adherence to authority to exist.

In contrast to this emphasis on transmission, critical pedagogy emphasizes transformation. The goal of critical pedagogy is the transformation of the self and the society. The role of teachers is transformed from "clerk of the empire" (McLaren, 1989) to "teachers as intellectuals" (Giroux, 1988). Teachers and students engage in inquiry together and produce knowledge rather than consume knowledge. "Critical pedagogy asks how and why knowledge gets constructed the way it does, and how and why some constructions of reality are legitimated and celebrated by the dominant culture and others are not" (McLaren, 1989, p. 169).

Multiculturalism

In the area of pedagogy, the necessity of including notions of race and diversity has manifested itself in the form known as multiculturalism, or multicultural education. Christine Sleeter, in an article entitled "What is Multicultural Education?" (1992) discusses the various approaches teachers ascribe to when taking into account notions of diversity. She elaborates five approaches to multicultural education. They are: 1) teaching the exceptional and culturally different, 2) human relations, 3) single group studies, 4) multicultural education, and 5) education that is multicultural and social reconstructionist (p. 5). The last approach is the orientation that most critical scholars would take toward multicultural education. This approach begins by discussing "contemporary justice issues that cut across diverse groups, using disciplinary knowledge to examine them and create ways of affecting change" (p. 7). As with critical theory more generally, the ultimate goal of this approach is to have students learn to take action on social issues, specifically those that have to do with issues of diversity. In her article in this volume, Sleeter discusses how teachers' specific attitudes about and awareness of issues of race and diversity can affect whether or not students are encouraged to engage with this kind of learning.

Many critical scholars and teachers of education question the basic assumptions traditionally associated with multicultural education. Cameron McCarthy (1990), for example, argues that the various approaches taken to the relationship between race and education too often do not "offer viable explanations or solutions to the problem of racial inequality in schooling" (p. 56). Most approaches view problems of racial and class inequality as the result of individual inadequacies due either to genetic deficiencies or "cultural deprivation." In these conservative and fundamentally racist points of view, the problem leading to differences in academic or economic achievement (which generally fall along both racial and class lines) is located firmly in the genes, or families of individual students. Approaches to the study of multiculturalism and education therefore too often remain at the level of individual human relations, in attempts to use schools to reverse these "inferior" cultural values and attitudes.

Schools are not seen in these approaches to inequality as sites of "differential power relations and structural inequality" (McCarthy, p. 56). To understand these relations, the larger social context must be taken into account. In this way, McCarthy's approach takes seriously the contributions to the study of schooling and inequality made by reproduction theory. McCarthy critiques multicultural education as it has been organized and practiced as a "direct consequence of the efforts of the state to redirect minority challenges to the persistence of racial inequality in American schools" (p. 38). In other words, what gets practiced in schools under the rubric of multiculturalism is a result of political struggle between the state and racial groups, whereby the state has managed to regulate and control the interests of those groups through school policy, curriculum, and pedagogical practice.

Most scholars in the critical educational community would agree that multiculturalism is not limited to notions of race. Current discussion of multiculturalism includes interest in issues of race, class, gender, and sexuality; the broad and intersecting spectrum of diversity as it weaves together to shape the lives of real people. We believe these issues will concern all educators as the decade continues.

Phenomenology

While the primary focus of critical theories of education is on the transformation of oppressive social and economic structures through education, other critical scholars focus on the individual experience of those dehumanizing processes. These scholars take a view that the processes of schooling can lead us away from ourselves. In "Sanity, Madness, and the School" (1976), William Pinar indicates that schooling, organized according to "the banking system," has grave psychological effects, and can even destroy the self.

Phenomenology has been used in various ways by various scholars to investigate the "lived experience" in schools. Phenomenologists begin their project with questioning how phenomena—"the things themselves"—present themselves. Consciousness becomes a major category for the phenomenologist.

Beyond a simple expression of "introspection," Maxine Greene explains that consciousness refers to an "experienced context" or "life world." The phenomenologist postulates his or her life world as central to all that he or she does—research or teaching—and, as a consequence, focuses upon the biographic situation of each individual, as opposed to the more social, structural focus of critical theory.

Ordinarily the individual is unaware of his or her life world; he or she is immersed in it. He or she is said to take the natural attitude of "taking for granted the reality and legitimacy of daily practical life" (Greene, 1973). As Greene observes: "Ordinary ways of perceiving have to be suspended: questions have to be posed. The individual has to be jolted into awareness of his own perception into recognition of the way in which he has constituted his own life world" (Greene, 1973, p. 21).

One approach to this study of the way our lives have been constituted is through autobiography. William Pinar and Madeline Grumet in *Toward a Poor Curriculum* (1976) discuss the notion that autobiography helps us to disclose that lived world suspending our ordinary ways of perceiving.

> We make use of autobiographical reflection, theater (Grotowski's), and hatha yoga to penetrate our public masks, the masks which keep us dissociated from our experience. With penetration comes the freedom to comprehend the nature of our involvement in the academic discourses, and with their teaching and learning (Pinar & Grumet, 1976, p. vii).

Autobiography is thus a way of practicing the phenomenological search for "the things themselves" as they come to affect individual experience. And education is a metaphor for the dialogue a person has with the world of that experience. The autobiographical method explores this dialogue as a means toward individual human freedom.

Post-structuralism

Post-structuralism begins from the argument that "things in themselves" can never finally be known, because anything we attempt to "know" must be expressed through language or some other symbolic form. That is, "the world," "the self," "experience," "knowledge," "pedagogy," all these are words, metaphors, or signs that we create to try to say something about the world, and as such they are always already distanced from and different from the world. Moreover, they *create* what can be known, experienced, and learned as we create and use them. That is, these words do not emanate from the objects that they represent; rather they mediate between the object and our understanding of it, and indeed in relation to other words, create our understanding.

In this view, all experience must be understood as filtered, and thus meaningful only through the "symbolic order"—the systematic organization of language, signs, and thus culture. Culture, and even the self or subject—the "I"—is a text, a complex interweaving of metaphor, signs, interpretations, and practices that operate to create our everyday understandings of our lives and the world around us. Nothing may be known of experience before or outside of text or language, because it is language and text that mediate between the world and our knowledge of it. Thus, the search for the origin (of what it finally means to be human, what experience is, and how we came to *be*) is ultimately caught in the paradox of re-presentation.

Because of our capture in a symbolic system, there is always, in the words of Jacques Derrida (1974), an "originary differance" at play in the process of knowing. This "originary difference" is expressed in the concept "differance," which Derrida creates from the French verb *differer,* meaning both to differ and to defer. With this deliberately ambiguous term, Derrida strives to undermine the notion that meaning, knowledge, and therefore the self are stable, predictable entities. Rather, meaning is made of the infinite play or relation between signs. Meaning is never immediately present in a sign or text, but is always made via what the sign is *not,* or via what is *not* in the text. One way to understand this is through our conception of time. We say we live in the present, but the present never really exists except in its relation to the past and the future. As soon as we say "present," it is already gone, slipping away into the past or forever in the future. The same can be said for the "self." The self is never immediately present to us, because we are always caught in the movement of time and representation; the self is never the same, never present to itself moment to moment. And this precisely because we only have language through which to try to imagine what "self" or "time" or even "education" might mean. As soon as a statement is made, there is always something else to be said, another metaphor, another question, another answer to supplement the last indefinitely. Thought and thus education operates in an endless, indefinite, supplementary process.

Thus a text (which could be a classroom, a movie, a book, anything in which meaning is created, expressed, and read) is not simply the object created from the intentions of an author (or a teacher), but includes those excluded or excess meanings manifested in our reading or listening. Each time we read, we are also in the process of writing, creating the text. There are never stable boundaries between this reading and this writing, or this teaching and this learning. Everything that we read/write is always only a rewriting of another reading. Michel Foucault puts it this way:

> Interpretation can never be brought to an end, simply because there is nothing to interpret. There is nothing *primary* to be interpreted, since fundamentally, everything is already interpretation; every sign is, in itself,

not the thing susceptible to interpretation but the interpretation of other signs (Foucault in Descombes, 1980) (italics added).

Foucault takes this conception of the effects of interpretation into a social and historical analysis of discourse, knowledge, and power. As Jennifer Gore's article in this book will elaborate, for Foucault, discourses, and the institutions and practices that support them, are social forces that motivate and guarantee the production of knowledge. We come to "know" what is "true" only through our attempts to say something about the world and the practices and institutions (including schools) that arise through these discourses. That is, we create our truths, which in turn frame, regulate, and control our lives. The truth is nothing more or less than our attempts to read/write the world. And power is not necessarily negative, a tool of oppression, or a possession of some and not of others. Rather, power in Foucault's work is the effect of our attempts to act in the world, to use discourse, to say something.

Thus, this perspective would find fault with some of the original ideas of critical pedagogy, which as you will recall seeks to "empower" students and teachers and thus assumes a notion of "power as property" or "power as dominance," something to be possessed and used against and sought by those who don't have it. A post-structuralist educator drawing on Foucault would seek to understand power as an effect of differential social relations. Power operates in all our discursive practices; our words, our practices, our theories will have specific effects on the lives of others. No theory or method or form of pedagogy can ever be innocent; no approach to teaching is inherently liberating or free of the effects of power.

What could this conception of reading and writing, of knowing, indeed of being itself, mean for our understanding of curriculum and pedagogy? Several authors in this book take up this question, deconstructing our commonsense notions of "pedagogy," "curriculum," "teachers," and "schooling." Their work asks us to reconsider such formerly taken-for-granted assumptions of what it means to be educated, what knowledge is, what power is.

Feminist Theory

Feminist theory is a broad and far from unified body of work. It is comprised of multiple theoretical perspectives, methodologies, disciplinary interests, philosophies, and even goals. Generally, feminists share a common interest in understanding and improving the lives and relations between women and men, economically, socially, culturally, and personally. Feminists generally agree that, historically, women have not enjoyed the same power and privileges as men either in the public or private spheres. We live our daily personal and professional lives in a society that is structured and organized by PATRIARCHY. While most feminists take patriarchy as a starting point of their critique, there is broad disagreement and debate among feminist scholars and teachers concerning the extent of and reasons for gender discrimination.

PATRIARCHY: A system organized around principles and practices of male domination.

The work of liberal feminists, for example, focuses primarily on equality of educational opportunity for women within existing economic and political structures. Liberal feminists introduced important analyses of sex-role stereotyping in classroom practices and curriculum and of the unequal representation of women in classroom materials, which they argued, led to unequal opportunities for girls. While these studies helped open the way for more in-depth studies of girls' experience in schools, critical feminist scholars and educators, drawing on the principles of critical theory, argue that liberal feminism overlooks the conditions of gender discrimination, power, and privilege produced in existing social and economic structures. They are interested in the ways these complex processes and structures help to create gendered identities that keep unequal relations between men and women in place.

Critical feminists define gender as "the socially imposed dichotomy of masculine and feminine roles and character traits. Sex is physiological while gender . . . is cultural (Warren, 1973, p. 181). What it means to be a "man" or "woman" (as opposed to male or female) gets produced and reproduced within specific social, economic, and political relations, and has specific differential effects on the lives of real men and women. Girls and women learn specific behaviors and attitudes, beliefs about themselves as girls that keep them in inferior relations to boys and men. Gender socialization and identity formation begin at infancy, and continue through all kinds of organized social life throughout our lives. Schools play a major role in this reproductive process.

Drawing on reproduction theory, critical feminists have focused on the ways that schools systematically perpetuate both classed and gender inequalities, arguing that capitalism and patriarchy are closely interwoven and interdependent.

Critical feminists look at all the processes, policies, and practices of schooling that function to reproduce unequal gender relations in society. They argue that the social relations of schooling, both what is included and excluded in the curriculum, differential teacher expectations for girls and boys, hidden messages in instructional techniques, classroom organization, and administrative structure, all can contribute to the construction of lowered self-esteem and MARGINALIZATION for girls as compared to boys.

But, as with other critical theorists of education, feminists also argue that girls and women are not simply passive recipients of these processes. They find ways of resisting what goes on in schools, and are active participants in the construction of meaning and identity. Thus, some feminists critique the overly deterministic perspective of the Marxist orientation in favor of a view of the lives of teachers and students that takes into account their personal experiences in relation to the cultural system of the institution. Nancy Lesko (1988), for example, has examined the ways in which girls construct identities as "rich and populars" or "outcasts" depending upon their relations to the organized expectations and values of a Catholic high school. Other studies examine

---

MARGINALIZATION: As Martel and Peterat discuss in detail in this volume, "marginalization" refers to the position held by women and other cultural groups in relation to cultural norms and values that are dominated by a white male perspective.

processes of "becoming feminine" in punk subcultures (Roman et al., 1989), through romance novels (Christian-Smith, 1991), or among female clerical students (Valli, 1985). For feminists drawing on phenomenological perspectives, the personal lives of both female students and teachers provide accounts of the complex and often contradictory ways that girls and women construct personal identities in response to school bureaucracies and general cultural processes.

Post-structuralist feminists are especially concerned with the ways that discursive practices and the textual weave of meaning that constitutes our culture construct our sense of what it means to be a man or a woman; how the symbolized practices, processes, materials, and relations in schools contribute to the construction of gender inequities.

For all these feminists, the implications of the theories drawn on to analyze what happens in schools are born out in visions for pedagogical practice in classrooms. Feminist pedagogy is the attempt to disrupt the taken-for-granted assumptions about what it means to be a man or a woman, assumptions that maintain exclusive realms of privilege and power for boys and marginalization for girls. Feminist teachers draw upon diverse disciplines and theories to ask critical questions about the way we live our lives as men and women, questions that, as part of the general voice of the critical educational community, demand that we take seriously the politics of identity, compassion, and caring, equality of opportunity and outcome. Put simply, though it is no simple matter, feminists are concerned with what it means to live ethical lives, lives that willingly and critically and actively engage the practice of justice, freedom, and happiness when considering the educational lives of girls and boys, women and men.

We do not claim to have given you a full explanation of these points of view; clearly this would be impossible. Rather what we have shared with you in this introduction is a glimpse of the intellectual and political landscape you will survey as you explore the essays collected in this book.

Suggestions for the Use of This Text

Some Thoughts on Reading

Let us take a moment to speak about reading and this text. Our students talk often to us about the difficulty of the reading assignments we give them. It seems that there are two difficulties that they refer to and that you too will no doubt confront as you begin to read the essays collected here: one is new vocabulary, the other new ideas and concepts. There is the difficulty of dealing with vocabulary that is new to you. Our students come to class saying, "We needed a dictionary to read this!" It's difficult not to find this earnest exclamation amusing. Oh, we realize that our students have struggled and that the assignment may have been frustrating, even maddening sometimes. And we have taken this problem seriously by asking the authors in this text to re-member their audience and to pay attention to the language and vocabulary that they use. We too have experienced this each time we pick up a text written from an unfamiliar perspective. It is simply impossible to have enough "prior knowledge" to escape this problem of unfamiliarity and lack of vocabulary if one wants to explore the world through reading. Our education demands that we struggle with new languages, academic languages as well as cultural lan-guages. And, after all, education *ought* to cause one to struggle, to stretch, to wonder, to scratch one's head. Just as it is our responsibility as editors to ask our authors to keep their language as straightforward as possible, while say-ing what they need to say, it is your responsibility as learners to take seriously your education. To take the time to learn new vocabulary, concepts, and uses of words. We have tried to help you in this struggle to learn new vocabulary through the use of *glossary notes* that appear at the bottom of appropriate pages. When you see a word highlighted in the text of an essay, the definition will appear in a footnote, as you have seen in this chapter.

The concepts, ideas, and questions raised by many of the articles in this book may also be foreign territory for many of you. You may feel very lonely in this landscape for a while. Some of the questions and points of view may even cause confusion or emotional distress. That is part of what the student meant by feeling turned inside/out. Try not to run and hide. Or slam the book shut in the defensive anger of not understanding. Too often we miss the most beautiful vistas because we lack the courage or confidence to venture forth to the edge of the unknown. Allow yourself to explore the confusion. Wander, look about, ponder the strangeness of this landscape. Just what is it about its geography that is so strange?

We invite you to read as though this were fiction, a strange adventure novel or series of short stories. A post-structuralist might say, in fact, that each of these pieces is a sort of fiction, since the perspectives presented come from each author's sense of what is important to say, his or her attempt to "make sense" of a particular problem. Any attempt to say something about the world is in some sense a fiction, never divorced from the author's questions, joys, or pain, and never separate from the reader's history or life experiences either. In this sense, you are also the author of these essays. Every reading is thus a kind of writing. The more you relax, and cease to pressure yourself to understand (as though there were one set of explanations or answers to your questions), the better you will become at writing your own understandings/interpretations, and thus, at connecting the ideas, questions, and issues in the essay with your own life. That is, after all, what becoming educated is about—a kind of making sense of one's own life through the works of others in order to turn one's at-tention, care, and compassion outward again toward the world.

This, of course, does not mean that trying to understand what the author is saying is not important. After all, those of us who write or teach do not do so without the desire to say something to someone. Most of us try very hard to communicate to others what we feel matters. That is what teaching is, and that is what writing is too, for poets, historians, philosophers, curriculum theorists, choreographers, musicians. And even though one's reading of what we have said or written can never exactly repeat what we "meant," and may in fact create much more than we ever meant, it is important to try to hear and even summarize what the main thesis is in any given work. Clearly this task is different when reading poetry, or listening to a lecture on molecular biology, or trying to make sense of an essay on the history of social studies. But still, we try to do it. We do it in every daily conversation, and with every form of expression we engage in. We do it because we desire to communicate with and to express ourselves to others. This is precisely what makes education possible.

So, we invite you to read with these questions in mind: What is this person trying to say to me, to teach me? And, what does it matter, to me personally, and to me as an educator? We invite you to engage in the struggle of reading and of learning, not to shy from it. To expect the struggle as a necessary part of the joy of learning, to come to welcome it as one would welcome any other joyful experience. Of course this means beginning to realize that these texts do not loom over you with any preordained authority, though some may seem to or even pretend to.

It also means that your reading is always also a writing, a kind of unavoidable interaction of your life, thoughts, questions, yearnings with the questions, problems, hopes of the author. What gets read is never anything other than this interaction; indeed, the text itself does not exist outside your reading of it.

Guiding Questions and Questions for Discussion

So write your reading. Write in the margins. Give the text your questions, your joy, your anger, your wonder, your voice. We suggest that you keep a journal where you might record these responses. In fact, at the beginning of each chapter we remind you of two *Guiding Questions*. What is the author trying to say or teach? and What is the significance of what you read here for you personally and for you as a teacher? It is important not to skip the first question. Try to understand what the essay is about before expressing a response.

We also offer two other *Guiding Questions* that ask you to consider the ways in which the essays engage the theoretical perspectives discussed above. What are the perspectives drawn on by the author to make the analysis? and How do they help to inform our practice in classrooms? We hope the use of these introductory questions and the journals will help to prepare you to engage with your classmates in discussion about the ideas included in this book. At the end of each essay are *Questions for Discussion* offered by the authors to promote additional thought about the issues or problems addressed.

Teachers as Researchers

At the end of each chapter there is also a section entitled *Teachers as Researchers*. This phrase indicates our commitment to encourage our students and users of this book to begin to identify themselves as producers of meaningful interpretations of the processes, practices, policies, relations, and experiences of education. Too often both students and teachers are seen as either consumers or simply transmitters of others' research. We see teaching as a richly interpretive process whereby teachers are constantly engaged in constructing knowledge of their students, of their practices, of their classrooms, of pedagogy, of the politics of school life, and so on. We know that there is research going on in classrooms all of the time, as part of the everyday responsibility of teaching, but teachers seldom identify themselves as creators of knowledge, and are seldom treated as such by the general public or by those they work for. This is all part of the general politics of knowledge that we discussed earlier. The effects of this are that teachers (along with administrators, university people, the state, research foundations, and the general public) often view the responsibility for creative change through research as originating someplace else, and thus give away much of the political power that they otherwise could utilize to change the contours of their daily lives and work (see Grinberg's essay in this volume).

We believe that teachers could have a greater impact on what happens in schools if they began to identify themselves as capable of creating change through their own research. Thus, we include in this text suggestions for activities or projects that will help to prepare the ground for such identities, and such action. The hope is that as students you will begin to take the time (with the help of these authors) to learn how to organize and carry out a piece of research about some dimension of education. We want you to gain confidence in asking questions that are meaningful to you, problematizing your lives as teachers. We want you to become skilled teacher-researchers, gleaning as much as you can; but more than this, we want you to learn to feel comfortable with your own ability to problematize and create as educators. With these goals in mind we have asked each author to suggest projects that will help you to research further the topics that they introduce with their essays.

It is our hope that the pedagogical apparatus of this book—the Guiding Questions, Questions for Discussion, Glossary Notes, and Teachers as Researchers sections—will help you to interact with these essays as much as possible, and even to begin to identify with this critical educational community. To be critical means a willingness to act in the world, which includes acting on one's self through reflective practice, as a means of creating spaces of life for oneself and others. It means being concerned with ethics; that is, with considerations of the consequences or effects of one's actions on the world. This includes an awareness of the tension between authority, knowledge, and diversity; the ways that knowledge and power intersect to form specific relations in social life. In education, this means a willingness to explore schools' relation to the social hierarchy, asking who controls curriculum development and policy, what forms of knowledge are considered "real knowledge," and how these relations affect our ability to think and act in the world. To think about education in such a way may well expand the specific study of schools to a broader understanding of educational experiences and meaning in social life. It may mean that we begin to consider curriculum as the sum of what is possible to learn in the world.

The editors and contributors are committed to opening dialogue and discussion with our students and the users of this book. We believe that the questions asked and perspectives offered shed light on educational institutions, relations, and practices in ways that could lead to the transformation of the quality of life not only in schools, but in the world more generally. Of course, this transformation depends upon our willingness and courage to engage together as teachers, students, and scholars of education to ask questions and make challenges to what exists, both in the world and in ourselves, if the two can ever truly be separated. It means, again, a willingness to look carefully at our own belief systems and to have the courage to shift our patterns of discourse and behavior, to turn our perspectives and our conduct inside/out, as a matter of concern for the world. Thus, we define education as related to a more general practice of freedom[1] through ethics, "as a form to be given to one's life . . ." to engage a type of knowledge in a way so as to modify not only the thought of others but one's own as well" (Foucault, 1989, p. 303). We offer this book in the spirit of such worthy work, which is, after all, the work of educators.

notes

[1] For a more detailed historical analysis of "the practice of freedom" through the study of Social Foundations of Education, see "The Practice of Freedom: A Historical Analysis of Critical Perspectives in the Social Foundations," by William Reynolds and Rebecca Martusewicz in this volume.

references

Apple, M. W. (1979). *Ideology and curriculum*. New York: Routledge & Kegan Paul.

Bowles, S. & Gintis, H. (1976). *Schooling in capitalist America*. New York: Basic Books.

Christian-Smith, L. (1991). Readers, texts, and contexts: Adolescent romance fiction in schools. In M. W. Apple & L. Christian-Smith (Eds.), *The politics of the textbook* (pp. 191–213). New York: Routledge.

Derrida, J. (1974). *Of grammatology* (G. C. Spivak, Trans.). Baltimore: The Johns Hopkins University Press.

Descombes, V. (1980). *Modern French philosophy*. Cambridge: Cambridge University Press.

Foucault, M. (1989). *Foucault live: Interviews 1966–84*. New York: Semiotext(e) Foreign Agents Series.

Freire, P. (1971). *Pedagogy of the oppressed*. New York: Continuum.

Geertz, C. (1973). *The interpretation of culture: Selected essays*. New York: Basic Books.

Giroux, H. A. (1981). *Ideology, culture and the process of schooling*. Philadelphia, PA: Temple University Press.

Giroux, H. A. (1988). *Teachers as intellectuals: Toward a critical pedagogy of learning*. Granby, MA: Bergin & Garvey.

Greene, M. (1973). *Teacher as stranger.* Belmont, CA: Wadsworth.

Lesko, N. (1988). *Symbolizing society: Stories, rites and structure in a Catholic high school.* London: The Falmer Press.

McCarthy, C. (1990). *Race and curriculum.* New York: The Falmer Press.

McLaren, P. (1989). *Life in schools: An introduction to critical pedagogy in the foundations of education.* New York: Longman.

Olson, P. (Ed.). (1981). Rethinking social reproduction [Theme issue]. *Interchange, 12*(2–3).

Pinar, W. F. (1976). *Sanity, madness, and the school.* Meerut, India: Sadhna Prakashan.

Pinar, W. F. & Grumet, M. R. (1976). *Toward a poor curriculum.* Dubuque, IA: Kendall Hunt.

Pinar, W. F., Reynolds, W. M., Slattery, P., & Taubman, P. M. (in press). *Understanding curriculum: A comprehensive introduction to the study of historical and contemporary curriculum discourses.* New York: Peter Lang.

Roman, L. et al. (1989). *Becoming feminine: The politics of popular culture.* Lewes: The Falmer Press.

Sleeter, C. (1992). What is multicultural education? In *Kappa Delta Pi Record.* Fall, pp. 4–8.

Spring, J. (1991). *American education: An introduction to social and political aspects* (5th ed.). New York: Longman.

Valli, L. (1985). *Becoming clerical workers.* London: Routledge & Kegan Paul.

Warren, B. (1973). *Feminine image in literature.* Rochelle Park, NJ: Hayden.

Willis, P. (1977). *Learning to labour: How working class kids get working class jobs.* Hampshire, England: Gower Press.

chapter 2

Deconstruction and Nothingness

Some Cross-Cultural Lessons on Teaching Comparative World Civilization

Edward K. Berggren

guiding questions

1. What is the author trying to say or teach?
2. What is the significance of what you read here for you personally and for you as a teacher?
3. What are the perspectives drawn on by the author to make the analysis?
4. How does this analysis help to inform our practice in classrooms?

> *True Reality: Of this there is no academic proof in the world;*
> *For it is hidden, and hidden, and hidden.*
>
> Jalaludin Rumi (in Idries, 1968, p. 203)

> *Everything is just as it is.*
>
> Abe (1991, p. 203)

**Education as history; history as education. The concepts are too big for any text, let alone for a short essay. I can only touch the surface here of what makes these two categories and their inseparability so essential to our lives. History and education encompass everything we do. History, as I read it, is about temporality, the dimension in which all learning and living take place; EDUCATION (PEDAGOGY) is about learning, or that space in which history takes form and shape. Our lives open to time or historicity in an endless educational process. Education is like water moving in snakelike fashion through the geography of existence, cutting out deeper and deeper riverbeds, opening always to new life, opening into the sifting deltas and into the great seas—the oceans of existence, time and space. There is no end to this process, nor is there a beginning. Learning and history thus meet everywhere as interwoven fabrics. Is it simply an accident that so many civilizations arose around rivers, whose waters became so entwined with the fabric of life?

To the extent that history and education seek to give or to open life, seek to overcome the past and thereby recreate a wholesome world, they will have to recall, open onto, or indicate something of what I will provisionally call the ethical; in pointing in this direction, they are pointing to what life *ought* to be. The quest here is toward an open life, or alternatively, a becoming consciousness and involvement in our connectedness with others. The ethical concerns that by which, through which, or in which we open to Otherness and the Other thereby becoming detached from or break down self-centeredness.

**Education and history both imply the ever renewed possibility of overcoming the past, no matter how evil that past might be. Our choice of what to include or what to exclude may be figured around the tropes that best promote a number of ethical qualities, which themselves stand outside any representational account. At this point, we might use pedagogical pointers that can help indicate the ethical space that is silenced within the pervasive representational

I owe thanks to Professor Rebecca Martusewicz for her many editorial comments, on which she went well beyond the call of duty, but most of all for her encouraging and friendly dialogue and criticism on innumerable points throughout the essay. She has made sure that this piece remained a labor of love.

This essay is not composed in the standard "journalistic" or "essay" style. I have decided to use the device of separated aphorisms or reflections as part of a wider effort to mimic the poetic and metaphoric paths of thinking, learning, teaching. These aphorisms or reflections are marked with double asterisks. Hyphens are used with a similar intent of shattering illusions of unity, objectivity, or obviousness which can accompany mechanical writing.

EDUCATION (PEDAGOGY): I will use these terms roughly in the same sense to describe those fields concerned with learning in all its breadth.

discourses currently dominating the human sciences (and thus pedagogy) in the West. Education and history present themselves as spaces in which ethics is offered as an opening toward the Other.

**Thought is ever subject to a deconstruction unto no-thing-ness, where the fluid character of being leaves no room for anything positive to stand. Ethics begins, perhaps, in the movement toward this awareness of our groundlessness, in a movement that Zen refers to as an enlightenment. But perhaps I have simply substituted ethics for what the Zen tradition has called nothingness, śūnyatā, or what Heidegger has called Being. At this point (or, "in the final account") I can only mark a path that, as Taoism reminds us, cannot be named.

**What can inspire us to move forward today in what must appear as a river thickly polluted with evil and violence? What, if not a calling, which we might try to name as hope, peace, love, and compassion? But "voices" or tonalities are never simply given: they come as mysterious messages that demand a hearing. From where this calling comes, we cannot say, for that place is not re-presentable. It stands outside space and time in the scientific sense of these terms. This is why I teach history with a constant ear for the religious and the ethical, for the dimension which transgresses the boundaries of representational language—language that insists we have solid "evidence" or "pictures" of delineated "objects" of study.

The question that confronts me here is: How does one teach history in a world where contemporary educational institutions have renounced responseability to this calling, this ethical and religious challenge to the contemporary crisis of civilization? We are so used to looking for scientific and human responses to our crisis that we forget that the very condition for such a response is some kind of guidance, some kind of direction. How can one attain guidance and direction in the space and time of the ethical and religious? To begin with, perhaps, we need to find a place from which one might hear, in which one might escape the "white noise" that crowds in upon us from all directions. Education worthy of its name would help us reach such a place.

**I have learned enormously since graduate school and my doctoral thesis; mostly, I have learned there is an enormous amount of things that I must now un-learn. If, with e. e. cummings, kisses are a far better fate than wisdom, at least wisdom is a far better fate than knowledge, and especially historical knowledge, which is increasingly characterized by avoidance, resistance, and forgetfulness. I speak, then, of my own personal journey through history to what more and more reminds me of the Buddhist notion of no-thing-ness (śūnyatā). I admit, however, that standing at this strange non-place, I do not quite know where to go. I write and teach, then, in *hope* of a response and a direction. This much is clear: As soon as one begins to radically question the central concepts of history, one also questions the central concepts of pedagogy (and vice versa) as well as of self-identity; these conceptions are welded in the same crucible. The same enframing assumptions give these "fields" the illusion of separateness and of internal coherence just as they provide an illusory sense of identity.

**The questions raised by the thinkers with whom I have been engaged haunt me day and night. They have changed my life, my way of viewing the world, space, and time. I offer them to you that they may haunt you as well, that they may sow in you the same kinds of vegetation that they have planted in me, and that you may in turn disseminate them to students and friends, urging history more and more toward the field of openness which Buddhists call śūnyatā.[1] Perhaps we need something like scarecrows to keep the evil demons away. Perhaps what we need today more than ever is to be frightened, shaken, and awakened so that we may, collectively, change our ways of seeing, feeling, hearing, witnessing, confessing, testifying, and loving. The cries of the suffering, the destruction and pollution of the earth, the face of violence and injustice everywhere call out to us in anger, misery, pain, and sorrow. History can be one way of listening to these voices, now raised in chorus, a chorus increasingly shattering the rigid doors of academia. To listen, we need new ears. I write and teach history in a tuneful turning toward these voices, which hauntingly cry out to us to listen and become testimony to a past that needs change and to confess our responsibility for change in the present. Teaching and history, then, enter into a complex relationship that tries to respond to a world of violence by turning it toward love, justice, and compassion. Part of this movement takes us from a historical language of violence to one of compassion; one's very voice changes along with one's hearing.

**The work of Ludwig Wittgenstein has helped me undo illusion after illusion[2] and has led me to stop doing anything like conventional history. The dominant forms of historical discourse often perpetuate our culture of violence by repeating illusions that hinder dialogue with other peoples and that, in other words, impede learning and thinking. For example, under the guiding illusion that science or some form of representational discourse is the primary, if not the exclusive, route to historical and pedagogical truth, our historical pedagogy and pedagogy of history often treats other societies (or rather, the "TEXTS" of other societies) as "primitive," "backward," "less advanced," "less developed," and "more traditional." More often implicitly than explicitly, this illusion of our superiority is created by reading history exclusively within Western narratives. We have acted as if our own culture were the only, or best, way of viewing the world, and so we continue to find universal texts on or about world civilization that treat the texts of other cultures as mere evidence for the story of world civilization at hand.[3]

This style of history may simply be an attempt to isolate our texts (texts on/of our society), and thus ourselves, from those of other societies and to reiterate the message that we are above, beyond, and outside of the boundaries of "traditional" societies, which are radically Other in a negative sense ("modernization" will make them like us). One of the most successful ways to reiterate the illusion of their Otherness is to write history that repeats the bifurcation between traditional or less developed cultures (often referred to as

---

TEXT: I use "text" here in the metaphorical sense of one of its roots, *texere*, meaning to weave, or *texture*, as in a woven fabric made of many threads (here meaning fibers).

"primitive"), on the one hand, and modern, developed or "advanced" cultures, peoples and civilizations on the other.

Concepts like "Other," "tradition" and "modernity," which are parts of the enframing conditions of modern history and education, need to be held under constant suspension and suspicion. They should be constantly questioned so as not to obfuscate the similarities between us "moderns" and the "primitives" or the similarity and difference between "our" culture or civilization and "Other" civilizations and cultures.

**I try to speak from a fluid position informed by traditions that are foreign to much, if not most, of Western history. These traditions are now part of my memory. I, as it were, become expression of (for) them. They are my teachers. They have taught me to ask questions that I now carry with me always like the lingering reminiscences of a lover. This re-tention of a certain style of questioning helps me deal with my loss of faith in the Western cultural tradition—history in particular—which seems to me to be on a disastrously wrong course, like the oil tankers that leave in their wake a lingering death and destruction. The course of history has led to the unquestioned acceptance of certain values that, in turn, legitimate and perpetuate in its wake a culture of violence: violence against children, against the earth, against other sentient creatures, against the sacred. It is to this violence that a re-thinking of history should speak and respond: history thus becomes a calling.

**Too often the texts from "traditional" societies—most often the religious texts—speak to me about sacred time in such a way that I can imagine the present in terms of historical degeneration much more easily than I can imagine historical progression. But the historical metaphors of "degeneration" and "progression" are posed in terms of binary opposition that are more obfuscating than helpful. How are we to imagine historical "change"? How do we differentiate significant change from historical repetition? Historical creativity here involves an ongoing project of creative thinking and writing for each act of historical interpretation.

**Most of the intellectual arsenal of Western metaphysics (those metaphors often used to legitimate its self-conception, which gets manufactured and re-produced in the various disciplines)—truth, objectivity, self, science, reason, and knowledge—have lost their TOTALIZING appeal to me. These values, when taken as ends in themselves or when taken without further question, seem increasingly harmful as idols in a culture of narcissism and aggression. The worship of these idols makes opening to other peoples and traditions all the more difficult because the idols imply a certain type of closure to the Other, who may speak in other styles of discourse. The pretension is that these values somehow help us reach "rock bottom," truth, or reality, or that their enframing assumptions yield something like completeness or coherence.

TOTALIZING: A concept implying a kind of total and closed worldview that reduces "life," "existence," "meaning," and "language" to processes that can be represented or explained in something like scientific or theoretical systems.

The Enlightenment tradition, much of which I'll refer to as modernity, often speaks of freedom and equality as the endpoints for the expansion of representational knowledge. But this tradition falls by its own standards, because it now reproduces itself in monster bureaucracies of knowledge, intimately linked to military, business, and other unwholesome enterprises that rob us of our voices and of our wealth.[4] Universities—the focus of Enlightenment dreams of liberation—have become modern castles for new privileged classes. Schools now work through the manipulation and the exploitation (often through direct theft) of students from all classes; electronic moats have replaced traditional moats and walls. Using mechanisms similar to those of the middle ages, schools serve as centers of regulation, protection, and redistribution of power and privilege, and they rob the majority of their voices and freedoms. May history help us out of this situation by rediscovering new ways of imagining and practicing education.

** Some contemporary schools of Zen Buddhism along with deconstruction, have radically questioned the central concepts with which this tradition of violence legitimates itself. Zen and deconstruction honestly confront Western historical culture's claims to liberation and justice with that culture's violent and obsessive applications and practices. Pedagogy is just one domain where one finds myriad forms of this violence put into practice on a daily basis.[5] One need only visit "inner city" schools, which often function as places of incarceration and discipline; one need only reflect on widely accepted practices like testing and grading, which fulfill purposes of selection, hierarchization, and exclusion, when they fulfill any function at all; one need only consider how thought is straitjacketed and punishment administered within the arbitrary boundaries of "the disciplines."

** Today, with a certain HEGEMONY of Enlightenment or representational style historiography dominating the discourses of history departments, Zen and deconstruction may serve to openly question the major figures of speech (tropes) around which history is written.[6] We teachers must continue such questioning if we are to open ways of thinking, feeling, living, and loving that might begin to change or halt this civilization gone violent, psychotic. Part of the task is to construct histories that re-call and re-member existential moods described or

---

HEGEMONY: I use this term, which I take from Antonio Gramsci, one of the most creative of the twentieth-century marxists, to describe the processes by which language or discourse becomes increasingly limited or mystifying under certain conditions—for example, the people in power limit the use of language (say by burning books, or controlling the press, or making schooling difficult to attain). A society may likewise "administer" language, which increasingly directs us to the inessential or nonethical, as when one can describe violence in double-talk. Many examples of both cases of hegemony can be found in the language "surrounding"—as in news "coverage"—our recent "war" with Iraq, beginning with the notion that this was a "war," rather than, as Chomsky has called it, an instance of state terrorism. (See Noam Chomsky, "The 'Gulf War' In Retrospect," in *War After War*, ed. Nancy Peters [San Francisco: City Lights Books, 1992], 14.) One might also reflect on concepts like "smart bombing," or the notion of a "Desert Storm," or of some of the new murderous weapons—"antipersonnel" weapons—with names like "Beehive" and "Adam." The language of the war was of course regulated by news "media" and the "armed forces." A good pedagogical exercise would be to have students try to invent a sensitive, ethical language by which one might describe "war" in its various forms of terror and violence.

anticipated within all of the great religious traditions, which speak of love, compassion, charity, and justice. It is not as if we are completely in the dark, without voices to guide us, but we seem to require hearing aids.

**I offer here, then, a series of reflections, reminiscences, and questions that I hope will help in the mammoth project of "deconstructing" history and the education of history as currently practiced in the Western world. The purpose of such a deconstruction is to open historical thinking, moving it in directions other than those now practiced and moving it into other dimensions that might deal more adequately with history's domain—temporality and memory, space and distance. Can there be a "proper" domain of time and distance?

With few exceptions I see a profound lack of self-questioning within contemporary history—much less so than in any of the other "human sciences." As a teacher, I have felt tremendous pressure when trying to introduce alternative historical styles, given the hegemony of a kind of pseudoscientific style in most history texts and courses. This pseudoscience works by reproducing history around a number of metaphors usually drawn from the natural sciences. One speaks, for example, of "explanation" of historical "events" as if these terms were fairly unproblematic. One reduces temporal meaning to quasi-scientific geographies of space and time and then speaks as if one were "open" and "critical." Are we being fair to so many other cultures and discourses (or so many of "our own") which *live* and speak of something like the sacred? Why has history forgotten or forsaken the category of the religious, the ethical, and the philosophical?

**In an effort to creatively work out our lives through historical teaching, I advocate a mixture of styles, genres, and metaphors, which might combine elements of poetry, music, dance, painting, and narrative. Let us purposely cross traditional boundaries—interdisciplinary as well as cultural—to disseminate new ways of living and writing about time, distance, otherness. Most importantly, as we work to dislodge the Eurocentric dimensions of our historical (and other similar) curriculum, let us advocate the use of other, non-Western traditions—traditions which often already have a healthy fusion of genres and have had since time immemorial. This creative mixture of styles and genres would provide just one attempt to re-think and re-live time, along with its pedagogy.

**By persistently questioning representational languages and thinking at the crossroads or margins of cultures and civilizations, DECONSTRUCTIVE (OR POST-STRUCTURAL) criticism and Buddhism, provide inspiration and hope by open-

---

DECONSTRUCTIVE (OR POST-STRUCTURAL): I use "post-structural," "post-modern," and "deconstructive" in similar ways. Although there is a vast literature trying to make fine distinctions between these concepts, I find most of these debates futile. After all, the project of post-structuralism is to get rid of the "proper," of the notion that there are essences behind certain terms and hence some unique property or set of properties which could be used to rigidly demarcate the boundaries of a given subject. Deconstruction would urge us beyond easy conceptual bifurcations and into the often murky waters of intertextuality. I take the same kind of approach to the concept of Buddhism, which I use here (to borrow from Wittgenstein) as a ladder with which to help my students see the emptiness of all "things." Deconstructive criticism, on my reading, talks of the supplementary movement in which signs are linked in endless chains of signs, where the definition of any one sign would take us endlessly from sign to sign were we not to arbitrarily settle upon some kind of boundaries.

ing escape routes for pedagogical imagination and historical thinking. In applying some of the themes within these two traditions, I hope to initiate renewed invention and creativity for both the teaching and the writing of history.[7] There is, of course, risk here; there is no guarantee of success. One works constantly under the guidance of hope. How would we describe a history and pedagogy of hope? Teachers and students need to discuss seriously how we can bring hope and peace into being through our pedagogical practices.

** Because Buddhism, like deconstruction, presents no rigid boundaries around itself, the genres are mixed in an effort to practice what I teach. I do not assume that Buddhism or deconstruction has an essence or fixed nature, other than the important recognition that there are no fixed natures or essences. Each use of language involves us in a paradox: every claim we make can be deconstructed by pointing to the various contexts in which the meaning of words, phrases, and texts change. For example, how can one speak of "Buddhism" in light of the indeterminately many schools of Buddhism and the openness of language used therein? (Each school, for example, as an open tradition of interpretation of its tradition, wherein each school is open to indefinitely many interpretations.) One might ask the same of "deconstruction." I use "Buddhism" and "deconstruction," then, as signs or entry points for re-thinking history, "points" or "pointers" that erase themselves in that act of historical writing, which henceforth creates its own boundaries and limits, but does so at least partly conscious of what it is doing.

I hope that I am capturing a sense of the Buddhist notion of "enlightenment" in this recognition of the non-boundedness or inter-connectedness of everything. The notion of connectedness, or co-dependency, is another way to speak of "emptiness" or of "no-thing-ness" at the heart of being. Derrida speaks in terms of supplementarity, traces, and differance. Lyotard speaks of the differend. These terms or signs are all indicators of that which lies "beyond" discourse, opening up a space for its very possibility. Buddhists use the analogy of the eye that can never see itself. The eye (I) is the condition of sight, yet it cannot perceive itself. What is the relation of the eye (I) to sight? To time and compassion? We need to meditate upon such relations and all of the implications they have for the writing of history.

** According to Buddhist teachings, the "highest truths," or the "mark" of wisdom (prajña), are achieved by non-conceptual, experiential "seeing" of the no-thing-ness or emptiness of everything, and especially by "realizing" the emptiness of self, or non-self. On this reading, "self," as traditionally conceived in the West—and think about how much our history texts rely upon this concept— is an illusion. Or rather, true self is no-thing.

The process in which this awareness comes (arrives, happens) is said to open onto (into) wisdom, a concept that implies more than just an awareness of truths that are beyond representation (beyond language, if language is taken as a system of signs that has a correspondence with objects outside of itself). Wisdom here also implies a readjustment of our lives in accordance with this new insight into no-thing-ness. One of the most important and ideal existential *moves* to make is the move into compassion. One "be-comes" compassion; one comes into being as compassion, which comes forth into a now emptied vessel. In this movement, we "re-turn" from enlightenment or nirvana in order to help all other sentient creatures attain something of this awareness and the attendant state of compassion. It is not accidental that the no-thing-ness, which is supposed to initiate the turn toward compassion, is often interpreted as love.[8] Christ, I recall, also said that in order "to follow" (i.e., to love), one would have to lose oneself.

** My descriptions and claims already open up to the co-dependence of a series of terms—concepts, awareness, language, experience, wisdom . . .[9]—which can only be defined in terms of one another, and then endlessly worked out until the investigator either "sees" that there is nothing that will close the chain of signifiers or else tires of this "game" and stops somewhere, settling, with the pragmatist, for incomplete knowledge or dogmatically claiming to have reached a "ground."

The attempt to "ground" (or "lay the foundation for") disciplines, experiences, knowledge, reason, or ethics is one of the characteristic metaphorical moves of what one could call "modernity." In "modern" thinking, one seeks grounds, or foundations as final reference points that would stop the endless dissemination of meaning opened by nothingness, or what Derrida has called differance, supplementarity, and the TRACE . . . Buddhism has tried to move us somewhere else with this realization of no-thing-ness: it has tried to indicate the existential realization of this non-place as love. Here Buddhists call on religious language to describe a realm of experience that cannot be represented in either ordinary or specialized scientific or philosophical language.[10] Why would this "realm" be any less subject to history than that of violence, of which our texts are so replete?

** Much in history hinges on how we approach the most viable or immediate evidence given to us. This evidence—even at the level of direct experience—is ever subject to interpretation and narration. Each event can be the subject of indefinite redescription and reinterpretation; "knowledge" of events is thus never accomplished. Perhaps this state of affairs is best described by the notion of textuality, a metaphor that seems to me a nice way of capturing the complexity of our existential situation. We are given, so to speak, texts. In this we are gifted. Again, that which we experience, or "in" which we live, is (can be thought of as) textuality. Textuality implies that experience can never fully close, that meaning is always a task.

All this, of course, is a series of metaphors for describing the layeredness or the geography (more metaphors) of experience, meaning, and consciousness.

TRACE: Derrida's signs, such as supplement, trace, arche-writing, are also used to indicate the non-conceptual "space" or fissure which allows for experience, culture, consciousness, language. . . . I here translate Derrida into Buddhist language, suggesting that we read his series of marks as gestures toward dependent co-origination or dependent co-arising. I do not suggest that I have achieved an accurate or exclusive translation, but rather another way of trying to think about similarity and difference. Sometimes "wisdom" (prajña) is described as such a process of trying to think about the similarity and difference of/between all things. See, for example, the excellent work on Zen by Christopher Ives, *Zen Awakening and Society* (Honolulu: University of Hawaii Press, 1992), 42 ff.

Texts, as the metaphor suggests, are woven bits of material (yet another metaphor). In fact, one way to define text would be as indefinitely "thick" compilations of metaphors: fabrics woven out of metaphor upon metaphor into a strange kind of magic carpet which winds up at one point as experience. We get somewhere in history by weaving metaphor upon metaphor and then riding upon our carpet.[11] Through metaphor, shall we say, the world comes to us, is created, is written . . . Perhaps time is simply the accretion of metaphor upon metaphor. . . .

**In being "based upon" metaphor—or better, strung out on metaphor—history and education are similar to any other discipline. Both turn on the weaving together of strings of metaphors. There is no end to these strings: one may simply stop thinking or writing (say, using our text as a tool) but the next moment of consciousness extends the string by one or more new metaphors. The past and the lesson of or on the past, then, is quite literally (figuratively speaking), a string of metaphors. What kind of reality is that? Metaphors are sometimes called "turns" of phrases. They are also called "figures" of speech. Defining metaphor would involve us again in an infinite regression of metaphors. (How would one come up with non-metaphorical definitions of "figure" or "turn"?[12]) Nothingness, we might say in Buddhist parlance, lies at the heart of metaphor, but this is just the start of a new string of metaphors in a fabric without beginning or end. Time. Buddhists speak of impermanence wherein each moment flows into the next in circular motions, but such descriptions take us round again to another metaphor, albeit circumspectly.

**To rephrase and reiterate, I accept here (in paraphrase) Lyotard's[13] concise definition of postmodernity: it is a time when all of the traditional metanarratives about self and world are thrown into question. The traditional metanarratives—that is, theories or stories that attempt to tell us about experience in general or to give coherence to the past—have fallen into suspicion because of the recognition that there are indefinitely many ways of coming to the world, of forming a world, of living a world. There are indefinitely many possible worlds—logical, to be sure, but most importantly for us, existential. Whichever world we choose, it becomes, in turn, subject to indefinitely many possible interpretations because one can always create another interpretation of that world. In any case, our interpretations hinge upon metaphors, rules, initial enframing assumptions, and countless other choices that are arbitrary constructs; that is, they are subject to choice and indefinitely open to indeterminable criteria of selection and re-adaptation—aesthetic, pragmatic, ethical, . . . Our worlds turn, as it were, in seas of metaphors. There is, in the final instance, no way of determining which of these metaphors is to guide us in our thinking, acting, writing, singing. . . . We are free, in other words. There is no end to interpretation, no end to writing. Illusion would, in part, consist in the belief that one had indeed encountered final truth.

**Illusion and violence find a common ground here: the notion that one comes to an end, that one has reached "base", that one has a feeling of certainty and upon this ground can "prove" that this path is the right, only, and true path. But don't I respond to violence and evil? Don't I recognize it and act with determination? I respond to acts of violence and evil, or try to, though more often than not, I stand back and ask what might be done or I simply turn away. None of this implies that I know what constitutes either the violence of these acts or the basis I use when I act with conviction. We might say that here is one of the places where one encounters the mystery and the calling, here is the point where we are called to response with the freedom to refuse response. Here, also, is the space that must be kept open, for it is so liable to close, and the point where our listening connects or disconnects us with others. History and pedagogy might act here as existential dynamite to unclog the dammed rivers of existence.

**History, then, is, in part, the remembrance of a time of illusion, a time when humanity lived without freedom and consciousness partly because of its illusions. History can then be read and taught in Buddhist terms as the re-cognition of a past with a view to opening to a non-illusory present and future. Buddhists speak of "skillful means" (upaya). One way to teach history is as a skillful means for achieving freedom and compassion. Such achievement would unfold differently at each and every moment. In Buddhism, each moment is in and of itself unique while connected with the rest of time. Writing history would thus mean standing at the crossroads of indefinitely many temporal points, which link in many directions and open indefinitely many possibilities of reflection and creativity. Each point could then be seen as the possibility of rupture, freedom, change . . . emptiness and compassion.

Each historical and pedagogical move involves us in a choice. Which narrative, for example, shall I use to enframe an illusory past? Which assumptions shall I choose to present time without illusion? How will I make sure that the reader or student remains aware that I am inventing one of many possible times? How will I write about time, while holding no-thing-ness, as it were, before the student's eye (I)? One suggestion is to read our texts with a view to their metaphors, understanding that every phrase carries us along through turns and figures until we are caught in labyrinths. We may be, then, like Roethke's love: moving in circles, and those circles moving, becoming martyrs to motions not our own.[14]

**Deconstruction and Buddhism emphasize the movement "beyond" dichotomies and the entangling labyrinths in which history is so often written and in which our imaginations and our lives are so limited: society-individual; primitive-modern; self-world; beginning-end; cause-effect; . . . Nothingness would point to the space opened by a thinking of that which gives way to such dichotomies. If time has no beginning or end, no inside or outside—like meaning, language or culture—then how shall we write history without getting stuck in our bifurcated mazes without end or beginning?

**I find the Buddhist notion of samsara appealing. In fact, history might be read as the remembrance of samsara, which is often translated "birth-and-death" and which is used to indicate the transient world of suffering in which we are caught until we learn to free ourselves of it, as we free ourselves of illusions. Foremost amongst the illusions is that of the self. The aim is to detach ourselves from suffering or grasping (or the cyclical reenactment of birth and death) and realize our "original face": no-self, that which stands before or beyond language, being, and time, yet yields to these events as their "condition."

In this reading, one might imagine one direction of history and education as the coming to awareness of that series of illusions—the cycle of birth and death—and then the movement "beyond" those illusions. As Joyce has written: "History . . . is a nightmare from which I am trying to awake.[15] Buddhism responds to such a call with its concepts of wakefulness, enlightenment, and wisdom: the realization that underlying what one once took as "self" is really no-thing-ness, emptiness, the same lack which lies behind anything and everything. It seems to me that deconstruction takes us to a similar place: metaphor, poetry, movement, time. We wind up with that which escapes representation. Emptiness. Impermanence. Time . . . and Otherness.

** The historical and educational questions I raise here may be taken as kōans. Kōans are Zen Buddhism's skillful means of trying to present and think through fundamental paradoxes in which we get caught when we rely unquestioningly upon our thinking tool boxes: language, concepts, and reason. Kōans are meant as pointers, signs, or ciphers, which direct us "elsewhere"—away from faith in these mere tools to "authentic faith," existentially mooring us before the mystery of the universe and toward no-thing-ness and a turning to compassion. For Buddhists these kōans are but another means to take us to the field of śūnyatā or nothingness, zero-ness, or again, emptiness. These indicate another dimension of existence and can be compared to love as the loss of oneself.

One such kōan helps us contemplate how language takes us to nothingness. "Language is like a finger pointing at the moon," goes the kōan. It's message is multiple: Don't confuse the finger with the moon; it's a long way from the finger to the moon; language is as distant from reality as a finger is from the moon . . . What does it mean for a finger to point to the moon? Shall we say that language "points" to a world in a gesture that transcends language or that simply uses language? That language—whatever it is—and everything else in existence can only be represented with signs like fingers? That everything becomes a sign of everything else? The moon can equally be considered a language using the finger: the moon points back at the finger with its moonlight, which, in turn, indicates the sun, or equally the finger, the moon, language, self, light, space . . . All become bound up in indeterminately many relations so that language points, like the finger or the moon, to everything else in existence. Or that, upon reflection, any one of these "things"—finger, moon, language—can drop out of the realm of thinghood and become a pointer to everything else, and thus the sign of no-thing, the emptiness that stands somewhere at the heart of things.

** May history be like a finger pointing at the moon.

questions   for   discussion

1. How do historical bifurcations like "modern/primitive" or "modern/traditional" distort the workings of culture or civilization and help reproduce Eurocentric styles of history and other forms of imperialist culture? You

might think about all of the ways in which contemporary civilization is indeed "primitive" and all of the ways in which traditional societies are "modern" or "progressive." Do these kinds of bifurcation serve any function except obfuscation of complex realities?

2. How does the close reading of the texts of other cultures (in this case, the texts of Zen Buddhism) subvert traditional representational historical discourses in which the texts from other cultures are used for the purpose of supporting a totalizing interpretation of history or for other utilitarian purposes?

3. What kinds of decisions are necessary in order to stop the deconstructive questioning of historical (or temporal) texts and to move toward construction of historical narratives? Is it even possible, in good faith, to construct assertive or positive historical narratives given the indefinitely many narratives from within which one might work and the profoundly problematic assumptions that one must buy into in order to begin? Can history, in other words, ever divorce itself from philosophy?

4. How might one mix historical genres, styles, or methods in order to come up with open and "productive" historical discourses that serve to open up our culture (and historical culture in general) to other cultures or styles of thinking about time?

t e a c h e r s   a s   r e s e a r c h e r s

Take any world civilization text and locate the historical metaphors, narrative plots, and teleological assumptions within which the history is written. Show how these might lead to Eurocentric, homocentric, or other violent forms of boundary setting and exclusion. Try to come up with alternative ways of thinking history.

s u g g e s t e d   r e a d i n g s

The following bibliography concentrates on the works from the Buddhist tradition that I have found most helpful and that may not be familiar to readers in America. However, I have also included other works I consider important for linking up education, deconstruction, and history.

Abe, M. (1985). *Zen and Western thought*. Honolulu: University of Honolulu Press.

Abe, M. (1991). Emptiness is suchness. In F. Franck (Ed.), *The Buddha eye*. New York: Crossroad Publishing.

Abe, M. (1992). *A study of Dōgen: His philosophy and religion*. New York: State University of New York Press.

Coward, H. (1990). *Derrida and Indian philosophy*. Albany: State University of New York Press.

Coward, H., & Foshay, T. (1992). *Derrida and negative theology*. Albany: State University of New York Press.

Derrida, J. (1976). *Of grammatology*. (G. C. Spivak, Trans.). Baltimore: Johns Hopkins University Press.

Dōgen. (1985). *Moon in a dewdrop: Writings of Zen master Dōgen*. (K. Tanahashi, Ed.). San Francisco: North Point Press.

Ermarth, E. D. (1992). *Sequel to history: Postmodernism and the crisis of representational time*. Princeton: Princeton University Press.

Franck, F. (1991). *The Buddha eye: An anthology of the Koyoto school*. New York: Crossroad Publishing.

Gross, R. M. (1993). *Buddhism after patriarchy: A feminist history, analysis, and reconstruction of Buddhism*. New York: State University of New York Press.

Gudmunsen, C. (1977). *Wittgenstein and Buddhism*. London: Macmillan.

Hajime, T. (1986). *Philosophy as metanoetics*. (T. Yoshinori, Trans.). Berkeley: University of California Press.

Idries, S. (1968). *The way of the Sufi*. New York: Dutton.

Ives, C. (1992). *Zen awakening and society*. Honolulu: University of Honolulu Press.

Jenkins, K. (1992). *Rethinking history*. New York: Routledge.

Lyotard, J.-F. (1988). *The differend: Phrases in dispute*. Minneapolis: University of Minnesota Press.

Nishitani, K. (1982). *Religion and nothingness*. (J. Van Bragt, Trans.). Berkeley: University of California Press.

Ulmer, G. (1985). *Applied grammatology: Post(e)-pedagogy from Jacques Derrida to Joseph Beuys*. Baltimore: Johns Hopkins University Press.

Wittgenstein, L. (1953). *Philosophical investigations* (3rd ed). (G. E. M. Anscombe, Trans.). New York: Macmillan.

notes

[1] I would like to thank Professor Charles Strain of DePaul University's Religious Studies Department for his help and his ongoing dialogue on a number of Buddhist texts and their relations with history and ethics. His questions and criticisms have made me rethink in countless ways the nature of deconstruction, Buddhism, and history. For an attempt at an interreligious dialogue between Western and Eastern perspectives on history, with a focus on Buddhism and social commitment, see his "The Open Kingdom: Peter Hodgson's *God in History* in the Light of Interreligious Dialogue" (paper delivered at the Conference of the American Academy of Religions, November, 1992).

[2] In particular, under the wonderful guidance of a particularly enlightened reader of Wittgenstein, Dr. Ranjit Chatterjee, Wittgenstein (and Ranjit) have helped me get over the feeling that there is something "special" about mathematics, science, or language. They have helped me see that these are tools, just like any screwdriver or pliers, and that it is the *use* of the tool that we need to examine. I have made the ethical question primary in the sense that no matter how sophisticated some kind of technology may seem, the important question is: How is any tool used? Even a screwdriver, after all, can be used as a weapon, as can mathematics when it figures in the making of bombs. Dr. Chatterjee is currently working on a book on Wittgenstein as a Jewish thinker. He has published a number of articles on Wittgenstein, among which see his "Judaic Identity and Motifs in Wittgenstein," in *Jews and Austrians in the Twentieth Century*, ed. Robert S. Wistrich (New York: Macmillan,

1993); "Reading Whorf Through Wittgenstein," in *Lingua,* 67 (1985): 37–63; and "The Battle For Intelligence: Wittgenstein as Educator" (unpublished manuscript available on request, 1989).

[3] As Dominick LaCapra has nicely put it, "In a sense, historians are professionally trained not to read. Instead they are trained to use texts in rather narrow, utilitarian ways—to 'strip mine' or 'gut' them for documentary information. Indeed, historians tend to appreciate texts to the extent that they provide factual information about given times and places," Dominick LaCapra, *Rethinking Intellectual History: Texts, Contexts, Language* (Ithaca: Cornell University Press, 1983), 339.

[4] See, for example, Jonathan Feldman, *Universities in the Business of Repression: The Academic-Military-Industrial Complex in Central America* (Boston: South End Press, 1989).

[5] *All* pedagogic action . . . is, objectively, symbolic violence insofar as it is the imposition of a cultural arbitrary by an arbitrary power." Pierre Bourdieu and Jean-Claude Passeron, *Reproduction in Education, Society and Culture,* trans. Richard Nice (London: Sage Publications, 1977), 5. This work, though couched in the kind of scientific jargon I would deconstruct, does a nice job at describing some of the violent dimensions of education. It provides few hints, however, about how one might escape the educational machine of symbolic violence.

[6] I do not for a moment want to suggest that these are the only means to these ends: I am discovering similar themes in Judaism, in Amerindian religions, in Sufi writers, and in many other places. Quite simply, I speak from where I am.

[7] Both are terms that I hope will in turn be deconstructed: history treats of everything, since everything is in time; pedagogy is likewise that which pertains to any experience of learning, which, ideally, would be every moment of one's life. We might perform a Wittgensteinian move here and ask about all the different senses that would emerge if we looked at all the ways history and pedagogy are used. The terms eventually evaporate when confronted with indefinitely many meanings, each dependent upon a different context.

[8] "Love is a concrete relationship of transforming mediation in which self-negation turns into self-affirmation. . . . Love is nothingness, and at the same time, nothingness is love." Tanabe Hajime, *Philosophy as Metanoetics* (Berkeley: University of California Press, 1986), 265, cf. 273 and 292. Also, see Keiji Nishitani, *Religion and Nothingness* (Berkeley: University of California Press, 1982), 277–285.

[9] I use ellipsis points ". . ." to indicate the unending series of signs into which we would be led if we kept questioning in an open and ongoing way. Derrida sometimes "marks" this ongoing process through his own selection of metaphors: chain of supplementarity, the trace, differance, etc. He emphasizes that he is using these marks in a nonrepresentational way. Buddhists might mark these processes as indicative of the dependent co-origination of things, their impermanence, their emptiness . . . The name, in any case, is unimportant; what is important is the "seeing" into the "emptiness" of "things."

[10] "It is my view that the unique characteristic of the religious way of life, and the basic difference between religion and philosophy, comes to this: in religion one persistently pushes ahead in a direction where doubt becomes a reality for the self and makes itself really present to the self. This sort of real doubt may, of course, show up in philosophical skepsis, but philosophy tends to transfer it to the realm of theoretical reflection, and within those confines to seek an explanation and solution of the problem." Keiji Nishitani, *Religion and Nothingness,* trans. Jan Van Bragt (Berkeley: University of California Press, 1982).

[11] Thought experiment: take any sentence, and "see" how it is "built" of metaphors. "We get somewhere in history by piling up metaphors upon metaphors." Where is it we get? And what is it like to be "in" history? How does one "pile" a metaphor upon another? Does "under-standing" simply consist in recognizing and repeating, with familiarity, metaphors? Of standing-under a mountain of metaphors? Or of swimming in them, breathing them . . .?

[12] The inability of philosophical discourse to escape metaphor is one of the topics of Jacques Derrida's "White Mythology: Metaphor in the Text of Philosophy," in *Margins of Philosophy,* trans. Alan Bass (Chicago: University of Chicago Press, 1982), 209–272. The article is difficult and not recommended for beginning students of Derrida. I recommend Christopher Norris's *Derrida* (Cambridge: Harvard University Press, 1987) as a starting point and translation of some of Derrida's philosophical gestures.

[13] Jean-François Lyotard, a contemporary French philosopher, is often credited with popularizing the term "Postmodern" in his book *The Postmodern Condition: A Report on Knowledge,* trans. B. Massumi (Minneapolis: University of Minnesota Press, 1979). Lyotard is at his best in a later work, *The Differend: Phrases in Dispute* (Minneapolis: University of Minnesota Press, 1988).

[14] Theodore Roethke, "I Knew A Woman," in *The Collected Poems of Theodore Roethke* (New York: Anchor Books, 1975), 122.

[15] James Joyce, *Ulysses* (New York: Vintage, 1986), 28.

chapter 3

Antiracist Pedagogy in a College Classroom

Mutual Recognition and a Logic of Paradox

Ann Berlak

guiding questions

1. What is the author trying to say or teach?
2. What is the significance of what you read here for you personally and for you as a teacher?
3. What are the perspectives drawn on by the author to make the analysis?
4. How does this analysis help to inform our practice in classrooms?

For the white person who wants to know how to be my friend
The first thing you must do is to forget that i'm Black.
Second, you must never forget that i'm Black.

Pat Parker (1990, p. 297)

If the many non-black people who produce images or critical narratives
about blackness and black people do not interrogate their perspectives,
then they may simply recreate the imperial gaze—the look that seeks to
dominate, subjugate and colonize. This is especially so for white people
looking at and talking about blackness . . . Their ways of looking must
be fundamentally altered.

bell hooks (1992, p. 7)

Introduction

By the second week of class, there are nineteen of us. Men: two Latino, one
African-American, one Asian-American, seven white (as I thought of them
then—a few weeks later the designation I had come to prefer was European-
American); women: one African-American and seven white. One of the white
women and the African-American woman are the teachers. I am the white
teacher. The course, which meets twice a week in one-and-a-half-hour sessions,
is required of all students at the small progressive college where I teach. It is
called Humanities I.[1]

I had met my coteacher only briefly. Once I had seen her perform a poetry
reading; my impression was of a powerful presence. In her introduction to the
reading, she described an experience with a white woman from which she had
concluded, "We certainly didn't have much in common." The comment had
troubled me. Somehow it mattered to me that M—— would come to feel she
and I had something in common.

My uncharacteristic willingness to share my position as teacher with a
stranger, to enter into so much unknown, reflected my intense desire to untan-
gle some of the complexities involved in dealing significantly with racism and
other forms of oppression in classrooms. I had chosen to coteach with M——
because she was an experienced facilitator of workshops based on a particular
model for unlearning racism—a model which also addresses classism, sexism,
oppression of gays, lesbians and bisexuals, and anti-Semitism.[2] We were, as far
as we knew, among the first to use this model as the basis for a college course.

Though I saw race as a socially constructed category (West, 1982), I was
searching for an antiracist teaching process that celebrated racial differences,
that problematized rather than reinforced the view that in an ideal world race
wouldn't matter. However, I believed there "had to be more to anti-racist education than a celebration of differences, as if all are equally valued" (Murray,
1991, p. 7). I wanted students to understand that racism refers "not just to
personal attitudes and prejudices, but to power relations which determine and
then justify how society is arranged. . . .(that) there is more to fighting racism

than changing personal attitudes" (Murray, p. 7).[3] Further, I hoped that, as a result of the course, students would be better able to ally with one another across their differences for the purpose of building institutions that embody justice, respect, and the absence of oppression (Ellsworth, 1990; Young, 1990, p. 319).

I hoped teaching this course would help me understand more clearly how these commitments might be realized in practice, what shifts in values, attitudes, and thought processes would occur, and what methods would accomplish my intentions most successfully. For example, I wanted to clarify, both for myself and for the European-American students, whether to approach overcoming racism as a matter of self-interest (whites are also hurt by racism) or in terms of outrage at the unjust treatment of others.[4] I also wanted to clarify what the students of color were to gain directly from the course. I knew that if the people of color were there primarily to assist in the education of European Americans the conception of the course itself was fundamentally flawed.

Little seemed to have been written about what classroom practices—readings, interactions, and activities—would help me move toward my goals (Ellsworth, 1989, p. 7; Sleeter, 1991, p. 22). Particularly, there were few complex, contextualized accounts of teachers' struggles to accomplish similar intentions. Some analyses described antiracist teaching as a process of presenting theories and frameworks that exposed racist illusions, answered racist perspectives, and analyzed overt and institutionalized racist practices (All London's Teachers Against Racism and Facism [ALTARF], 1984, p. 13; Rattanis, 1992). Though I believed this could be of some value, my own experience (Berlak, 1989) suggested that such an approach could address neither the powerful psychological and material interests European-American students had in maintaining racist views nor the largely unacknowledged white privilege deeply embedded in the structures of modern discourse in the West, which "finessed easy resolutions such as the elimination of race prejudice by knowledge or the abolition of racism under socialism" (West, 1982, p. 50 and chap. 2).

I wondered if it was even possible to advance significantly toward my goals in our, or indeed in any, classroom. Sharon Welch (1991, pp. 95–98) has suggested certain conditions for socially emancipatory conversations that enable the breaking of race and gender hierarchies to occur: Participants must include sufficient numbers of persons who are members of less powerful groups (see also Franzen & Helmhold, 1991, p. 50); members of different groups must grant each other sufficient respect to listen to other ideas and be challenged by them and to recognize that their lives are so intertwined that each is accountable to the other; members of the more powerful groups must not be able simply to leave the conversation; and the group must engage in material interaction with one another—that is, they must work together. Did the low proportion of people of color in our class and the fact that members of the group could leave the class at will (though not entirely without consequence) doom the project in advance? Was Welch correct that "material" interactions are prerequisite to mutual respect and accountability, and, if so, would classroom interactions count as "material"? Giroux wrote, "Students must be given the opportunity to engage in anti-racist struggles in their efforts to *link schooling to real life*" (1991, p. 255, emphasis added). To what extent, I wondered, would what happened in our classroom count as "real life"? To what extent could any classroom, bounded by the calendar and the clock, ever be a site where recognizing and dismantling oppression are truly significant acts?

These questions and the stories of Humanities I that follow arose in a historical context of increasing racial and cultural diversity in the United States and of new forms of racism on the rise (Winant, 1990) in a society where racism is attributable not only to individuals but also to institutions and structures that insure some people have less access than others to material and intangible resources, the intangible including self-confidence and self-esteem (West, 1992, p. 11). The recession economy was characterized by widespread backlash against affirmative action programs, much public talk about reverse discrimination, and various racial and ethnic groups blaming one another for their economic dislocation. It was a time when educators at all levels were debating intensely how the schools should respond to these phenomena. These debates were formulated at the university level in terms of the role the "canon" should play in the curriculum and the importance of students learning to view the social world from non-Western as well as Western perspectives. In elementary and secondary schools the controversies were argued in terms of what multicultural means, the value of Afrocentric curricula, and whether state and local districts should adopt textbooks that some consider multicultural and others consider racist.

It was in this context that the faculty at our college decided to require a course that would engage students in examining their location in race, class, gender, and sexual orientation hierarchies. The hope was that this course would put students in better positions to form alliances across differences and thus to work together to overcome institutionalized injustices.

In the next section, I briefly present the structure of and rationale for the model we used. Then I tell my story of the model-in-practice in Humanities I, interspersing some experiences from workshops I attended during the semester that were based to varying degrees upon the model. The next sections are alternative readings of Humanities I, and represent attempts to clarify questions about antiracist teaching I began with and some questions that arose along the way. The reader should keep in mind that the issues and events surrounding the issue of racism that I report on are just a fraction of the story of the course, which dealt also with classism, sexism, anti-Semitism, and heterosexism, issues which certainly equaled racism in their interest and complexity.

The Model and the Model-in-Practice
//////////////////////////////////////

The model we worked with was designed a decade ago to help members of the working class overcome their divisions and differences so they could build more successful alliances against what was seen as an unjust political and economic system. Thus, the model focused on the range of oppressions that at any given time are seen as interfering with alliance building among working-class members. Presently, the social divisions most frequently considered when doing this work are racism, sexism, heterosexism, adultism, and anti-Semitism.

Liberation Theory

The fundamental premise of the theory underlying the model is that no one is born oppressor or oppressed; we are all born into a society already "polluted" with negative attitudes and beliefs about more and less powerful groups of people—children, women, members of racial and ethnic groups, and so forth. This pollution is perpetuated by every social institution, and it is through contact with these institutions that new generations are inducted into multiple and shifting memberships in dominant and subordinate groups. The terms *multiple* and *shifting* point to the fact that I, for example, am a member of some dominant or more powerful groups—middle class, white, and adult. At the same time, I am also a member of the subordinate groups Jews and women.

We defined oppression as systematic pervasive routine mistreatment of individuals on the basis of their membership in groups which are disadvantaged by institutionl power imbalances in a particular society. Oppression involves normalized mistreatment—invalidation, denial, nonrecognition of the complete humanity of the targeted group—as well as instances of violence.

Those who are objects of oppression are called, in the model, targets of that oppression.[5] Nontargets are socialized, though to varying degrees, through exposure to systematic, institutionally transmitted misinformation to believe and act on the basis of the prevailing social judgments about the targets, that is, to internalize domination. Targets are socialized to varying degrees to accept these judgments about themselves, to internalize oppression. Internalized oppression and domination arise in spite of resistance by both targets and nontargets to incorporating these judgments. All people experience being targeted for some period of time during their lives because all are at one time children. Adultism—the systematic, institutionalized mistreatment of children—is a form of oppression to which we all are subjected. This oppression we experience as children prepares us for roles as both oppressors and oppressed.[6]

The purpose of the unlearning racism process is to contribute to undoing the effects and eliminating the causes of oppression. The assumption is that the process will advance both targets' and nontargets' abilities to become allies to members of their own and other groups, and as allies to work to reduce oppression at individual and institutional levels.

The Model-in-Practice

The model can be described in terms of five activities: power shuffles, context settings, separate meetings of target and nontarget groups or caucuses, Speak Out and Reflect Back sessions, and making commitments to future action. The syllabus I pass out on the first day of class reflects my intention to integrate these activities with readings from a text composed primarily of first person accounts of experiences with racism, sexism, adultism, class oppression, anti-

Semitism, and, as labeled in the model, heterosexism. In retrospect I see a vague plan to alternate responsibility between M—— and myself; I taking the lead when we respond to the text, and M—— taking the lead when we learn directly from one another's experience as structured by the unlearning racism model.

The process of "unlearning" the "isms" involves encountering and exploring each oppression in turn, customarily beginning with race.[7] We, however, begin with a three-week examination of adultism. We hope beginning here will encourage class members to recognize our commonalities and to develop a sense of community that will hold us together when we begin examining the issues that divide. M—— and I separate the class into four groups that are as heterogeneous as possible. Among the limitations to heterogeneity is, as far as we can tell from results of a questionnaire, the lack of gay/lesbian/bisexual or female students of color. Because of the racial composition of the class, each group has only one student of color.

During the next three weeks, students read to others in their groups and discuss the autobiographies, focusing on their childhood experiences, we have asked them to write. With few exceptions, students tell of childhoods characterized by some degree of physical, sexual, or emotional abuse. We are amazed at the recounting of so much pain. We wonder whether such experiences are overrepresented in our college, if the student body here is atypical. In the small groups we also discuss accounts of childhood presented in our texts in order to broaden the array of childhood experiences we know something about. We consider liberating, as well as oppressive, experiences and the ways we and the children whose lives are described in the readings have resisted internalizing the critical messages transmitted by adults. We also look at what these experiences suggest about the institutions—families, schools, laws—of the societies in which we have come of age.

Toward the end of the third week, the energy in the groups dwindles. I wonder what's going on. One day after class I'm approached by about half the women in the class. They tell me they can't abide the sexism that is running rampant in three of the four groups. They tell me they're being talked over, ignored, and put down and that they don't feel like sharing with their groups any more. Laura asks to be moved into a different group; she "can't learn in a group with Jason because he is so sexist." M—— and I agree on another group she can join. At a subsequent class shortly thereafter, I notice that Gil, one of the two Latinos and a member of Laura's new group, is sitting apart from the others, writing. After class Laura tells M—— and me that when she entered the group to which she had been transferred, she asked everyone's names. When Gil's turn came, he answered, adding, "You can remember me. I'm the tall, dark, and handsome one." She responded to him, she tells us, by saying, "F___ you." The next day Gil hands me what he had been writing during class: his rendition of and puzzled reaction to his interaction with Laura.

So much for our plan to postpone conflict, division, and dissension.

We have our first Speak Out. Each of the four groups stands before the others in the class for about fifteen minutes and the members extemporaneously complete, when they are moved to do so, each of three statements:

"What I want you to know about me and my group . . . ," "What I never want to see, hear or have happen again . . . ," and "What I expect from my allies . . ." When it is their group's turn, those speaking out speak from the viewpoint of children. We listen in silence to statements of the following sorts:

> I want you to know that when my father was drunk he used to beat me.
> I never want to hear an adult say, "You're too young to understand."
> I expect my allies [i.e., adults] to listen to me and take what I say seriously.
> I expect my allies to always intervene if they see someone abusing a child.

Immediately after the Speak Out is completed, the Reflect Back session takes place. Those who listened complete the phrase, "I heard you say . . .," by repeating as close to verbatim as possible a statement made during the Speak Out. In this one oppression only, we are members of neither a target nor a nontarget group, since we were all targeted as children and are all nontargets now as adults. After each group has had its turn, we sit in a circle on the floor and discuss the experience. We are all quite moved and, at least momentarily, united.

The beginning of the fourth week. We're ready to move officially to what divides us. M—— will take the lead. We begin with the power shuffle. All members of the class stand on one side of the room in silence. M—— makes it clear that students are free not to participate at any time. She begins by asking, "Will all of those who are African Americans walk across the room. . . . Stand for a moment and see who is with you. (Len has walked across the room and is standing there alone.) See who is left behind. Notice how you feel to have walked across. Notice how you feel to have stayed where you are." Silence for several moments. "You may return."

This process is repeated for a dozen or more designations of groups that are oppressed in our society. Among them are the poor and working class, women, disabled (Susan walks across the room with her cane), gays, lesbians, bisexuals, Latinos, Asians, Jews, children of alcoholics or persons addicted to drugs (only three students remain in place for this), and finally, those who have been children.

Everyone has been both target and nontarget. The power imbalances of society, as well as the multiple places in which each of us stands, have been presented and represented experientially. The mood is somber. There are tears. When the exercise is over we talk about how deeply and inexplicably moving the power shuffle has been.

Next we take up racism. M—— gives the context setting, laying out the theory that supports the model, including the concept of internalized oppression. This context setting transmits information on racism that is designed to counter the systematic misinformation that institutions sanction and perpetuate. It clarifies how institutions reward and condition nontargets to accept their roles as perpetrators, and how targets internalize and express their oppression, sometimes violently or self-destructively. M—— tells us how, after years of self-reflection, she has come to recognize her own internalized oppression, a deeply buried desire to be white. She states explicitly that there is no place for blame or guilt in the theory, that no one asks to be born into an oppressor position or to internalize racist views.

We then divide into target and nontarget caucuses. In our class this means the four men of color and M—— in one group, the rest of us in the other. The assumption behind dividing the group on the basis of target/nontarget status on each oppression is that only in separate groups can members of either group do the work that makes building alliances across differences possible.[8] In their separate group the people of color will have "the separatist space (that) often facilitates coming to . . . critical consciousness" (hooks, 1991, p. 35); they will identify and examine their internalized oppression, and "locate that marginal space of difference inwardly defined" (hooks, 1991, p. 15).

In the European-American caucus we discuss several questions: How does it feel to be in this group? What do we know about our heritages? What aspects of our heritage are we proud of? How were we socialized into racism and how did we resist? How have we been hurt by racism? These questions encourage us to consider our attitudes toward our European-American heritages, because unless European Americans know and respect their own cultures, they will not respect, nor gain enough respect from, other white people, leaving them unable to support and learn from each other. When they cannot get help from one another in overcoming their racist and Eurocentric conditioning, their only alternative is to seek it from people of color, a burden that is not properly theirs (Ellsworth, 1989; hooks, 1984). Further, in order for people of European descent to feel empathy for the loss entailed by the destruction of the cultures of nondominant peoples, they must have some notion of what it means to have lost one's culture.

We discuss how we feel to be in the white group. Some acknowledge discomfort. Laura resents it; she doesn't "know why we have to look at differences." Others welcome the opportunity to talk about race in the safety of the caucus. Next we consider what we like about being European-American. It's like pulling teeth. Few of the whites know anything substantial about their heritages. Most express dismay that they are white and feel, in fact, that being white is being nothing. Only Susan expresses pride, speaking proudly of her radical Irish forebears. I respond to the question by claiming some pride in being Jewish, which is not exactly fair, since the assignment is to identify strengths in our nontarget heritages. Bob deals with the question by calling attention to the eighth of his heritage that is native American. I feel fairly certain the discussion of pride has been of little worth.

Though they don't want to talk about white pride (even the words stick in their mouths), what they do want to talk about surprises me. Laura says, "I know this is racist but if my grandparents from Italy made it, then why can't blacks and Hispanics?" She adds that when she was in high school she wanted very much to be accepted by the black students, who rejected her, calling her a honkey. She says perhaps she should just accept the abusive treatment "to make up for the abuse that they received." Joyce and Paul describe experiences similar to Laura's, labeling the harassment they received "reverse racism." In the context setting we had talked at length about the psychological and social effects of racism on its targets, including how the institutional violence of racism can evoke violence and anger in individuals. I realize again that information does not in itself significantly dismantle racist conditioning. I re-present information on the differences between the experiences of Latinos and African Americans on the one hand and European-American immigrants on the other. I reiterate that oppression involves institutionalized imbalances of power, thus the harassment of whites by members of oppressed groups is not and should not be seen as a reverse racism (though it is certainly unfortunate and hurtful), but I am under no illusion that elaborating this view once again gets to the heart of the matter.

The European-American students ask these questions in the safety of the separate caucuses because they know they have incorporated racist views and are, at least on a conscious level, eager to excise them. On the night after the European Americans met in their race separate group, Adam writes that he is always afraid he'll "say something wrong" about race. Rachel, on the same night, writes:

> In theory . . . all humans are created equal. In practice, well, I don't have a lot of practice. I grew up in an all white town. When I see a black woman on the street I am acutely aware that I do think "black woman." While I know that doesn't imply anything derogatory, and that her color is very much a part of her, I wonder if a great deal of racism doesn't come from that sort of instant classification, and why I don't just think "human." I look forward to the Speak Out when we will all come together and I will perhaps be able to clarify this for myself.

Nov. ——. Today we have the Speak Out by the people of color. I prompt: "What I never want to see, hear, or have happen again. . . ." Len (the African-American man) contributes only once, "I never again want to see my children stopped by a policeman because they are black." M——, Gil, Joel, and Richard (the Japanese American) speak of both the joy and pain of being members of their groups. I misstate the third question. Instead of saying, "What I expect from my allies . . .," I say, "What I *need* from my allies. . . ." M—— corrects my formulation. "It's not 'need.' We don't *need* anything from you." I know my choice of words angers her. The European Americans reflect back, "I heard you say. . . ." It's six o'clock. The class is dismissed. I leave feeling something has gone wrong.

Jerry, a European-American student, writes in his journal that night:

> I don't know why but I didn't feel nearly as emotional and as much sympathy for the racism Speak Out (as the Speak Out on adultism). Consciously, I am not a racist, but I think I was so bombarded by racist views where I grew up in Alabama that I literally can't feel anything subconsciously. During the Speak Out I felt angry because I wasn't feeling a lot of sympathy.

Adam, a gay white man, wrote later about the same event:

> My feeling was we'd spent quite enough time on racism. The Speak Out
> made me feel very strange. I wanted to reach out to these people, under-
> stand their pain, but I was removed, unable. The closest I could come was
> identification with their anger. It wasn't enough. I can never really under-
> stand. I was disturbed for days. There was something in the way, an invis-
> ible barrier I didn't know how to cross.

He later comes to see me in my office, troubled. "I wasn't moved by the
Speak Out. Not like the last time [the adultism Speak Out]. There was a barrier. I felt like M—— was dramatizing. I feel guilty because I think it's my racism that keeps me from feeling." I tell Adam I feel the same way.

(Two weeks later, at a Speak Out by people of color at a weekend workshop
using the model, an African-American man tells us he wants us to know that
he now crosses the street when he sees a white woman approaching, because
he knows that she is likely to be afraid of him. This statement affects me more
powerfully than any other at the workshop and classroom Speak Outs by the
people of color. I wonder why.)

The day following the racism Speak Out, M—— is absent. In his journal
Adam described his feelings as he entered class:

> When we reconnected for the next session I was relieved to discover I was
> not a complete neurotic, others had also been disturbed. I said "hello"
> to a classmate, a person of color. He said "hello" in a different way than
> usual.

I am slated to conduct the class on this day. I plan to lead a discussion of an
excerpt from Ellison's *Invisible Man*. As we begin, Gil interrupts. He wants to
hear the white people's reaction to the Speak Out. Joel, the other Latino, and
Len agree. I respond that the model explicitly stipulates that the nontargets
listen to the targets at a Speak Out and show that they have listened by reflecting back what they have heard, but that the nontarget groups are not to express
to the target groups their feelings about the Speak Out. I explain the reason for
this as I understand it: The Speak Out and Respond Back attempt to reverse the
power relations that prevail outside, as well as inside, the classroom, where
people of color are always listening to whites. I tell them that if M—— were
here I'd be glad to negotiate this, and that I intend for us all to critique the
model, but only after we have given it a chance. We move to the discussion of
Ellison. Low energy in the class.

Nov. ——. M—— returns for the following session and we begin the context
setting on sexism. We have spent three weeks on racism and only six weeks
remain to deal with sexism, heterosexism, social class, anti-Semitism, and a
wrap-up. It's time to move on.

Gil, one of the Latinos, interrupts M——'s opening sentence:

> You want me to think about how I'm a sexist. But we're not done with
> racism. I want to know what the white people thought about the Speak
> Out. We were told it would be dealt with later. That's what happens to

people of color all the time. People of color are always being told to wait. We need some compensation. We were the givers. We shared and we came home empty-handed. I paid my money. I have a right to know this.

I am caught entirely by surprise.

We discuss the issue raised by Gilberto for the remaining hour and a half of the class. Following are some of the statements made:

> John (a white male): I thought we would sit around like we did after the Speak Out on adultism and talk about what we felt.
>
> Len: The atmosphere is different in this class today. What is it you [whites] don't want to say? It's a thing of vulnerability.
>
> M—— (to Len): Why do you need to hear what white people think? That's our internalized racism.
>
> Jerry: I thought people of color were fed up listening to us.
>
> Len: I didn't inflict racism on them. It's a two way street. There's racism here in this room. Right after our Speak Out I wanted to hear them. But it's too late now. We missed the chance.
>
> Joel: We feel an emptiness. We need a recognition of emptiness. I am in solidarity with Gil. When M—— came back today, our allies should have raised the issue.
>
> Sam (white male): I listened to you [people of color] in the last class. I thought you felt your concerns were addressed.
>
> Gil: You didn't help us speak up. You guys weren't good allies.
>
> Laura: Let's have a vote on what to do. This discussion is a big waste of time.
>
> Sam: We shouldn't give in to their internalized oppression.
>
> Laura: That's a pretty racist thing to say.
>
> M——: When I started talking about sexism, you interrupted. Ann was right about what she did. I would have left the class if the white people had started talking about how they felt about what we said in the Speak Out.
>
> Ann: I felt split. I felt a responsibility to M—— to respect the model, and I wanted to have the people of color get what they wanted. And I was thinking of the fact that each day we spend on racism is one day less for sexism and heterosexism. I think I was in an impossible position. One thing for certain. This class reflects some of the major contradictions out there in the society. It's certainly not easy. But we didn't think it would be easy. I don't think that this can be resolved.

After class M—— and I agree that we have done the only thing we could have done today: used our authority to refuse to authoritatively resolve the issue and move the class on. On the next day, however, we did move the class on, though no one felt resolved. Gil told us he had gotten some of what he wanted: "I stopped the class."

Later that week Len assessed the situation in a private conversation with me:

> It's not totally bad to try to discuss these things in an educational manner. If we discussed it outside of class, there'd be friction. I hope it's a form of

enlightenment, but I feel we're still in limbo. I don't feel we've completed the cycle of racism. I want to *know* you. I want to know what you think. In order to understand me, you [whites] need to ask me questions."

M—— told me she thought that Len's wish to continue the dialogue reflected his desire to take care of whites. "It's his internalized oppression," she said.

Rachel wrote of that class in her journal:

> I was very angry at the direction the class took today, and yet I found myself unable to express that anger because to do so would likely have been perceived by myself and others as racist. I respect Gil's feelings. However, I felt that the way he diverted the class *when* he did was disrespectful of the women in class. . . . It was frustrating to think that the two target groups could have problems of respect between them. I was also frustrated that though many solutions were suggested we failed to resolve the problem . . . It's painful that a group that seemed so together after the adultism discussion couldn't come together on this problem. I suppose that any kind of growth involves pain. I just hope that pain doesn't become a brick wall.

Sam wrote:

> I feel a bit excited and even in awe of my capacity to change. This surprises me because if anyone would have told me at 4:30 this afternoon that in the next hour and one half I would: be accused of having said only racist statements during this time, have it pointed out to me that I was not a good ally, . . . accuse my instructors of avoiding pointing out an example of what we're learning in the actions of classmates [What he wanted was for us to confirm his labeling of the men of color's desire as internalized oppression.], come face to face with my own racism, and still feel good about myself, . . . I would have told you you were no doubt talking about someone else. I was frustrated with Ann and M—— for not providing focus in what was becoming a free for all. But then I looked at what happened. A real concern about the reality of racism in a progressive institution in a "safe" humanities class was addressed. In a flash it came to me. The words I said were not inherently racist, but in the context of the class some of my statements were racist . . . It took a breakdown in the class to teach me how to live what I am learning.

Adam wrote:

> The men of color wanted to know our feelings, our questions. I wanted to share with them how I felt then. I was confused about how to be an ally. The tension in the room was very difficult for me to endure. Something was happening I didn't understand and I felt defensive. After sitting with it for a couple of days I understood better what occurred. Although I'd successfully extricated racial jokes and slurs from my conscious speech, my attitude about wanting to move on came from an unconscious, racist

place. The target group felt swept under the rug. The class taught me more about racism than any of the others. Truthfully, I was worried that we wouldn't get to hetero-sexism if we spent another day on racism. I felt something was going to be taken away from me to make room for "them."

Adam told me several months later that he had recognized that another layer of his desire to move on was his wish to be an ally to the women in the class.

Take One on the Model as Practiced

Differences within Groups and Individuals

Like all practices, the practice in our classroom was both liberating and op- pressive. It dispelled racist (and sexist, etc.) concepts, myths, and misinforma- tion, and it perpetuated them; the very process that illuminated and privileged racial and ethnic differences also elided, erased, and collapsed differences, dif- ferences between individuals as well as differences or complexity within groups.

Let us first consider the power shuffle and the separation into multiple and shifting target and nontarget groups. By requiring participants to claim mem- bership in racial categories, these activities acknowledged, perpetuated, and deepened a way of categorizing people that has served, paradoxically, both as a basis for justifying some groups' power over others and as a basis for estab- lishing identity, a sense of self-worth, and community (West, 1982). Requiring people to claim membership in multiple and shifting groups (gender, class, age, as well as race) acknowledged, perpetuated and deepened the participants' un- derstanding that they and others view the world from multiple positions and that others recognize their multiple roles; that people are multidimensional, holding target status in some categories and nontarget status in others. Thus, the activities formalized and privileged affinity groups based upon racial/ethnic likenesses within the groups and differences from others (Ellsworth, 1989), while embodying that racial/ethnic categories are not the only important ones. The activities also structured recognition of some of the power imbalances asso- ciated with these differences in the present political and historical context.

In Humanities I, the ethnic/race separate group meetings and the Speak Out highlighted similarities within two racial/ethnic categories—people of color and European Americans—and differences between them. The explorations in the caucuses encouraged awareness of similarities within and differences be- tween the groups, moving beyond more widely recognized and "innocent" cat- egories of difference, such as food preferences and celebrations, to consider the different historical and contemporary experiences that shape the ways target and nontarget racial/ethnic groups see themselves and one another and act in the world. Thus challenged was the assumption students, particularly European- American students, often make that they shouldn't see racial differences: Sarah, chastising herself about her "tendency to instant classification," asks, "Why don't I just think human?"

Paradoxically, however, while calling attention to similarities within caucuses and differences between the two groups, the model shadowed differences within groups and complexity within individuals. One way it did this was by attending to a limited array of differences. The limits upon the array were in part inevitable, a function of limited time and the composition of the groups. In our class we used "people of color" as the target category because a single African American does not form a group. Even if our class had been more racially diverse, some differences would inevitably have been elided. The differences between Asian Americans' experiences and African Americans' experiences might have been acknowledged, but all significant differences among African Americans and among Asian Americans—age, class, gender, family's country of origin—could not possibly have been recognized. There could never have been enough time to explore the wide variety of differences within any racial/ethnic group.[9]

Another way to think about this is that the classroom processes failed to convey fully that the effects of membership in multiple groups are not merely additive. The meaning of being an African American or a European American is significantly different for a woman than for a man, different for those men aged twenty-five than for those aged fifty. The model, while allowing people to claim membership in different groups, distorts the experience of women and men by separating consideration of their race from consideration of their gender, a separation that conveys the idea that there is an essential gender free black, Latino, or white experience. Of course the same goes for all combinations of statuses (hooks, 1990, p. 28; Spelman, 1988, p. 125).[10] Although a false unity is imposed through the process, there is a diversity expressed, as individuals share experiences with one another in the caucus groups and Speak Outs, that teaches and embodies these irreducible differences.

What is more, the process of categorizing is inherently oppressive, not only because it erases the complexity of individuals and variations within the group, but also because, like all such processes, it reflects the power of those who do the naming, of those who decide which differences will be recognized, reinforced, and created (Spelman, 1988, p. 150). When "unlearning racism" we are asked to walk across the room when a particular group is named or to stand where we are, to go into one group that is named or into another. The creation of a multiheritage or multiracial category addresses this problem but cannot solve it. Does a Spanish-speaking white woman who lives in the United States but who was born in Spain and brought up in Argentina, who has limited English proficiency, and who identifies as a Latina belong in a mixed heritage or Latina or any target group? What percentage of native American heritage would put Bob in the native American rather than a multiheritage group? Who should draw the line? No model or process of categorizing can be innocent of power or fully recognize the complexity of individuals, all the differences within groups of individuals, and how the relationship of difference to oppression changes over time and differs from place to place. Thus, our classroom process inevitably reproduced stereotypes and power even as it also effectively worked against them.

Conflicts between Statuses

Since each oppression is taken up in turn, the model does not call attention to conflicts between the interests of various statuses. It provides no place to examine public policy issues—affirmative action, for example—that encapsulate these conflicts, so it does not show how a politics of race can suppress issues of gender and how a politics of gender can marginalize racial issues.[11]

In our class, however, the model-in-practice forced us to confront some of these contradictions, and it was this confrontation that seemed to result in the most significant shifts in our readings of the world. Let us consider our struggle about whether the European Americans should be allowed to respond to the people of color after the Speak Out in these terms. That situation may be viewed as a pedagogical moment when "an opportunity of classroom practice holds the potential for profound shifts in perspective and meaning," as an uncanny moment "when that which has been made invisible (even though it is ever present), . . . makes itself known" (Ellsworth, 1990, p. 9–10). It was one of those moments when students and teachers "are most receptive to uncovering how they are invested in their own meaning-making practice" (Lewis, 1990, p. 476).

One way of looking at the controversy about continuing or closing off conversation after the Speak Out on racism is to consider how individuals and groups first read the situation from their differing and often conflicting initial viewpoints, and how they then repositioned themselves and reread the experience through different sets of lenses.

The men of color immediately read the events in terms of antiracist discourse. Gil: "People of color are always being told to wait." The initial responses of the European Americans came from within a racist and Eurocentric discourse; the whites initially neither saw the issue from the perspective of the men of color, nor recognized the significance of the power imbalance in the class with its tiny number of people of color, the missing teacher of color on that day, and the presence of a European-American lead teacher. My surprise that the issue was still hot for Gil on the day that M—— returned indicates to me my own initial Eurocentric, racist positioning. However, it appears that Gil's insistence that we consider his viewpoint prompted at least some of the European Americans to adopt his reading of the situation, as suggested by the journal entries of Sam, Adam, and Rachel and by my own analysis of this event.

The women, including myself and M——, on the day she returned, and at least one gay man also read the situation through the lenses of other oppressions in which we had personal investments. Rachel, M——, Adam and I looked at the event from a feminist standpoint. Rachel expressed in her journal what M—— and I were both acutely aware of, that Gil's interruption was formulated in opposition to the examination of sexism. It is also possible that M—— and I read the situation through our own internalized sexism; I later wondered if we would have allowed ourselves to be derailed from our plans for the day if we had been interrupted by a female student. M—— read the situation from an antiracist, as well as feminist, position, though her antiracist perspective led her to a position that was the opposite of Gil's, that the men of color's desire to hear from the European Americans was an indication of internalized oppression that should not be satisfied.[12]

When we faced the class the day that M—— returned, she and I each, without discussing it with one another, took for granted and communicated to the students that we could neither dismiss the issue summarily nor grant the men of color's request; that we would assert our authority by refusing to say what should be done, and in this way indicate there could be no easy, satisfactory resolution to our predicament; that some of the contradictions of the society outside the classroom were within us and among us, suggesting opposing and contradictory responses; and that the repressed had returned and would return again. In that moment I think it seemed to all of us that the classroom was "real life." It also seemed to me that M—— and I did indeed have something in common, the differences in our perspectives, perhaps only momentarily, resolved.

Take Two on the Model

Questions remain. What might we have done in class to encourage the European Americans to feel greater empathy for those targeted by racism? What might we have done to increase the likelihood that the whites would more easily identify the racism implicit in both our failure to recognize the intensity of the men of color's desire and our closing off of the conversation about it? What was it that the men wanted from us, and should "we" have given it to "them"? To what extent did and do these questions suggest problems with the model or problems with the ways we put the model into practice? What changes should we try next time?

There are many plausible ways of looking at these questions. I will look at them through the lenses of what I, drawing upon the work of feminist psychoanalyst Jessica Benjamin (1988), call mutual recognition theory.

Mutual Recognition Theory

Benjamin's theory is intersubjective: it maintains that the individual grows through relationships to others (p. 19–20). Benjamin argues that in order to develop and maintain a sense of self—to feel alive—to realize authorship and agency (p. 12), and to know she feels and is, a person needs another to recognize her. "Near-synonyms" Benjamin proposes for the concept of recognition are: "affirm, validate, acknowledge, know, accept, understand, empathize, take in, tolerate, appreciate, see, identify with, find familiar, . . . love" (p. 15–16).

Central to the theory is that recognition must be mutual. For recognition to be mutual, it must occur between persons who *see one another as both like and unlike themselves.* This is so, first, because your recognition of me is only of value to me if I see you as an other, a separate self, i.e., a self that is different from myself. But in order for your recognition of me to be of value, I must also be aware that you are like me—that we have a shared reality, that you are contacting my mind (p. 37). Thus, interaction with others with whom one feels both sameness (the sense of shared reality) and difference (the sense that it is a separate other that is sharing one's reality) must occur simultaneously for it to contribute to one's feeling of aliveness and agency, of being a self.

This recognition is mutual in the sense that I must see you as both like and separate from me in order to find your recognition of me enlivening, and you must, in fact, recognize me by seeing me as both like and unlike yourself. If I do not recognize you, I can receive nothing from you and your recognition of me is meaningless (p. 35). For this reason effacing the other leads ultimately to winning nothing. "The result is negation, emptiness, isolation" (p. 35). One can only feel alive in the presence of an equal other.

Mutual recognition theory acknowledges interpersonal need and dependence as against bourgeois autonomy and the ideal of the autonomous individual.[13] For Benjamin, denial of dependency on the other is a mystification (p. 187). Confrontation with an independent other is a real condition of development and change, a simultaneous process of transforming and being transformed by the other (p. 49). The theory also acknowledges that human relationships will involve conflict: one must at times collide with an outside other in order to recognize the differences both parties require to enliven one another.

Understanding others as they understand themselves and being understood as I understand myself are ideals that can only be approximated, and then only in quite particular circumstances. In part this is because to recognize sameness and difference in relation to another requires that we know ourselves and others. Yet the degree to which we can know both ourselves and one another is limited. The notion that each person can understand the other in relation to oneself presupposes both conscious awareness—I am conscious of my motivations, fears, and so forth—and the ability to express or confirm that knowledge accurately and unambiguously to others (Young, 1990, p. 310). Then, of course, the other person may misunderstand what I mean; misunderstanding is always possible (p. 310–311).

A Logic of Paradox

Recognizing that the other person is outside our control and yet needing her (Benjamin, 1988, p. 221), experiencing sameness without obliterating difference, achieving separation without isolation, maintaining connection without losing self (Tarule, 1990, p. 160), holding on to "differences between" without undermining unity, and living with the tension between ethnocentricity and multiculturalism require what Benjamin calls a logic of paradox. Benjamin assumes such paradox is often experienced as painful, even intolerable (Benjamin, p. 50). She argues that the process of mutual recognition, which depends upon the holding of paradox, therefore, often goes awry (p. 49). Breakdown can occur through either assertion or denial of sameness or of difference.

We need to consider how power differentials affect the process of mutual recognition in order to further illuminate our grapple with racism in Humanities I. "Both the assertion of difference and the denial of difference can operate on behalf of domination" (Spelman, 1988, p. 11). Whether such assertions and denials contribute to domination partly depends on who defines the likeness or the difference, who says which likenesses and differences are relevant, and who is like or not like whom. Such definitions are strongly influenced by institutionalized power imbalances in the society; among the privileges of the more powerful are creating and ordering categories of likeness and difference. Thus, it is usually the more powerful group that identifies the similarities and the differences between themselves and subordinate groups (it is white women who claim "marriage is slavery"), in this way rendering invisible particular characteristics that are significant for the less powerful (such as the differences between marriage and slavery) (Spelman, p. 12). And when the logic of paradox dissolves through the assertion of difference and the denial of sameness by members of more powerful groups, the different qualities attributed by the more to the less powerful are most often those devalued by the society and its institutions (for example, the less powerful being described as lazier or more irrational). The acceptance by a dominated individual of a dominator's definition of either the likenesses or the differences between them is one part of the process we have referred to as internalized oppression.

Finally, Benjamin accepts that periods of denial of recognition are inevitable. The best that can be hoped for is a continuing, evolving dynamic balance between the two processes: "If the denial of recognition does not become frozen into unmovable relationships, the play of power need not harden into domination. [B]reakdown and renewal are constant possibilities" (Benjamin, 1988, p. 223).

Using the Mutual Recognition Theory

Meeting in target/nontarget caucuses provides an opportunity for people who share experiences relative to particular oppressions as either targets or nontargets to deepen their mutual recognition within that group. However, this deepening is by no means assured. In order for both target and nontarget caucuses to provide opportunities for deepening mutual recognition, they must encourage awareness of both similarities and differences on a range of qualities. The focus in our caucuses was more upon similarities than differences within the groups. In the white caucus we dealt inadequately with both how we were like one another and how we differed from each other, in part because we lacked information about how historical and contemporary institutions and experiences have contributed both to our lack of awareness of white privilege—our racism—and to our resistance to racism, i.e., the antiracist and egalitarian elements of our heritages.

To what extent did our activities promote mutual recognition between whites and people of color? It appears to me that the Speak Out/Reflect Back activity advanced recognition of differences between the two groups without contributing significantly to their understanding of commonalities between them. Though the study of adultism had highlighted significant commonalities between the groups, the class had not yet examined the effects of oppression on gays/lesbians/bisexuals, Jews, poor and working-class people, and women. Later sessions illuminated for European Americans who are targets of other oppressions (white women, white gays/lesbians/bisexuals) the effects of being targeted (for example, low self-esteem and lack of respect for other members of one's group) which they share with people of color.

This clarification of differences and de-emphasis on commonality between whites and people of color may help us understand why class members did not generally experience the outcome Benjamin claims for mutual recognition but, in fact, experienced the reverse—what some described as deadness, emptiness, and lack of feeling. One way to frame this is that those sentiments reflected the breakdown of the process of mutual recognition, which resulted from our refusal to continue the conversation between the targets and nontargets that began in the Speak Out and Reflect Back. That conversation may be seen as an initial movement toward mutual recognition, which highlighted differences between the two groups. Closing off the conversation after the Reflect Back exercise embodied the crucially important need to call attention to (and, at least symbolically, redress) a significant difference between whites and people of color—the power differential between them—by requiring nontargets to listen but not to respond. But by interrupting the process at this point, by stopping the conversation, both nontargets and targets were prevented from learning more about both the similarities/differences *within* the separate groups and the similarities/differences *between* them. The members of neither target nor nontarget groups could know to what extent their responses to the Speak Out were both idiosyncratic and shared by other members of their caucus, and the targets and nontargets could not learn how their responses to the Speak Out were both like and unlike one another's.

The no-response-by-nontargets was especially limiting for the men of color, who could not check out how the white people reacted to the Speak Out. They could not, therefore, discover to what extent they were understood and could not, as a consequence, learn more about how white people differ from one another and are like and unlike themselves.[14] Thus, the no-response-by-nontargets converted what might be seen as a recognition of a power differential, which could have been part of an ongoing process of mutual recognition, into a breakdown of the ongoing dynamic balance between recognition and denial. Members of the less powerful group were essentially powerless in the face of the denial. Len and Joel said as much: "We were the givers. And we came home empty handed."

The men of color had made themselves known; Len suspected the European Americans were unwilling to do the same. "What is it the whites don't want to say?" Though it is surely true that members of target groups know the dominant group better than nontargets know them (Spelman, 1988, p. 161), Len's plea, "I want to know you. I want to know what you [nontargets] think," indicates that that knowledge is not always felt to be satisfactory. The request by the men of color to hear the white people's response to the Speak Out may be seen as a request to decide which qualities of likeness and difference are significant, a request that was denied. Perhaps Len suspected that the European Americans didn't want members of their own or the target group to know what they had (not) felt. Perhaps the phrases "We feel an emptiness" and "I need a recognition of emptiness" indicate that the men of color suspected that, though they may have been listened to, they had really not been heard, seen, and known. Our failure to recognize the depth of their desire to continue the conversation might be seen as corroboration of this suspicion.

Let us now briefly consider the interruption of the conversation in terms of its effect upon members of the nontarget group. My own experience of a deepening sense of mutual recognition occurred when I saw how I, a white woman, appeared to an African-American man. I came to recognize more deeply not only that he differed from me (I grasped that he must always be aware that he evokes fear; I have never evoked that type of fear), but also that he shared my reality—like myself he knows fear and does not want to evoke it. At that moment I simultaneously grasped his recognition of my likeness to, and difference from, himself; I recognized a new (for me) dimension of the subjectivity of (some) members of his group. The model made that moment possible, but then prevented us from exploring what that moment meant to one another; it provided no opportunity for members of target and nontarget groups to reflect together upon such interactive processes.

Where am I in all of this? One way of positioning myself is between M—— and the men of color, with their opposing interpretations of stopping the conversation. I also feel myself drawn toward alternative responses to the question of whether targets (in this case people of color) "need" whites. I am persuaded that to continue expanding our knowledge of who we are in the world we—both targets and nontargets—must continue to learn about how we are like and unlike those with whom we interact, however infrequent, distant, or indirect the interaction. Mutual recognition is, therefore, in the interests of all of us, though it may in fact be particularly oppressive for members of subordinate groups to be unrecognized by those with power, since one attribute of power is the ability to define the worth and reality of the less powerful. It is in this sense that denial of dependency is a mystification.

Yet, M—— saw the men of color's need to hear what the whites thought as evidence of their internalized oppression and rejected my implicit assumption that people of color "need" anything from their allies. Who am I to interpret the "needs" of others, especially others who are members of subordinate groups?

From the perspective of mutual recognition theory, disruptions in the process of mutual recognition are inevitable, but renewals of such fissures must remain constant possibilities. No teaching moment can be met with a technology

(Ellsworth, 1990, p. 4; Lewis, 1990, p. 487). I do not know what I will do next time. Perhaps after some time has elapsed, I will let the conversation continue and allow, even encourage, students to share with one another our responses to the process we have engaged in together.

Such ongoing conversations will not, however, be occasions for the achievement of mutual recognition, though they may move us in that direction. As long as conversations about racism and other forms of domination occur in institutions where people of European origin, with Eurocentric perspectives, predominate in the administration, faculty, staff, and student body, the conversation will be severely limited. When people of color are outnumbered and relatively powerless, we cannot be assured there will be a Gil who will take the risk of asserting his difference.

And, for many reasons, there will be limits to any institution becoming truly multicultural as long as it is part of a society where people of European origin and/or perspective have superior power to shape the material circumstances and subjective reality of others. At best such conversations can increase the likelihood that people who engage in them will recognize that others with whom we share our cities, states, nations, and the planet are separate and feeling human others who are profoundly like and unlike ourselves. Two years after the events I have written about, almost a third of the student body has participated in Humanities I. The quality and number of ongoing conversations between students, between faculty and students, and between administration, students, and faculty have increased, and the faculty, student body, and curriculum have become more diverse and more responsive to difference. Yet, we have only just begun, within a social context where, statistics clearly indicate, the welfare of people of color both in this country and abroad continues to worsen.

q u e s t i o n s   f o r   d i s c u s s i o n

1. In what ways is the argument made in this article relevant for devising curriculum to address sexism, class injustice and heterosexism? What are some significant differences among the "isms" and of what significance for curriculum and pedagogy are the differences?
2. How would you respond to a student who told you, "I don't think it makes any difference what race people are. I just see people as human beings"?
3. How and what did you learn about race and ethnicity as you were growing up? What are some of your earliest memories? Of what relevance is this self-analysis for you as a teacher?
4. To what extent and at what age do you think it's appropriate to discuss racism in the classroom? What are the assumptions upon which your views rest?

t e a c h e r s   a s   r e s e a r c h e r s

Devise a plan for finding out how students at the grade level you plan to teach think they are both like and different from people their own ages who are of races/ethnicities different from their own. Share the results of this research with your classmates. Discuss with your classmates what you think would be appropriate objectives for teaching about racism with the students whose views you have investigated. Devise a curriculum sequence that will address racism with these students and try it out.

s u g g e s t e d   r e a d i n g s

Ellsworth, E. (1989, August). Why doesn't this feel empowering—working through the myths of critical pedagogy. *Harvard Educational Review, 59*(3).

hooks, b. (1984). *Feminist theory from margin to center.* Boston: South End.

Miller, A. (1983). *For your own good.* New York: Farrar, Strauss & Giroux.

West, C. (1993). *Race matters.* New York: Farrar, Strauss & Giroux.

n o t e s

[1] Some of the demographics have been altered slightly to protect the privacy of individuals.

[2] The construction of the model is attributed to Erica Sherover Marcuse. Workshops based upon the model were conducted under the auspices of New Bridges, an organization that no longer exists under this name.

[3] In this paper I use the terms Eurocentric and racist interchangeably; a future project might explore the implications of differentiating these terms for analyzing classroom antiracist pedagogy.

[4] See Welch (1991, p. 96), Minnich (1990, p. 34), and Lewis (1990, p. 485) for discussions of this issue. To anticipate my argument, I came to reject this dicotomy.

[5] Those of us who have worked with this model are acutely aware of distortions inherent in the language, particularly the terms *target* and *nontarget*. These terms, like all language, can belie our intentions; all language is unsatisfactory in an unjust world. We are particularly concerned that the terms *target* and *nontarget* convey that people who are targets of a particular oppression are helpless victims, or are only targets. The only way to avoid such distortion is to assure that the connotations of all terms are always open for review and discussion.

[6] See Miller (1983) and Berlak (1989) for the connections between childhood experiences and failures of outrage and empathy.

[7] Workshops commonly begin with race because it is presumed to be the most divisive and difficult, the one that must be faced head-on before the others can command serious attention. The problem of where to begin is not inconsequential, as Spelman (1988) argues persuasively. (See note 10.) We found that students were more able to become involved in the course after the "ism" which they felt most targeted by had been the focus of discussion.

[8]This rationale for meeting in caucuses parallels the argument for women-only consciousness-raising groups.

[9]Nevertheless, at one workshop I attended questions were continuously posed to encourage participants to focus on differences among members of a caucus group.

[10]Spelman (1988) presents an extremely useful metaphor for thinking about this issue. She postulates a series of doors through which individuals must pass, and asks us to consider how important the order of the doors is. Imagine a series of doors. The first set says "man" or "woman"; second: each man and each woman then passes through a door for either white or person of color; third: each member of these four groups then passes through the door naming his or her social class. She asks us to consider the difference the order of the doors makes, who labels the doors, who chooses the order, and who decides who may pass through a door.

[11]A next step would be to explore how such issues could be integrated with the curriculum and pedagogy we developed for Humanities I.

[12]A further analysis would consider how class members and the two teachers shifted their readings of the events through various discourses about authority in classrooms.

[13]When Benjamin uses the terms *bourgeois autonomy* and *the ideal of the autonomous individual,* she is referring to the view that individual authority and autonomy in a capitalist economy are illusions. To believe that workers are "free" to choose their work, for example, one must ignore the limited range of options open to her or him.

[14]One way to provide for continuing the conversation would have been through the sharing groups we set up for discussion of autobiographies. However, because in each of these groups there was only one person of color, there could be no semblance of conversation among equals in these groups and therefore we did not often use them. (See Ellsworth, 1989.)

r e f e r e n c e s

All London's Teachers Against Racism and Fascism. (1984). *Challenging racism.* London: ALTARF.

Benjamin, J. (1988). *The bonds of love.* New York: Pantheon.

Berlak, A. (1989, Summer). Teaching for outrage and empathy in the liberal arts. *Educational Foundations.*

Ellsworth, E. (1989, August). Why doesn't this feel empowering—working through the myths of critical pedagogy. *Harvard Educational Review, 59*(3).

Ellsworth, E. (1990). *Education for a politics of difference.* Paper presented at the meeting of the American Educational Research Association, Boston.

Ethnic fraud stirs up furor over standards. (1991, January 14). *San Francisco Chronicle.*

Franzen, T., & Helmhold, L. (1991, February). What is to be done? *Woman's Review of Books, 8*(5).

Giroux, H. (1991). *Postmodernism, feminism, and cultural politics.* Albany: SUNY Press.

Hall, S. (1981). Teaching race. In A. James (Ed.), *The school in multicultural society.* London: Harpers.

hooks, b. (1984). *Feminist theory from margin to center.* Boston: South End.

hooks, b. (1990). *Yearnings.* Boston: South End.

hooks, b. (1991, February). Challenging patriarchy means challenging men to change. *Z Magazine.*

hooks, b. (1992). *Black looks*. Boston: South End.

Lewis, M. (1990, November). Interrupting patriarchy; resistance and transformation in the feminist classroom. *Harvard Educational Review, 60*(4).

Miller, A. (1983). *For your own good*. New York: Farrar, Strauss & Giroux.

Minnich, E. (1990). *Transforming knowledge*. Philadelphia: Temple University Press.

Murray, N. (1991, January/February). Is the playing field really equal? *Rethinking Schools*.

Parker, P. (1990). For the white person who wants to be my friend. In Gloria Anzadula, *Making face, making soul*. San Francisco: aunt lute foundation.

Rattansi, A. (1992). Changing the subject? Racism, culture and education. In J. Donald & A. Rattansi (Eds.), *Race, culture and difference*. Newbury Park, CA: Sage.

Sleeter, C. (1991). *Empowerment through multi-cultural education*. Albany: SUNY Press.

Spelman, E. (1988). *Inessential woman*. Boston: Beacon Press.

Tarule, J. (1990, Summer). Mapping the moral domain: A contribution of women's thinking to psychology and education. *Educational Studies, 21*(2).

Urwin, C. (1984). Power relations and the Emergence of language. In J. Henriques (Ed.), *Changing the subject*. London: Methuen.

West, C. (1992). *Prophecy and deliverance: An African-American revolutionary Christianity*. Philadelphia: Westminister Press.

West, C. (1993). *Prophetic thought in postmodern times*. Monroe, ME: Common Courage Press.

Welch, S. (1991). An ethic of solidarity and difference. In Henry Giroux (Ed.), *Post modernism, feminism, and cultural politics*. Albany: SUNY Press.

Winant, H (1990). Postmodern racial politics in the United States: Difference and inequality. *Socialist Review*.

Young, I. (1990). The ideal of community and the politics of difference. In Linda J. Nicholson (Ed.), *Feminism/postmodernism*. New York and London: Routledge.

chapter 4

Marxism and Education

Alan A. Block

guiding questions

1. What is the author trying to say or teach?
2. What is the significance of what you read here for you personally and for you as a teacher?
3. What are the perspectives drawn on by the author to make the analysis?
4. How does this analysis help to inform our practice in classrooms?

Perhaps now especially, as mainstream discussion of education increases in volume and prescription, and as marxism is gloatingly dismissed in American public debate as irrelevant and/or fatally flawed, the alternative discourses of marxism have most to contribute to the discourses of education. Despite the turbulence in Eastern Europe over the past several years, marxism is not bankrupt, though many speak its demise. Indeed, it would be an error to equate the fate of marxism with the failure of any of the governments of any of the individual states which have espoused a marxist (or marxist-leninist, or any variant appellation) orientation. First, it must be noted that there is not a single marxism; rather, there are many interpretations of Karl Marx, each of which calls itself *marxism*. Like all philosophical perspectives, the range of strategic positions identified as marxisms is situated across a wide spectrum. The possibility of movement across this spectrum, and the wide variety of positions available along it, does not invalidate the spectrum itself but merely creates a question of individual placement along it. Second, there ought not to be an equation between marxism and communism; they are not synonymous terms. Communism could disappear from the earth and marxism would still exist.

Why is this? Because marxism is a way of viewing society and is not, like communism, a system of governing it. Marxism presents a perspective from which to view, not a prescription for society. Of course, a marxist understands that a changed perspective would necessarily produce the impetus for change. Karl Marx, from his particular stance in the middle of the nineteenth century, asked certain questions and in the quest for answers arrived at the belief that given certain conditions—history, which he defined as the actual lived experience of people—the progress of society would lead to a social system organized by principles he referred to as communism. Though Marx spoke from a specific historical setting, and though he spoke of the inevitable coming of socialism, it was his system of investigation, not the specific prescriptions he avowed, that is marxism. Marx misunderstood certain aspects of his society and misrepresented certain potentialities; hence, his counsel that the specter of communism, which haunted Europe, would soon overtake it did not come to fruition. From our present-day perspective, Marx's several errors are clearly visible. His erroneous prognostications for society, however, do not invalidate the system now known as marxism because the system itself helps explain Marx's own misconceptions. It is an incomplete understanding of Marx and his writings that results in the mistaken equation between marxism and communism and that gave rise to so much contention in the history of the United States. Nonetheless, because marxism is what it is, its discourses have much to contribute to our understanding of education, and thus, I would like to begin with a necessarily brief and delimited explanation of certain marxist language, which we can then employ to discuss contemporary education.

What Is Marxism?

Marxism is a philosophical system, which, like all philosophies, attempts to identify and study the basic facts of reality and our relationship to them. What is reality and if we can know it, then how can it be known? What is a human being? What motivates a human being and how does she or he come to be so motivated? What might or ought a human being do in this world? Is change possible? Though Marx avowed he was a philosopher, he also believed that the problem with all prior philosophies—even those to which he was indebted— was that they attempted merely to interpret the world; the point of philosophy, Marx thought, was to change it.

> Hitherto men have constantly made up for themselves false conceptions about themselves, about what they are and what they ought to be. They have arranged their relationships according to their ideas of God, of normal man, etc. They, the creators, have bowed down before their creations. Let us liberate them from the chimeras, the ideas, dogmas, imaginary beings under the yoke of which they are pining away. Let us revolt against the rule of thoughts. Let us teach men, says one, to exchange these imaginations for thoughts which correspond to the essence of man; says the second to take up a critical attitude to them; says the third, to knock them out of their heads; and—existing reality will collapse. (Marx, 1988, p. 37)

Marxist philosophy may be seen as an attempt to answer the call of the above three voices: to understand the human being in his or her essence, to look critically at the thoughts that humans hold true and to expose their speciousness, and, by so doing, to obliterate those ideas from human consciousness and replace them with other, more vital propositions and realities.

Marxism is a system of thought which attempts to explain humanity and its social organization from a materialist, as opposed to an idealist, perspective. A materialist philosophy assumes that all reality consists of natural rather than supernatural or ideal things, and that therefore these "things," or phenomena, can be examined scientifically. As a materialist, Marx chose to select material production as the "crucial determinant" (Eagleton, 1991, p. 82) of human existence. Which is to say, that to a greater or lesser extent, all humans always have been engaged in the production and reproduction of themselves and the means of their existence. This production under conditions of real or artificially induced scarcity is history, declared Marx, and has so consumed human energies that it is hard to imagine that its effects could not be found in everything we do, including how we think and what we think about, even about ourselves. As Marx said,

> The way in which men produce their means of subsistence depends first of all on the nature of the actual means of subsistence they find in existence and have to reproduce. This mode of production must not be considered simply as being the production of the physical existence of the individuals. Rather it is a definite form of activity of these individuals, a definite form of expressing their life, a definite *mode of life* on their part. As individuals express their life, so they are. What they are, therefore, coincides with their production, both with *what* they produce and with *how* they produce. The nature of individuals thus depends on the material conditions determining their production. (1988, p. 42)

Thus, Marx's materialism suggests that the human entity—what other idealist philosophies would refer to as the human essence—can only derive from material production, and only in the study of material production and the relations entailed in that production can the individual be known.

> The production of life, both of one's own in labor and of fresh life in procreation, now appears as a double relationship: on the one hand as natural, on the other as a social relationship. By social we understand the co-operation of several individuals, no matter under what conditions, in what manner and to what end. It follows from this that a certain mode of production, or industrial stage is always combined with a certain mode of co-operation, or social stage. . . . (p. 50)

The idealist philosophers whom Marx criticized held that things were produced from ideas: that we produce chairs from our idea of chairs. Marx argued that ideas were produced from things, or rather, from the relations between things. For Marx, our idea of a chair derives from our experience with chairs, that is, with our relations arising from the mode of production involved in chairs. The ruler who sits atop a plush throne purchased from the public coffers and serviced by unpaid servants has different ideas about that throne, of chairs, than the people who produced it by the effort of their unpaid labor, or than the people who can afford no chairs so that the ruler may have his. As Marx said, "The production of ideas, of conceptions, of consciousness, is at first directly interwoven with the material activity and the material intercourse of men, the language of real life" (1988, p. 47). Those relations were always organized about production, which must also be recognized as consumption. It is useless to produce something that is not intended for consumption, which, in turn, is premised on the idea of future production. We consume something with the expectation that we can get more of it. Consumption is thus production, even as production is consumption. Hence, for Marx, our lives—and our ideas about life and ourselves—derive from the material aspects of the production and reproduction of our daily lives because that is what consumes so much, if not all, of our time.

Therefore, to understand society one had to study the means and relations of production. These relations of production exist between those who own, who operate or who, in some form, share the forces of production—the material forces which (re)produce life. And these relations exist not only between humans but also between those same humans and the means of production that they operate. After all, there is a difference between those who own machines but never operate them and those who merely work them and do not own them. Marx believed that because so much life was spent producing and reproducing itself, it was important to look at this (re)production in order to understand the human society. "Material production is 'primary' in the sense that it forms the major narrative of history to date; but it is primary also in the sense that without *this* particular narrative, no other story would ever get off the ground. Such production is the precondition of the whole of our thought" (Eagleton, 1991, p. 83). Thus, Marx's great work is *Capital*, an analysis of the forces and relations of production then dominant—capitalism. We will define capitalism as "a mode of production in which capital in its various forms is the principal means of production. Capital can take the form of money or credit for the purchase of labor power and materials of production; of physical machinery (capital in the narrow sense); or of stocks of finished goods or work in progress" (Bottomore, Harris & Kiernan, 1983, p. 64). It is the private ownership of such capital that characterizes capitalism.

Because Marx believed that the material conditions determined our ideas of reality, it followed that our social consciousness would stem from our relations deriving from production. In *The German Ideology* Marx said, "Life is not determined by consciousness, but consciousness by life" (1988, p. 47). And in *The Eighteenth Brumaire of Louis Bonaparte* Marx wrote that

> Upon the different forms of property, upon the social conditions of existence, rises an entire superstructure of distinct and peculiarly formed sentiments, illusions, modes of thought and views of life. The entire class creates and forms them out of its material foundations and out of the corresponding social relations. (1984, p. 47)

All morality, religion, metaphysics, all that we consider as productive of ourselves, "have no history, no development; but men, developing their material production and their material intercourse, alter, along with their real existence, their thinking and the products of their thinking" (Marx, 1988, p. 47). Our ideas, Marx argued, derive from our material lives, which are a result of our relations of production, or rather, our relations to the means and forces (including other humans) by which our lives are produced and reproduced. Marx said that "man's [sic] consciousness of the necessity of associating with the individuals around him is the beginning of the consciousness that he is living in society at all" (p. 31). Or, as marxist scholar Raymond Williams said, "What is knowable is not only a function of objects—of what is there to be known. It is also a function of subjects, of observers—of what is desired and what needs to be known" (1984, p. 17). Everything that we know—and the means by which we may come to know it—is based in the material conditions of our life.

Here is one place where the discourses of Marxism may begin to inform the discourses of education. Marx's materialism offers us the possibility of a perspective on education that is not held by idealist philosophers, those who argue that education rises above the material world and contains universal truths. For marxism, what is desired and what needs to be known—issues regarding the definitions, substances, and practices of philosophy—must be understood as based or grounded in the relations of production, which in capitalist society are inevitably unequal because of private ownership. What is known and desired, what may be known and desired are then also unequal—different—because the relations of production are "in the last instant" (these are Marx's ambiguous terms) economically determined and determining. The struggle over education passionately fought out in the public sphere today must be understood in its material roots, which marxism argues are "conditioned by the degree of development of [the] economic positions, by the mode of their production and of their exchange determined by it" (1988, p. 4). Thus, we must understand the relationship between this economic BASE and the SUPERSTRUCTURE—the forms of the State and the social consciousness, including the institutions that produce and are produced by that consciousness, which is so intimately associated with that base.

Base and Superstructure

///

How is it that there is a correspondence between this economic base and the superstructure which rises from it? Indeed, what is the base and what is the superstructure which so much of the marxist discourse concerning education depends? In his introduction to *The Critique of Political Economy*, Marx said that

> In the social production of their existence, men inevitably enter into definite relations, which are independent of their will, namely relations of production appropriate to a given stage in the development of their material forces of production. The totality of these relations of production constitutes the economic structure of society, the real foundation, on which arises a legal and political superstructure, and to which correspond definite forms of social consciousness. The mode of production of material life conditions the general process of social, political and intellectual life. It is not the consciousness of men that determines their existence, but their social existence that determines their consciousness. (1970, p. 21)

Marx's statement, which is repeated in variant forms throughout his work, suggests that the legal, political, religious, aesthetic, or philosophical forms by which we know society—the superstructure—are somehow "determined" by the economic base. This is consistent with the materialist nature of Marx's philosophical system. But the notion of the relationship between base and superstructure has been hotly debated in discourses of and about marxism, for within Marx's description one may find, *if one chooses*, the notion of a fixed and definite spatial relationship between the economic base and the superstructure which derives from and sits atop the base. I do not mean to engage here in this debate, which is a discussion regarding the notion of determinism, except to say that *within* marxist circles the debate concerns the relationship between base and superstructure—the extent to which the base exists in an absolutely determining relationship to the superstructure. Of course, *without*

BASE: In marxism, the base is either the economic structure of society—the mode of production— which determines the superstructure, or the real and often contradictory activities of human beings. The base limits the range of practices available in a social organization.

SUPERSTRUCTURE: In marxism, the superstructure refers either to the political, social, cultural, and philosophical forms that sit atop the economic base or to a related range of cultural practices that arise from the relations of production and that may have reciprocal effect on those relations.

marxist circles, the debate questions the very spatial metaphor itself. The view one takes regarding the base/superstructure relationship will delimit how one perceives the form and content of education. If one denies the reality of the metaphor, and therefore denies the relationship between the economic system and the social structures and consciousness that a society develops, then the educational system may be viewed as an organism independent of any specific social order, and education itself may be regarded as free from social influence and unfettered by prejudice. In this view, the values intrinsic to, and thus promoted by, education may be judged universally valid for and integral to society regardless of social position. These are arguments of such theorists as Allan Bloom (1987), E. D. Hirsch (1987), Diane Ravitch (1987), and Mortimer Adler (1982), who argue that everyone ought to receive the same education and that education ought to be understood as the delivery of materials deemed by consensus to be universally excellent and eternally valid.

But let us look at marxist perspectives on the relationship between base and superstructure and the insights on education to be gained from such a view. If, on the one hand, the superstructure is seen as directly determined by the economic base, then education may be considered an apparatus that is produced by economic relations and that is intended to reproduce those relations. Such is the argument of Samuel Bowles and Herbert Gintis in *Schooling in a Capitalist Society* (1976) and Pierre Bourdieu and Jean-Claude Passeron in *Reproduction in Education, Society and Culture* (1970/1990). Indeed, such views of education are grouped under the heading "reproduction theories." The educational researcher who accepts this viewpoint will be concerned with the ways in which the schools reproduce the social relations prevalent in the larger society in order to maintain the status quo and the existing relations of production and power. The notion of educational tracking is an obvious example of the reproductive mechanisms intrinsic to the schools.

On the other hand, we may understand the base in a far less rigid way. Those who accept this position regarding the relationship of base and superstructure understand the base not only as the economic activity of people but also as the real and specific activities of human beings engaged in economic *and* social relationships, which are meant to produce and reproduce themselves, as Marx had said. But, "these social and real and specific activities in which people are engaged in the process of (re)production carry fundamental contradictions and variations" (Williams, 1980, p. 35) that make the base dynamic. Consider the contradictions and complexities inherent in the relationship when a wealthy factory owner hires her or his child for a summer job. The economic base, rather than strictly determining certain practices, which would then have to be understood as merely products, now may be understood as setting limits to the range of acceptable ideas and practices. These limits are set by those who are positioned to exercise dominance over accepted social and cultural practices and are based in relations of production. Alternative schools are so named because they deviate from society's conventional definition of education, and they are declared valid for certain "alternative" students for whom the traditional education is not working. But the presence of alternative schools never calls into question the accepted definitions of education. The system *permits* alternative schools to exist and minimizes their effect by marginalizing them. The morality of conventional society permits jeans with ripped knees (though not those with ripped buttocks) to be worn to formal symphony concerts, provided that those ripped jeans meet certain social requirements—for example, that they are not malodorous or mud-stained. And yet, at a rock concert, the same value structure may not apply. A teacher legitimates a book for a school book report based on the definitions of literature developed from her or his own education and experience. The extent to which a teacher may deviate from this dominant position is carefully controlled by the dominant powers. Issues of tenure and academic freedom are called into play in such discussion. This interactive view of the relationship between base and superstructure is in contrast to that of more orthodox marxists, who attempt to understand cultural products as derived more or less directly from a rigidly organized economic base. For these theorists, all practices in the superstructure may be viewed as products of a determining base, and we have only to examine the products for their component parts, which ought to be easily discerned from the economic base.

Consider a Hispanic boy in an honors English class studying the works of Shakespeare as the quintessential example of literature. What if this student has an awareness of Hispanic literature? How will his opinions about Shakespeare be affected by that awareness and therefore be different from those of other students who know only the English-American tradition? Those who adhere to a strict base/superstructure model would address the student's behavior in economic terms: Literature is defined by the dominant powers—those whose relations to the means of production place them in strategic positions to exercise power—and what is not so defined is not literature. The reproduction theorist argues that the school structure forces the student to ignore and/or deny what she or he knows in order to learn what the school offers as knowledge. In this way, society produces what it considers an educated person and thereby reproduces itself. If the student resists education, the schools still reproduce the dominant society by imposing a structure that demands either conformity or exile, self or otherwise. Reproduction theorists see schools and education as derived from the economic base, which they then serve to reproduce.

The broader view would address a complex and often contradictory range of behaviors in this student. Here, the school as superstructure must be understood as a related range of cultural practices arising from those relations of production and reciprocally affecting those relations. What is literature—and knowledge—in that Hispanic student's class must be understood as resulting from complex social relations, which include his or her own engagement in the cultural traditions from which he or she derives. What occurs in the school— what the school is—can only be understood by examining the conditions by which certain practices are legitimated and others are excluded, not by studying how the component parts of the cultural product are derived from a solid base. What conditions exist that offer Shakespeare as knowledge and not Garcia-Lorca; why is Garcia-Lorca excluded; what results from this exclusion?

How is a student's knowledge of Shakespeare affected by his or her under-standing of Garcia-Lorca? What happens to a student's knowledge when his or her understanding of Garcia-Lorca is rendered meaningless by the presence of Shakespeare in the curriculum? Is this student's skill on percussion commen-surate with that of the fluent reader of Shakespeare? How are these various traditions to be understood in the educational hierarchy? This marxist view of the relationship between base and superstructure sees education as a practice whose *conditions of existence and operation* may be examined, rather than merely as a product whose component parts may be studied and anchored in a solid economic base. The educational researcher here must study the whole of society in which education occurs in order to discover those conditions of appearance and practice. Education is not merely a product, but a practice as well, that must be rooted in real social relations.

In either case, there is no doubt that a relationship exists between base and superstructure in marxist theories of education. Indeed, for many marxists, the schools are seen as the primary agents of domination—of exercising power—in contemporary society. Louis Althusser, a French marxist, suggests, for exam-ple, that the *educational ideological apparatus* is the dominant State apparatus installed in modern capitalist societies, and that "... the school ... teaches 'know-how', but in forms which ensure *subjection to the ruling ideology* or the mastery of its 'practice'" (1971, p. 133). And Raymond Williams says that the "educational institutions are usually the main agencies of the transmission of an effective dominant culture" (1980, p. 39). How is it then that the schools have attained and maintain this powerful position? This is a complex question to which there is no single answer. But marxism offers a language and a method with which to explain the form and content of the educational apparatus.

Indeed, Marx's materialist philosophy offers us a methodology with which to approach this problem. Remember that Marx said that consciousness does not determine life but that life determines consciousness, and that consciousness derives from the relations of material production. Those who own—control—the means of production are obviously those with the potentially greatest opportunity for exercising power. No one would willingly divest himself or herself of the possibility of power—position—and remember that, in a materi-alist philosophy, power and position derive from the ownership of the means of production. Nor would anyone willingly believe that his or her ownership and position are illegitimate, illegal, specious, unnecessarily cruel, or oppres-sive. Indeed, those who own the means of production—which ownership re-sults in certain relations of production from which derive consciousness—believe in the legitimacy of their position. To so believe is to accept the relations in society as natural, correct, and universally acceptable. Hence, the related cultural practices, which derive from what may now be termed the dominant class, will be a product of that class's thinking and will represent the ideas of the class that is dominant. Thus, Marx says,

> The ideas of the ruling class are in every epoch the ruling ideas; i.e. the
> class which is the ruling *material* force of society, is at the same time its

ruling *intellectual* force. The class which has the means of material production at its disposal, has control at the same time over the means of mental production, so that thereby, generally speaking, the ideas of those who lack the means of mental production are subject to it. The ruling ideas are nothing more than the ideal expression of the dominant material relationships, the dominant material relationships grasped as ideas; hence the relationships which make the one class the ruling one, therefore, the ideas of its dominance. (1988, p. 64)

You will recall that, according to Marx, consciousness derives from life and life is organized by and about the relations of production. Those who own the means of production, who organize their distribution and uses, occupy positions of greater power and hence may be seen as a ruling class. The individuals comprising this ruling class "possess among other things consciousness, and therefore think. As a result of their strategic position in society this ruling class determines the extent and compass of an age INCLUDING the production and distribution of the ideas of their age; their ideas are the ruling ideas of the epoch" (1988, p. 64).

What does this have to do with schools and education? First, it is clear that if the dominant ideas of the age are those of the ruling class, then legitimate knowledge will be defined by the class that is dominant. In a capitalist society, this class will be those who own and/or control the means of production. What is knowledge, and what is important knowledge, will be established by those whose interests are best protected by claiming legitimacy for their knowledge. Is astrology or astronomy a legitimate science, and how does one know? What counts as a fact? What is a fact?

Further, what knowledge is significant is also a result of strategic positions of the dominant classes. Is knowing how to open a locked car door without keys as equally worthy as knowing how to open a patient upon a table? Is dialect American English of equal worth with standardized American English? How do you know? Standardized tests, curriculum design, school structures—all can be shown to result from the ideas of the dominant class. And it is equally possible to show how the ideas of the subordinate classes are either marginalized or dismissed altogether. What effect does the emphasis on science and math in the national debate over education have on the place of art and music in the school curriculum? Is carving intricate wood figures an acceptable form of knowledge for admission to Harvard as compared to a perfect score on the math scholastic aptitude test? To what extent is the governing structure of the United States derived from native American society? What is the current debate over multicultural education? Whose interests are served on either side of the issue? Who ultimately makes these decisions? And by what right do they make them?

Second, if the ideas of an age are those of the ruling class, then the very structures of the school are conceived and organized by the dominant class based on its idea of education. And, because this class attains dominance through the relations of production and because consciousness derives from these relations, then reality—the structures which derive from thought—are based on the "natural relations" in which we find ourselves, but which marxism teaches us are actually a product of the material relations of production. The very *idea* of schools is intrinsic to the consciousness of the dominant class, which, from its position of dominance, has the power to establish schools. The structures of these would serve to legitimate the dominance of the ruling class, whose reality is to be reproduced in the educational apparatus because those structures would appear as natural. This is the marxist use of the term HEGEMONY.

> Hegemony supposes the existence of something which is truly total, which is not merely secondary or superstructural . . . but which is lived at such a depth, which saturates the society to such an extent, and which . . . even constitutes the substance and limit of common sense for most people under its sway, that it corresponds to the reality of social experience . . . (Williams, 1980, p. 37)

Thus, we need not think of this whole process as devious or consciously determined. Because our ideas of reality derive from the material conditions of our lives—which themselves derive from the relations of production—the notion of hegemony teaches us that it would be impossible to conceive a reality that was not based upon the very relations of production that organized the daily lives of the dominant class. Our very experience of reality depends upon our acceptance of the educational system. The very structures of education— the hierarchies of the schools, the structures of educational policies and politics, the development of curriculum, the licensing and practice of teachers, and the degree-granting power of educational institutions—derive from the ideas of the ruling class members, which are a product of their life—their relations of production. Needless to say, the subordinate class might have alternative ideas, but it clearly lacks power to supplant those of the dominant class.

Regardless of which view of the base/superstructure we adopt, marxism attempts to explain the structures and functions of schooling by situating the educational apparatus in the material relations within which it functions and which it serves. Reproduction theorists argue that the structure of education and the schools attempts to ensure the reproduction of society, thus maintaining the present power relations and leaving the dominant class in dominance. This is accomplished in the structure of the schools and the type of knowledge which is legitimated by it. On the other hand, it is argued that the structure and functioning of the system results not from conscious choice, but from the very center of consciousness itself: reality, our consciousness, can only be known based on the relations of production. Until those are changed, the possibility of an alternative reality is not only impossible, but literally unthinkable.

HEGEMONY: The web of institutions, social relations, and ideas by which reality is known in a particular social organization. Domination without force.

Alienation
//

In this necessarily brief and incomplete overview of the confluent discourses of marxism and education, one final topic must be addressed. We have shown how, as a philosophical system, marxism may have a great deal to offer to our understanding of education as a practice and as an institution, and we have shown how marxism attempts to problematize (make into a problem) the whole knowledge base on which traditional education rests. But we have yet to deal with a central aspect of life that Marx addressed most specifically early in his career, in his *Economic and Philosophical Manuscripts of 1844* (in Fromm, 1986), and that is crucial to an understanding of the role of marxism in explaining educational discourses.

This aspect is referred to as *alienation.* As an experience of the human condition, alienation has been explored for centuries from a variety of philosophical positions. Existentialists have attempted to explain alienation as a product of the human condition: we are each alone in the vast universe. The work of Jean-Paul Sartre and Samuel Beckett's *Waiting for Godot* are quintessential expressions of this position. Theologians have explained alienation as separation from God. But Marx, as a materialist philosopher, attempted to explain alienation as an inevitable result of the capitalist mode of production—the material conditions of the (re)production of life. In other words, Marx attempted to explain a philosophical condition previously ascribed as a product of ideal relations (to God, to the universe) as, instead, a product of the actual material conditions and relations. Marx said that humans experience alienation when they are separated from their own activities, their own products, their fellows, and/or from their species, and he attempted to explore how the material conditions in the production and reproduction of life result in alienation. Marx said in these early writings (which were not discovered until the 1920's) that

> Alienation is apparent not only in the fact that my means of life belong to someone else, that my desires are the unattainable possession of someone else, but that everything is something different from itself, that my activity is something else, and finally (and this is the case for the capitalist) that an inhuman power rules over everything." (Fromm, 1986, p. 151)

The experience of alienation results in a sense of powerlessness, of lack of agency, of an absence of subjectivity, or of identity. The experience of alienation is one in which nature, others and even the individual self is alien; the individual experiences each realm of existence as separate from and as standing above and against himself or herself as objects, even though these objects may even sometimes be the objects of his or her own creation. Alienation perverts all values because all spheres of life remain separate and independent from each other:

> The nature of alienation implies that each sphere applies a different and contradictory norm, that morality does not apply the same norm as

political economy, etc., because each of them is a particular alienation of man; each is concentrated upon a specific area of alienated activities and is itself alienated from the other. (Fromm, 1986, p. 146)

Hence, education as a separate sphere remains independent from the rest of society; appropriates objects for its own ends, which are then viewed as isolated from the rest of social life; and produces objects that are separate from the remainder of social life. Education as a product of alienation is a process that is itself alienating, and has as its product an alienated being. I would like to briefly explore how marxism explains the process of alienation experienced in the educational process.

First, schools in a capitalist mode of production must be viewed as themselves the products of alienation. Recall that the definition of the capitalistic mode of production stems from the notion of private ownership of the means of production—private property. However, Marx explained, private property is already a product of alienation and not merely productive of it. The idea of private property is merely the material manifestation of alienation. In other words, the whole notion of private property is a product of the particular mode of production rather than the provocation for it. Private property—and the individuals who own it—are material products resulting from the relations of production and are not ideal categories that history has actualized. The schools, then, must be seen as the products of the relations of production—as products of alienation—and they will ultimately represent in material form those same alienated relations. This derives from the relationship of the base/superstructure discussed above.

How is it, then, that private property derives from and merely continues the condition of alienation rather than being simply its product? Workers (including students, teachers, and the entire hierarchy of education), Marx argued, produce what does not belong to them, for which production they receive subsistence wages. In this work, the worker receives *both* an object for work and an object that will provide the means of subsistence—wages in the form of money. In these instances, the work is separate from the worker and the worker experiences alienation. On the one hand, the worker does not make his or her own work but rather, has it given to him or her; second, the work is done for an object—money—rather than for himself or herself; and third, the object produced from the worker's own labor does not belong to the worker but is, rather, set against the worker. It contains none of the worker because he or she may not sell it. Of course, the means of subsistence sustain the worker, but the work itself is not done for the worker, nor can the worker choose the remuneration or even the product produced; these are set by owners of production. All the worker can do is choose to sell his or her labor or not to sell it. In the labor process the worker is merely an object producing an object.

Now, as a result of his or her labor, the worker produces an *object* that does not belong to him or her. Now, if the product does not belong to him or her—if that object is alienated from the worker—then it must belong to someone else. Thus arises the idea of private property. In the factory model the object belongs to the capitalist, but so, too, does the worker, who has sold labor power to the capitalist. Hence, products of the workers do not belong to the workers; nor do the workers anymore belong to themselves. To obtain the means of subsistence, they have sold all that is yet available to them. Relations of production, which form in the historically particular mode of production, must reproduce these basic structures based on that mode of production. Institutions that arise in a specific mode of production must reproduce—or at least struggle to reproduce—and legitimate that mode of production and the relations which exist in this mode. In the capitalist mode of production, despite the rhetoric which argues that schools are community based, schools must be viewed as being always and already products of alienation. Hence, the possibility of national licensing criteria, curricula, and standards may arise despite the notion that schools are formed by, and function in and for, the communities where they are situated. Schools as institutions do not, then, belong either to the populace that they mean to serve or to the population that functions within them. As products of alienation, schools are set apart from the rest of society and their relations to society are denied and/or obscured. Marxist thought argues that all analysis of the school that doesn't acknowledge its material roots merely examines an alienated product.

> Man's reflections on the forms of social life, and consequently, also, his scientific analysis of those forms, take a course directly opposite to that of their actual historical development. He begins, post festum, with the results of the process of development ready to hand before him. (Marx, 1987, p. 80)

Marx would argue that, in order to be understood, the school must be studied as a form of thought that expresses with social validity the conditions and relations of a definite, historically determined mode of production. In the capitalist mode of production, the school is a product—commodity—and must, therefore, be viewed as a product of alienation. It has no relation to the rest of society against which it is set.

Second, marxism understands the process of education as necessarily alienating. The process of acquiring knowledge does not belong to the learner because it is not organized by the learner based on his or her own perceived needs and desires. For students, the educational process means that knowledge is never something they have, but something they must acquire. It is separate from them and resides in the institution and in the functionaries of it. The process is organized for them; as learners they have no say in what they will learn or in how it is to be organized. Their place in the system is set by others, as their movement through the system is determined by the system's structures and not their own. The means and manners of delivery of the prescribed body of knowledge is set outside of them without their input. As the knowledge is not theirs, but is rather an object that they may acquire, its presence or absence in them may be assessed by objective standards. There may, then, be procedures which address them not as subjects but as objects, or what Paulo Freire (1973) says, banks into which "knowledge" is deposited for future withdrawal without, of course, acquiring much interest. The sense of knowledge being without, as separate from the knower is the experience of alienation.

Of course, education is not only the experience of the student; all participants in the school must experience the alienating process. As a teacher, I have no say in my schedule, nor in the curriculum I am to teach, nor sometimes, as with basal readers, with the very methods I am to use. The existence of school hierarchy is an indication of the lack of control the individual experiences. We occupy positions in the educational system: we are objects in the structure rather than creators of it. Thus, if as Marx says alienation is experienced as the separation of the means of life from myself, then clearly the process of education is alienating.

Finally, the product of education is alienation. That is, the human produced by the educational process is an alienated human being. It ought to be now understood how marxists view education as the product of alienation and how the process of alienation is alienating. Thus, it is inevitable that the process of education results in a human being who is alienated.

> Since alienated labor: (1) alienates nature from man; and (2) alienates man from himself, from his own active function, his life activity; so it alienates him from the species. It makes *species-life* into a means of individual life. In the first place it alienates species-life and individual life, and secondly, it turns the latter, as an abstraction, into the purpose of the former, also in its abstract and alienated form. (Fromm, 1986, p. 101)

First, the process of education alienates the learner from the natural world by setting it apart from the learner as an object of study rather than as a means of existence. Nature is separate from the individual, and hence, the whole ecological disaster may be understood as a result of alienation. Second, the process of education alienates individuals from themselves because education is never something that the learners do by their own activity but rather is something that is done to them. They are essentially passive, using all that is left to them— labor power—to perform someone else's labor. "Man is simply a *worker*, and as a worker his human qualities only exist for the sake of capital which is *alien* to him" (Fromm, 1986, p. 110). Finally, education produces an alienated product as it handles and transforms knowledge into private property, which must be personally acquired and maintained, whose service is solely for the benefit of the individual. Recall that the whole notion of the individual rests on the concept of private property, itself the material manifestation of alienated labor. "Production does not only produce man as a *commodity*, the *human commodity*, man in the form of a *commodity*; in conformity with this situation it produces him as a *mentally* and *physically dehumanized* being" (Fromm, 1986, p. 111).

Education serves society. Or so it is said. Education prepares citizens to ensure the progress of society and the development of better lives for all. Or so it is said. Marxism offers a perspective on society that permits the educational apparatus to be viewed in an actual, as opposed to an ideal, social context, even as marxism explains that social context as an actual and material complex relationship between a base and superstructure. Marxism questions the seemingly natural and universal order in which the ideas of education remain unexamined by exposing the material roots of these ideas and by revealing the conditions of their appearance in history. Marxism provides a method and a vocabulary to explore the relationship between society and its schools and offers insight into that relationship based on a materialist philosophy. From this perspective, education is viewed as deeply embedded in the material world, and change in education is seen as demanding a change in that world. This requires at least a change in teacher education. In his third Theses on Feuerbach, Marx says:

> The materialist doctrine that men are products of circumstances and upbringing, and that, therefore, changed men are products of other circumstances and changed upbringing, forgets that it is men who change circumstances and that it is essential to educate the educator himself . . . The coincidence of the changing of circumstances and of human activity can be conceived and rationally understood only as revolutionising practice. (1978, p. 144)

Marxism looks at education as the potential agent of change in ways that many contemporary political and educational theorists hardly imagine. And it offers future teachers the opportunity for changed PRAXIS.

questions for discussion

1. How would marxist educational theorists respond to the government's program for improving education in the twenty-first century?
2. How would a marxist educational theorist respond to the charge that schools must pass on a common culture if the United States is to produce a literate population?
3. What would a marxist educational theorist say about standardized tests?
4. How would a marxist educational theorist set about restructuring the educational system in the United States?

teachers as researchers

A school district in an inner city is presently functioning on limited resources. Its scores on standardized tests are consistently low, and the drop-out rate is high. Despite an increased tax base, city revenues have not risen because of tax abatements given to real estate developers who have brought business and upper middle-class rents into certain de facto segregated portions of the city.

PRAXIS: The free creative and self-creative activity engaged in by humans in producing and reproducing themselves and thereby changing the historical human world and themselves.

Education dollars, as well as resources for other social programs, including police and fire departments, have thus far remained frozen.

Now, the teachers union is requesting not only a 4 percent across-the-board raise, but also a reduced class size. This proposed reduction in class size will result in a 3 percent increase in staff within the city schools.

A private TV channel offers monitors that will broadcast educational TV several hours every day for each classroom in a particularly poor neighborhood. This would not only bring new resources into a school badly in need of them, but would also alleviate the need to decrease class size because student manage-ability is expected to improve as a result of the children's natural interest in TV. The company offers research linking the increased performance on standard-ized tests to classrooms utilizing the TV channels sponsored by the company.

In exchange for the TV monitors and the free access to the educational chan-nels, the school must permit five minutes of every hour to be used for broad-casting consumer product advertisements.

The school board is about to debate the issue. Based on your understanding of this chapter, prepare arguments *for both sides*. Be sure to consider issues regarding the base and the superstructure and the place of education in that discussion. Of course, educational issues must be the focus of your arguments.

suggested readings

Althusser, L. (1971). Ideology and ideological state apparatuses. In *Lenin and philos-ophy* (B. Brewster, Trans.). New York: Monthly Review Press.

Aronowitz, S., & Giroux, H. A. (1985). *Education under siege.* Boston: Bergin & Garvey.

Bowles, S., & Gitnis, H. (1976). *Schooling in capitalist America.* New York: Basic Books.

Marx, K. (1984). *The eighteenth brumaire of Louis Bonaparte.* New York: Interna-tional Publishers.

Marx, K. (1988). *The German ideology.* (C. Arthus, Ed.). New York: International Publishers.

Ollman, B. (1988). *Alienation.* New York: Cambridge University Press.

Williams, R. (1980). *Problems in materialism and culture.* London: Verso Editions.

references

Adler, M. (1982). *The Paideia proposal.* New York: Macmillan.

Althusser, L. (1971). *Lenin and philosophy* (B. Brewster, Trans.). New York: Monthly Review Press.

Bloom, A. (1987). *The closing of the American mind.* New York: Simon & Schuster.

Bottomore, T., Harris, L., Kiernan, V. M., & Miliband, R. (Eds.). (1983). *A dictionary of marxist thought.* Cambridge: Harvard University Press.

Bourdieu, P., & Passeron, J. (1990). *Reproduction in education, society and culture* (R. Nice, Trans.). London: Sage Publications. (Original work published 1970)

Bowles, S., & Gintis, H. (1976). *Schooling in a capitalist society.* New York: Basic Books.

Eagleton, T. (1991). *Ideology: An introduction.* New York: Verso.

Freire, P. (1973). *Pedagogy of the oppressed.* New York: Seabury Press.

Fromm, E. (1986). *Marx's concept of man* (T. Bottomore, Trans.). New York: Ungar Publishing.

Hirsch, E. D. (1987). *Cultural literacy.* Boston: Houghton Mifflin.

Marx, K. (1970). *A contribution to the critique of political economy* (M. Dobb, Ed.) (S. Ryazanskaya, Trans.). New York: International Publishers.

Marx, K. (1978). Theses on Feuerbach. In R. Tucker (Ed.), *The Marx-Engels reader.* New York: W.W. Norton.

Marx, K. (1984). *The eighteenth brumaire of Louis Bonaparte.* New York: International Publishers.

Marx, K. (1987). *Capital, I.* New York: International Publishers.

Marx, K. (1988). *The German ideology* (C. Arthur, Ed.). New York: International Publishers.

Ravitch, D., & Finn Chester E., Jr. (1987). *What do our seventeen year olds know?* New York: Harper & Row.

Williams, R. (1984). *The English novel from Dickens to Lawrence.* London: The Hogarth Press.

Williams, R. (1980). *Problems in materialism and culture.* New York: Verso.

chapter 5

School Routines
and the Failure
of Curriculum Reform

Charles E. Bruckerhoff

Charles E. Bruckerhoff

guiding questions

1. What is the author trying to say or teach?

2. What is the significance of what you read here for you personally and for you as a teacher?

3. What are the perspectives drawn on by the author to make the analysis?

4. How does this analysis help to inform our practice in classrooms?

Introduction

//

A prerequisite for success in many occupations today is the ability to solve mathematical problems. However, at the time when technology offers mathematical problem solving its greatest challenge and promise, the youth who could benefit most have serious academic deficiencies (Romberg, 1988). Many of these children are poor, live in urban centers, and come from dysfunctional or historically disadvantaged minority or ethnic groups (National Center for Education Statistics, 1991). These urban children's school records show high absenteeism, low academic achievement, and drop out rates near or exceeding 50 percent. Not only are their chances for employment diminishing—their hopes for a good life are vanishing (Bruckerhoff, 1988).

Recognizing this condition, the National Science Foundation in 1988 awarded the Cleveland Education Fund a two-year grant of approximately $200,000. The grant's purposes were to enable Cleveland's intermediate-level mathematics teachers to reform their curriculum consistent with NCTM's new standards and to improve the urban children's mathematics achievement. Through meetings, lectures, workshops, and demonstrations, the mathematics teachers would reorganize the math curriculum, giving special emphasis to problem solving. Project participants would evaluate their effectiveness through pilot tests and revise curriculum accordingly. The project's key innovation tied teacher empowerment to curriculum reform. However, first-year results showed the teachers' mathematics problem solving curriculum and instruction were standard fare. What happened?

The teachers practiced solving the curriculum writer's word problems, returned to their schools to test the problems on their students, and then reported the results back to the curriculum writer. Through practice sessions and experimentation, the teachers were to learn how to solve the problems and how to organize the problems to best suit their students. In the second year this initial cadre of teachers would train other teachers, and so on until every Cleveland intermediate-level mathematics teacher knew this material.

The present report describes Cleveland's problem solving project from the project participant's viewpoint. The problem solving project operated on a standard, goal-directed curriculum development model. During the first year, the curriculum writer and a core of intermediate-level teachers established a curriculum-planning organization. The group met regularly, cooperatively solved math problems, and assigned problem solving lessons to their students. In time the core teachers were to disseminate their findings and train other math teachers.

However carefully prepared were the planning sessions, teachers complained about teaching and expressed skepticism about the project's effectiveness. For

This research was sponsored by the National Science Foundation and the Cleveland Education Fund. An earlier version of this article was presented for a Division B session at the Annual Meeting of the American Educational Research Association, April 16–20, 1990, Boston, MA. The author expresses appreciation to Michael Bossé for editorial assistance in preparation of the manuscript.

instance, during interviews teachers recalled short-lived initiatives and claimed that all their school programs suffered from excessive internal and external influences. The curriculum writer lacked theoretical background and was not a district employee. The math curriculum supervisor's scant involvement showed that administrative and ordinary curriculum development channels were uncoupled from the project. Local and national funding agencies gave teachers considerable latitude, underestimating the teachers' deficiencies in leadership and self-discipline.

The Cleveland teachers' effort to reform intermediate-level mathematics curriculum and empower themselves fell short. Halfway through its funding cycle, the problem solving project's reform language was rhetoric. What might have been a real curriculum innovation was an absurd academic exercise; it became typical school work (see Bruckerhoff, 1991; Ravitch, 1983; Wehlage & Rutter, 1987) by attempting to substitute one technical feature (problem solving) for another (traditional math) without considering the specific needs of the urban students. Cleveland's problem solving initiative lacked teachers' political, professional, and pedagogical intervention.

At year's end, despite reform language, district sanction, and financial support, math teachers' curriculum development and decision-making had scarcely changed. Due partly to neglect of duties and partly to misguided preference for routines or standard procedures, Cleveland's mathematics curriculum maintained a troublesome, uncomplimentary overlap between professional ethics, social context, and curriculum issues. The math teachers knew about the abandoned and sometimes belligerent and out-of-control urban children, but they were unable or unwilling to bring children and curriculum into intimate, mutually beneficial association. Teachers resisted the project's curriculum decision-making role and continued isolated, textbook-dependent practice. Some teachers' negative workplace mentality promoted waste, sloth, and frustration. District policy meant that direct instruction was the standard interpretive framework, rather than process-oriented curriculum theory. Teachers' practice emphasized explicit teaching and dependence on the standardized course of study.

The project's shortcomings are attributed to institutional policy, students' social context issues, and teacher resistance. This math curriculum innovation was small, narrowly focused, and short-term, but its message to reform-minded policymakers and educators is clear: real change is not the substitution of one thing for another. Making a substantive educational difference requires a change in principle (Bruckerhoff, 1988). If educators truly desire to improve urban children's problem solving and math achievement, the whole purpose of schooling, and not just the techniques, must change from inert subject-centered methodologies to student-centered pedagogical practices.

The grant's dual interest—to implement the new standards for school mathematics and empower teachers to make curriculum decisions—identify this project with the "second wave" of school reform (Judge, 1988). The first wave emphasized student performance improvement through routine achievement testing, closer attention to basics, and increased graduation standards. The second wave has emphasized teachers' professional development concerns.

While the first reform wave concentrated on students and curriculum and the second wave upon teacher training, neither reform wave tied curriculum development to urban community renewal. It is only through benign neglect that current educational policy, legislation, and institutional practices exacerbate the dichotomy between the child's experience and curriculum (Gordon & Bhattacharyya, 1992). Offering a problem solving curriculum package as a solution to the urban child's low math achievement without also offering urban community renewal overlooks poverty's powerful, negative effects and the sensitive relationship between the child and the curriculum.

Method

This article reports first-year effects of Cleveland's Problem Solving Infusion Project (PSIP). The researcher used field study methods—chiefly, recording descriptive and historical data gathered from observations and interviews with the curriculum writer, teachers, students, curriculum director, and project director. The field work was conducted during a six-month period from January through July 1989 and emphasized the natural history approach (Bruckerhoff, 1991; Smith, F., 1986). The researcher attended weekly faculty meetings; observed seven teachers' classrooms twice weekly for two periods each visit (N=12; 7 women, 5 men; 15–25 years experience; two retired and three discontinued involvement); and interviewed teachers, the curriculum writer, university faculty, building principals, and the mathematics curriculum supervisor. The field study's basic purpose was to record the mathematics teachers' collaborative behavior and the problem solving curriculum and instruction.

The discussion begins by presenting the teachers' views of the PSIP. Teachers acknowledged the importance of a problem solving curriculum for urban children, but only periodically supplemented the regular, standardized course of study with PSIP materials. Teachers' resistance to implementing the new math curriculum stemmed from their belief that students' low math achievement, students' poor social context, and the district's competency-based education policy discouraged creative and innovative teaching. Next, there is a description of the problem solving committee at work. Three characteristic teacher behaviors are identified: work sheet practice, shop talk, and grousing. The latter two, while very apparent, contributed little or nothing to the project. The math curriculum reform project gave teachers respite, review and practice, and extra pay. The next section presents the curriculum writer's explanation and remarks from the district mathematics curriculum supervisor. The former lacked recent urban experience and theoretical background, the latter had no project involvement. Because these two key individuals chose not to cooperate, the project was insulated from the school system's ordinary curriculum development channels. Cleveland's intermediate-level curriculum reform was a school routine accessory.

The Teachers' View
//

The teachers, who volunteered for the Problem Solving Infusion Project, usually spoke in terms that paralleled the project's language. For example, one project objective concerned emphasizing measurement and design of solid objects. When asked to comment about the math lab's manipulative collection, a teacher said:

> The math curriculum has to have an experience base because these kids don't have the same opportunities as advantaged kids. The math curriculum needs to become more physical. So, that's why I have them doing tessellations today.

Perhaps as often as once per week—usually the day after the curriculum workshop meeting—teachers guided their students through a problem solving or manipulative lesson, like drawing tessellations or other geometric figures. Teachers said that they were reluctant to include PSIP activities more frequently because the problem solving curriculum they were developing had no apparent relation to the district course of study. According to this same teacher:

> The activities of the problem solving project are so varied that the kids don't know where they come from and they coincide only now and then with the regular curriculum. For example, we might do some problems that have something to do with perimeter and find out later in the year where the project might fit in.

Because no one had used these materials previously, teachers and students were unclear about the PSIP subject matter in relation to the regular mathematics curriculum. This perceived mismatch led teachers to use the PSIP materials cautiously for bell work assignments or demonstration lessons mostly for the researcher's benefit. Why?

Compliance with a court-ordered desegregation ruling meant that the district had to administer an annual, competency-based, standardized test to monitor students' achievement of grade-specific math objectives. Explicit teaching to the course of study objectives was minimum school instructional policy. All Cleveland teachers were well aware that creative or innovative teaching (implicit in the PSIP project) risked students' low performance on competency-based tests and risked teachers' transfer, intensive supervision, or nonrenewal. Some teachers—facing real or imagined threats from their building principals—made the minimum, explicit teaching into their standard. One teacher summed up colleagues' resistance to change thusly:

> If a teacher has the class under control, gets good grades from the students, and so on, then the job is being done. Teachers are not required to be creative and innovative. Most teachers just want to do the routine, because that is what the system requires (competency-based course of study).

Teachers would say that typical student behavior and the school's workday organization (forty-minute class period and three-minute student rotation and class change time) prevented or discouraged their flexible use of building facilities and PSIP instruction. A teacher had this to say about using the school's math lab, which, at the school in question, was not located on the same floor as the math department classrooms:

> I'd like to use our building's math lab more often, but I've tried it and it's just about impossible. You need time to do a worthwhile project. It would take me most of the period just to get the kids to the right room (lab) and settled down. The lab materials are great and a break away from the regular classroom is good for all of us, but when I make time for manipulatives, I use the stuff down here.

The math lab's appeal notwithstanding, teachers knew that they could count on the regular classroom, complete with thirty student desks in five-by-six rows, to help maintain order and cover course of study objectives. On most school days, the math lab remained locked and empty.

Despite building level policies and practices to assure an orderly school day, teachers reported that students had low math achievement and poor study habits. Why—in the relatively stable school environment—did students' math scores remain low? Answering this question, one teacher said:

> How do you squeeze into the little time we have all of the work these kids need in math? It might be different if you could give the kids homework and they would do it, but they don't. Most of them take no books home after school or for the weekend. Some might take a notebook or a folder, but no books. Many kids come in on Monday, Tuesday, every day, with nothing. That's discouraging. Take this ditto sheet as an example, "Multiplying Fractions." They were to take it home over the weekend and finish it. This one paper is all I got back from one class. I got only a couple from another class and virtually nothing from the class I just dismissed.
>
> The kids bring in problems that make it very hard to teach. We have repeaters, overage kids, and messed up families. I have one boy in third hour whose parents have abandoned him. He's been in so much trouble with the law. It was the same with his three brothers. I've had them all. The foster homes have been a disaster for this boy. He does not know where he will be living next and may have to go to jail. When he's in class I have to be careful who sits around him because he'll start a fight over anything.

In the teachers' opinion (consistent with newspaper reports) the intermediate-level urban students had a well-below-average proficiency in essential math calculation skills and study habits. Teachers found this to be a difficult starting point that was made nearly impossible to remediate by the students' dangerous and alienating social context. The teachers' row-by-row seating and explicit instruction complemented the district's standard course of study and competency-based achievement testing. Teaching practices and school policies alike discouraged creativity or innovation and emphasized minimal standards.

Teachers were in full agreement that building principals determined the timing, manner, and extent to which teachers could make curriculum decisions. The following teacher quote explains why some PSIP teachers seemed to lack confidence in themselves—as well as mathematics—and to express fear and anger regarding empowerment issues:

> The administration is "beating up on teachers" for failing kids. Some principals demean teachers who consistently hold high standards and threaten these same teachers with lower evaluations. So, we keep two records: one we use for teaching and one we turn in to keep our jobs.

The expression "beating up on teachers" is a reference to harassment, which may include placing teachers on intensive supervision, threatening nonrenewal or transfer to an undesirable location, and ridiculing and shouting or getting physical with teachers—sometimes in the presence of students and colleagues. Taking into account that a majority of these teachers were women and most principals were men (or women following the system's ways), any inappropriate superordinate behavior was also sex abuse and discrimination. Partly in response to these conditions, veteran teachers would express no surprise at a colleague's preference not to question authorities or experiment with new materials and practices.

In the best of circumstances, one might expect that fresh, well-prepared recruits would replace retirees and tired out or incompetent colleagues, who quit or get fired. Instead, bad staffing practices contributed to the teachers' malaise, as the comments of one teacher made clear:

> We have staffing problems that just shouldn't be going on. A teacher will take a sick leave and a substitute will be brought in on a long-term appointment. It might be OK if the substitutes knew math, but in most instances they are certified in English or history. They start out the term with our students and before long the damage has been done because these people don't know math.
>
> The principal's hands are tied to people who work in the building. When someone retires or quits, the building gets to interview a new person. However, all of the interviewees are sent here from downtown. Recently, they had to hire three new people. There were only three people sent out for the interviews. No choice was possible.
>
> Moving in people who are good from another building is possible, but that has its problems, too. We would have to get rid of other people and we just can't get rid of somebody except for just cause (i.e., incompetence or moral turpitude).

Despite the PSIP proposal's intention to spread reform through the district's intermediate-level math curriculum, the PSIP teachers had a depressing outlook on themselves, colleagues, administrators, and the school system. For the foreseeable future, only accidental staffing changes would bring new reform-minded math teachers. Apparently, the PSIP teachers' only hope resided in building principal endorsements or noninterference and their math colleagues' professional development interests.

Recognizing the teachers' low-status position relative to the school system and its authorities, the weekly curriculum development meetings had a dual purpose: to prepare problem solving materials and to foster the teachers' curriculum decision making authority. In the teachers' view, these meetings produced mixed results, at best. A teacher described the PSIP's weekly writing workshops:

> At these meetings with the curriculum writer, we talk about the problems he's developed, work them out ourselves, take them back to the classroom to try them out with kids, and tell him what did and did not work. Then, he revises them.
>
> Once we have been through it, we will in-service the other teachers in these specific problems. Right now, it's like a testing period. We are taking all of the bugs out of it. The idea is to develop a workbook categorized according to the curricular area.

This description closely parallels the project's goals and objectives. However, this teacher and others also expressed skepticism that the project's implicit features undermined or did not support mathematical problem solving and teacher empowerment. The same teacher continued speaking:

> But is this problem solving? Or, are we just getting together to work out some neat problems? We play around with them and have our students play around with them. Some of us use them and some of us don't. I happen to know at least one person who does nothing with these materials. Is this empowerment? Are we really doing curriculum work?

Next, this teacher expressed what seemed to be a deep-seated concern:

> Our behavior at the meetings is so typical of teachers. I find myself getting caught up in the gossip and shop talk. Some of the teachers are coming for the money and that has little or nothing to do with math. We get paid for attending every meeting. Extra money is the reason some teachers come.

The PSIP intended to support teachers' collaborative curriculum development work. To the extent that teachers successfully carried out this work, urban students would learn mathematical problem solving and teachers would empower themselves. However, these teachers only did the work that was required of them and expressed doubt that the expected effects would be realized. Their comments also show that their participation included a negative workplace mentality and subtle forms of resistance.

To clarify further the PSIP's characteristics in its first year, the next section describes the problem solving committee at work.

The Problem Solving Committee at Work
//

In the 1989 spring semester, the curriculum writer, twelve teachers, and the researcher met at the math resource center two or three times per month for two or two and a half hours at a time. During these meetings, instead of writing and revising the PSIP curriculum, the teachers engaged in routine behavior that the researcher called work sheet practice, shop talk, and grousing. The practice sessions pertained to project concerns, but shop talk and grousing were deviations.

It was uncommon for all twelve teachers to be present at the meetings. Absences ocurred because of school district meetings, building level crises, or personal needs. The curriculum writer devoted the first several meeting minutes to introductions, relevant news, and small talk. Within a short time he adopted a businesslike demeanor, getting teachers seated at the table and ready to do *work sheet practice.*

Next, the curriculum writer distributed problem solving exercise handouts that he had prepared beforehand. He read the instructions and asked the teachers to complete the assignment. These instructions to the teachers were accompanied by a student work sheet packet, making up one problem solving unit. As soon as possible after each curriculum planning session, teachers were to use the materials as a pilot exercise with their students and report findings back to the committee. As they worked, the curriculum writer encouraged the teachers to talk about the exercise in terms of its immediate effects on them and their opinions about its possible effects on their students. Generally speaking, the teachers followed these instructions, but from time to time they diverged from their task to cite problems they had with a previous work sheet, discuss their students' misbehavior, complain about work, or talk about the news.

The teachers completed the exercises during three consecutive meetings, proceeding somewhat slowly one sheet at a time. The curriculum writer controlled the pace to allow ample time for examining the pedagogical implications. As the teachers worked out the problems, he worked and talked about what he was doing—sometimes taking the student's role and sometimes the teacher's. It was typical for the teachers to ask technical questions, such as "Should students use colored pens?" It was uncommon for the teachers to talk theoretically about problem solving, to discuss the exercise's mathematics teaching implications (for example, science of pattern or order), or to explore related teaching strategies (see Devaney & Sykes, 1988).

With the committee's help, the curriculum writer assembled at the end of the first year a more or less polished, intermediate-level, problem solving exercise collection. Many of the teachers had participated in the problem solving sessions, piloted the exercises, and reported results. There was some discussion about whether it would be better to have work sheets kept loose or bound. The workbook idea had more appeal because then the teachers would not have to copy materials.

When teachers were not involved immediately in math problem solving, they sometimes engaged in *shop talk*. The topics were wide-ranging but common to teachers. Sometimes the topic was a spin-off from the exercise. At other times it had a remote connection to the exercise itself, but a direct relationship to urban classroom competence. Practical knowledge and technical skill were the teachers' most frequent topics.

As an example of a spin-off, one teacher described how her class responded enthusiastically to a problem solving activity, but it disturbed teachers in adjoining classrooms. The other teachers acknowledged that they had similar reactions in self-contained classrooms. Because all of the teachers were not present to discuss this, they agreed to ask those who were absent to report on the same unit at the next meeting. The teachers then discussed classroom management techniques and student discipline. In the end they expressed their frustration about not catching students who are regularly disruptive and resolved that these students must be caught and expelled. How to deal with students, colleagues, and administrators was a popular shop talk topic.

A more frequent shop talk topic was instructional material—its choice, production, and use. For example, a teacher would state that paper use was causing a problem. Who was paying for this? What do we do if we run out? What about the complaints from other teachers in the building? Should we fun off 150 copies at a time or just enough for one class at a time? Another teacher would raise similar questions about thermofax masters and transparency sheets. What kind should we be using? How can we make sure that there are enough to go around? Should each school get a box of masters or should we keep them at a central location? Someone present would give a practical answer to each of these questions. For instance, at one point there was a discussion about the quality of writing on thermofax masters. As a solution, one of the teachers proposed using the type of mechanical pencil he had with him. This pencil was passed around for all of the teachers to examine. When the question seemed to be an administrative or clerical one, the curriculum writer took notes and told the group what he would do.

There were long discussions about using production equipment, such as the thermofax machine, overhead projector, screens, and ditto machines. Sometimes a teacher would impute that another teacher did not know how to use a machine correctly and that caused unclear copies. This would lead another committee member to give a detailed set of instructions on how to run the machine correctly, what materials to use or avoid using, and what to do if the machine broke down. Work sheet production took time and the teachers, perceiving themselves too short on time, seemed compelled to give out explicit machine operating instructions, including tips and short cuts.

Although the teachers' talk bore little direct relationship to the project's problem solving interest, some of it had a positive and professional aspect. Sometimes, however, it was a rambling complaint about the students and the misperceptions that administrators and other teachers had about the problem solving project and its participants. In brief, the teachers were *grousing*. This seemed to stem from a personal interest—for instance, "I want to get this off my chest"—and often the comments were made in negative and unprofessional terms.

When grousing about students, the teachers complained about the "weird results" they turned in, the students' low morale, and their boisterous or violent behavior. It was typical for a grousing session to begin when one teacher would tell what had happened that day at school. Then, other teachers would relate additional stories, pointing out how these were similar, sometimes more shocking, examples.

In one instance a teacher talked about using handouts instead of transparencies, saying, "All that these students really want are material possessions, like the handouts, and they want them immediately." A second teacher acknowledged that this seemed to be true, but added that it was at least a good basis for using different media. To this the first teacher said, "We work so hard and try everything and get the same kids who come in and refuse to do a damn thing. We all have them. I feel like, Jesus, am I accomplishing anything?" At this point all of the teachers began talking and the meeting lost its focus. The curriculum writer called for a ten-minute break. His action seemed to diffuse the emotional response and refocus the teachers' attention.

The teachers tended to view and treat the problem solving project as merely a technical or mechanical matter, rather than as an opportunity to examine the theoretical and practical aspects of their mathematics instruction (Hardy, 1967; Polya, 1991). By doing so, they kept themselves at a surface level instead of delving into a more meaningful and productive level of reflection, analysis, and critique. One got the impression that teachers' work consisted entirely of monotonous routines for tending machines, passing out work sheets, and monitoring students' behavior. There was little said about the pedagogical concerns of mathematical problem solving or critical analysis and reflection, which lead to the issues of empowerment and judgment. Collaboration with colleagues rarely occurred outside of the project.

Although—according to the project—teachers were to assume curriculum decision-making responsibility, they tended to focus attention on technique and on sustaining personal, and sometimes selfish, motives. The teachers missed an important craft opportunity: fostering teacher decision-making. Considering the project's goals, these behaviors lowered expectations and led to unsatisfactory results. The researcher saw the outcome as stemming from social context conditions for which the curriculum writer and teachers were unprepared or unconcerned, institutional structures that emphasized stability and certainty, and the teachers' being accustomed to a passive curriculum-planning role.

Another influence on the teachers' behavior was their apparent lack of knowledge and skill with higher-level organizational work. Some teachers knew that their materials and machines discussions had little to do with problem solving, and they recognized the gossipy lounge talk for what it was. Apparently, peer pressure, work day weariness, and their need for relief kept the teachers from raising the issue at meetings. As the quotes in the previous section indicate, the teachers did speak privately to the researcher about the committee's products and their classroom practice.

Teachers seemed unconcerned about the empowerment implications. Indeed, teachers never mentioned curriculum decision making. As the next section shows, the curriculum writer prepared problem solving materials and guided the teachers' practice sessions, but math curriculum reform and teacher empowerment also eluded him.

The Curriculum Writer
//

The PSIP curriculum writer was a high school mathematics teacher at a suburban school district. He had twenty-three years experience in mathematics teaching and curriculum development, mostly in suburban and small town settings, and a reputation for math curriculum development. However, his usual work environment, slight acquaintance with urban school children, and decision to work things out himself contributed to the gap between the urban child and the new math curriculum.

The curriculum writer began his account of the project by saying that it had gotten off to a late start in November because this was "a huge district where inertia is a natural part of it"—inertia was a deterrent to reform. The twelve teachers volunteered and, according to the curriculum writer, "were very enthusiastic about getting together to look at new materials and use them." However, he indicated that there was some confusion regarding the writer-teacher roles and relationships. The grant required teachers to "take a bigger share than they did in shaping the math problem solving curriculum. *They* should develop problem solving activities correlated to course objectives." The teachers resisted. They made it clear that they expected the curriculum writer to prepare all of the materials.

By February the curriculum writer had resolved the confusion. He said, "I simply concluded that nothing would be done by the group unless I worked everything out beforehand." According to the curriculum writer, the teachers' new role was "to work hard between meetings to make sure this stuff works." By mutual consent they adopted a typical manager-directs-and-worker-follows interaction framework. Despite the project's claims about teachers as curriculum developers, these teachers' curriculum reform would entail review and practice lessons. There were other compromises. In this statement, the curriculum writer describes and criticizes the writing project:

> The material we made concerns visual thinking and processing of information from visual to verbal and back again. There is a certain amount of problem solving, in that we give the kids a problem and see how they deal with it.
>
> I'm not operating out of any really conscious theoretical construct. A good problem solver may draw a picture, make a model or chart, list the steps, reread the problem.
>
> Each curriculum unit is a theme with a topic. It starts out fairly tame and then these wrinkles appear. These wrinkles are the problems for the kids. The problems at the end of the week are a real challenge.

The teachers report back to me in the committee whether the kids like it, whether they can complete it successfully, and whether they think the kids are learning something. A convincing factor is whether the kids take it home at night and bring it back the next day.

However, the feedback I get from the teachers isn't satisfactory. For one thing, I can't tell whether there is any growth among the kids. I'm hoping that we can do some testing. Also, we need to meet more often so that the teachers do more and more of this material.

For another thing, teachers and administrators are at cross-purposes. According to some administrators, we can do anything we want because nothing that the system does works. However, when you propose something new to the teachers, they will say that you have to ask the principals. Why? Because some principals would not agree to teachers using this material. Too many principals have traditional ideas about teaching and testing. They monitor their teachers, change grades, and penalize teachers who fail students.

The teachers have so little authority. They will say, "I don't dare flunk kids."

I have some other serious concerns. The teachers like doing these practice problems. The kids like it. But, I feel guilty about not having made a huge stack of curriculum materials. Right now our work is a bit free and I am a little worried about what happens when we move it from these 12 teachers out to the whole district.

I'd feel better if a psychologist said, "This is exactly what these kids need." Or, if some math expert said, "This is just the math they need." I don't have anybody who oversees the mathematical worth of what we are doing. We need somebody in the back of these classrooms watching this. I think these materials should be going to some kind of review board.

Things are not going well with the curriculum planning. For instance, I passed this material out at the meeting last week. We did page one and then I passed out page two. The teachers said, "We should make page two before page one." Then, I gave them page three and they wanted it before page one. When I passed out pages four and five, they did the same thing with these pages. They said these last two should go before all of the others. I thought the material at the end was the hardest. So, I was to go home and rewrite the pages, but not put the page numbers on them.

I'd like to bring in something that they think is really good and then they talk about the various ways in which they can do this, rather than my bringing something in and they all say, "Oh, we gotta fix this."

The teachers and the students worked out the mathematical problems, but the materials did not meet the project's goals. The curriculum writer lacked urban teaching experience and made too many concessions. Acknowledging the teachers' preference not to design their own materials, the curriculum writer compiled the materials himself and directed the teachers' review and practice sessions. Because the teachers would not assume curriculum decision-making responsibility, he hoped a school psychologist and math expert would validate the problem solving materials. The curriculum writer was uncomfortable with the risk or uncertainty associated with problem solving curriculum development, and he concluded that there should be a more rigorous curriculum design and an external board of specialists to review their products.

The late start, the teachers' voluntary appointment to the curriculum committee, and the wayward protocol also contributed to negative consequences. During curriculum development meetings, there was confusion about work roles, disagreement about results, and a missing theoretical framework. The teachers' remarks showed that they preferred an externally controlled curriculum, including pre-established problems and explicit processes. Also, the teachers and the math curriculum director wanted to publish a workbook. The curriculum writer expressed misgivings about the workbook idea because of its obvious parallel with commonly available textbook material.

The curriculum writer's perspective raises a number of questions, three of which are worthy of consideration. What is the nature of problem solving? What should be the teachers' curriculum development role? What resources or mechanisms should be used to evaluate these problems? The curriculum writer's comments suggest that the project gave too little attention to the theory of mathematics and curriculum (see Romberg & Carpenter, 1986). Lacking a theoretical construct, he sensed a need for confirmation from external agencies or experts and generally avoided the teachers as well as the district's course of study. The curriculum writer assembled a makeshift problem solving kit prior to the curriculum planning session and directed the teachers' problem solving practice during the sessions. Later, teachers would conduct pilot exercises with their students.

The teachers took a passive role in regard to problem solving and curriculum planning. Their preference to be passive had a negative impact on their assumption of responsibility for decision making (see Erickson, 1986; Maeroff, 1988). The curriculum writer's decision to "work things out beforehand" guaranteed that problem solving would be artificial for teachers. The teachers' compliance gave assurance that the students' problem solving would be artificial as well. The curriculum writer's dilemma—to publish or not to publish a problem solving workbook—foreshadowed the project's limited effect.

The curriculum writer rarely referred to the district mathematics curriculum director, who was chiefly responsible for mathematics curriculum development in compliance with state guidelines. For all intents and purposes, there was no relationship between the curriculum writer and the mathematics curriculum director. Contrary to the project's intent and to sound curriculum development policy, they chose not to collaborate. This was a serious flaw. The State of Ohio had recently passed legislation that required all districts to follow a course of study. Also, Cleveland public school policy stipulated that all teachers plan according to pupil performance objectives (PPO). A teacher's PPO was a detailed listing of content specific objectives for competency-based instruction. In theory at least, teachers, curriculum committees, and content area supervisors were to derive PPO's from specific knowledge bases and the district's course of study; in practice, the PPO list was made up from currently used textbooks and standardized achievement tests. From the math curriculum director's viewpoint, the problem solving project failed because it was not integrated with the course of study. He said:

> There are some things coming out of the problem solving project that are good, but it has some critical issues to deal with. Before they begin next year, they should have some kind of chart or plan that shows what should be produced and when. Let's imagine for a moment that the new school year is about to start. A math teacher has to know something about how to start out the year with problem solving.
>
> So, the project is kind of a hit and miss affair, in my opinion. It would be nice if they had enough activities, so that these could be coordinated with all of the chapters in the textbook. That way they could always be working with a concrete model. The bottom line is this: they have to give kids problems to solve. They've got to get the kids involved.
>
> Where are we with the first year of work in? I think they should have produced more by this time. The teacher empowerment thing is ticking off some of the other math teachers in the district, who are not on the committee. What if they get angry and decide not to use these materials once they are developed? Also, the committee consists of some people who are just there for the fifty bucks. They are willing to do whatever they are told, so long as they get paid. What are they going to do about all of that?

The mathematics curriculum director expressed a skeptical opinion and only alluded to the PSIP curriculum writer. The director wanted an explicit problem solving curriculum that was integrated with the district's course of study. From his perspective, curriculum planning for problem solving must emphasize pre-established conditions (see Smith, F., 1986).

As things stood, the project lacked direction and left too much to chance. The project's general openness led to poor results and may have caused the teachers' unprofessional conduct. Mathematical problem solving should be a preplanned classroom activity and not an open-ended, process-oriented teaching lesson. The curriculum director, like his central office supervisors, wanted teachers to follow the district's course of study. The curriculum writer and math curriculum director were far apart, and their noncollaboration assured that they would remain so.

Discussion

//

This account of the Cleveland teachers' Problem Solving Infusion Project shows how school routines can be a major deterrent to mathematics curriculum reform. According to the proposal, teachers would receive support for collaborative work and for assuming more responsibility in decision making. Cleveland's intermediate-level children would receive higher quality, up-to-date problem solving instruction, which would improve their mathematics achievement. However, less-than-professional conduct and school policy issues weakened the project's reform focus. In particular, the teachers' workshop behaviors were ill-suited to achieving the project's goals, but were effective resistance routines. The curriculum development plan and problem solving decision making were standard and vested in external authorities, namely the curriculum writer and district course of study. The teachers chose not to assume the necessary political, professional, and pedagogical interventionist roles.

Routinized operations were the end result for the curriculum writer and the teachers. From the curriculum writer's perspective, there was too little guidance. He believed consultation with a board of experts would relieve his anxiety about choosing the right mathematics problems, correct word problem sequence, and appropriate solutions. The curriculum writer thought that the difficulty he and the teachers were having would be resolved once they produced the workbook of word problems in conformity with Cleveland's pupil performance objectives. However, he acknowledged that the workbook might interfere with the new problem solving curriculum for the same reasons as published materials of bygone eras: workbooks stifle thinking and discourage creativity and innovation. His avoidance of the curriculum director, course of study, and pupil performance objectives suggest that he expected the old system to absorb the new work routines. His musings quoted earlier indicate that he thought there were serious discrepancies between the direction the committee was headed and the intent of the new standards. He was searching for sources of difficulty among students, teachers, schools, and their revised mathematics curriculum. Although the first-year results did not satisfy the curriculum writer, his tasks and conceptual framework matched the project's guidelines. He followed a rational plan for curriculum development, including goals, objectives, and time-line. His charge was to supply problem solving exercises and to train teachers to use these materials. He completed his work routines on time.

Interviews with PSIP teachers showed that they believed problem solving activities were important additions to the urban children's math curriculum. The teachers said that the explicit, textbook approach they used before the project was not satisfactory. They believed that the project's techniques could improve urban children's math achievement, particularly where problem solving lessons included manipulatives such as geoboards, containers, figures, rulers, and so on. However, these teachers also said that course of study requirements, children's low math achievement, and students' nonsupportive home life refocused their attention on standardized pupil performance objectives. From the teachers' viewpoint, the new math problems would be mere frills or distractions, unless they were made part of an official curriculum plan. The math teachers chose to stick with the district's course of study, even though they knew urban children require a much greater effort to achieve real success in a standard math curriculum. The PSIP teachers temporarily adapted the new routines to their jobs, but none believed that this project would succeed—and it wasn't. It seemed inevitable that their "reform" of problem solving would be coopted by the very thing they were trying to replace—the routinized and irrelevant status quo.

This project was also stymied by the institution's competency-based, standardized course of study. Indeed, the system's overdependency on routine jarred with experimental curriculum planning. Clarifying the practice-experiment distinction is very important for promoting curriculum change. However, traditional school organizations confuse practice with experiment, value established routines, and create frustration over using innovative or creative techniques. A curriculum reform project devoted to practice, such as Cleveland's, would be a study in contradiction.

John Dewey noted that the intention of his "Chicago Experiment" was *not* to develop a "practice school, nor (in its purpose) what is now called a 'progressive' school" (1936, p. 464). His position on experimental curriculum planning is instructive. Dewey's main point is this: an experimental curriculum supports the continuous pursuit of understanding that is *both moral and intellectual* (p. 465). Intellectually, curriculum planning includes the selection and study of subject matter with consideration for its best reorganization and presentation to particular students. In this way experimentation is a constituent feature of the teacher's interactions with students. Experimentation is not a detached series of continual practice exercises. Concerning the moral aspect, today there is an epidemic of disadvantaged children. Their daily lives are steeped in poverty, hunger, hopelessness, violence, drug and alcohol abuse, AIDS, transience, homelessness, and adolescent parenthood. The personal and social aspects of childhood in cities like Cleveland make solving the problem of education an evident and especially difficult moral imperative.

Continual emphasis on practice obscures the real value and function of reform and experiment in curriculum planning and postpones the day when moral and intellectual education benefits will accrue to these children. That some of these teachers were deficient in math knowledge and some were indifferent is manifested in the teachers' continual practice of word problems. In the least, many lacked an understanding of what could make mathematical problem solving a vital interest to these children. In either instance, an intensive effort should be undertaken to improve the teachers' grasp of mathematics.

When math teachers planned to use PSIP methods and materials, they perceived themselves and their students at risk regarding school schedule and policy requirements. Systematic teaching and competency-based learning were the district's most highly regarded strategies for insuring compliance with Ohio's education policies and Cleveland's court-ordered desegregation. These policies and practices subtly discouraged teachers from functioning as autonomous professionals. Teachers would risk losing their jobs when deviating from the course of study. Teachers' behavior at the project meetings—understandable but not acceptable—suggested that routinization had become commonplace, even definitive. With the first year of the project behind them, their decision making would involve no more than adjusting minor details while teaching word problems, which was not different from their previous role. Unacknowledged resistance to reform was an inherent feature of this traditional system.

The unsuccessful curriculum reform project in Cleveland presents several suggestions for future initiative. In the first place, teachers have a moral obligation to provide effective problem solving instruction to urban children and to assume rights and responsibilities appropriate to their occupation. Systems do not make moral and intellectual decisions; people do. Second, a city, like Cleveland, has a moral responsibility to trust its public school teachers to be more responsive to children's needs. Public *trust* must be the central feature of curriculum reform, otherwise the "second wave" of reform will be piecemeal and ineffective (Darling-Hammond, 1988). Third, mutual improvement of problem solving instruction and urban children's mathematics achievement depend upon a research program devoted to intensive inquiry of process-oriented teaching and learning (Romberg & Carpenter, 1986). Fourth, comprehensive improvement of an urban education program requires policymakers to promote students' learning as the teachers' primary responsibility; to make individual schools into consistent, intensive, and flexible institutions for educating children; and to coordinate a network of local services for the social and physical welfare of children. Finally, any effort to improve America's urban public schools must be linked to the particular city's plans for urban renewal and reconstruction. In the end desperate children will learn problem solving and will know that a formal education offers hope for tomorrow.

questions for discussion

1. Drawing upon your personal experience and this article's description, explain the social conditions of American children who live in poverty.
2. How would you characterize the relationship between poor children, public school curriculum, and public policy?
3. In your opinion, why did these teachers behave as they did? What would you suggest to improve the situation?
4. What is a theory? What is a curriculum theory? Should a person who teaches mathematics know math theory? What about other subject matter? Is there a relationship between subject matter theory—mathematics, physics, linguistics, sociology, history, art—and curriculum theory? What are the limits or dangers of theory? Explain.
5. If you believe that education can have a positive effect on America's minority and poor children, what should that effect be and what public policies, instructional practices, curriculum theory, and school organization would promote these results?

teachers as researchers

In attempting to reform the curriculum of schools, teachers need to play an essential role. Interview practicing teachers as to what conditions would be necessary for teachers to work together for curriculum reform. What would be the initial steps in the development of this reform and what would be the priorities be?

suggested   readings

Apple, M. W. (1986). *Teachers and texts: A political economy of class & gender relations in education.* New York: Routledge.

Apple, M. W. (1993). *Official knowledge: Democratic education in a conservative age.* New York: Routledge.

Aronowitz, S., & Giroux, H. A. (1985). *Education under seige: The conservative, liberal and radical debate over schooling.* South Hadley, MA: Bergin & Garvey.

Cuban, L. (1984). *How teachers taught: Constancy and change in American classrooms 1890–1980.* New York: Longman.

From risk to renewal. *Education Week, xxii*(30), pp. 1–34. (See previous issues of this periodical for additional information.)

Giroux, H. A. (1988). *Teachers as intellectuals: Toward a critical pedagogy of learning.* South Hadley, MA: Bergin & Garvey.

Kliebard, H. (1986). *The struggle for the American curriculum: 1893–1958. New York: Routledge & Kegan Paul.*

McNeil, L. M. (1986). *Contradictions of control: School structure and school knowledge.* New York: Routledge & Kegan Paul.

references

Bruckerhoff, C. (1988, May). *Removing the stigma of disadvantage: A report on the education and employability of 9–15 year old youth at risk* (National Commission for Employment Policy Monograph No. 88–09). Washington, D.C.

Bruckerhoff, C. (1989). *Teachers on the board: The Cleveland collaborative for mathematics education.* Paper delivered at the annual meeting of the American Educational Research Association, San Francisco, CA.

Bruckerhoff, C. (1991). *Between classes: Faculty life at Truman High.* New York: Teachers College Press.

Darling-Hammond, L. (1988). Policy and professionalism. In A. Lieberman (Ed.), *Building a professional culture in schools* (pp. 55–77). New York: Teachers College Press.

Devaney, K., & Sykes, G. (1988). Making the case for professionalism. In A. Lieberman (Ed.), *Building a professional culture in schools* (pp. 3–22). New York: Teachers College Press.

Dewey, J. (1936). The theory of the Chicago experiment. In K. C. Mayhew & A. C. Edwards (Eds.), *The Dewey school* (pp. 463–477). New York: Appleton-Century Company.

Erickson, F. (1986). Tasks in times: Objectives of study in a natural history of teaching. In K. Zumwalt (Ed.), *Improving teaching* (pp. 131–48). Alexandria, VA: Association for Supervision and Curriculum Development.

Fullan, M., Bennett, B., & Rolheiser-Bennett, C. (1990). Linking classroom and school improvement. *Educational Leadership, 47*(8), 13–19.

Gordon, E., & Bhattacharyya, M. (1992). Human diversity, cultural hegemony, and the integrity of the academic canon. *Journal of Negro Education, 61*(3), 405–418.

Hardy, G. (1967). *A mathematician's apology.* Cambridge, MA: Cambridge University Press. (Originally published 1940)

Homans, G. (1950). *The human group.* New York: Harcourt Brace and World.

Judge, H. (1988). Afterward. In A. Lieberman (Ed.), *Building a professional culture in schools* (pp. 222–31). New York: Teachers College Press.

Maeroff, G. (1988). *The empowerment of teachers: Overcoming the crisis of confidence.* New York: Teachers College Press.

National Center for Education Statistics. (1991). *Digest of education statistics, 1991.* (NCES Publication No. 91–697). Washington, D.C.: U.S. Government Printing Office.

National Commission for Excellence in Education (1983). *A nation at risk: The imperative for educational reform.* Washington, D.C.: U.S. Government Printing Office.

Polya, G. (1991). *How to solve it.* Princeton: Princeton University Press. (Originally published 1945)

Popkewitz, T. (1988). Culture, pedagogy, and power: Issues in the production of values and colonialization. *Journal of Education, 170*(3), 77–90.

Ravitch, D. (1983). *The troubled crusade: American education 1945–1980.* New York: Basic Books.

Richardson, V. (1990). Significant and worthwhile change in teaching practice. *Educational Researcher, 19*(7), 10–18.

Romberg, T. (1988, May). NCTM's curriculum and evaluation standards: What they are and why they are needed. *Arithmetic Teacher, 35,* 2–3.

Romberg, T., & Carpenter, T. (1986). Research on teaching and learning mathematics. In M. Wittrock (Ed.), *Handbook of research on teaching* (pp. 850–73). New York: Macmillan.

Schorr, L. (1989). *Within our reach.* New York: Doubleday.

Smith, F. (1986). *Insult to intelligence.* New York: Arbor House.

Smith, L. (1988). *Educational innovators: Then and now.* New York: The Falmer Press.

Snider, W. (1990, February 7). Cleveland school officials move to avert state takeover. *Education Week,* p. 5.

Waxman, H., & Walberg, H. (1991). *Effective teaching: Current research.* Berkeley: McCutchan.

Wehlage, G., & Rutter, A. (1987). Dropping out: How much do schools contribute to the problem? In G. Natriello (Ed.), *School dropouts: Patterns and policies* (pp. 70–88). New York: Teachers College Press.

6

///

Representation, Self-Representation, and the Meanings of Difference

Questions for Educators

Elizabeth Ellsworth

Elizabeth Ellsworth

guiding questions

1. What is the author trying to say or teach?

2. What is the significance of what you read here for you personally and for you as a teacher?

3. What are the perspectives drawn on by the author to make the analysis?

4. How does this analysis help to inform our practice in classrooms?

///

For the past twenty-five years, many artists, political activitists, and students of media, literature and other cultural forms have radically challenged and changed the ways they think about language, images, and the creation of meanings within and across cultures. Concerned with how forms of cultural expression such as art, film, television, and writing both re-present *and* produce social relations and social inequalities, they have made "representation" a key issue in their actions and debates. They have used the term "representation" to refer to the processes that people and social groups use to interpret and give meaning to the world, and to the mediation of those meanings by and through language, stories, images, music, and other cultural products.

Teachers and educational institutions interpret and structure meanings into curriculums, and they mediate and produce official school knowledge through language, images, stories, and ways of interacting in classrooms. In this sense, curriculums and teaching practices can be understood as acts of representation, and teachers and students can be understood as active participants in the social construction of meaning. Because of this, contemporary theories of representation offer serious and interesting questions to educators. Whether consciously or unconsciously, educators are always acting upon assumptions and beliefs about representation—such as how we "know" what something "means;" how we determine the "correct" or "official school" understandings of people, things, and events; and how we understand the relations between images, stories, language, and "reality."

People in marginalized social and cultural groups in the United States are trying to have some effect on how their lives are characterized and defined by curriculums and teaching practices. The ways that educators participate in the processes of representation have serious consequences to these efforts. Once again, Asian-American, African-American, Latino/a, Chicana/o, Puerto Rican, and native American students and community members are focusing the nation's attention on the persistence of institutionalized racism in education. They are demanding the right to self-representation in schools and universities— the right to be full participants in constructing official school knowledge about their experiences, histories, needs, ways of knowing the world, social positions, and senses of selves. They are demanding that their individual and collective self-representations be visible, respected, and considered legitimate forms of knowledge and topics of study.

These demands grow, in part, out of refusals to be assimilated—that is, refusals to give up distinctive social identities and communities, which have been shaped by histories of exploitation and by creative self and group definition in the face of exploitation. Women and men of color, white women, people with disabilities, people for whom English is an additional language, gay men and lesbians, and marginalized groups are struggling to represent and define themselves, their histories, experiences, and futures in ways that support viable communities and social identities, which refuse to be assimilated into the dominant culture. They/we are doing this in the educational field (curriculum development, teaching practices, school organization, and community control of schools) as well as in the media, law, medical and political institutions, and the family.

Struggles over representation and self-representation in schools and universities are not new.

> The first successful assault on the liberal myth of the university's political neutrality in the postwar period was the work of the civil rights movement; as segregated schools and universities across the country were compelled, sometimes by force of arms, to admit black children and black women and men to study, the notion that the university (or any classroom) stood above political questions or outside the structures of power was discredited. (Rooney, 1989, p. 9)

The resurgence of feminism in the 1970s and the establishment of women's studies in universities are in part legacies of the civil rights movement of the 1950s and 1960s. These movements have sustained ongoing struggles to revise the official curriculums of schools and universities by addressing Eurocentric, masculinist, and class biases and by incorporating scholarship by and about marginalized groups. People involved in civil rights movements, feminisms, and the establishment of new academic disciplines and school practices have generated perspectives, histories, and self-definitions that now disrupt assumptions and practices of entire academic fields. They have shaken the very foundations of disciplines such as anthropology, history, sociology, literary criticism, communication, law, and medicine. Scholars, activists, and artists whose work is grounded in these movements have developed and expanded new areas of interdisciplinary studies. These include ethnic studies such as African-American, Chicano/a, native American, and Asian-American, as well as critical cultural studies, gay and lesbian studies, and the "third wave" of feminist and womanist studies launched by women of color through critiques of white, middle-class feminism and its institutionalization as women's studies.

The CANONS of all traditional academic disciplines in the West were institutionalized during times of violent and blatant racism, sexism, colonialism, and exploitation of human and natural resources. People working in the new disciplines mentioned above have demonstrated how official curriculums and "the canon" continue to naturalize, justify, and extend those dynamics into what is taught in schools and how it is taught. Through such demonstrations, they have formed strong and influential arguments that all knowledge is socially constructed and linked to power and its interests. That is, meanings are not direct reflections of the world or of people, but are actively made and always mediated by interests and histories of dominant groups and by previous and current cultural representations and understandings. From this perspective, making sense of the world is seen as a process of selecting signs and symbols from the diverse and often contradictory images and connotations currently circulated by social groups. The meanings available for selection are always in competition for power and legitimacy within the culture. Once selected, the meanings are combined by artists, writers, curriculum developers, students, and teachers in ways that try to support the position(s) they have

CANON: A body of principles, rules, standards, or norms.

taken up (consciously and unconsciously) within those struggles. Curriculum materials and media that result from such a process can never "force" us to agree with the intentions of their producers. Rather, they act as "invitations" to students and teachers to take up particular perspectives and actions in the ongoing production and contestation of meaning within and among social groups. These invitations to adopt views that are invested with particular interests are accompanied by "encouragements" to accept the invitation. For example, curriculums often encourage students and teachers to make official school knowledge "their own" through implicit and explicit guarantees of certainty, familiarity, success, power, safety, validation, pleasure, and recognition.

The struggles and analyses of people who have been exploited and made invisible by dominant meanings of "woman," "poor," "black," "disabled," "gay," or "lesbian," for example, have shown that the "foundations" and canons of academic disciplines do not represent neutral "facts" or a pre-given "reality." Rather, they represent the experiences, desires, and political interests of the social and cultural groups that were in the position to name and shape the histories, experiences, and meanings of their own and other social groups. The argument that meaning is the product of social and political interaction seriously undermines a number of claims that support dominant Western thought and education. These include claims that there are absolute universal truths that can be known, that there are single identifiable origins and causes of events, that there is an essential and common human nature or experience, that there are universal human goals, and that a utopian future that benefits everyone can be envisioned. The image of the scientist or educator as one who speaks with certainty, authority, and a single "correct" perspective from which to represent the world is under serious attack by those who have suffered under institutionalized scientific and educational authority.

What some have called the "crisis in representation," then, is not merely a crisis of confidence in the abilities and appropriateness of received perspectives to understand and make sense of the world. It is also a political crisis in which marginalized groups refuse to be "represented" in the sense of spoken for, defined, or assigned meanings by anyone other than themselves. Struggles for political self-representation have become theoretically and practically intertwined with struggles for symbolic self-representation. Women and men of color, white women, working-class members, and impoverished people, for example, were systematically barred as full, welcome, and valued participants in deciding whose histories would be written and taught, whose experiences and expressions would be worthy of the labels "literature" and "art," whose versions of "reality" would count as "science," or whose ways of learning would count as "education."

Diverse, and sometimes contradictory, educational initiatives have resulted from the political struggles and theoretical developments concerning representation. They take the forms of mandated multicultural and gender-balanced curriculums; community-controlled bilingual schools in which racial, ethnic, and language differences are seen as strengths to be built upon rather than deficiencies to be remedied through assimilation to the dominant norm; culturally specific curriculums and teaching strategies; and cultural immersion and cultural survival schools.

What does it mean, then, to be studying the "social foundations" of education at a time when various social groups and scholars are challenging and rejecting the very notion of "foundation"? As diverse and often antagonistic groups struggle against assimilation and for self-representation, the search for "educational foundations" becomes extremely problematic and charged with inescapable political, cultural, economic, and social consequences. "Foundation" implies a single, firm, enduring, and fixed base on which to build our ideas and practices as educators. It implies a base of shared meanings about what knowledge is worth teaching and how it should be taught. The assumption is that educators have agreed, or can be convinced to agree, to share these founding meanings because they have some basis in "fact" and "reality."

Yet, the political, institutional, and intellectual conflicts I discussed earlier demonstrate the very real limits to just how much of what some assume to be "shared" culturally, socially, and intellectually is, in fact, not shared across deep and often irreconcilable differences of power relations and interests within U.S. society. Traditionally, educators concerned with curriculum theory and development have framed the study of foundations in curriculum with this question: What knowledge should be taught in schools and how should it be taught?

In the past fifteen years, however, educators who are developing the areas of the sociology of knowledge and cultural studies in education have argued that instead of asking what knowledge should be taught in schools and how, we must ask: *Whose* knowledge has been seen as worth teaching, and who has benefited? *Whose* knowledge should be taught and why? These educators have traced the operations of the "selective tradition" in how curriculums are developed and organized. Apple, following Raymond Williams, defines the "selective tradition" as "the ways in which from a whole possible area of past and present, certain meanings and practices are chosen for emphasis, certain other meanings and practices are neglected and excluded" (1979, p. 6). Research on this topic has shown that curriculum policymakers and developers have selected for official school knowledge those meanings and practices that serve the interests of dominant groups and legitimate their ways of making sense of the world. This has led to school curriculums overwhelmingly organized around individualization, for example, as opposed to cooperation and group location.

The question of *whose* knowledge should be taught in schools implies a "who" to teach about and a body of knowledge available for inclusion in existing curriculums. Yet, many social and cultural groups, struggling to survive economically and culturally under the exploitations and violences of sexism, racism, and classism, have been excluded from the process of writing histories and from the canons of art and literature. They have had few resources to devote to developing and presenting self-representations in ways capable of dislodging the lies and misinformation that have shaped how they are represented in and to their own communities and to the dominant culture.

Each day, students and teachers are met by curriculums and teaching practices that re-present the dominant culture, with little or no acknowledgment of how that very culture is profoundly shaped by its ongoing efforts to differentiate itself from those groups considered outsiders, "Others." According to members of marginalized groups, such learning environments perpetuate internalized oppression, whereby students find it difficult to foster senses of self and group that could help stop demeaning representations and erasure. Despite often violent efforts to eliminate them, rich cultural and social identities have survived and thrived in marginalized groups. However, they have often been forced to do so in fragmented, coded, and isolated forms that pose the least threat to dominant groups.

For someone in a social or cultural group that has been made invisible, marginalized, and misrepresented through efforts to perpetuate its subordination and exploitation, the question of *whose* knowledge should be taught is necessary, but not sufficient. Groups whose social or cultural identities and knowledges are not articulated in the terms needed to provoke curriculum change in schools and universities, or whose forms of identities and knowledges are not effective within and responsive to changed and changing circumstances, must engage, at some point, with the politics of representation. Under such circumstances, the following questions about representation also become crucial: How will I/we *construct* my/our knowledges, histories, and cultural identities *as,* for example, white working-class women, black lesbians, white men with disabilities, Menomonie Indian women?" Addressing such questions requires more than adding information about marginalized social and cultural groups to the already structured curriculum. It requires actively and creatively rewriting and reconstructing marginalized cultural and social identities and knowledges in ways that address the challenges and opportunities of the present.

Such creative writing and rewriting of identities is an ongoing process in all social and cultural groups. Sometimes, it results in the construction of *new* social identities. For example, in the past twenty years, struggles to name and oppose sexism, racism, heterosexism, oppression of people with AIDS, discrimination against persons with disabilities, and so on, have created contexts in which naming and organizing around new social identities have become strategically necessary in order to oppose social relations and interactions that are oppressive and exploitative. The possibility, desire, and political need to designate oneself as a woman of color, gay man or lesbian, person living with AIDS, and so on are the result of struggles to name and make visible oppressed social positions that have been historically denied, have gone unrecognized by those not living them out, or have resulted from new and unprecedented social and political circumstances. For such groups, the project of constructing knowledge about their social positions, histories, cultures, and social identities is absolutely essential. Such knowledge enables marginalized groups to construct cultural-ethical positions from which to negotiate existing oppressive power relations. It is from an understanding of historical selves that meaningful futures can be constructed.

The formation and re-presentation of cultural and historical selves and social positions is not simply a matter of selecting and combining knowledges and meanings that are already available. It is also a matter of participating in the ongoing social construction of knowledge—in the writing and rewriting of history and social identities. What is at stake when we ask "whose knowledge" will be taught in schools is the "who" in "whose knowledge." What is at stake is our senses of ourselves and Others, and what it is we "know" about ourselves and Others.

The insistence by some artists, political activists, and cultural critics that social identities are constructed, not discovered, and their rejection of the myth of a single, universal, collective human story confront educators with questions such as these: How will we as teachers and students understand our work as a process of constructing representations of ourselves, of others, and of the world in our classrooms? How will we do this in ways responsive to the contexts we are in and to the constantly shifting power relations among us? What does it mean to be teaching during a time when many students and teachers are members of marginalized groups that are struggling to develop languages and styles of self-representation able to sustain communities of difference as they resist assimilation?

Students and teachers of difference, who struggle to transform what is taught in schools, are faced with this strategic question: How can we, how will we construct knowledge about and representations of groups that have been marginalized in and through education in ways that render continued marginalization unintelligible?

Curriculums, teaching practices, and school policies are attempts to constitute relationships between and among teachers and students. Stories about our own and other social and cultural groups attempt to set us in particular relations to ourselves and to others. For example, the curriculums and teaching practices we use and/or construct as teachers tell stories "as," "about," "to," "for," "with," and "at" our own and other social and cultural groups. Each of these orientations between the teller of the story and the subjects of the story enacts a particular social and political relationship that profoundly affects the meanings that will be constructed by listeners. For example, speaking "as" may take the form of autobiography, or of "speaking out" *as* a member of a particular social and cultural group against representations imposed on oneself and one's group by those occupying different social positions. Speaking "about" implies that the speaker/teacher does not share the social and political location of the group being represented, and is in a position to name, describe, analyze, and/or represent a group whose histories and meanings he or she does not live out. Speaking "with" implies that the speaker/teacher does not share the social position of the group he or she is representing, but is connected to that group by shared commitments and a history of shared struggle, and has demonstrated an ability to respond meaningfully in support of that group in ways that have been welcomed and valued by its members. Speaking "to" or "at" implies a direct address to the audience, one that acknowledges and represents the social, intellectual, ideological, or political distance between the speaker/teacher and the audience, and that heightens the awareness and consequences of the distance by maintaining it and using it as the very occasion and justification for speaking or teaching. Speaking "for" implies that the speaker, policy, curriculum, or teaching practice in some way represents—stands in for—those who cannot speak for themselves in a particular context and makes present and visible meanings and perspectives that, it is assumed, would otherwise be absent or missed.

Which of the above "speakings" do various curriculums and teaching practices enact and *why?* What is it about specific classroom contexts that make some relations of speaking more appropriate, more acceptable, more urgent, more strategic, more "educational," or more supportive of the struggles of marginalized groups than others? What meanings and power relations get enacted when we as educators speak "for," "to," "about," "with," or "as" social positions we do not live out in our own bodies? How have relations of speaking "to," "for," "about," "with," "as," or "at" become codified and institutionalized within various conventions of curriculum design?

Teacher education classes have access to rich, powerful, and urgent poems, novels, short stories, essays, films, videos, and other artistic self-representations by people from marginalized groups about their social and cultural experiences with education—of going to school and teaching in schools. They can be used to raise questions about the many ways that various curriculums and teaching practices based on speakings "about," "to," "for," and "at" have injured passions for learning, undermined self-confidence and senses of self and group worth, and led students and teachers to disassociate from their own social and individual histories and to disdain and/or be ashamed of their own groups. Socially and culturally grounded stories of schooling and teaching challenge students and teachers to become responsive to what happens when the "collective human stories" told in official school curriculums, policies, and practices repeatedly exclude the languages, experiences, perspectives, needs, images, and popular cultural forms of all but a few dominant groups. What happens to passions for learning and teaching when this exclusion is not accidental, but is instead linked implicitly and explicitly, consciously and/or unconsciously, to judgment about the worth, correctness, desirability, beauty, and intelligence of various social and cultural groups? What happens to passions for teaching and learning when expectations and rewards for learning and teaching hinge on assimilating oneself to the mythical universal human story and hiding one's own social and cultural histories and differences?

Suppose we agree with those who argue that meaning is not absolute, given, or something we can simply "read off" of the world. Suppose we agree that it is a constantly changing product of social struggle that shifts and functions for particular purposes. Then, paraphrasing Brenda Marshall, we are challenged to pay attention to how meanings get constructed and used, by whom, and for what purposes in schools and curriculums. "As a result, the *responsibility* of interpretation is highlighted" (1992, p. 70). Rather than searching for a reassuring foundation and universal truth, this perspective challenges us to become response-able (that is, able-to-respond) to our active participation in interpreting the world—not only as individuals, but also as members of groups and communities and as people who develop and teach curriculums.

questions for discussion

1. What relations of speaking "to," "for," "about," "with," and/or "as" are set up between this article and its readers (students *and* teachers)?
2. What relations of speaking "to," "for," "about," "with," and/or "as" are set up between this book and its readers (students *and* teachers) when the book poses lists of questions like this one at the end of chapters?
3. How might the answering of questions like this one in a book like this one become an opportunity for students and teachers to engage in acts of self-representation?
4. Describe a current situation involving attempts by a marginalized group or groups to affect the terms in which they are represented in school and/or university curriculums. How might teachers, administrators, and students respond to these attempts in ways that acknowledge and engage with their active participation in the social construction of meaning?

teachers as researchers

Some educators have suggested that there are serious gaps in educators' understanding of the difficulties of teaching within and across social and cultural differences in classrooms. Initiate a research project that documents your difficulties and successes in teaching about and across cultural differences. Identify which particular perspectives, resources, and practices help or hinder your efforts and reflect on how and why they are and/or are not useful to you.

suggested readings

Anzaldua, G. (1990). *Making face, making soul: Haciendo caras.* San Francisco: Aunt Lute Foundation.

Donald, J., & Rattansi, A. (Eds.). (1992). *"Race," culture and difference.* London: Sage Publications.

Perry, T., & Fraser, J. W. (Eds.). (1993). *Freedom's plow: Teaching in the multicultural classroom.* New York: Routledge.

Kahn, D., & Neumaier, D. (Eds.). (1985). *Cultures in contention.* Seattle: The Real Comet Press.

Simpson, R., & Walker, S. (Eds.). (1988). *Multicultural literacy: Opening the American mind.* St. Paul: Graywolf Press.

r e f e r e n c e s

Apple, M. (1979). *Ideology and curriculum.* London: Routledge & Kegan Paul.

Marshall, B. K. (1992). *Teaching the postmodern: Fiction and theory.* New York: Routledge.

Rooney, E. (1989). *Seductive reasoning: Pluralism and the problematic of contemporary literary theory.* Ithaca: Cornell University Press.

Enticing Challenges

An Introduction to Foucault and Educational Discourses

Jennifer M. Gore

guiding questions

1. What is the author trying to say or teach?
2. What is the significance of what you read here for you personally and for you as a teacher?
3. What are the perspectives drawn on by the author to make the analysis?
4. How does this analysis help to inform our practice in classrooms?

> *No discourse is inherently liberating or oppressive. The liberatory status of any theoretical discourse is a matter of historical inquiry, not theoretical pronouncement.*
>
> Jana Sawicki (1988a, p. 166)

For many, this statement will seem odd, if not simply wrong. In this chapter, my aim is to demonstrate how such a position can be supported and why it matters within the field of education. Both the statement above, and this chapter, are framed by the work of French social philosopher, Michel Foucault. Foucault's work, first published in English as early as 1965 (Bemauer & Keenan, 1988) has profoundly influenced thinking in many arenas of social theory about many aspects of social practice, including, quite recently, education. In part, the magnitude of his influence results from the degree to which his ideas, while challenging existing understandings, are compelling and persuasive.

Sawicki's statement characterizes the major Foucauldian challenges I want to highlight. While there exists an expanding and sophisticated body of literature, debate and analysis on the work of Foucault, my goal here is simply to explore consequences of Foucault's view that truth and power are linked to each other through contextually specific practices. I begin this task with an elaboration of Foucault's ideas on power and knowledge, focusing on his notion of 'regimes of truth'. Next, I consider applications of Foucault's analyses to education. Finally, I review implications of Foucault's challenges.

Before I begin, a brief note on the use of "discourse" is necessary. The notion of discourse in use here is not that of linguistics where the primary concern is with the structure of language. Rather, discourse is used here as it is by Foucault and within poststructuralism, where the focus is much more on the content and context of language. Discourses, in the context of specific historically constituted power relations, and invoking particular notions of truth, define the actions and events that are plausible, rationalized or justified in a given field. Hence, by referring to discourses, my intention is to signal a concern not so much for what words mean as for the way words, sets of statements, and related practices function (Bové, 1990).

Regimes of Truth, Power-Knowledge, and Disciplinary Power
//

Foucault's (1980) notion of "regimes of truth" is central to the part of his work I want to present here. In itself, the term conjures up visions of "truth" used in ways that control and regulate. Dramatic examples come to mind whereby versions of "truth" have had horrific consequences of oppression and violence, such as Hitler's visions of a pure Aryan race or South Africa's policy of apartheid. As Foucault (1980) explains the term: "'Truth' is linked in circular relation with systems of power which produce and sustain it, and to effects of power which it induces and which extend it" (p. 133). Thus, I argue, it is not just in the "dominant" or "dominating" discourses of any society that it makes sense to talk of regimes of truth (Gore, 1990a, 1993). If truth and power are "linked in circular relation," if truth exists in relation to power and power operates in connection with truth, then all discourses can be seen to function like regimes of truth.

To elaborate, Foucault (1980) says:

> Each society has its regime of truth, its 'general politics' of truth: that is, the types of discourse which it accepts and makes function as true; the mechanisms and instances which enable one to distinguish true and false statements, the means by which each is sanctioned; the techniques and procedures accorded value in the acquisition of truth; the status of those who are charged with saying what counts as true. (p. 131)

Consider the "politics of truth" in education: Briefly stated, discourses based in the discipline of psychology and linked to particular notions of science have been more readily accepted than other types of discourses; scientific reason has been the primary means by which these discourses are sanctioned; empirical techniques have held primacy in the production of truth; professional, scientific and intellectual status has been accorded to those charged with saying what counts as true. Alternative or competing discourses, while having to function in the context of this general politics of truth in education, construct their own versions of truth, of what counts, of who is sanctioned to speak, and so on. That is, they can also be seen to function like regimes of truth.

In order to more fully understand "regime of truth" I want to draw attention to Foucault's use of power and knowledge (*pouvoir* and *savoir*). It is helpful to begin by clarifying what power and knowledge, in his usage, are *not*. First, despite his arguments about the connection of power-knowledge, Foucault (1983a) was quite emphatic that power and knowledge are not identical:

> When I read—and I know it has been attributed to me—the thesis "knowledge is power" or "power is knowledge," I begin to laugh, since studying their *relation* is precisely my problem. If they were identical, I would not have to study them and I would be spared a lot of fatigue as a result. The very fact that I pose *the question of their relation* proves clearly that I do not identify them. (p. 210)

Second, Foucault breaks away from the standard definitions of power and knowledge. He reverses the standard articulation in which power works only in negative ways and in which truth or knowledge can reverse, erase, or challenge the domination of repressive power (Dreyfus & Rabinow, 1983; Keenan, 1987). This standard definition of the relation of power and knowledge is found in much self-proclaimed radical educational discourse, whereby through consciousness raising and the process of education (generally), dominant powers can be unmasked to reveal the "truth" and, as a result, increase the potential for overthrow of the capitalist and/or patriarchal system. Knowledge, from this perspective, offers revenge to the evils of power. Instead, Foucault's notion of power-knowledge challenges assumptions that undistorted truth can be attained (Diamond & Quinby, 1988); it "delimits the intellectuals' dreams of truth's control of power" (Bové, 1988, p. xviii). I should emphasize at this point that my reference to radical educational discourses does not implicate those discourses as somehow more dangerous than other educational discourses simply because they hold a standard conception of power. Indeed, this standard conception of power is shared with "mainstream" educational discourses when they engage with, for example, organizational structure or teacher empowerment.

Foucault expresses his alternative, and for me compelling, understanding of power and knowledge and their relation as "power-knowledge." In his view, power is not necessarily repressive since it incites, induces, seduces, makes easier or more difficult, enlarges or limits, makes more or less probable, and so on (Foucault, 1983b). Furthermore, power is exercised or practiced rather than possessed and so circulates, passing through every related force. For instance, in education, it is clear that power is not solely in the hands of teachers. Students, as well as teachers (and parents and administrators and governments), exercise power in schools. In order to understand the operation of power in any context, we need to understand the particular points through which it passes (Foucault, 1980). In this sense, Foucault draws attention to the need to reconsider some of our assumptions about schooling and to look anew and more closely at the "micropractices" of power in educational institutions.

In Foucault's analyses of power he was especially concerned with forms of "government," drawing on the sixteenth-century meaning of this word, which "did not refer only to political structures or to the management of states; rather it designated the way in which the conduct of individuals or groups might be directed: the government of children, of souls, of communities, of families, of the sick. . . . To govern, in this sense, is to structure the possible field of action of others" (Foucault, 1983b, p. 221). Foucault argued that modern forms of government reveal a shift from sovereign power which is overt, visible, and located in a monarchy to "disciplinary" power, which is exercised through its "invisibility" via normalizing technologies of the self. Traditionally, power was what was seen, what was shown and what was manifested:

> Disciplinary power, on the other hand, is exercised through its invisibility; at the same time it imposes on those whom it subjects a principle of compulsory visibility. In discipline it is the subjects who have to be seen. Their visibility assures the hold of power that is exercised over them. It is the fact of being constantly seen, of being always able to be seen, that maintains the disciplined individual in his [sic][1] subjection. (Foucault, 1977, p. 187)

This notion of disciplinary power is vividly illustrated in Foucault's presentation of Bentham's Panopticon, an architectural structure, primarily created for prisons, whereby individual cells on the periphery of the building surround a central tower. The backlighting created by inner and outer windows enables observation of each cell from the central tower while at the same time ensuring that the inmates cannot see if they are being observed. "Hence the major effect of the Panopticon: to induce in the inmate a conscious and permanent visibility that assures the automatic functioning of power" (Foucault, 1977, p. 201). Disciplinary power thus becomes internalized:

> He who is subjected to a field of visibility, and who knows it, assumes responsibility for the constraints of power; he makes them play spontaneously upon himself; he inscribes in himself the power relation in which he simultaneously plays both roles; he becomes the principle of his own subjection. (Foucault, 1977, pp. 202–203)

Considered in the context of school education, this notion of disciplinary power helps explain the self-regulation of students who maintain behaviors even when the teacher leaves the room. I turn now to a closer focus on education and a consideration of both Foucault's work in this area and the implications of his work.

On Education

Although Foucault did not carry out a detailed analysis of schools, it is clear that he saw schools and formal education as playing a part in the growth of disciplinary power. In *Discipline and Punish,* under a chapter titled "Docile bodies," Foucault (1977) outlines early pedagogical innovations and the model they provided for eighteenth-century economics, medicine and military theory. Later in the book he asked "is it surprising that prisons resemble factories, schools, barracks, hospitals, which all resemble prisons?" (p. 228). These resemblances Foucault articulated emerged from the focus of his studies on the mechanisms that construct institutions and institutional experiences, and not on the people within those institutions.

> It is sometimes said, too hastily, that Foucault was the one who studied the mad, the sick and prisoners. . . . Yet he wrote [the Birth of the Clinic, Madness and Civilization, Discipline and Punish]. He did not collect patients' laments, nor did he capture the confessions of captives or set out to surprise the mad as they went about their tasks; he studied the mechanisms of cure and the mechanisms of punishment. He turned to institutions, he took his bearings from their buildings and their equipment, he sounded out their doctrines and disciplines, he enumerated and catalogued their practices and he published their technologies . . . as a result of which, instead of contemplating the insane, the prisoner or the poor person like a vase on a table, he preferred to study confinement, to understand imprisonment and to analyse assistance. (Barret-Kriegel, 1992, pp. 193–4)

Students, themselves, recognize these mechanisms that Foucault studied when they utter the expression "this school is like a prison." Consider some of these mechanisms.

The pedagogical process embodies *power relations* between and among teachers and learners (defined either narrowly to refer to the actors in institutionalized education or broadly to refer to other pedagogical relations such as those of parents and children, writers and readers, and so on) over issues of *knowledge:* what is valid knowledge, what knowledge is produced, whose knowledge, and so on. Pedagogy relies on particular techniques of *government*, the development of which can be traced historically/archaeologically (see for example Hamilton, 1989; Hunter, 1988; Jones & Williamson, 1979; Luke, 1989; Meredyth and Tyler, 1993), and produces, and reproduces at different moments, particular rules and practices. Increasingly, pedagogy has emphasized self-disciplining whereby students are to keep themselves and each other in check. Following Foucault, the specific techniques/practices which elicit such behavior might be called *technologies of the self*. These technologies are enacted at the site of the body; eyes, hands, mouths, movement. For example, in many classrooms students quickly learn to raise their hands before speaking in class, to keep their eyes on their own work during a test, to keep their eyes on the teacher and appear to be listening when the teacher is giving instructions, to stay in their seats, and so on. We can say that pedagogies produce particular political regimes of the body. Such technologies of the bodily self can also be understood as manifestations of the internal (mental) self, how people identify themselves. Pedagogies, in this analysis, operate as regimes of truth. Disciplinary relations of power-knowledge are fundamental to the processes of pedagogy. Whether self-imposed, imposed by teachers, or imposed on teachers, as Foucault (1977) puts it: "A relation of surveillance, defined and regulated, is inscribed at the heart of the practice of teaching, not as an additional or adjacent part, but as a mechanism that is inherent to it and which increases its efficiency" (p. 176).

Mechanisms of power-knowledge operate not only in relation to pedagogies argued for in educational discourses—that is, in relation to particular social visions and instructional practices enacted in the name of pedagogy—but also in relation to the pedagogy of the arguments that characterize specific educational discourses, that is, to the arguments themselves (Gore, 1993). Foucault (1978) argued that "it is in discourse that power and knowledge are joined together" (p. 100), hence:

> We must not imagine a world of discourse divided between the accepted discourse and excluded discourse, or between the dominant discourse and the dominated one; but as a multiplicity of discursive elements that can come into play in various strategies. . . . Discourses are not once and for all subservient to power or raised up against it, any more than silences are. We must make allowances for the complex and unstable process whereby discourse can be both an instrument and an effect of power, but also a hindrance, a stumbling-block, a point of resistance and a starting point for an opposing strategy. Discourse transmits and produces power; it reinforces it, but also undermines and exposes it, renders it fragile and makes it possible to thwart it. . . . There is not, on the one side, a discourse of power, and opposite it, another discourse that runs counter to it. (pp. 100–102)

Radical or "emancipatory" discourses are not exempt in this analysis. Thus, when radical educational theorists draw on Foucault to claim that we can consider *dominant* educational discourses (those produced by the dominant culture) as "regimes of truth,"[2] they fail to emphasize Foucault's point that "everything is dangerous" (1983c, p. 231).

Keenan (1987) argues that "*because* the articulation between power and knowledge *is* discursive, then the link can never be guaranteed. . . . It is unpredictable. . . . The discourse that makes [the link] possible also undermines it, precisely because power and knowledge *are* different" (pp. 17–18). Sawicki (1988b) makes this point also in her analysis, framed by Foucault and feminism, of identity politics and sexual freedom. Where she refers to "sexuality," I have substituted "pedagogy" in order to demonstrate the relevance of the argument to my own intellectual and practical concern with discourses of radical pedagogy (See Gore, 1990a, 1990b, 1990c, 1991, 1993).

> Discourse is ambiguous . . . a form of power that circulates in the social field and can attach to strategies of domination as well as to those of resistance. Neither wholly a source of domination nor of resistance, [pedagogy] is also neither outside power nor wholly circumscribed by it. Instead, it is itself an arena of struggle. There are no inherently liberating or repressive [pedagogical] practices, for any practice is co-optable and any capable of becoming a source of resistance. After all, if relations of power are dispersed and fragmented throughout the social field, so must resistance to power be. Thus evaluating the political status of [pedagogical] practices should be a matter of historical and social investigation, not a priori theoretical pronouncement. (pp. 185–186)

Some examples may be helpful at this point. Consider the circle-seating formation so common to progressive pedagogical practice. The circle is frequently employed to shift the classroom interaction away from the direct control of the teacher. The circle counters the traditional classroom in which "Stillness is the achievement of the science of *super-vision,* an arrangement of persons in collective units accessible to constant surveillance. By arranging students in rows, all eyes facing front, directly confronting the back of a fellow's head, meeting the gaze only of the teacher, the discipline of the contemporary classroom deploys the look as a strategy of domination" (Grumet, 1988, p. 111). The circle opens the possibilities for every student to voice her or his opinion and to be heard. With students sitting on the floor or on portable chairs they are freed from the restrictive confines of their desks, separated from each other.

Most of us who teach have used a circle-seating arrangement at some time, with these kinds of intentions. Foucault, Sawicki and others (e.g., Walkerdine, 1985, 1986) help us to realize that there is nothing inherently liberating about this practice, even when located within a radical discourse, and nothing inherently oppressive about rows. On the one hand, the circle can require of students a greater self disciplining, taking responsibility for behaving "appropriately" without the "look" of the teacher. On the other hand, the partial privacy allowed by the traditional placement of desks, whereby one is under the surveillance or supervision primarily of the teacher, might be forfeited as students come more directly under the surveillance of their peers as well. The student who prefers not to speak up is less obvious when all desks face the front, as is the student who cannot afford new shoes, who blushes, who is bored, and so on. I am not trying to make an argument for a return to rows of desks—I continue to use the circle-seating formation in my own practice. I am arguing that supposedly "liberatory" educational practices have no guaranteed effects.

As another example, consider the practice (often well intentioned) of acknowledging the contributions of marginalized people by adding such events as "Women's History Month" and "Aboriginal History Month" to the school curriculum. The effects of such a practice can be quite conservative in terms of continuing to place the experience of white men at the center and maintaining all other experience in a marginal position. Even curricula that aim to more radically transform the perspective from which social life is viewed can overlook other marginalized groups. For example, in efforts to deal with race, class, and gender, other oppressive formations such as heterosexism and ageism often prevail. There are no guaranteed effects.

Conclusion
//

As I see it, this analysis of our location within relations of power-knowledge, disciplinary society and regimes of truth allows us to begin to identify the features of particular discourses and practices which have dangerous, dominating, or negative effects. Looking again at the mechanisms of educational institutions, questioning the "truth" of our own cherished discourses, examining that which causes us to be what we are—all open possibilities for change. Indeed, shortly before his death, Foucault said, "All my analyses are against the idea of universal necessities in human existence. They show the arbitrariness of institutions and show which space of freedom we can still enjoy and how many changes can still be made" (1988, p. 153).

Regimes of truth are not necessarily negative, but rather necessary. Knowledge and power *are* linked, often in productive ways. Just as power can be productive, so can the power-knowledge nexus in and through which one carries out one's work be productive. The point of employing regime of truth to analyze radical educational discourses, as I have done elsewhere, is not to engage in a "politics of the pointing finger" (Morris, 1988, p. 23). The lack of reflexivity among radical discourses is hardly surprising in light of their struggle to legitimate themselves among "mainstream" educational discourses. Rather, I employ regime of truth as a technology of self, encouraging us to be more humble and reflexive in our claims for our teaching, acknowledging that there is deconstructive work to be done within our own domain as well as outside of it. Foucault challenges claims to truth and claims to innocence in all educational discourses.

Foucault's analyses of power-knowledge raise doubts about the possibility or desirability of ever giving a final answer to the question: Which pedagogical discourses and practices are liberating? (Sawicki, 1988b) His politics, "designed to avoid dogmatism in our categories and politics as well as the silencing of difference to which such dogmatism can lead is a welcome alternative to polarized debate" (p. 187).

But where does this kind of analysis leave us? There have been many criticisms of Foucault's work on the basis of historical accuracy, methodological rigor, and political consequences; it is on the latter that I should like to focus. Some critics have argued that Foucault leaves us with no way out of disciplinary power, that in his joining of power-knowledge Foucault has removed the basis for the practical political linkage of the two (e.g., Anderson, 1983; Habermas, 1986; Taylor, 1986); some claim that Foucault's analyses leave us only with pessimism; some argue that his work is antithetical to feminist projects (e.g., Balbus, 1988). These arguments stem from particular readings of Foucault and from particular intellectual, political, and professional agendas (Bové, 1988). Bové argues that many academics misread Foucault "to blunt the political consequences of his critique of their disciplines', their discourses', and their own positions within the knowledge/power apparatus" (p. xi).

Others have argued that "Foucault's own reluctance to be explicit about his ethical and political positions is attributable not to nihilism, relativism, or political irresponsibility, but rather to his sense of the dangers of political programs based on grand theory" (Sawicki, 1988b, p. 189). My view is that Foucault (1980) left questions of specific tactics, strategies, and goals to those directly involved in struggle and resistance, hence his notion of "specific" intellectuals working within specific sectors "at the precise points where their own conditions of life or work situate them" (p. 126). As Foucault (1983b) argued:

> A society without power relations can only be an abstraction. . . . To say that there cannot be a society without power relations is not to say either that those which are established are necessary, or, in any case, that power constitutes a fatality at the heart of societies, such that it cannot be undermined. Instead I would say that the analysis, elaboration, and bringing into question of power relations . . . is a permanent political task inherent in all social existence. (pp. 222–23)

It is to this political task, in the sector within which I work, that I direct my current research and teaching energies in the ongoing struggle to identify the regimes of truth in which I participate.

q u e s t i o n s   f o r   d i s c u s s i o n

1. How does Foucault's conception of power-knowledge differ from other conceptions of power and knowledge?
2. Provide examples of ways in which the Panopticon might operate in schools. Consider the effects of disciplinary power on teachers and students.

3. For what reasons, according to Foucault, might teacher intentions in curriculum not be realized?
4. Specify ways in which your professional work as a teacher might construct and be constructed by "regimes of truth."

teachers as researchers

Foucault's notion of power begins with "micro" level identification of exercises of power. In classrooms, observe teacher and student behavior for micro practices of power and consider whether they are necessary to the process of teaching and learning.

Taking Sawicki's notion that there are no guarantees, attempt to document in classrooms the multiple outcomes that arise from teacher or student actions. Look for cases where outcomes are much like those expected or sought.

suggested readings

Ball, S. (Ed.). (1991). *Foucault and education.* London: Routledge.
Diamond, I., & Quimby, L. (Eds.). (1988). *Feminism and Foucault: Reflections on resistance.* Boston: Northeastern University Press.
Gore, J. (1993). *The struggle for pedagogies: Critical and feminist discourses as regimes of truth.* New York: Routledge.
Foucault, M. (1980). *Power/knowledge: Selected interviews and other writings, 1972–1977* (C. Gordon, Ed.). New York: Pantheon Books.
Sawicki, J. (1988). *After Foucault: Humanistic knowledge, post-modern challenges.* London: Rutgers University Press.
Steedman, C., Urwin, C., & Walkerdine, V. (1985). *Language, gender and childhood.* London: Routledge & Kegan Paul.

notes

[1] It should be noted that French is a highly gendered language. The "individual in his subjection" is a literal but not faithful translation. *L'individu* has no feminine equivalent.
[2] See, for example, McLaren (1989, p. 181).

references

Anderson, P. (1983). *In the tracks of historical materialism.* London: Verso Editions.
Balbus, I. (1988). Disciplining women: Michel Foucault and the power of feminist discourse. In J. Arac (Ed.), *After Foucault: Humanistic knowledge, postmodern challenges* (pp. 138–160). New Brunswick, NJ: Rutgers University Press.

Barret-Kriegel, B. (1992). Michel Foucault and the police state. In T. J. Armstrong (Ed. and Trans.), *Michel Foucault philosopher* (pp. 192–198). London: Harvester Wheatsheaf.

Bemauer, J. & Keenan, T. (1988). The works of Michel Foucault 1954–1984. In J. Bemauer & D. Rasmussen (Eds.), *The final Foucault* (pp. 117–158). Cambridge: MIT Press.

Bové, P. (1988). Foreword: The Foucault phenomenon: The problematics of style. In G. Deleuze, *Foucault* (pp. vii–xi). Minneapolis: University of Minnesota Press.

Bové, P. (1990). Discourse. In F. Lentricchia & T. McLaughlin (Eds.), *Critical terms for literary study*. Chicago: University of Chicago Press.

Diamond, I., & Quinby, L. (Eds.). (1988). *Feminism and Foucault: Reflections on resistance*. Boston: Northeastern University Press.

Dreyfus, H. L., & Rabinow, P. (Eds.). (1983). *Michel Foucault: Beyond structuralism and hermeneutics* (2nd ed.). Chicago: University of Chicago Press.

Foucault, M. (1977). *Discipline and punish: The birth of the prison*. New York: Pantheon Books.

Foucault, M. (1978). *The history of sexuality: Volume 1: An introduction*. New York: Vintage Books.

Foucault, M. (1980). Truth and power. In C. Gordon (Ed.), *Power/knowledge: Selected interviews and other writings 1972–1977* (pp. 109–133). New York: Pantheon Books.

Foucault, M. (1983a). Structuralism and post-structuralism, interview with G. Raulet (J. Harding, Trans.). *Telos, 55*, 195–210.

Foucault, M. (1983b). Afterword: The subject and power. In H. L. Dreyfus & P. Rabinow (Eds.), *Michel Foucault: Beyond structuralism and hermeneutics* (2nd ed.) (pp. 208–226). Chicago: University of Chicago Press.

Foucault, M. (1983c). On the genealogy of ethics: An overview of work in progress. In H. L. Dreyfus & P. Rabinow (Eds.), *Michel Foucault: Beyond structuralism and hermeneutics* (2nd ed.) (pp. 229–252). Chicago: University of Chicago Press.

Foucault, M. (1988). The political technology of individuals. In L. H. Martin, H. Gutman, & P. H. Hutton (Eds.), *Technologies of the self: A seminar with Michel Foucault* (pp. 145–162). Amherst: The University of Massachusetts Press.

Gore, J. M. (1990a). The struggle for pedagogies: Critical and feminist discourses as regimes of truth. Unpublished doctoral dissertation, University of Wisconsin-Madison.

Gore, J. M. (1990b). Pedagogy as "text" in physical education teacher education: Beyond the preferred reading. In D. Kirk & R. Tinning (Eds.), *Physical education, curriculum and culture: Critical studies in the contemporary crisis* (pp. 101–138). London: Falmer Press.

Gore, J. M. (1990c). What we can do for you! What *can* "we" do for "you"?: Struggling over empowerment in critical and feminist pedagogy. *Educational Foundations, 4*(3), 5–26.

Gore, J. M. (1991). On silent regulation: Emancipatory action research in preservice teacher education. *Curriculum Perspectives, 11*(4), 47–51.

Gore, J. M. (1993). *The struggle for pedagogies: Critical and feminist discourses as regimes of truth*. New York & London: Routledge.

Grumet, M. R. (1988). *Bitter milk*. Amherst: The University of Massachusetts Press.

Habermas, J. (1986). The genealogical writing of history: On some aporias in Foucault's theory of power (G. Ostrander, Trans.). *Canadian Journal of Political and Social Theory, 10*(1–2), 1–9.

Hamilton, D. (1989). *Towards a theory of schooling*. London: Falmer Press.

Hunter, I. (1988). *Culture and government: The emergence of literary education*. London: Macmillan Press.

Jones, K., & Williamson, K. (1979). The birth of the schoolroom: A study of the transformation in the discursive conditions of English popular education in the first-half of the nineteenth century. *Ideology and Consciousness, 5*(1), 59–110.

Keenan, T. (1987). The "paradox" of knowledge and power: Reading Foucault on a bias. *Political Theory, 15*(1), 5–37.

Luke, C. (1989). *Pedagogy, printing and Protestantism*. Albany: State University of New York Press.

McLaren, P. (1989). *Life in schools: An introduction to critical pedagogy in the foundations of education*. New York: Longman.

Meredyth, D., & Tyler, D. (1993). *Child and citizen: Genealogies of schooling and subjectivity*. Institute of Cultural and Policy Studies, Griffith University.

Morris, M. (1988). The pirate's fiancée: Feminists and philosophers, or maybe tonight it'll happen. In I. Diamond & L. Quinby (Eds.), *Feminism and Foucault: Reflections on resistance* (pp. 21–42). Boston: Northeastern University Press.

Sawicki, J. (1988a). Feminism and the power of Foucauldian discourse. In J. Arac (Ed.), *After Foucault: Humanistic knowledge, postmodern challenges* (pp. 161–178). New Brunswick, NJ: Rutgers University Press.

Sawicki, J. (1988b). Identity politics and sexual freedom: Foucault and feminism. In I. Diamond & L. Quinby (Eds.), *Feminism and Foucault: Reflections on resistance* (pp. 177–192). Boston: Northeastern University Press.

Taylor, C. (1986). Foucault on freedom and truth. In D. C. Hoy (Ed.), *Foucault: A critical reader* (pp. 69–102). Oxford: Basil Blackwell.

Walkerdine, V. (1985). On the regulation of speaking and silence: Subjectivity, class and gender in contemporary schooling. In C. Steedman, C. Unwin, & V. Walkerdine (Eds.), *Language, gender and childhood* (pp. 203–241). London: Routledge & Kegan Paul.

Walkerdine, V. (1986). Progressive pedagogy and political struggle. *Screen, 27*(5), 54–60.

chapter 8

From the Margin to the Center

Teachers' Emerging Voices through Inquiry

Jaime Gerardo A. Grinberg

guiding questions

1. What is the author trying to say or teach?
2. What is the significance of what you read here for you personally and for you as a teacher?
3. What are the perspectives drawn on by the author to make the analysis?
4. How does this analysis help to inform our practice in classrooms?

Autobiography and the Individual as Part of the Inquiry

In the following pages I will partially explore autobiography as a starting point for teacher inquiry and then discuss the issues and tensions connected with inquiry as a form of validating and transforming teachers' pedagogies, emerging voices, and power arrangements. *Teacher inquiry* and *teacher-researcher* will be alternative ways to call for the same activity. They refer to the concept of teachers as producers of systematic, valid, and reliable knowledge connected with classroom and school curriculum, pedagogy, and learning. The range of research paradigms and inquiry questions is large. Currently, for instance, narrative inquiry and literary criticism are valid forms of constituting knowledge about practice. Teacher-researcher also emphasizes the ethical and political dimensions of the curriculum, the hidden curriculum, and the classroom processes. Furthermore, autobiography becomes a central piece of the inquiry because the inquirer is not neutral and invisible.

I do believe in being overt about who I am in anything I write or present to an audience. I won't hide myself under the veil of objective analysis or critique. I act in self-interest—not always my best interest. I used to be a good writer; however, I hated writing. I decided to start to write what I feel and think in a way that I like. Therefore, for those who will read this chapter and expect a conventional format for a flow of an argument, I apologize. At times my "voice" may impress you as aggressive. It is not my intention to be so, but it is an authentic way of expressing myself. Please accept me. I am apologetic because I don't want to alienate but to invite you to share my ideas and concerns as they are today in relation to some issues that are very important to me. In a sense, I am looking for dialogue, for conversation, not for quotation or citation. For me it is also important to introduce myself because my ideas evolved directly from my experiences with schooling, education, and teaching. In turn, there is a dynamic of shape and change. My personal experiences were interpreted by my ideas, perceptions, perspectives, and views. Narrating part of my stories helps me (and you as a reader) to clarify the temporality and intentionality of the ideas presented as contingent to a regime of truth that might challenge power arrangements in the relationship between, on the one hand, pedagogy and, on the other, research as production of legitimized and validated knowledge about classroom and school life.

My Story

As you may notice from my writing, English is not my native language. Actually it is my third language. Spanish, "Castellano," is my native language. I was born in Argentina, a South American country with many European immigrants, rich natural resources, nice people, good food, and great music. However, the political system was corrupted and the country suffered three different periods of military dictatorship during my school years. I attended public schools—all-boys schools—with a very traditional disciplinary system and with a strong emphasis on the European white male version of liberal education.

Because of family reasons, for some years I lived in Uruguay, traditionally a democratic country that ended up with leftist terrorism and with a reactionary military government. I remember from Uruguay a school content and organization very similar to the Argentinean except that the schools weren't all-boys anymore. When, in 1973, there was a final consummation of a military *golpe* (coup) to end the democratic system, high school students and teachers were politically resistant to the new dictatorship. Several schools and college buildings were occupied in protest. The military government (*junta* in Spanish) not only wanted to physically control the schools by having police and army in the buildings, but also wanted to control the content of what should be taught and learned and by whom it should be taught and learned. Because of a centralized, national unique curriculum, there were not a lot of alternative textbooks for classroom use. Without enough time and resources to produce new ones, the "new" curriculum had to rely on the old textbooks for a while. Several books were prohibited to read or possess at school or home, but what did the junta do with the old textbooks that were needed for instruction but that had "subversive" ideas in their chapters or references, like explaining theories of democracy, marxism, or psychoanalysis? The solution: students and teachers had to staple together those pages that the Ministry of Education indicated. Certainly, the measure in many cases wasn't implemented and teachers actively defied the attempt to control free access to information and knowledge.

This experience shaped my perception of the potential role of the teacher in trying to build a democratic community, at least in the sense of trying to present more perspectives about knowledge than just the official, "approved," censored versions. Since then, I have felt the urgency to act through teaching in order to defy injustice. My first experiences, whether as a tutor in a literacy project in marginalized barrios or as a youth leader, were rather nonformal. Particularly, the tutoring experiences shaped my beliefs and understanding about the close relationship existing between education, access to knowledge, and social arrangements. Because of the repression and lack of freedom, South America wasn't "livable" anymore and I chose to leave.

As a young teacher I preferred to teach in an innovative type of educational experience in Israel (Hebrew became my second language). I chose to join a group of teachers who were living in the community in which the school was located. The story I will tell has several similarities with those of many immigrants, legal and illegal, when they go to a new place. This is also true of several Latino families and children immigrants to North America.

The community where I taught had enormous social problems. Most of the population was composed of immigrants from North-African and Near-Asian countries. The tremendous cultural shock experienced by these immigrants also alienated the young first generation of Israelis. First of all, the immigrants had to adapt to a dominant occidental mentality, which saw their behaviors as "not fitting civilized culture" and which had a very different set of values and traditions. Second, the language barrier, the lack of material resources, and the lack of skills to become part of a specialized workforce in an industrial society were devastating. Most immigrants came from countries where their main trade was either agriculture or small commerce. Thus, circumstances forced the immigrants to occupy the lower layers of the social stratum doing unskilled jobs for very low salaries. Furthermore, several families unable to find jobs had to live on welfare. The combination of cultural alienation, marginal low incomes, decrease of self-esteem, and life dependency on the bureaucratic control of the state affected the relationships between community members and public institutions in a negative and distrusting atmosphere, which did not exclude schools. Living in the community and knowing the families and the youngsters not just in a job-related situation helped me to develop understandings and sensibilities toward multicultural education, ethnic differences, class, and gender, inside and outside the classrooms.

In this community I lived and taught for three years in an elementary school. For one year I worked in the alternative high school, which was physically located in a shelter. Many of the students were defined as juvenile delinquents who had developed a tremendous mistrust toward authority. This attitude also extended toward the expectations they had of the educational system and their personal aspirations. Many years later, when I found myself reading Willis's *Learning to Labour* (1977), I was surprised by the similarities between that work's "lads" and the students I worked with. It was not the system alone that marginalized them. The students had AGENCY. They chose to reject dominant culture by reproducing a counterculture that glorified their marginality. As a teacher committed to transforming relations of domination, this situation presented a dilemma: How could I foster appropriate pedagogies and content that would not reproduce a dominant culture that alienated them but that would challenge their own glorification of marginality? There were no winners.

The above experiences not only shaped my understanding of cultural diversity and social marginality, but also taught me a lot about pedagogy, cooperative inquiry, and the role of the teacher as curriculum developer and as agency for social transformation. As a teacher, I had to search for strategies and techniques that fitted the characteristics of each classroom and of each student. Knowing the curriculum wasn't enough to implement it. Although I was well equipped with theoretical principles and some experience, I had to adapt myself to a new environment and students very different from those I had in the past. There was a need to constantly revise, adapt, and change teaching and content and to develop new curriculum and methods that responded to the needs and characteristics of the students and the community. Knowing how to plan, how to select objectives, and how to use different methods like cooperative learning or a direct lesson design were not enough. There was much need for systematic reflection and inquiry, not just about the broader social issues,

---

AGENCY: In this context, "agency" means the active involvement of the individual in shaping and controlling social and institutional arrangements.

but also about classroom life and about how to facilitate an environment of respect that would enhance all of the students' reading of the world.

At times, however, students' perception of the curriculum and of what they learned did not fit my goals and objectives. I used to meet every evening with my roommates, who were also teachers in the same project. Our purpose was to reflect, discuss, share, and develop new ways to improve our practices. What we perceived as needed for the students drove our lessons and unit designs. Although I was very enthusiastic, I now realize that my students' voices were silenced by both the declared and the hidden curriculum and that even my pedagogy did, in a sense, patronize instead of liberalize, as I wished. I settled the objectives according to my ideas and perceptions of the curriculum. I had the answers and I directed classroom life according to a preconceived plan for "liberation." I formulated the agenda of transformation and I was "empowering" students. Neither students nor parents were directly involved in the shaping of the curriculum. Their voices and intentions were never challenged because they were not heard; they were silenced by my emancipatory pedagogy. What a contradiction! I wanted to model after Freire's (1970) literacy projects through dialogical pedagogy, but I just implemented monologues. I was ready to follow a recipe of steps instead of learning from the people and the context where I was living. I was incoherent because I tried to forward an agenda constituted only by me. No wonder there was student resistance. Looking back at this experience makes me very sensitive to the need to support teachers in the field who want to engage in transformative praxis. It also makes me wonder about the implication of unreflective and uncritical methods with which many teachers become familiar during their teacher preparation. Although I wanted to alter unjust power arrangements, I just perpetuated them with my monological method.

Now, after years of study, I emphasize reflection and inquiry when I teach about the meaning and nature of pedagogical practices. Skills will be of little help if there is no contextual connection. They will be of little help if teachers only apply ideas without evaluating why to use them, when to use them, and who ultimately is being served by one technology or another. A systematic study by the teacher of his or her own practice is a sine qua non for a teacher to learn from experience. This learning could be done either individually or cooperatively with other practitioners and/or researchers—for example, in action research projects. Teachers and teacher educators have to be sensitive to the difference between being a technician, as good as one might be, and being a reflective critical practitioner who constantly challenges the ways we come to construct knowledge about teaching and learning. It is critical for a teacher to search for the underlying assumptions that penetrate and perpetuate our everyday practices. A critical, reflective teacher tries to connect students' lives with worthwhile content by reconstructing knowledge that should be emancipatory.

It is my view that schools and any form of educational institution or activity should always be concerned with the effects on the life of the learner. Nowadays most schools serve rather custodial (just keeping students in a building) and social stratification purposes to fit unjust social arrangements instead of creating conditions for learners' empowerment, understanding, and respect for each other. My concern is with the welfare of the children, youngsters, and adults involved in the educational effort. Education should be primarily concerned with developing lifelong communities of learners and constructing meaningful understandings of and engagement with subject matter that will challenge the elitist arrangement of access to privileged knowledge and that will emphasize democratic values, social justice, and equity for everybody's children.

Teacher Commitment

Today more than ever, the teacher-researcher movement is pushing the field to look anew at how to build reflection, inquiry, and critique in pedagogy and curriculum. An educator who only consumes knowledge produced by other colleagues without pursuing personal and collective research agendas suffers a deskilling dependency that favors perpetuation of asymmetric power arrangements. If the focus of the educator's activity is good teaching for serving the child, the community, and oneself, then there is a need for thoughtful and SYSTEMATIC INQUIRY.

I want to emphasize one more time that it is imperative we commit ourselves to transform unjust social arrangements in order to make schools safe and democratic places where children and youngsters can grow, have access to meaningful experiences and knowledge, and learn to be socially and politically empowered. However, I always wonder what we mean by empowering. How can we transform power arrangements in schools in a way that will allow self-empowerment for students, teachers, and administrators, and eventually for parents and communities?

We have more power than we think. Power is arranged, negotiated. If knowing is a form of power and doing research is producing knowledge, then our research can be powerful. What matters is us, the teachers, the researchers, the teacher-researchers. Is our question leading toward making the world a better place? Do we need "data" in order to make sense of the world? We should not dismiss easily those who say that empirical data, at times, just disturb good thinking. Sometimes our credibility is enhanced if we cite authorities and I wonder if this is not just a form of good plagiarism, which makes our work academically sound but without any meaning for classroom life. Maybe we are depriving ourselves more than we can figure out. We can excuse ourselves and say "research says." Instead, we should challenge the purposes of our and others' research. Whose interest is being served? Are we just accommodating ourselves?

SYSTEMATIC INQUIRY: A consistent and substantial gathering of information, as well as its analysis, interpretation, and critique, and subsequent action. The data should be collected during a prudent period of time and could be gathered in several different ways.

Is there a true commitment to a liberatory pedagogy? I sometimes ponder this question when I read some educational journals. Are we to be mere spectators who observe and analyze, at best, the relation of school and society? How do we account for change? Which change? Whose change? We should try not to disconnect ourselves from life, from schools and other formal and informal educational settings, from classrooms, and from all the children, particularly the homeless children, the children of addiction, and the children of abuse. For committed teachers, asking and searching for answers to these questions engage them in an inquiry that pushes not only thinking, but also action in challenging dominant knowledge about school practices and classroom pedagogies.

If education is understood as a social process, then the intersubjective dimension of what is being valued as legitimate knowledge influences teachers' perceptions of their own practice (Greene, 1979) and of their working conditions. These dominant perceptions of valid knowledge about classroom life are tested and shaped by teachers in light of others' meanings and purposes, not necessarily those of the participants. The agenda is imposed from the outside and it is foreign to the voices of children, teachers, and caregivers. Thus, this process not only deskills teachers (McLaren, 1989) but fundamentally undermines any possibility of intellectual growth and sociopolitical transformation. Teachers and others ". . . undervalue their (teachers) natural ontological capacities for reflecting and learning from experience" (Hollingsworth, 1990). If my personal perception, which was also influenced by my readings of Dewey (1899/1964) and Freire (1970, 1973), that education can be a means for social change is correct, then teachers are central actors in such transformation. Teaching, in this view, is a tool to further social reform, democratic life, and human improvement. Teachers and students are part of a community involved in learning from, making sense of, transforming, and constructing experience and knowledge. But, is this community's ways of knowing being validated or challenged as a legitimate equal in the educational system?

Teacher as Researcher

Teachers have been neglected as generators of knowledge by academic research. Furthermore, in the knowledge base for teaching (Shulman, 1987), teachers' ways of knowing, teachers' ways of questioning, teachers' voices, are either ignored (Cochran-Smith & Lytle, 1990) or, at best, just acknowledged as implicit knowledge. For instance, Traver (1987) points out in *The Handbook of Research on Teaching,* 3rd ed., that schoolteachers ". . . do not appear in person, nor as authors, nor with the specifics of knowledge and day-to-day experiences that teachers use and have . . . (they) are represented as numbers, or clusters of behaviors . . ." (p. 443).

As consumers of research, teachers are usually informed by others about the realities and conditions of their own classrooms and students. Teachers, then, resist theory because it situates neither the classroom context, nor the students and teachers' biographies. The self has been alienated, covered, and silenced by traditional educational research paradigms. Yet, those who practice know that teaching is personalized and that life in the classroom requires personal involvement and interpretation if the intention is to care, to respect, and to nurture the whole student. Although teachers develop theory from their own practices and work conditions, the teachers themselves and the educational establishment do not recognize these theories. Therefore, becoming producers of research and, in consequence, of knowledge may change power arrangements in the educational system, as well as validate and/or challenge unrevised practices. There is a need for our active political involvement as educators and educational inquirers in shaping our institutions and social arrangements also through research. For this to happen, we have to recognize the importance of challenging the dominant ways of knowing about classrooms. There is also a need for teacher narrative that includes students' voices as a powerful source of knowledge about teaching and learning, thus challenging theories driven by artificial laboratory experiences.

The notion of teacher-researcher is not new. For instance, in 1931 Lucy Sprague Mitchell wrote:

> Our aim is to help students develop a scientific attitude towards their work and towards life. To use this means an attitude of eager, alert observations; a constant questioning of old procedures in the light of new observations; . . . an effort to keep as reliable records as the situation permits in order to base the future upon actual knowledge of the experience of the past. (p. 251)

It doesn't matter whether we call the activity of critical inquiry research, inquiry, reflection, or something else. The meaning of the activity and its consequences in terms of a compromised agenda to foster an emancipatory pedagogy are what matter. Sometimes language is appropriated by technicians who are interested in maintaining efficiency, complicity, silence, and control. The consideration of accuracy in language reminds me of a passage from Wittgenstein's *On Certainty*:

> I once said to someone—in English—that the shape of a certain branch was typical of an elm, which my companion denied. Then we came past some ashes, and I said "there, you see, here are the branches I was speaking about." To which he replied "But that's an ash"— and I said "I always meant ash when I said elm." (1972, p. 86e)

Teacher's Voice

What do teachers who have engaged in systematic inquiry have to say? I conducted a study to find out how some such teachers made sense of their experiences (Grinberg, 1992). These teachers were taking a class about teacher as researcher.

The teachers realized that their daily practices were based on a certain type of unrecognized research and that a more systematic and organized way of collecting and analyzing information by themselves, and/or in cooperation with peers and with university people, could have a great impact on those practices. This realization—teachers are able to produce meaningful research—was a form of validating their craft and activity. Inquiring into their own teaching became a powerful means for professional growth. Being able to perform research and critically consider and reflect about practices, working conditions, and possible actions is potentially empowering for teachers because they ought to be the main source of knowledge production about their own classrooms. Thus, validation of practice through systematic inquiry opens space to legitimize teachers' voices. This also has a political dimension because legitimization alters relations between teachers, who traditionally have been at the bottom of the educational hierarchy, and the rest of the educational system. Validation brought not just proudness of teachers' work, but also intentionality. Teachers told me:

> A teacher's voice means she/he has some input on what is taught and how it is taught. It is real a case of teacher's power and influence.

> To me, this means that I can believe the validity of my own voice and reflection. Also other professional teachers' voices can be valued, as well, to feel that what we think is important . . . for a change.

> Sometimes teachers' voices aren't heard. Teachers' voices need to be encouraged by allowing them to verbalize their own teaching experiences.

Redefining Research

Before engaging in their inquiry projects, the teachers I interviewed assumed research was alien to their abilities and classrooms (Grinberg, 1992). Many thought that being a teacher-researcher involved reading about what others did and that an inquiry project meant only literature review in the library. The teachers' perceptions before they started their projects are illustrated in these comments:

> Research means . . . be required to do enormous library research on some topic.

> I thought that the project would focus on very structured research, with many hours spent in the library. The professor would direct how and what we would research.

After starting their projects and looking at their practices and contexts, at their classrooms, and at their schools, the teachers' perceptions about inquiry shifted because they were in charge of their own projects. The topics teachers chose to research and the ways of collecting information were very varied. For instance, one project was to find out how to make the only computer in a classroom accessible to all the students. Another project focused on students' perceptions of ability grouping for reading activities. Use of portfolio assessment was a popular topic for research as was school reform. Yet many projects took a narrative format and became papers on topics like school organizational change; the allocation of resources; the perpetuation of gender stereotypes in textbooks; the role of special education in labeling, perpetuating alienation, and relating with the socioeconomic background of many children in a specific school district; or the relationship between the teacher, the school building, and the parents. The projects ranged from concrete classroom needs and practical solutions to large social issues and their connection with school life.

Teachers started to recognize that being reflective and systematic about their experiences involved some knowledge that they possessed. They started to see teaching as a form of research, but not always to see the difference between technological implementation and critical practice. For these teachers, their personal experiences and biographies intersected with the topics of inquiry to build a new critical view. Validation of past and present practices helped them break from dependency. Keeping systematic and consistent records of actions and thoughts, of students, and of classroom events informed teachers' inquiries. Their voices said:

> . . . Teaching as research means learning from my experience. I reflect (and now write) and look at what I can change and how I might go about creative change in the environment I work in.

> . . . having unveiled and reflected on my autobiography. I feel that teachers should be encouraged to document their experiences.

> My concept of teaching as research is mainly a crystallized form of a concept I've held intuitively for a long time . . . pursuing your own thoughts in more formal ways if that will further your thought processes and, secondly, recording what you find.

Inquiry, Caring, and Pedagogy

Ethics of caring (Noddings, 1984) was recognized by many teachers not only as a desired approach to classroom life, but also as something that has been in place in most classrooms but has gone unvalued. A pedagogy that values trust, caring, and sharing can validate teachers' practices. It also opens channels to value process and risk-taking rather than production alone. Some teachers labeled this pedagogy as feminist. They encountered in feminist theory a validation of their practices. This relationship between classroom practice and feminine ways of understanding the world, they told me, was a consequence of engaging in personal and pedagogical explorations about themselves as teachers and as women. Referring to their meaning of feminist pedagogy, they said:

> This is the nurturing aspect of teaching (both male and female) which focuses on the growth of the individual and the ability to recognize the evolving process vs. simply the end product. This is the philosophy that keeps me bucking the product orientation of our district.

Feminists have fought to change society just as teachers must.

A caring, valuing pedagogy . . . peace.

Certainly, there were also some tensions. For example, one person interviewed said about feminist pedagogy that

I don't feel comfortable with the term. Why should we call it feminist? I value some things but is there a need to label? to distinguish? . . .

Other concerns were also expressed:

If we focus only on the final products . . . this is wrong. But how about performing on standard tests? How about academics? I don't think [sic] should be a tension but we have to think more about it . . .

In the type of classroom that I have . . . I am not sure how I will give up my power . . . I need to work with my students . . . social skills . . .

Emerging: Moving from the Margin to the Center

The teachers I quoted above had just started a process. The first big transformation came through the validation of their own practices. This in itself is good but problematic. My concern is that the rhetoric of "we know our classrooms, ourselves, our students" may also validate unhealthy practices. Isolated reflection and inquiry may be dangerous. On the other hand, it is less of a concern if some problematic issues in our classrooms or schools can be shared with colleagues. Having the chance to talk with each other about meaningful situations in our classrooms, to share and shape each other's questions, to discuss data in any format, or just to support and ask questions can be very powerful. These opportunities help to construct understandings for a sense of community that challenges traditional cultures in schools. Sadly most schools do not facilitate this type of professional growth (Cochran-Smith & Lytle, 1992). As expressed by one teacher:

This is too bad that we (teachers) don't have opportunities in our work place to do this type of thing.

This teacher refers to meetings in which they shared their experiences, successes, failures, and questions. It started with personal explorations and became a process of individual and social validation of teaching practices. This validation moved toward raising important questions about the nature of power relations within the research community and the nature of valued forms of knowledge production about education. This process also started to question how academic authority constructed teachers' lives.

In my view, this questioning and challenging about making sense and producing knowledge in a different relationship with authority in schools and academia has a positive transformative capacity. It also shapes and redefines the intellectual and practical roles of the scholar. This is potentially what Sartre (1974), the French writer, philosopher, and activist, called marginal power, which takes a form of democratizing power arrangements to have ownership over changing and organizing one's life. Sartre opposed the notion of Marcuse (Kellner, 1974–75), the German-American scholar, that the intellectual can always formulate or elaborate the interpretation of reality and the goals for social transformation. According to Sartre, the academic intellectual can polish the intellectual worker's thought but cannot produce it. Teacher educators who support the production of knowledge by teacher-researchers recognize the intellectual formulation of the teacher. These formulations can be polished by educational scholars in the same way that teachers should polish academic elaborations. This establishes a new relationship that alters power arrangements. For me, a teacher who is now in the academia and who has a deep concern with the power implications of knowledge production, the move from the margins to the center challenges hegemonic educational regimes of truth. Eventually what is being proposed is a less oppressing regime of truth within contingent emancipatory energy. From my past experiences as a teacher of marginalized populations, I have also learned about the potential oppression involved in new regimes of truth like those I described earlier. However, "The new revolutionary strategy seeks to seize and expand marginal power to provide space for developing new institutions, ways of relating and values as a prelude to the construction of a liberated society" (Sartre, Gavi, & Victor, 1974–75, p. 193, cited in Kellner).

I am a strong believer in the positive role that critical and collegial inquiry can play in transforming life in the schools. However, education is much more than schooling, and the transformation of society takes much more than making schools livable places for teachers, students, families, and administrators. Schools in general do not recognize the research done by teachers and do not create any structural conditions to facilitate or stimulate collegial inquiry among practitioners.

Although I strongly support any form of collegial inquiry, I understand there are involved some tensions that might disturb a trusting relationship among colleagues, particularly when institutional arrangements take part in the process of creating the conditions for facilitating teacher empowerment. In reformulating the regime of truths, we continually have to question power arrangements and ask ourselves who is being silenced and why. Remember my story in which I fooled myself by creating an illusion of emancipation while my pedagogy was a monologue of liberation that excluded anyone else.

At this point, then, I am asking questions, not answering them. Please pay attention to the language of possibility, not of affirmation: What is the interest of academia or teacher educators in developing or helping to develop teacher-researchers? Why engage in collaborative inquiry or in action research or any other label imposed from the academia? Is it all about schools and learning? Why present in conferences? Why writing? Do teachers have to do it? Do teachers have to follow the academic modes of promotion? And what about teachers who don't want to engage in any type of writing or inquiry?

Another question that comes to my mind is: Do those teachers who narrate their stories, but who have no relations with teacher educators or academic research, call their work research? Who is labeling it research, the practitioners or teacher educators? What implications has this label? Why the word research? Whose interest is being served by labeling activities, stories, biographies, research? I am not questioning if this is research or not. It is the connotation of having to adopt academic language that makes me wonder.

Regardless, if teachers are to engage in doing research, teacher educators have a very important role. Who will prepare or help teacher-researchers to conduct systematic inquiry? However, is this another instance to promote a false approach to professionalism that only benefits teacher educators? (Labaree, 1991, 1992)

One last, but not least, consideration is how teachers and teacher educators account for students' narratives. What role do they play in the formulation of reality? And what about families (I refer to a rather broad concept of family, which means caregivers for our students)? When we involve ourselves in the rhetoric of expertise (in this case, doing research of any type) we distance ourselves from the nonexpert—in this case the child or the caregiver. Where are their voices? Isn't it dangerous to ignore them? Isn't the expertise of our research moving the institution of schooling away from its communal, democratic roots? (See Welker, 1992, for a discussion of expertise. His discussion of Jane Addams' views of schooling is particularly helpful.)

Finally?

To answer the basic question—what do we have to gain from supporting and researching our own practices and other teachers' practices—is not a simple, single task. However, beyond rhetoric, making sense of our lives to help improve ourselves and our students' lives is powerful enough. If there are different personal interests and power struggles involved, it is important to clarify where we stand. I do think that socially committed teachers and teacher educators have much to gain from forwarding teachers' systematic critical inquiry. Without my own autobiographical and pedagogical inquiry, I have doubts that I would have been able to recognize my strengths and serious limitations as a transformative teacher. My hope now as a teacher educator is to challenge the reproduction of a celebration of marginality on the part of alienated teachers.

To conclude, I would like to quote what for me captures the spirit of empowerment to alter unjust power relations:

> If I am not for myself, who will be for me?
> If I am for myself only, what am I?
> If not now, when?
>
> (Pirkei Abot, Talmud)

questions for discussion

1. How did I come to know what I know and believe about teaching, learning, students, subject matter, classrooms, schools, and/or education at large?
2. What are these ideas, perceptions, ways of knowing, beliefs, and understandings?
3. How do I "picture" myself as a teacher? Where is this picture coming from? Is this picture complete?

teachers as researchers

Write your autobiography as a learner using the following guidelines to help focus your writing. This narrative will be a starting point for further systematic inquiry. Please notice that you do not have to answer all of the questions or refer to all of the topics. Rather, you will have to select what to write about. The selection process is important, because you will have to elaborate and give yourself time to rethink what your choices are and why.

When writing your autobiography, be sure to make clear what you mean by terms or ideas you express. If you use labels, you should clarify and explain what these labels mean to you. If you write about learning as fun, you will have to carefully explain what you mean by fun and how you know you have learned or someone else has learned something. If you say that you love children, you will have to explain what you mean by loving and how it takes place. In short, a good strategy for clarifying and explaining ideas is to give examples. Sometimes giving more than one example is useful to reinforce the meaning of the idea. Remember that some ideas and examples may have multiple interpretations. Thus, make sure you analyze your perspectives and consider other perspectives as well. However, there are times when we are not sure about what something means or how the idea or examples can be interpreted differently. In these cases I encourage you to speculate with alternatives. It is O.K. to be inconclusive on some points and leave them as open questions. Just make sure you ask those questions.

You do not have to write only about schooling. Furthermore, I highly encourage you to refer to experiences outside school that shaped the ways you came to think about education, about yourself, and about children. Perhaps a book, a play, a movie, or a trip influenced your beliefs and ideas. You might want to explore those experiences and what you have learned from them. Perhaps friends, fictional characters, siblings, parents, or other relatives had a strong impact on your perspectives of what education is and how it connects with life. I suggest you also explore this line of inquiry about experiences and beliefs.

In school there were experiences in and out of classrooms with teachers, peers, and other people that probably had an impact on your life. Refer to these stories. Of course, there were negative and positive experiences. Try not only to describe the two types of experiences, but also to contrast ideas, values, and feelings. See if you can identify the characteristics of teachers who positively or negatively shaped your beliefs about teaching, learning, children, yourself as a learner, and subject matter knowledge. As always, try to give examples if your memory helps you.

The autobiography is an opportunity to clarify beliefs and connect them with experiences you had in and out of school. Realizing what these beliefs are and seeing how they have developed gives you a better perspective from which to make reasonable choices and to reject, challenge, and validate your own and others' perspectives. Questions you may address are (you don't have to follow this order or answer all of them):

1. How did I come to know what I know and believe about teaching, learning, students, subject matter, classrooms, schools, and/or education at large?
2. What are these ideas, perceptions, ways of knowing, beliefs, and understandings?
3. What experiences in and out of school have influenced and shaped the ways that I know?
4. What does becoming a teacher mean?
5. Who is a teacher, what is a teaching? Why?
6. How do I picture myself as a teacher? Where is this picture coming from?
7. Is there room for revising my beliefs and ideas? Is the "picture" complete?

The above questions are a general guide to help your focus. You can be more specific if you like. There are no rules on how to write the autobiography. However, if this helps you, you can be creative. For instance, some people find it important to include pictures or poems because for them it is a way of conveying meaning. Take risks! Think unthinkable things! Let your imagination grow! Be an independent thinker, which also means that instead of thinking of what others want from you, think of what you want from yourself. Remember that you are the focus and source of knowledge.

suggested readings

Barrit, L., Beekman, T., Bleeker, H., & Mulderij, K. (1985). *Researching educational practice.* North Dakota Study Group Evaluation.

Bolster, A., Jr. (1983) Toward a more effective model of research on teaching. *Harvard Educational Review, 53*(3), 294–308.

Cherryholmes, C. (in press). Reading research. *Curriculum Inquiry.*

Clark, C. (1990). What you can learn from applesauce: A case of qualitative inquiry in use. In E. Eisner & A. Peshkin (Eds.), *Qualitative inquiry in education* (pp. 327–338). New York: Teachers College Record.

Cochran-Smith, M., & Lytle, S. (1990). Research on teaching and teacher research: The issues that divide. *Educational Researcher, 19*(2), 2–11.

Connelly, F. M., & Clandinin, D. J. (1990). Narrative and story in practice and research. In D. Schon (Ed.), *The reflective turn: Case studies of reflective practice.* New York: Teachers College Press.

Elasky, B. (1989). Becoming. *Democracy and Education* (Occasional paper No. 3, pp. 6–13).

Goodson, I. (1991). History, context and qualitative methods. In I. Goodson & R. Walker (Eds.), *Biography, identity & schooling,* 114–136. Bristol, PA: The Falmer Press.

Grumet, M. R. (1992). Existential and phenomenological foundations of autobiographical methods. In W. Pinar and W. Reynolds (Eds.), *Understanding curriculum as phenomenological and deconstructed text,* pp. 28–44. New York: Teachers College Press.

Hollingsworth, S. (1990). Teacher as researchers: Writing to learn about ourselves—and others. *The Quarterly of the National Writing Project & the Center for the Study of Writing, 12*(4), 10–18.

Traver, R. (1987). Autobiography, feminism, and the study of teaching. *Teachers College Record, 88*(3) 443–451.

Walker, R. (1991). Making sense and losing meaning. In I. Goodson & R. Walker (Eds.), *Biography, identity & schooling,* pp. 107–113. Bristol, PA: The Falmer Press.

Wile, K. (1989). Voter information persons. *Democracy and Education* (Occasional paper No. 3, pp. 16–19).

references

Cochran-Smith, M., & Lytle, S. L. (1990). Research on teaching and teacher research: The issues that divide. *Educational Researcher, 19*(2), 2–11.

Cochran-Smith, M., and Lytle, S. L. (1992). *Communities for teacher research: Fringe or forefront?* Currently under consideration for publication.

Dewey, J. (1938). *Experience and education.* New York: Macmillan.

Dewey, J. (1964). The school and social progress. In R. D. Archambault (Ed.), *John Dewey on education: Selected writings* (pp. 295–310). Chicago: The University of Chicago Press. (Original work published 1899)

Freire, P. (1970). The adult literacy process as cultural action for freedom. *Harvard Educational Review, 40*(2), 205–225.

Freire, P. (1973). *Education for critical consciousness.* New York: Seabury Press.

Greene, M. (1979). Teaching: The question of personal reality. In A. Lieberman & L. Miller (Eds.), *Staff development: New demands, new realities, new perspectives* (pp. 23–35). New York: Teachers College Press.

Grinberg, J. (1992). *Teaching as research: Issues, tensions and validation through collegial conversation.* Paper presented at American Educational Research Association, San Francisco.

Hollingsworth, S. (1990). Teachers as researchers: Writing to learn about ourselves—and others. *The Quarterly of the National Writing Project & The Center for the Study of Writing, 12*(4), 10–18.

Kellner, D. (1974–75, Winter). Jean-Paul Sartre, Philippe Gavi, Pierre Victor, *On a raison de se revolter* [Book review]. *Telos, 22,* 188–201.

Labaree, D. (1991). *Research says: Teacher professionalization and the science of teaching.* Unpublished manuscript, Michigan State University, East Lansing, MI.

Labaree, D. (1993). Power, knowledge, and the rationalization of teaching: A genealogy of the movement to professionalize teachers. *Harvard Educational Review,* forthcoming.

McLaren, P. (1989). *Life in schools.* White Plains, NY: Longman.

Mitchell, L. S. (1931). The cooperative school for student teachers. *Progressive education, 8,* 251–255.

Noddings, N. (1984). *Caring: A feminine approach to ethics and moral education.* Berkeley: University of California Press.

Shulman, L. (1987). Knowledge and teaching: Foundations of the new reform. *Harvard Educational Review, 51,* 1–22.

Traver, R. (1987). Autobiography, feminism, and the study of teaching [Essay review of *The handbook of research on teaching,* 3rd ed., M. C. Wittrock (Ed.)]. *Teachers College Record, 88*(3), 443–452.

Welker, R. (1992). *The teacher as expert: A theoretical and historical examination.* New York: SUNY.

Willis, P. (1977). *Learning to labour: How working class kids get working class jobs.* Farnborough, England: Saxon House.

Wittgenstein, L. (1972). *On certainty.* G. E. M. Anscombe & G. H. Van Wright (Eds.). New York: Harper & Row.

The Social Construction of "The Problem of Teenage Pregnancy"

Nancy Lesko

guiding questions

1. What is the author trying to say or teach?

2. What is the significance of what you read here for you personally and for you as a teacher?

3. What are the perspectives drawn on by the author to make the analysis?

4. How does this analysis help to inform our practice in classrooms?

In its December 9, 1985 cover story, *Time* magazine proclaimed that teenage pregnancy was a crisis, a problem that "rends the social fabric." However, in a booklet published in the same year, the Children's Defense Fund listed statistics that placed the peak of births to women under twenty in 1970, fifteen years earlier. If the number of births to women under twenty was declining, how was it possible that in 1985 there was a crisis?

This article explores one account of this apparent discrepancy by examining the social context in 1985, specifically the areas of social demographics, relations between men and women, and the economy. This analysis suggests that "the problem of teenage pregnancy" is a way of talking about other, broader problematic areas in American life and helping to create public-policy dispositions. This analysis interprets the problem *of* teenage pregnancy to be a problem *for* white, middle-class people who see in teenage pregnancy an increase in births to poor women, who are disproportionately women of color. Without explicitly stating this, the "problem of teenage pregnancy" taps into fears of an American society which is predicted to be increasingly composed of persons of color, lower-class or poor, who live in single-parent families.

Several assumptions undergird the following analysis. First, I assume that there is no "naturalness" or inevitableness about which problems arise and are accepted as legitimate, major public problems. There is also no necessity about who will be seen as responsible for a public problem. In this view, public problems are constructed as legitimate and important by certain social groups with certain kinds of interests or perspectives. Part of this construction of a problem is the apportioning of responsibility for the crisis onto certain social shoulders. Joseph Gusfield has analyzed both the temperance movement (1986) and the problem of drunk driving (1981) in this way. In the case of drunk driving, he notes that there are several alternative ways that drunk driving and accidents resulting from it could be considered. The blame for the problem of drunk driving could be placed upon traffic management and be seen primarily as a transportation problem. The responsibility for improving the situation would then fall to traffic planners, who would devise better public transportation or more roads, so inebriated drivers could travel with more safety. This view seems strange at first reading, but it is just as reasonable as putting responsibility upon the individual driver, and defining the problem as individual lack of willpower or reckless behavior or socially irresponsible behavior. In this latter definition of the problem, the correction of the problem lies with individual drivers who must police their own behavior or be charged with recklessness or irresponsibility.

The very fact that there are alternative ways to define a problem and alternative ways to assign responsibility for its existence is strong evidence that other factors—socially contextual factors—will help determine which definition of the problem will occur and which social groups will be viewed as responsible for causing it. The social groups responsible for the problem are simultaneously seen as the only ones who can improve the situation.

Gusfield's approach to analyzing public problems is twofold: He looks at the rhetoric around the problem, to see how the problem is defined, what language is used, and what images are used. Second, he closely analyzes the historical period for other conflicts, stresses, changes, or difficulties. He locates a problem as it is discussed in several social arenas, e.g., how drunk driving is discussed in courts and in public service announcements. As the problem is discussed and defined across various social realms, clues to its many layers of meaning are amassed.

Similarly, this analysis of the construction of the problem of teenage pregnancy first examines the imagery and rhetoric used to establish the problem and then situates it in the socioeconomic context of the mid-1980s. In the process, I will argue that the real problems are changing social demographics, gender relations, and economic shifts. All of these separate problems, evidence of social change, are discussed by implicit and explicit re-idealization of the white, middle-class, and patriarchal nuclear family. When teenage pregnancy is defined as the problem, the solution is the stability and order attendant with the white, middle-class nuclear family. Implications of this analysis include that the problem of teenage pregnancy is part of a conservative, antisocial (Barrett & McIntosh 1982), antiwelfare movement with class, race, and gender positions.

Images and Rhetoric of the Problem of Teenage Pregnancy

The dominant images of the problem of teenage pregnancy are meant to alarm. Two images are most consistently associated with teenage pregnancy. The first is that of a young woman standing sideways, with full, pregnant, sexual body. Her full body is juxtaposed with her childlike face. That juxtaposition is meant to startle, to seem out-of-place, and, thereby, to alarm. The second image connected with the problem of teenage pregnancy presents a young woman with a child or a baby on her lap or in her arms. There is always an empty look on the young woman's face, which can be read as ambivalence or an "I don't care" attitude. This photo alarms in the attitude portrayed, implicitly toward the child and the mothering situation. The young woman is ambivalent toward her offspring: some days she has an attitude of a real mother, other days she may not want to be bothered.

Accompanying such photos are texts which express in words and anecdotes the same alarm for the future through a description of three interrelated problems of teenage pregnancy: sexual irresponsibility, bad mothering, and hopelessness. These themes were present across articles in *Time* and in publications from the Alan Guttmacher Institute (the research arm of Planned Parenthood) (1981) and the Children's Defense Fund (1985).

Sexual Irresponsibility

An eighteen-year-old's comments set off in a box in the *Time* article exemplify the lack of seriousness: "I was going to have an abortion, but I spent the money on clothes." A seventeen-year-old remarked, "I had birth control pills in my drawer. I just didn't take them." The girls are portrayed as either lacking knowledge about reproduction, overly casual about their actions, or blinded by the glamour of out-of-wedlock births to Hollywood stars.

Given the "obvious" (from a middle-class adult perspective) reasons for postponing sexual relations or using contraception (e.g., truncation of schooling, likelihood of being poor, likelihood of single parent families), the failure to postpone or to use contraception can only be read as pathology or stupidity. A researcher for the Rockefeller Foundation shook her head about why lower-class girls do not think about their futures:

> Middle-class girls tend not to have babies because Mother would kill them if they did. [For lower-class groups] it's the big shoulder shrug. They don't get abortions. They don't use contraception. It's just not that important; they don't have a sense of the future. (*Time*, December 9, 1985, p. 87)

Likely to Be Bad Mothers

Time chronicles the mothering of Desiree Bell, who at fifteen resented her first son.

> I used to punch myself in the stomach . . . The first year I wouldn't play with him. He didn't talk until he was nearly two . . . I would say I traumatized my own son. (December 9, 1985, p. 87)

In addition to physical or psychological abuse, young mothers are less likely to seek prenatal care, which might affect the baby adversely, for example, through poor nutrition. Very young girls have an increased chance of low birthweight babies, who are prone to "serious mental, physical, and developmental problems that may require costly and possibly even life-long medical care" (*Time* 1985, p. 79). In this subtheme, teenage mothers are portrayed as delinquent for failing to place the care of children as their single and highest priority.

Emotionally Disabled: Worthlessness and Despair

The *Time* authors wrote: "[The true root of teenage pregnancy] may be a sense of worthlessness and despair" (December 9, 1985, p. 90). This third subtheme suggests that an "emotional disability" of hopelessness for a decent future leads to pregnancy. Having hope of a better future, i.e., striving for upward mobility, is linked to economic self-sufficiency; the emotional antecedents of self-sufficiency are hope in one's future and a belief that good things are attained through hard work.[1] Without such hope, teenage mothers see a life stretching before them characterized by poverty.

The discussion of the costs of teenage pregnancy for taxpayers follows the description of the true root of the problem. "It has been estimated that overall, the U.S. spends $8.6 billion on income support for teenagers who are pregnant or have given birth" (*Time* 1985, p. 87). This third subtheme describes teenage mothers as social problems because they are emotionally disabled or hopeless of better futures. As a consequence, society will have to support many of these girls and their children through welfare. Their lack of self-sufficiency, and its attitudinal roots, is their third deviant characteristic.

Teenage mothers are social problems because they are sexually irresponsible, likely to be bad mothers, and unlikely to be self-sufficient. In order to question this view of the problem, the next section examines the actual statistics from different perspectives, attempting to specify *for* whom the statistics are a problem.

Looking Again at the Problem of Teenage Pregnancy
//

Joseph Gusfield's analysis of the temperance movement in *Symbolic Crusade* (1986) presents a portrait of the late 1800s and early 1900s that counters common sense. Gusfield argues that during these turn-of-the-century years when temperance activists were advancing, alcohol use was declining. Immigration, however, was increasing. Gusfield portrays alcohol use as associated with immigrants, especially Irish and Germans, but with the lower classes generally. Given the changing social demographics, Gusfield reads the temperance movement as a way middle-class WASPs reestablished their norms and values as superior to those of the immigrants. Alcohol use symbolized broader cultural, racial, and socioeconomic differences. By outlawing the use of alcohol, teetotaling WASPs denigrated immigrants' cultural beliefs and practices as being socially problematic and leading to individual and family problems. Middle- and upper-middle-class WASPs did not explicitly devalue the immigrants' lives, but did so by defining their attitudes and practices as socially problematic.

Similarly, teenage pregnancy became a problem when the number of births to women under twenty was declining. The births to U.S. teenagers across the last forty years are as follows (Children's Defense Fund 1985):

Births to women under 20

1950	425,000
1960	594,000
1970	656,000
1980	562,330
1982	522,981
1983	499,038

These statistics identify the peak of births to women under twenty in 1970, with a consistent decline since. How then do we explain the announcement of a "crisis" of teenage pregnancy in 1985? To answer this question, we must look at the context in which a social problem is created, just as Gusfield examined the social context in which alcohol was defined as a problem.

Changing Social Demographics and Teenage Pregnancy

There is widespread anxiety over the changing composition of American society. For example, in a special *Education Week* issue entitled, "Ready or Not, Here They Come" (May 14, 1986), the authors heralded a dramatically changing school population in the next twenty years. This population will be increasingly black, Hispanic, and from single-parent families, which are predominately poor. "A country without a middle class majority will simply not be the America we have known," wrote the authors. Even in this brief excerpt and in the title, a dichotimization of "they" and "we" is established. "We" (that is, white, Eurocentric, middle-income) are the legitimate people of America, being taken over by "them" (that is, people of color, linguistic minority, and poor). The April 9, 1990 cover story of *Time* was entitled: "The Changing Color of America." In addition, the birthrate of white, middle-class adults is declining, so that the births to lower-class people, and especially to teenagers, stand in even starker relief. The social demographic changes are very much in evidence and form one important level of what the problem of teenage pregnancy signifies in the 1980s and 1990s.

I propose that we reread the problem of teenage pregnancy in light of changes in social demographics and of middle-class decline. Making teenage pregnancy a national problem now can be seen as an attempt to reaffirm middle-class values of rational life-planning, self-sufficiency, and striving for upward mobility. It is an attempt to scare young women and men into conforming to and affirming a life ordered by reason, delayed gratification, and an expectation that such actions will be rewarded with a good job and a decent place to live. The crisis of teenage pregnancy is also a warning that young people who violate these norms—who do not adhere to the path marked "This way to the middle class" with its proscriptions of sexual activeness and denial of the limited upward mobility for people of color—will be abandoned, declared as "getting themselves into trouble" or having "bad values" (Baca Zinn, 1989; Hill Collins, 1989).

Gender Relations and the Problem of Teenage Pregnancy

The problem of teenage pregnancy is represented by images of young women alone with children. This is another important level of its meaning and connects directly to a different set of statistics. Although the total number of births to women under age twenty has diminished, the percentage of those births to unmarried women has increased:

Per cent of births to unmarried women under 20

1950	14%
1970	30%
1982	51%

Thus, we see that the family contexts of the births to women under twenty is an important part of the problem. The births, even though declining in numbers, are increasingly to single mothers. Women's position in relation to marriage and the fathers of their children is also part of the problem, albeit not headlined. The problem is not just that young women are having children, but, more importantly, that they are having children outside the bonds of marriage. This is not directly stated in any document, but can be found in popular culture, specifically in movies and television.

One popular film, *Fatal Attraction,* and one television documentary, "The Vanishing Black Family," illustrate some of the issues entangled in this denigration of single mothers. In *Fatal Attraction,* a big box office success, the character played by Glenn Close is a single woman, sexually assertive, and, later, pregnant by a man (Michael Douglas) who is already married with a daughter. Douglas tells her that he will pay for an abortion. If she refuses that route, then she is "on her own." He refuses to see her, talk to her, discuss the issue with her. Close's single mother-to-be is to obediently disappear and leave Douglas's nuclear, patriarchal, middle-class family in peace. Only after such stonewalling does the single mother-to-be resort to violence, matched by the biological father's violence. However, from the camera's viewpoint, only the woman is "crazy," for demanding economic and emotional support from the father. She deserves to be eliminated by Douglas and his legitimate wife in the line of duty—protecting the nuclear family's boundaries. After Close is killed in their bathroom, the closing shot of the film is a close-up of a family photo: Douglas, his "good" wife (that is, docile, dependent), and his "real" daughter. The viewer can imagine that a jury would acquit the husband and wife, declaring the murder justified by self-defense.

In *Fatal Attraction,* the independent, sexually assertive woman, who will not have an abortion, is portrayed as crazy and is eventually killed by a married couple. This morality tale positions single mothers as direct threats to patriarchal family isolation; in turn, single mothers are dependent upon middle-class families for support (via taxes and social welfare programs). The self-preservation of the couple produces a logic in which only Close (although the child was conceived by Close and Douglas) is villainized; only Close is killed; only Close *pays* for a child out of wedlock.

Bill Moyers' documentary, "The Vanishing Black Family," similarly villainizes black women, who are presented as pathological for having children without support from a husband or father. The logic behind this program is: Only a nuclear family, one with a mother and a father in the house, is a real family (thus, the title, "The Vanishing Black Family"). To conceive and bring children into poverty is a form of abandonment or neglect. A woman is not a good mother if she brings children into poverty. Black men are irresponsible for fathering children, with no ability to help support or raise them (although Michael Douglas's white, middle-class character appeared justified to refuse economic and emotional support to his child).

The gender dimension of the problem of teenage pregnancy relies upon aspects of both of these popular presentations and strongly suggests that the problem is single mothers, not teenage mothers. Single mothers are presumed to be sexually assertive, in that, as the *Time* issue on teenage mothers states, no one wants to be a virgin. Second, single mothers are not to *demand,* but must accept the consequences of their sexuality and docilely ask for help. No one is responsible to help them, because they are "bad women" who have broken the rules of decency. Like criminals, they have no rights. Third, these two films suggest that only intact families with husband and wife should have children. Poor people (synonymous with single mothers) who knowingly have more children must be immoral or stupid.[2]

These two films are explicit in their biases toward poor and single mothers, many of whom are women of color. The problem of single motherhood is a problem *for* middle-class, reason-centered, patriarchal families. It is a problem that is corroborated by social structures that reinforce nuclear family advantages (e.g., tax structures) and make it extremely difficult to survive in a family which is not nuclear and patriarchal (Barrett & McIntosh, 1982).

From the above descriptions and analysis, we can see that the problem of teenage pregnancy, more aptly titled, the problem of single mothers, is a negative valuation of any child-rearing environment that does not adhere to the idealized white, middle-class, nuclear family. This idealized environment was created over the last century, as the work of raising children came to be defined as women's full-time labor (Macleod, 1983; Smith-Rosenberg, 1985). The benefits for the nation-state of such nuclear families are enormous (Carter, 1988). Families carry the entire burden of educating and training future students and workers. The state bears no cost, but businesses and government reap the benefits of people trained to be self-interested, high-achieving individuals. Business and government look to the family to carry the extensive child-rearing costs; middle-class women have been educated to believe that children need full-time, personal attention in order to be psychologically and intellectually developed. At the same time, societies look to strengthen family units during transitional periods when other social institutions are shaky (Carter, 1988).

The mid-1980s through the present qualifies as such an unstable period. There is a major relocation of workers from industrial to service and information provider jobs. New immigrants call into question our identity through the movement for bilingual schooling (Ovando, 1990). Ronald Reagan's legacy is a more starkly class-divided society, with more people economically worse off than ten years ago. In this environment, attention to the idealized nuclear family has heightened, while the actual condition of families deteriorated.

> During the 1980's, while the U.S. engaged in the largest military build-up in peacetime history, investing $1.9 trillion in national defense, $10 billion was cut from programs serving poor and moderate-income families and their children. As 2.1 million children dropped into poverty, the number of American billionaires quintupled. And as wealth was generally redistributed upward, nearly every statistical indicator of quality of life— the poverty rate, real income, homelessness, access to health care and affordable housing, the increase in low income, no benefit jobs—translated into the abuse and neglect of children. (Carter, 1991, p. 33)

The Family and the Problem of Teenage Pregnancy

The discernment of the problem of teenage pregnancy relies upon maintaining a yardstick of a normal, white, middle-class nuclear family. The construction of a "problem" necessarily implies a non-problem or "good" situation. This is the social form that young women and men should be striving for and if they are not, then they are not "like us" (the definers of the problem). For low-income, youth of color to believe in striving for the Cosby family image, they must strongly deny the structural inequality and racism which they have experienced. The blindly optimistic or indefatigable upwardly mobile individual is a stock character in our social mythology, e.g., Horatio Algiers, and it is having a revival. The rules by which Horatio must live are well-known: no despair, no immediate gratification, no children. Complete devotion to the task of getting ahead is required. Of course, the chances have never been the same for women, especially for women of color.

Following Gusfield, the resurrected, idealized nuclear family serves to establish white middle-class, nuclear family norms as the proper ones. When they remain in place, despite changing demographics, gender relations, and economics, young women who violate those norms can be relegated to a category of loose women or bad mothers, thus garnering neither social empathy nor social resources. When the norms of the upwardly mobile, nuclear family prevail, we have norms by which to evaluate other behaviors as bad, pathological, and dangerous. These individuals and groups—here, single mothers and single mothers of color—can be written off as undeserving of social empathy and social resources because the public rhetoric of problems identifies them as pathological. In this way, the construction of the problem of teenage pregnancy is directly linked to the distribution of resources in the coming welfare wars (Abramovitz, 1988; Fraser, 1990). If single mothers can be constructed as a social problem with its "roots" in their attitudes of hopelessness, then these women do not deserve to be supported with public funds.

It is my position that the problem of teenage pregnancy, which is a problem of single motherhood, was constructed in the mid-1980s as part of a broad-based social policy aimed at keeping women in their place (patriarchal families) by decreasing social empathy for and willingness to provide public funds for their support. If single mothers, especially black mothers, can be constructed as undeserving, social sympathy will be manipulated in support of further reductions in welfare. Additionally, the resurrection of white, middle-class nuclear families who could bear the costs of extensive education to produce good future workers would nicely serve business and state leaders. The construction of the problem of teenage pregnancy is part of broad social engineering toward reprivatization and dismantlement of the welfare state support of women and children. This social engineering operates on both the symbolic, or normative, level and on the functional—production of future workers—level. It is a multilayered, multifaceted construction of social policy and opinion.

Conclusion
//

I have urged that we rethink our automatic acceptance of teenage pregnancy as a major social problem. This analysis calls the problem into question by looking at the diminishing numbers since 1970. Using an analytical strategy that sees a public problem as symbolic of broader social conflicts, I propose a different view of teenage pregnancy by recontextualizing it in the changes occurring in mid-1980s America: demographic shifts, economic shifts, and changes in gender relations.

The conception of a problem of teenage pregnancy reasserts the values associated with the middle-class, self-interested, patriarchal family and pathologizes people who do not conform, notably single mothers. At the same time, this pathologization supports a policy of diminished resources for single mothers. On another side, the reassertion of the nuclear family backs the privatized, rather than state or business, support of the extensive education needed to produce white-collar workers, or the inculcation of the work ethic in blue-collar workers in the new service and information economies. Such a reading of the problem of teenage pregnancy clarifies how it exploded into a national issue, because within it are widely experienced conflicts over socioeconomic position, gender relations, and racial fears.

This analysis indicates that we need to be cautious in our acceptance of social problems. We need to be alert to who is defining the problem, which groups of people are given responsibility for creating the problem, and the language and images used to create and communicate the problem to others. In attempting to rethink a social problem, it is imperative to place it into its historical context and to understand what changes were occurring simultaneously. In these ways, we minimize the manipulation of our views on social policy and maintain alternate ways of seeing and talking about social life.

q u e s t i o n s   f o r   d i s c u s s i o n

1. According to the author, what broader social conflicts are central to the perception that teenage pregnancy is a major social problem in the late 1980s and 1990s?
2. How does the ideal, middle-class nuclear family seem to be the solution to the social problems of the 1980s and 1990s?
3. What limitations does the nuclear family have as "the solution" to the problems of population changes, gender relations, and economic shifts?
4. Following from this analysis, what things (e.g., attitudes, public policies) might change if we renamed the problem of teenage pregnancy as "the problem of single mothers"?

teachers as researchers

Choose a current "problem" in education. For whom is it a problem, or from whose perspective is the problem defined? What can you understand about the social construction of this problem? That is, can you investigate answers to some of the following questions:

- What is the history of the articulation of this problem?
- What other social conflicts or changes were occurring simultaneously with the creation of the problem?
- Does the language used to define the problem constrain how we think about the issue and possible responses?

suggested readings

Jones, E. F., Forrest, J. D., Henshaw, S. K., Silverman, J., & Torres, A. (1989). *Pregnancy, contraception, and family planning services in industrialized countries.* New Haven: Yale University Press.

Omolade, B. (1986). *It's a family affair: The real lives of black single mothers.* Latham, NY: Kitchen Table:Women of Color Press.

Rains, P. M. (1971). *Becoming an unwed mother: A sociological account.* Chicago: Aldine.

Sanders, J. (1992). *Before their time: Four generations of teenage mothers.* New York: Harcourt Brace Jovanovich.

Sidel, R. (1986). *Women and children last: The plight of poor women in affluent America.* New York: Viking.

Solinger, R. (1992). *Wake up little Susie: Single pregnancy and race before Roe v. Wade.* New York: Routledge.

notes

[1] An alternative view of upward mobility is provided by Joel Spring (1989) who argues that most mobility in U.S. history was directly connected to a changing economic structure, with mass expansion of blue- and white-collar jobs. Without such structural expansion of the economy, tenacity, optimism, and hard work will amount to little. See Spring's Chapter 4.

[2] This last point connects with pro-choice activists whose reason-centered world leads them to have children only under optimal circumstances. Pro-choice activists have children when economic and personal resources can be maximized in the care and raising of a child. Any other approach to having children is seen as incomprehensible. From this rational-centered view, neither poor nor single women would ever have children.

references

Abramovitz, M. (1988). *Regulating the lives of women: Social welfare policy from colonial times to the present.* Boston: South End Press.

Baca Zinn, M. (1989). Family, race and poverty in the eighties. *Signs: Journal of Women in Culture and Society, 14*(4).

Barrett, M., & McIntosh, M. (1982). *The anti-social family.* London: Verso.

Carter, E. (1988). Intimate outscapes: Problem-page letters and the remaking of the 1950s German family. In L. Roman, L. Christian-Smith, & E. Ellsworth (Eds.), *Becoming feminine: The politics of popular culture.* London: Falmer Press.

Carter, S. (1991, January). Children of crisis. *Z Magazine.*

Children's Defense Fund. (1985). *Preventing children having children.* Washington, D.C.: Adolescent Pregnancy Prevention Clearinghouse.

Fraser, N. (1990). *Unruly practices: Power, discourse and gender in contemporary social theory.* Minneapolis: University of Minnesota Press.

Gusfield, J. (1986). *Symbolic crusade.* Urbana: University of Illinois Press.

Gusfield, J. (1981). *The culture of public problems.* Chicago: University of Chicago Press.

Guttmacher Institute. (1981). *Teenage pregnancy.* Alan Guttmacher Institute. New York: Family Planning Perspectives.

Hill Collins, P. (1989). A comparison of two works on black family life. *Signs: Journal of Women in Culture and Society, 14*(4).

Macleod, D. (1983). *Building character in the American boy.* Madison: University of Wisconsin Press.

Ovando, C. (1990, August). Politics and pedagogy: The case of bilingual education. *Harvard Educational Review, 60*(3), 341–356.

Smith-Rosenberg, C. (1985). *Disorderly conduct: Visions of gender in victorian America.* New York: Oxford University Press.

Spring, J. (1989). *American education: An introduction to social and political aspects* (4th ed.). New York: Longman.

chapter 10

Margins of Exclusion, Margins of Transformation

The Place of Women in Education

Angéline Martel &
Linda Peterat

guiding questions

1. What are the authors trying to say or teach?
2. What is the significance of what you read here for you personally and for you as a teacher?
3. What are the perspectives drawn on by the authors to make the analysis?
4. How does this analysis help to inform our practice in classrooms?

Women are drawn to education for its promise of individual advancement, of social and economic improvement. The rights women gained in the past century and a half to enroll in postsecondary education and, more recently, in professions such as engineering and medicine were hard fought struggles. But women's presence as teachers in the public school system is readily recognized; Geraldine Clifford notes that "at no time between 1870 and 1970 did teaching fall below fifth place on the list of the ten leading occupations of all women in the labour force" (1991, p. 111). Because women have gained access to various realms of education and have achieved majority participation as students and teachers in public schools, one might, at first glance, perceive women's participation and presence in education as nonproblematic. Yet, if we examine more closely the experiences of women in education and insert them within a reflection of the nature of education systems, we begin to perceive other realities; we see more clearly the complexities and contradictions in women's experiences as well as the purposes and interests inherent within education systems.

Our present social system is described as patriarchal, which implies that it accords to certain men (and men as a general category) certain rights, privileges, and freedoms not granted to others. In its normal daily practices, our education system, like the other social systems of politics, economics, and religion, serves as a foundation to sustain and recreate patriarchy (Leck, 1990). If we grant a naturalness to the normal daily practices that occur in and constitute our educational systems, to the meaning of education, and to what it means to be educated, we grant a continuity to education as a foundation of patriarchy. Our intent in this essay is to explore the ways in which the normal daily practices in education culturally construct gender relations, along with an associated vision of the world, which fundamentally oppress women.

In the following, we explore women's experiences in schools in order to understand the ways in which education serves as a foundation of a patriarchal society. Women's experiences in schools offer examples of how women are marginalized, positioned, and contained in powerless and supportive positions. In the first part, marginality is viewed as a structural exclusion constituted in relation to what is valued and contained in the curriculum and in relation to the social interactions of schooling. Our examples are drawn from young women's experiences in intermediate and secondary schools. However, in the second part, we see within women's marginalized positions the ways in which marginality may be turned to an advantage for women (and men) in the long and short terms and the ways in which it offers the necessary conditions for resistance and transformation. Our overall orientation attempts to restore an ecological view of human experiences, particularly of women's; we do so by constantly introducing the fundamentally indivisible dimension of body-and-mind-experience.

An earlier version of this essay appeared in 1988 as "A Hope for Hopelessness [sic]: Womanness at the Margin in Schools," *Journal of Curriculum Theorizing*, 8 (1): 103–135.

Marginality as Structural Exclusion

The Curriculum

Women are excluded from the curriculum through limited definitions of knowledge and knowing and through the valuation of *some* school subjects and not others as core knowledge. Our schools ascribe to the ideal of objective knowledge—abstract, value-free, and factual. Knowledge is COMMODIFIED, assumed to exist externally, detached as fact, able to be possessed, and given. Generally, the teacher is viewed as possessing knowledge, which students may also come to possess in exchange for diligence and work. In this way knowledge and mind, as the locus of mental labor, are separated from the body and established in a relationship of power and authority between student and teacher. In assuming and enacting a mind and body separation, knowledge is (apparently) neutralized and commodified. This is a process of exclusion in which what is valued as knowledge is men's knowledge posing as knowledge for all (Spender, 1982).

The value placed in schooling on factual, apparently disinterested and "universal" knowledge has constructed a dominant core of school subjects: mathematics, biology, grammar, physics, and chemistry. Such construction and fragmentation of school subjects are testimony of the itemization of knowledge possible when notions like abstraction and objectivity are created. This destroys knowing through interrelationships of ideas and contexts and removes the body-mind connection. It is only rarely, and with giggles of unfamiliarity, that students are encouraged to measure their feet, smell a flower, create a crazy sentence, gaze at a fly, or slam a door (to hear the noise of course)! School subjects that could offer an occasion for reflection on EMBODIED LIFE are coerced to replicate the dominant core. Social studies becomes a chronology of battles and kings within geographical confines and castles. In health, students learn how an apple is digested, emphasizing the function of gastrointestinal juices and carbohydrates. In second languages, it is assumed students must learn vocabulary and grammar if one day they want to communicate with someone. Physical education becomes techniques of arm and body movements, of hitting a ball or scaling a hurdle. And so the prevalent mode of knowledge is multiplied within and through the school subjects.

Objective knowledge, posing as interest-free, has eliminated women and their bodily difference as one of its sources and, at the same time, has claimed their mindful allegiance through the claim of universality. Sheila Tobias (1978) has discussed occasions when women did not behave as expected in experiments to test psychological and sociological hypotheses; if they skewed or distorted the data, they were eliminated from the results. Women are treated

COMMODIFIED: Made into a commodity—something to be used and/or exchanged.

EMBODIED LIFE: Life as experienced through the body, sensually, day to day experience of life.

as aberrations rather than as indications of the limitations of a particular theory. Abraham Maslow's theory of motivation and self-actualization is limited by being based on traditional male values, which place self-esteem and self-actualizing needs on higher planes than affiliation needs (Shakeshaft & Nowell, 1984).

The domination secured in schooling by such knowledge—posing as factual, disinterested and universal—reveals the oppressiveness of such a dominant core. Valuing and defining knowledge in only one way becomes the standard against which all knowing and human value and potential are measured. For example, and with some concern, George Posner quotes a college admissions officer who states, "Math is a measure of the degree of academic rigor in a student's academic program; grades in math are a measure of intelligence" (1992, p. 2).

Schooling favors males: it is associated with the traditional male sphere of public life and action. The very linking of education with schooling and the restriction of the definitions of education to the public sphere suggest that what goes on outside the school is not education, thus devaluing such activity. In this sense, the family and its "education" activities become a matter for the private sphere, the sphere of women and mothers. This is the distinction made by Jane Roland Martin when she shows that education includes only the so-called productive sphere of life to the exclusion of the reproductive. Martin states: "Education, like politics, is defined in relation to the productive processes of society, and the status of women and the family are 'a-educational' as well as a-political" (1982, p. 137). In delimiting the field of education, the body—woman's body, particularly, with its power of reproduction—is relegated to a sphere where its powers and importance in society are made invisible, excluded from the male mainstream, and devalued.

This denial and elimination are problematic if we consider phenomenological philosopher Merleau-Ponty's (1973) claim that it is our bodily presence in the world that makes knowing possible. He states that it is through the body that we can speak the world, because the world in turn speaks to us through the body. For women, what appears as objective and disembodied knowledge is, in fact, men's bodily knowledge implanting a male-bodily stance in the world.

If we consider the word "knowledge" we recognize its references to the valued knowledge of patriarchy. When it refers to em*bodi*ed knowledge, the word "knowledge" becomes negative as in "carnal knowledge"—knowledge that in common parlance refers to passions, animality, worldly knowledge. Patriarchal knowledge attempts to control and fragment the totality of knowledge, namely embodied knowledge, by exclusion and devaluation. Thus, there is a sharp distinction between the transmission of valued knowledge of the public sphere and the devaluation of knowledge of the private sphere, the realm of carnal knowledge. Such a distinction is a testimony of excluding the body from the core.

Let's consider a lived example for every female: the moment of menstruation. First, we have to ask why biology and sex education lessons in school focus on contraception and anatomy (both male and female) and exclude a very large part of women's sexuality, from menstruation to ovulation, from pregnancy to birthing, from sensation to desire. The lessons render visible in the curriculum the moments in which males partake; they fail to acknowledge women's own bodily experiences (Fine, 1988). Second, while menstruation is excluded from the official curriculum, it is very much a part of every young woman's experience. The image that students get of menstruation, mostly through talking among themselves, is a negative one. Sandra Lewis, in a poem entitled "There Is No Real Problem of Pain," speaks of the grade eight name for IT: "The Curse."

> After class the giggling boys
> what do you do when you get IT
> while driving a car?
> Stop at a Kotexaco Station. (1982, p. 19)

Yet women do not always feel negative about menstruation. Lewis also says:

> I can proclaim my womanhood
>   proudly
> but only to other women
> and even then, with a whisper. (1982, p. 19)

Thus, women in schools create their own celebrations on the margin of the formal curriculum. Exclusion forces them to find their own corner. L. K. Tobias speaks about one lunch hour at school:

> We girls sat chatting in the sun on the school steps at the south entrance. That day I shall relish above all other school days. We, each in turn revealed to the group experiences with our monthly "periods". . . Some of the younger girls surprised us as they spoke up: other sat listening attentively. Our talk drew to an end and we linked arm around waist until there was a chain of about twelve of us spanning the school yard, laughing and dancing in the sun while our younger sisters, cousins and friends watched.
>
> In retrospect, we had intuitively initiated ourselves into womanhood . . . (1982, p. 8)

The exclusion of such an important moment in women's life from the conversation and concerns of the explicit curriculum cannot be a chance happening. Margaret Sutherland suggests one reason why women's menstruations are viewed as negative by patriarchy and schooling: "It could be argued that above all menstruation brings us awareness of not being in full control" (1981, p. 77).

Lewis echoes:

> And he says, god you're a
> bitch, what's your problem
> anyway, got your period?
> and frowns at that sign of weakness.

I feel guilty about those
little spots,
that lack of control
over my own body. (1982, p. 19)

Menstruation reminds a woman that complete control of her body is not possible. In this reminder, patriarchy asks: How can you be so illogical, irrational, as to let your blood flow? Inadequacy and guilt speak loudly.

At the same time, menstruation reminds everyone of mortality. Lewis states: "Passing months remind me of my own mortality" (1982, p. 19). Menstruation is a flaw for the patriarchal system that values de-bodied knowledge; it is a reminder that the mind has no control over some happenings, eventually over death.

Perhaps there is an added interpretation to the blatant exclusion and the negative overtone of menstruation. When women value their bodies and view menstruations positively, they become a celebration of power (Zelman, 1991). At first, menstruation is a hope and a promise of children. It is a passage into realization that life will be transmitted again. Menstruation viewed as the blood of death in patriarchy becomes a celebration, the blood of life. An Ojibway woman speaks in these terms:

So many times I have heard the traditionalists speak of the "power" a woman has during menses. The way they tell it is positive and spoken of with reverences. The terms they use are poetic and meaningful: "Changing Woman"—"My grandmother is visiting me". The "rites of passage", puberty ceremonies were/are looked upon as gifts to women, a time of joyful recognition in the change from girlhood to womanhood. (L. K. Tobias, 1982, p. 9)

With the words "power of women," we realize that patriarchy negates women and relegates them to the margin because women's power and success are deeply threatening to the status quo (Walkerdine, 1989). Patriarchy brings its power to bear on women's bodies, and schools are an institution where it does so. If any bonding occurs among women in education, it is on the margins and it is likely to reinforce women's marginal positions and diminish their self-esteem in relation to the core values and ideals of schooling.

Very early in schooling, team sports for boys help them bond while channelling their bodily energies and experiences. Jon Young (1985) noted that boys tend to play sports-oriented, organized games during recess while girls don't focus on such obviously team-oriented activities. The importance of team sports for men becomes interesting when we consider the games played as metaphors of sexual politics. Games like hockey, tennis, racketball, baseball, badminton, and golf involve a sticklike object representing the male sexual organ. The object of such games is to direct and control the ball representing the female ovum/womb. When the ball becomes larger, the game involves only the control of the ball: basketball, football, and soccer are examples. In these sports men/boys bond together to act out the symbolic interplay of gender in patriarchy. In these games the power of the womb/egg is diffused; it is brought under the power of the male. The very activities of bashing, throwing, pushing, kicking, and hitting carry in them a devaluing of the ball-womb-woman-egg. One does not treat an object with such harshness and desire to control when one holds it in respect. Team sports are a part of schooling very early on in life. They serve to establish a bonding between men and to incarnate bodily the sexual politics of the patriarchal system.

Team sports for men, while creating a spirit of kinship, again exclude women from the valued activities of schooling. In the sexual politics of sports, women become the objectified other: the ball. Women, when included, serve to support their marginality. As spectators and sponsors or cheerleaders and fundraisers, they are allowed to continue the glorification of the male. When women participate in team sports, they do so among themselves because they, it is thought, cannot compete with men; yet, women are forced, in their games, to adopt the rules and the mindset of patriarchy. Thus women's alternatives are either exclusion from the valued activities or co-optation to the norms and forms of those activities if participation is to occur.

Michel Foucault suggests that in an institution's denying and regulating, we as participants in the institution realize what it is that is important (Sheridan, 1980). We might say that in denying bodily difference at the surface level, we as participants experience body as making all the difference. Abstractness, detachment from self, and denial pose as covers for the gender identification process that is the real learning. Females coming of age in our society are situated in a total network of social relations which, while denying them, define their social existence as marginal. But the body does not relinquish its powers so easily. What is denied at the structural surface level survives as a deep undercurrent, and so schools are saturated with sexuality.

The rhymes, jokes, and stories of children are part of the informal playground and hallway interactions in schools. These interactions contain lessons of identity and are evidence of the "naturalness" by which gender is constructed. Here is an example from personal experience.

> I found in my twelve-year-old son's pocket the following joke and the fact it was a wrinkled note tells us that it was passed along as a hidden object, a forbidden thought.
> "Did you know that Eve was the first salesman?
> She exchanged an Apple for a Wang!"

We first note the gender-excluding language: salesman; then the derogatory tone to women because it is inserted in the story of women's "downfall" and first sin. This boy is (as other boys are) internalizing a negative attitude toward women. However, what this story indicates is that the body-sexuality is an undercurrent moving through and below the official curriculum. The boy perhaps did not know what the word "Wang" means, but he could well guess the context of the joke and its reference to body was intuited.

We have observed young girls singing the following skipping song in widely separated North American cities, which attests to the central part it has in a young girl's culture.

I met my boyfriend at the store
He bought me ice cream
He bought me cake
I went home with a belly ache
Mama, mama I think I'm sick
Call the doctor, quick, quick, quick.

Doctor, doctor, will I die?
Count to five and you're alive.
One, two, three, four, five
I'm alive.

Interpreting this song, the world of traditional male and female roles unfolds before marriage takes place. This is the world of children in adult roles. The boyfriend meets the young girl at the store and he does the buying. She is passive and fragile. She doesn't control her eating and overindulges. The mother becomes the helper by calling the doctor. She is saved by the great white knight, the doctor. However, the sexual parallel of the story is hardly disguised. It can be read as a story of premarital sexual relations, of pregnancy, of the fear of death in childbirth, and of rebirth. One, two, three, four, five could in reality be the one to nine months of pregnancy. Children spontaneously dramatize real life sexual politics in their play. Their body is very much present but not in the formal curriculum.

Women are excluded from the formal curriculum of schooling in that their social participation, achievements, and experiences are underrepresented in the information selected and transmitted in the school subjects. Pat Mahony (1988) writes that "whether one looks at . . . the way in which knowledge is framed, or the content of curriculum subjects, the same picture emerges. The content of education is overwhelmingly oriented towards male interests" (p. 80). Patricia Galloway (1980) examined the material used in forty-two English courses in the curriculum of Ontario and found women were barely represented among the authors of the material. Mathematics textbooks, materials, and course content have been found to reinforce the perception of mathematics as a male domain.

When women's experience finds no resonance in the formal curriculum, Spender suggests that the absence and invisibility of women is internalized as doubt:

> We doubt our own feelings and ideas. We search for words which encode
> our meanings, which describe how we feel and think, but the words are
> not there. So we doubt more. Each day of our lives we are informed that
> women do not count, that we are wrong, that our different descriptions
> and explanations are ridiculous or unreal. If we try to insist on their va-
> lidity, we can be discounted again, as aggressive or emotional (unfemi-
> nine or feminine, but either way is wrong). (1982, p. 53)

Invisibility assigns nonexistence to women who wonder, who doubt their experiences and their very presence. A recent survey by the American Association of University Women confirms that girls between the ages of nine and sixteen experience a great loss in self-esteem. When asked in elementary grades how often they felt "happy the way I am," 60 percent answered "always." By high school that figure had dropped to 29 percent (Daley, 1991). The question of presence and absence in the curriculum leads to the physical presences (and apparent absences) of children in schools. It begs the questions: How do males and females and teachers relate to each other? What network of interconnections develops in schools?

School Interactions

The social interactions in schools that occur between students and between students and teachers influence the identities-in-formation of young people. The abundance of research in this area shows that women are again marginalized in their presence or, when acknowledged, serve as a negative reference group for males.

Dale Spender (1982) has illustrated that we, as teachers, are often unaware of the extent to which our sex biases influence our interactions in the classroom. Even when teachers *think* they are spending equal time interacting with boys and girls, they are interacting twice as frequently with boys as with girls. When teachers interact with girls more than one-third of the time, the teacher and the boys in the class perceive it to be more than one-half of the time. Boys are more likely to be disruptive in class, and they more frequently secure the teacher's attention and response. A high interaction cycle with boys is set: Teachers give more attention and offer more praise and encouragement. Boys talk more, make more demands, and question and challenge more (see also Sadker & Sadker, 1986). Classroom interaction is dominated by boys' talk, boys' questions. A teacher comments:

> It's a bit harder to keep the boys' attention during the lesson . . . at least that's what I've found so I gear the subject to them more than I do the girls who are good at paying attention in class. (Clarricoates, 1978, pp. 356–357)

In the interactions between teacher and students, girls are silenced; they become spectators, wallpaper flowers, listeners of the boys who, given more time and attention, form the dominant valued core and command the action of the classroom. This command places boys foremost in the minds of teachers as they plan classes so that teaching in very specific ways is directed to boys. For example, teachers report:

> —The girls will read anything so I always choose a book that will interest the boys.
> —Nearly all of the books have male characters because the girls don't mind reading about males, but the boys won't read about females.
> —Boys are very particular. They won't have anything to do with things that are "sissy" you know. So we read lots of stories about adventures and spies, that sort of thing. (Spender, 1978, pp. 3–4)

In schools, girls also form a negative reference group for boys. They represent a category that boys find despicable and do not want to identify with (Stanworth, 1983). Consider a young boy's reaction to being called "a sissy" or "a girl." Spender states:

> The boys do not like girls, that they find them inferior and unworthy, and even despicable—is a conclusion hard to avoid when observing and documenting evidence that boys frequently make insulting and abusive (often sexually abusive) comments to girls. There is also evidence that more often than not teachers do not take them to task for this behaviour—it is considered 'natural' for boys to hate girls. (1982, p. 5; see also Walkerdine, 1989)

Sue Lees (1986) points out that girls do not have the power of language, particularly abusive language, available to use against boys. She states that "there are no words that amount to an attack on their [boys] whole personality or social identity" (pp. 31–32), or to "formulate their sexual experience" (p. 54). Thus, everyday discourse excludes, marginalizes, and silences the power of women.

Girls learn early that their presence and participation in the classroom are more often than not undervalued by the teacher. They learn they are inferior and despicable in the eyes of boys. Both these lessons set the stage for self-doubting, which permits the establishment during adolescence of the internalized, devaluing other. This is illustrated by Elizabeth Fennema (1980), who found that, up to a certain age, when girls were asked whether they were capable of being mathematicians, and whether they liked, enjoyed, and were competent at mathematics, they invariably answered yes. The boys said no: girls could not be mathematicians. During adolescence, many of the girls changed their opinions and began to state that girls could not do math. They denied their own experience and took on the perspective of the boys when they reached the age at which boys' opinions became important. Sadker, Sadker, and Steindam (1989) state, "Girls are the only group who enter school scoring ahead and 12 years later leave school scoring behind" (p. 46).

The marginality of women in schools has been shown by probing valued/devalued knowledge, the formal curriculum, and interactions in schools. Primarily this marginality has surfaced through exclusion and devaluation. Women as a result develop a negative self-identity based on doubtfulness, women as other, and underestimation. This experience is akin to that of racial and ethnic minorities, who also gravitate around the center core of the patriarchal dominant figures.

Marginality as a Condition of Transformation

Using the word "marginality" recognizes that the margin is bordering a valued center. It is a statement pertaining to the structural conditions of a society. Furthermore, the negative connotations that the patriarchal system has integrated into this word tell us that margin is always in reference to another entity, never on its own grounds. Thus, women and minoritized groups are on the margin of societies to the extent that they do not participate in or influence normative thinking and action. They remain on the periphery with interests and experiences other than those sanctioned by the core. At times, however, marginalized groups enter the core. Then they become valued by the core because they allow the continuation of the status quo or because they buy the merchandise that it sells.

We shall now attempt to show that the word "margin," as well as the phenomenon it describes, can be inverted on itself. Instead of being a condition naming the verge of disaster, the word "margin" can name an invitation to change. Just as the white spaces around the words of a written page can become a place for reflection, spaces for the writing of new words, so "margins" can point to the possible, to outside the limits of the core or to outside the written script. Instead of being the expression of repression, exclusion, and devaluation, the margin should be taken on its own ground: as the hope of future possibilities.

The Naming of Marginality

A feeling of hopelessness often accompanies the life of marginalized groups. For minorities, marginality is experienced as an erosion of one's being, or one's children's being, to the dominant group, often arousing cries of despair. This process can be named "assimilation."

Their condition, however, is similar to that of women. Although ethnic and racial minorities are easily identifiable, women and girls in schools are taken for granted as part of the "normal" population and not identified as a minoritized group. Because they are taken for granted, it is harder to show their being as socially constructed. This is so for two reasons. First, the dominant male culture finds it difficult to recognize its domination of the half of the population that is ever present, and yet absent, like the air we breathe. Second, it is also difficult for women and girls to name the feelings of marginality that are experienced, but that seem so natural while they make up one's self-identity in relation to the dominant group.

The Possibilities of Transformation

However, the naming and the concurrent realization of marginality fosters a deeper understanding of social life, of exclusion; it is the seed for transformation. When women begin to see their exclusion and devaluation in everyday happenings in schools, they can begin to ask questions about the patriarchal way of being. They can name the domination to which they are subjected. They can name the characteristics of the genderized female. They can name patriarchy and they can identify its features like a landscape. Mitrano has pointed out that patriarchy is a way of viewing the world:

> Regardless of its origins, patriarchy soon came to mean more than
> political leadership or lines of descent. It came to mean a mind-set, a

world view, a perspective through which all reality was (and is) viewed.
(1981, p. 15)

It is the very way of viewing, of thinking, that marginalization can challenge.
Indeed, it is the very existence of a mind-set that can be questioned. Thus,
being at the margins, women are able to question the very idea of domination
as "normal" in every human relation. The limit of the possible is to question;
for example: Can human relations take place in a nondominant context? When
patriarchy attempts to envision what matriarchy might have been at the dawn
of history, it becomes another system of domination; the patriarch is only
replaced by the matriarch. Yet, women in their lives can understand the
possibility for a system where domination might not exist. It is marginality that
will allow a genuine probing beneath domination and that may lead to a different network of relations.

In questioning the hold of the patriarchal mind-set on social relations, the
experience of marginality can also help question the way patriarchy sees
the mind. Revaluing embodied experience and bodies themselves becomes a
spontaneous alternative to the very notion of "mind-set." Marginality then
allows women to discover and value a suppressed realm of their lives in which
wholeness is valued. The despair encountered by the realization of marginality
creates a paradox: realizing one has something to lose by not being marginalized, one's being a woman. Marginality thus shifts from an attention to the
dimension of a power struggle to a celebration of being a woman. In the living
of marginality, in the questioning that it fosters, lies the discovery of a new
world. The body informs the mind and the mind informs the body. Then
a harmonious balance may appear, alternate relationships emerge. Beyond a
questioning of domination, marginality brings a wholeness of body and mind
capable of inverting the status quo. The first hope of questioning that marginality brings (questioning the patriarchal mind-set) then introduces a second layer of hope: that of joining body and mind in a celebration of new
social networks.

By excluding and devaluing women's bodies, patriarchy has searched for
an ideal of rationalized, intellectualized society. The mind through instrumen-
tality has become the powerhouse of patriarchy. The third hope of marginality
leads to a broader societal change: that the harmony of body and mind might
form the bases of social networks. While the first two levels of hope focused on
women, the social networks require that men and their bodies be valued. The
powerhouse of domination that patriarchy has set has also excluded many
men, and, although this exclusion was not the subject of this essay, we need to
indicate here that many efforts have been made by men to press in the same
direction as marginalized women. Men, too, have been in some ways marginalized by patriarchy. This is where the feminists meet phenomenologists, her-
meneutists, minorities, children, adolescents, older-aged persons, people from
less-industrialized countries, and so on.

The ultimate hope of marginality is in changing social networks. Perhaps
one day, because of marginality, the center core will itself be transformed into

another margin in such a way that everyone, every group will find and value its place. Spender puts it this way:

> If and when the world is described and explained from the multiple perspective of human beings (and not just the dominant group), if and when knowledge is encoded by all, all forms part of the record for all, we will not be living in a patriarchal society as we know it today. (1982, p. 38)

The ultimate hope of marginality is a very long-term hope. It is the hope that a celebration of women, just like a celebration of minorities, of children, of phenomenologists, etc., can transform the patriarchal system. In the meantime, marginality brings a final hope, that of guarding against the illusion of change.

Much rhetoric has been devoted to showing how the situation of women has changed. Promises of equal opportunities, equal salaries, equal job expectations seem near realization. Yet the rhetoric of equality takes place on the grounds of patriarchy. According to Jane Gaskell women are not gaining equality. They are, in fact, becoming more marginalized. As an example, she concludes on the subject of school that:

> Schooling can help a girl, relative to other girls but it is not effective in overcoming group differences between males and females . . .
>
> Men who get a teaching certificate are more likely to be employed in higher paying jobs not related to education [while] the tendency for women to revert to traditional jobs increases as time since graduation increases. (p. 229)

The hope in marginality is that it helps cut through the illusory rhetoric of change and it allows women and men to see that in fact the patriarchal system has not relinquished its dominant hold.

Living on the margins is a way of being for women in a patriarchal system. As long as the social network is a system and as long as it is patriarchal, there must be no illusion of change. Patriarchy is the rule of the patriarch with its dominating mind-set and its mind-set of domination. The very naming of patriarchy is a realization that the matriarch and her daughters are excluded from the core: it is a way of guarding against illusion. When our naming of the social network can be changed and when that naming coincides with a valuation and inclusion of women, then perhaps women will not need to remind themselves of their marginality.

Can final words tell us what the formal education institution of schooling in patriarchy is for marginalized women? Mary O'Brien comments on the contradiction for women, invoking social transformation and formal education: "Educational systems and school curricula are structured hierarchically and are profoundly conservative: educational institutions are bastions of male supremacy and ruling class power" (1983, p. 3).

Women need to remember their marginal status and refuse to learn the school lessons of devaluation and exclusion. This refusal becomes their real education as the etymology of the word "ex-ducere" requests that it be.

A Word on the Notion of Equality

As for the notion of equality, we suggest that to become equal would mean entering the dominant core of the patriarchal system. Equality is competition in patriarchal terms and every woman who achieves equality must marginalize herself at the same time for:

> What we need to appreciate is that the problem of sexism and education will not be overcome by inserting some positive images of women in the curriculum, by appointing a few more women to senior posts or even by encouraging girls to stay longer at school and reach the relatively higher standards of their brothers so that they no longer "underachieve". (Spender, 1982, p. 37)

That some women enter the valued patriarchal core can be only a temporary solution that may, in the end, allow a diffusion of the domination center. Women at the center need to marginalize themselves with their sisters. While working at the center, women must remind themselves that their being "woman" is at the margin. As long as a woman moves to the center, she serves to reinforce the structure of domination. She enters the patriarchal game: individual women may win but women as a community may lose. But when women return to the margin, they strengthen the hope for long-term transformation.

Conclusion
//

We have not spoken about sexism in this essay because we attempted to probe more deeply into education as a foundation of patriarchy. Sexism is one way of naming the exclusion and devaluation that patriarchy imposes on women. It points to a profound living of marginality. As we shift from experience to social structure, we realize that patriarchy as status quo is the organizing force for social relations. Realizations of sexism are part of the questioning that the margin allows.

Women are marginalized by exclusion and devaluation through knowledge, the formal curriculum, and interaction in the classroom, but marginality is a hope for social transformation, both for women and men.

q u e s t i o n s   f o r   d i s c u s s i o n

1. From your observations in school classrooms, can you detect ways in which schooling can be said to "favor" males?
2. What evidence can you find (by observing in classrooms) of the ways in which it can be said girls are excluded from the curriculum?

3. Focus your classroom observations on individual boys and girls in various classes. In what ways do you see differences in their responses, actions, and participation in classes taught by women?
4. Think of your own experiences as a student in school:
   a. What (and whose?) values were implicit in the way your classes were organized and taught?
   b. Were some school courses different? In what ways? Why?
   c. What view of knowledge was implicit in the way most of your courses were taught?
   d. Can you agree with the values that shaped your own schooling experiences? Why or why not?
   e. If you are to assert alternate values, what would you do differently as a teacher?

teachers as researchers

In what ways is gender constructed in any school subject? In what ways does the culture and context of schooling contribute to the marginalization of women in education?

suggested readings

Forman, F., O'Brien, M., Haddad, J., Hallman, D., & Masters, P. (Eds.). (1990). *Feminism and E.D.U.C.A.T.I.O.N.* Toronto: Centre for Women's Studies in Education. Ontario Institute for Studies in Education.
hooks, b. (1984). *Feminist theory from margin to center.* Boston: South End Press.
Rich, A. (1979). *On lies, secrets, and silence.* New York: Norton.
Sears, J. (Ed.). (1992). *Sexuality and the curriculum.* New York: Teachers College Press.
Weiler, K. (1988). *Women teaching for change.* New York: Bergin & Garvey.

references

Clarricoates, K. (1978). Dinosaurs in the classroom: A reexamination of some aspects of the hidden curriculum in primary schools. *Women's Studies International Quarterly, 1*(4), 353–364.
Clifford, G. (1991). 'Daughters into teachers': Educational and demographic influences on the transformation of teaching into 'women's work' in America. In A. Prentice & M. Theobald (Eds.), *Women who taught* (pp. 115–135). Toronto: University of Toronto Press.
Daley, S. (1991, January 9). Girls' self-esteem is lost on way to adolescence, new study finds. *The New York Times,* p. B1.
Fennema, E. (1980, January). *Success in math.* Paper presented at Sex Differentiation in Schooling Conference, Churchill College, Cambridge.

Fine, M. (1988). Sexuality, schooling, and adolescent females: The missing discourse of desire. *Harvard Education Review, 58,* 29–53.

Galloway, P. (1980). *What's wrong with high school English? . . . it's sexist . . . un-Canadian . . . outdated.* Toronto: O.I.S.E. Press.

Gaskell, J. (1983). Education and women's work: Some new research directions. *The Alberta Journal of Educational Research, 29*(3), 224–241.

Leck, G. (1990). Examining gender as a foundation within foundational studies. *Teachers College Record, 91*(3), 382–395.

Lewis, S. (1982). There is no real problem of pain. *Canadian Woman's Studies/Les Cahiers de la femme, 4*(1), 19.

Mahony, P. (1988). How Alice's chin really came to be pressed against her foot: Sexist processes of interaction in mixed-sex classrooms. In R. Dale, R. Ferguson & A. Robinson (Eds.), *Frameworks for teaching* (pp. 80–90). London: Holder & Stoughton.

Martin, J. R. (1982). Excluding women from the educational realm. *Harvard Educational Review, 52*(2), 133–148.

Merleau-Ponty, M. (1973). *The prose of the world.* Evanston, IL: Northwestern University Press.

Mitrano, B. (1981). Feminism and curriculum theory: Implications for teacher education. *The Journal of Curriculum Theorizing, 3*(2), 5–85.

O'Brien, M. (1983). Feminism and education: A critical review essay. *Resources for Feminist Research, 12*(3), 3–16.

Posner, G. (1992, March). Institutional roles of school subjects: How schools limit access to knowledge. *Association Canadienne pour/Canadian Association for L'étude du Curriculum Studies, 2,* 8–10.

Sadker, M., Sadker, D. & Steindam, S. (1986, March). Gender equity and educational reform. *Educational Leadership,* 44–47.

Shakeshaft, C., & Nowell, I. (1984). Research on theories, concepts, and models of organizational behavior: The influence of gender. *Issues in Education, 2*(3), 186–203.

Sheridan, A. (1980). *Michel Foucault: The will to truth.* New York: Tavistock.

Spender, D. (1978). The facts of life: Sex differentiated knowledge in the English classroom and the school. *English Education, 12*(3), 3–4.

Spender, D. (1982). *Invisible women: The schooling scandal.* London: Writers and Readers Publishing Cooperative.

Stanworth, M. (1983). *Gender and schooling.* London: Hutchinson & Company.

Sutherland, M. (1981). *Sex bias in education.* Oxford: Basil Blackwell.

Tobias, L. K. (1982). My grandmother is visiting me. *Canadian Women's Studies/Les Cahiers de la Femme, 4*(1), 8–9.

Tobias, S. (1978). Women's studies: Its origins, organization and prospects. *Women's Studies International Quarterly, 1*(1), 85–89.

Walkerdine, V. (1989). *Counting girls out.* London: Virago.

Young, J. (1985). *Ethnicity, race and education.*

Zelman, C. (1991). Our menstruation. *Feminist Studies, 17*(3), 461–467.

chapter 11

Guardians of Childhood

Rebecca A. Martusewicz

guiding questions

1. What is the author trying to say or teach?

2. What is the significance of what you read here for you personally and for you as a teacher?

3. What are the perspectives drawn on by the author to make the analysis?

4. How does this analysis help to inform our practice in classrooms?

> *What is this Reason that we use? What are its historical effects? What are its limits, and what are its dangers?*
>
> Foucault (1989)

Seizing upon a moment of great fervor for public education and increasing demand for teachers sweeping the nation early in the nineteenth century, Catherine Beecher passionately wrote,

> Where do we find such an army of teachers . . . not from the sex which finds it more honorable, easy and lucrative to enter the many roads to wealth and honor. . . . It is woman who is to come at this emergency—woman, whom experience and testimony have shown to be the best, as well as the cheapest, guardian of childhood. (Woody, 1929, p. 462)

As these words suggest, it was widely held during the Victorian era that women were inherently more suited to teach young children. Indeed, it is no accident that today a large majority of teachers are women. Our contemporary assumptions and definitions of what it means to be a teacher have been produced through historical shifts in the definition of woman and her relation to children. These shifts took place in a complex weave of social and political interests, economic transformation, and accompanying institutional development. Moreover, our current experience as teachers within the organization of educational institutions can be traced to these historical and social changes.

Importantly, as this essay will demonstrate, women themselves were central in developing a DISCOURSE that endowed traditional values of motherhood and domesticity with new meaning. This transformation of meaning and identity, made possible through a convergence of socioeconomic, political, and religious changes, opened the door to new social and SUBJECTIVE possibilities for women. The installment of women into the previously exclusive male realms of public education and later into higher education must be understood as accomplished within this context of shifting systems of meaning that transformed the definition of womanhood and teaching.

Economic Changes
//

The shift from agrarianism to industrialism is often mentioned as important in considering the changing roles of women. At the turn of the nineteenth century the United States was still primarily an agrarian nation made up of small, independent yeomen and craftsmen. The colonial woman was most often domestic manager and manufacturer in that she baked, spun, sewed, and brewed all the

DISCOURSE: The complex weave of textual practices and relations through which we communicate and produce meaning about the world.

SUBJECTIVE: Refers to a position of personal identity; the "I" as subject; in poststructuralist theory this "I" is constructed within relations of discourse and power, and is never stable.

goods that her family needed to survive. Though this economic role was seen as secondary to men's, women's labor was critical to success and prosperity, and hard work was accepted as both necessary and valued in both sexes (Cott, 1977, p. 19).

By 1830, however, this could no longer be said of most American families. As industrialization grew, small independent farms in the Northeast were run out of business by large commercial organizations; men uprooted their families and moved to the cities to find work. Women found their lives and identities being radically transformed. No longer needed to produce the necessary daily goods and excluded for the most part from the newly expanding world of business, women were exiled to a new social position. From principal producers of the nation's goods, they became transformed almost overnight into consumers of now factory-produced goods. This change had considerable impact. As Ann Douglas has pointed out, both for middle-class women married to and tending "productive" men, as well as for working-class women toiling in sweatshops for low wages, female labor was devalued and female identity was necessarily redefined (Douglas, 1977, p. 54).

Social and Political Changes

Congruent with these economic changes were particular social and political changes. Along with migrating rural families, a constant flow of immigrants swelled the cities, keeping unemployment high and wages low. Coupled with this growing urban population, a new political ideology of democratic individualism contributed to the fears of social and political anarchy. A group of men seeking to remedy these problems organized a movement for public education. Through a system of common schools, the educational reformers set forth a plan to provide the proper instruction to create a morally responsible citizenry, thus restraining the chaotic tendencies of Jacksonian Democracy (Tyack & Hansot, 1982). A major problem facing these men was a shortage of able teachers, and many turned to women as a solution.

Fundamental to the philosophy of the Common School reformers and helping to reshape family and community life in New England were major changes in traditional religious structures. One such shift was the increasing attention focused on women by the clergy. As men became more involved in practical matters of the secular world, nineteenth century Puritan ministers found that participation in religious affairs became an increasing concern of women. Women, though seldom the majority with regard to actual church membership, began to fill more church pews than men on Sunday and were more often the organizers of religious meetings and events in the community (Douglas, 1977; Kuhn, 1947).

That women and clergymen became closely associated can be understood in relation to the changing conception of the child, rather than merely as an economic consequence. Unquestioned, and fundamental to orthodox Puritanism before the mid-nineteenth century, was the belief that life on earth was only a preface to an eternal existence in heaven or hell. Devoted Puritans were expected to pray for a conversion experience during which they would come to acknowledge themselves as inherently sinful, yet worthy of God's grace and mercy. Only through this process of inward salvation were men and women allowed membership to a particular church and access to heaven's gate (Slater, 1977).

Directly related to this belief was the doctrine of infant damnation. Often related by historians to an extremely high infant mortality rate, this doctrine condemned those children who died before experiencing conversion to spend eternity in the fires of hell. The concept of original sin, then, played a crucial role in shaping Puritan theology and family life.

By the middle of the eighteenth century, however, this doctrine was beginning to be challenged. The liberal ideas of the Enlightenment philosophers were having a profound effect on the Puritan religious structure as human nature and the conception of man were redefined. Out of John Locke's theory of the "tabula rasa" came a new understanding of the child born into the world pure and innocent. As the traditional concept of predestination came increasingly under fire, the doctrine of infant damnation became the center of great theological debate. A new liberal religious movement was initiated in which the child was redefined as capable of growing into grace with God without the trauma of conversion. A celebration of childhood was enacted that greatly altered the meaning and form of parenthood. Specifically, the meaning of woman and her relation to her children was transformed as she became defined as the natural celebrant of infancy. Motherhood along with childhood, as categories of meaning produced in social relations, shifted to give women new responsibility and new status in relation to the home.

Clearly these theological transformations had an impact on the changing structure of the family. In addition to the increasing attention being directed at the child, families in general began to be characterized by increasing mutual affection. Before the Revolutionary War, marriage was principally an economic relationship arranged by parents. By the nineteenth century Puritan stress upon personal affection in marriage was giving children more autonomy in choosing a spouse, and women were waiting longer before marrying (Degler, 1980, p. 14).

Taken together these social, political, and economic changes introduced important shifts in familial relations, re-presenting and repositioning women as the focal points of nurturance and moral guidance. The period between the Revolutionary War and approximately 1830 was one of intense social and cultural transformation that sent men to search for the American Dream in a new external world of work and isolated women and children within the internal, private realm of the home. With these socioeconomic changes, a myriad of discursive changes came together to produce complex new patterns in the social relations of women's lives, and consequently changes in the meaning of womanhood itself. Looking carefully at the intersecting lines of discourse, inspired in part by women's desire to push beyond the bounds of their oppressive social positions, one can begin to see not only the reshaping of female identity within the home, but small openings in the male-dominated structure of meaning that had previously excluded women from any participation in the public sphere.

Domestic Reform and the Discourse of Motherlove

///

> She is made guardian of morals; servant of man, servant of the powers that be, she will tenderly guide her children along appointed ways. The more resolutely optimistic a society is, the more docilely will it submit to this gentle authority, the more the mother will be transfigured. (Beauvoir, 1953, p. 173)

Whereas the preindustrial, colonial period saw women denied significance in the political sphere and access to formal education (Kerber, 1980), the next century witnessed traditional signs associated with womanhood—domesticity, patience, nurturance—crystalize into new forms signifying moral superiority that elevated women into the idolized position of caretaker of the nation's future. Through a variety of forms—novels, poems, essays, sermons, and speeches— a discussion of women's childrearing practices and responsibilities, women's education, and women's general social responsibilities took place that recast Victorian womanhood.

Authorized by the aforementioned political, social, and economic shifts, a discourse on womanhood transformed the meaning and practice of bourgeois women's lives, assigning to them the moral responsibility of educating America's children. Womanhood was produced as a sign within a particular restricted discursive framework, represented by the division of life into male and female spheres.

In what has been referred to as the domestic reform movement, advocates of a new social position for women created a discourse which accentuated the differences between men's and women's worlds. Denigrating the male-dominated business world as an arena of selfishness, ambitious competition, and degradation of the soul, they heralded the female sphere as an "oasis" of virtue, peace, and moral salvation. The home, once signifying family cooperation and productivity, was now the sign of protection and relief from the economic sphere, and woman's domestic labor, once important for its contribution to economic prosperity, was now necessary in the provision of shelter and comfort away from economic pursuit.

> O! What a hallowed place is home when lit by the smile of such a being; and enviably happy the man who is lord of such a paradise. . . . When he struggles on in the path of duty, the thought that it is for *her* in part that he toils will sweeten his labors. . . . Should he meet dark clouds and storms abroad, yet sunshine and peace await him at home; and when his proud heart would resent the language of petty tyrants . . . from whom he receives the scanty remuneration for his daily labors, the thought that

she may suffer thereby will . . . bid him struggle on, and find his sweet reward in her gentle tones and soothing kindness, and that the bliss of home is thereby made more apparent. (Cott, 1977, p. 70)

As Nancy Cott points out, though there was ample "antipecuniary bias in domestic rhetoric," there was no direct challenge to the modern organization of work. She writes that, "the values of domesticity undercut opposition to exploitative PECUNIARY standards in the work world by upholding a 'separate sphere' of comfort and compensation, instilling a morality that would encourage self-control, and fostering the idea that preservation of home and family sentiment was the ultimate goal" (Cott, 1977, p. 69). But the analysis must go further than this.

The discourse being produced by the domestic reformers did more than uphold a separate female sphere, or instill particular values of morality to be communicated through women; it produced a new bourgeois woman. This woman, though newly endowed with social value in the form of moral superiority, remained man's opposite, his servant, mother of his children, and necessary to the reproduction of his labor. She remained the Other, defined and differentiated, as always, in relation to man. The definition of man as competitive and hard was necessary in the production of woman as caring and tender. She remained isolated from his economic interests within the naturalized subjective position as his gentle servant, caretaker of the future of the moral Republic. Self-denial and a willingness to live for others, naturalized as female characteristics, signified woman's special usefulness to society. The touted "true work" of woman was the happy maintenance of her home and care of her family. Upon marriage, she was initiated into her "unique vocation," and was expected to fulfill her duties as self-sacrificing wife and mother. Cott is right in her commentary that the domestic reformers did not challenge the economic system. The bourgeoisie had no desire to dismantle the burgeoning economic apparatus so dear to its success. Rather, the positioning of woman as REPUBLICAN MOTHER would help ensure its survival.

Woman, re-presented in terms of the procreative function of her body, would be the new guardian of the moral order as defined by bourgeois HEGEMONY. The discourse of domestic reform, drawing on a liberalized theological rhetoric, introduced new meaning for woman as both a category of social meaning and as a social subject. Beyond her differential relation to man, woman's newly defined relation to the child was the key to the shift in her subjective position.

PECUNIARY: Having to do with finances or financial relations. In this case, it refers to the economic and business interests that surrounded and impacted the lives of those who worked in industry.

REPUBLICAN MOTHER: A term used to describe women's special status as caretakers of the nation's future citizenry.

HEGEMONY: Put most simply, this term means domination without force, but such domination occurs through the complex day-to-day experience of practices, beliefs, and relations through which particular interests get expressed.

It would eventually provide women with a strategy for escaping isolation in the home, carrying them into the male-dominated realm of education and knowledge.

Prescriptions for a stable society that was to eminate directly from harmonious family life dominated the literature of domestic reform. Referring to the need for moral guidance in effecting the Good Society, reformers initiated a discussion of woman's responsibility in educating the nation's future citizenry. Within this discussion the influence of religious doctrine and of protestant ministers themselves is clear.

As pointed out earlier, religious discourse, in the face of radical philosophical and social change, was moving away from an emphasis on predestination to a more liberal interest in effecting earthly moral reforms, particularly from within the family, as a means to eternal salvation and social amelioration. Many ministers, among them the Reverend John S. C. Abbott, turned to women in the millennial quest for a harmonious society.

> It is maternal influence, after all, which must be the great agent, in the hand of God, in bringing back our guilty race to duty and happiness. Oh, that mothers could feel this responsibility as they ought . . . A new race of men would enter upon the busy scene of life, and cruelty and crime would pass away. (Kuhn, 1947, p. 36)

Within the developing Unitarian theology, as well as within some shifting Calvinist rhetoric, the child was no longer defined as inherently sinful and evil but as potentially good or evil depending upon the environment into which he was born. In light of this concept, parental guidance was considered of paramount importance in assuring that he chose his path wisely. According to the doctrine of "Christian Nurture" set forth in 1847 by Horace Bushnell, a young minister fiercely opposed to the strict Calvinist doctrine of conversion, the acquisition of grace by the child was to come from "nurturance and internal growth." The need to preserve the child's natural purity while preventing sin placed crucial importance within the naturally nurturant realm of the home. Thus, "the child" signified by "innocence, purity, and potential virtue" became a new sign within a shifting network of meaning that functioned to re-present woman. The mother, "by virtue of an organic power," was attributed the central position in guiding the child toward the development of Christian character (Sklar, 1947, p. 162).

Cott points out that the emphasis on the mother as central in forming the character of her children "departed from (and undermined) the patriarchal ideal [prevalent in the colonial period] in which the mother, while entrusted with the physical care of her children, left their religious, moral and intellectual guidance to her husband (Cott, 1977, p. 86). Without actually denying paternal authority, new knowledge about womanhood, functioning as God's truth, was created, assigning to women "naturally" maternal instincts of compassion and nurturance and submitting her to the service of God, her country, and her husband.

The Influence of the Popular Media and Women's Publications
///

By midcentury this vision of republican motherhood dominated the essays and stories by female authors in popular ladies' journals like Sarah Joeseph Hale's *Ladies Magazine,* which merged with *Godey's Ladies Book* in 1837, and *Ladies Repository,* which was edited by Sarah Edgerton. Stories portraying middle-class woman's ". . . duties, her influence, her mental and moral culture, her social ministry to the human heart . . ." centered around family life, portraying the heroine as a pure and virtuous young wife and glorifying her maternal role as the anchor of society (Cott, 1977; Douglas, 1977; Kuhn, 1947, p. 43).

Drawings and prints found in these magazines or used as the frontispieces in novels or didactic texts also contributed to the discourse on motherlove. They provide us with a beautiful visual example of the woman that this discourse produced. One such drawing is the frontispiece of *The American Woman's Home,* a text written by Catharine Beecher and Harriet Beecher Stowe. It features a young woman who is surrounded by her husband and children as she reads. Her lighted face is the focal point of the picture while the others form a halo around her. She holds a small child on her lap while a little girl sits at her feet with a doll on her own lap. The message produced for and by nineteenth-century women by this scene is clear: with woman, the self-sacrificing, nurturant mother-wife, lies the responsibility for the protection of domestic harmony and the survival of the bourgeoisie in the face of increasing social degeneration (Beecher & Beecher Stowe, 1869).

Indeed, though moral guidance and the nurturance of the soul was empha-sized as woman's special responsibility, the insurance of the family's physical health also became an important concern. The coupling of a healthy family life with a stable and healthy nation linked the Christian discourse of motherlove and republican motherhood to a growing medicoscientific discourse. Within such texts as Sarah Hale's *Manners,* Catharine Beecher's *Treatise on Domestic Economy,* and Lydia Child's *American Frugal Housewife,* among a host of others, female readers were instructed in practical matters of health, food, clothing, infant care, and other household duties in the hope that "correct knowledge would lead to a corresponding correct action" (Beecher, 1843; Child, 1835; Hale, 1868).

The daily activities of the American housewife were put under close scrutiny with specific recommendations made for the insurance of healthy bodies and minds. In turn, the American housewife put her own family's body under sur-veillance. Guided by advancements in domestic knowledge, the mother could most carefully and scientifically regulate her family's activities, insuring the healthy development of her children and fulfilling her role as guardian of the social order.

New knowledge about the nature of woman—produced in a complex web of religious, economic, and social transformation—endowed these women writers with the authority to seek the truth within their assigned private sphere and to prescribe remedies for potential threats to the social order found there. In this way, the social construction of the bourgeois woman functioning in shifting regimes of truth ensured the perpetuation of a male-dominated economic system and way of life. By the turn of the twentieth century, the medicoscientific attitude would overshadow the theological as the basis for justifying women's place in relation to knowledge and the public sphere.

For the women writing during the early nineteenth century, however, religious commitment still dominated their efforts to carve out new social positions for women. In this struggle, a number of women within the domestic reform movement pushed the religiously supported discourse on the nature of woman into an insistence on knowledge for women.

Motherlove and Female Education

Inspired by a truth attributed to God's word, and driven by the desire for economic and social freedom, these women, most notably Sarah Hale, Emma Hart Willard, and Catharine Beecher, urged the discourse of motherlove beyond the doorstep of the home by insisting on the necessity of education for women. For example, Hale wrote:

> If God designed woman as the preserver of infancy, the inspirer or helper of man's moral nature in its efforts to reach after spiritual things; if examples of women are to be found in every age and nation, who without any special preparation have won their way to eminence in all pursuits tending to advance moral goodness and religious faith, then the policy as well as justice of providing liberally for feminine education, must be apparent to Christian men. (Kuhn, 1947, p. 45)

If women were to carry out the tasks and duties prescribed to them in their special vocation, then it was essential that they be exposed to those bodies of knowledge that, as Willard hoped, would "enable them as mothers, to do all that enlightened reflectiveness can for the happiness of the beings entrusted to them" (Kuhn, 1947, p. 129).

Not only was new knowledge about woman being produced in this discourse, but knowledge about knowledge. That is, a discourse on knowledge for women developed in conjunction with a new construction of the middle-class woman that would catapult them into social relations outside the private realm and into the male-dominated public sphere.

Early practical examples of the interest in knowledge for women are the schools for girls founded, among others, by Willard and Beecher, and moreover, the curricula that were set out for women in these schools. In 1814, Willard began a boarding school for girls in Middlebury, Vermont where she became intensely interested in forming what, in her words, would be "the design of effecting an important change in education, by the introduction of grade schools for women, higher than heretofore known (Willard, 1861). By 1821 she had sowed the seeds for another institution, the Troy Seminary for Female Education in New York state where she stressed that education for women would differ as much from that of men as "women's character and duties" differed from men's. Equally committed to the promotion of education for women's vocation, Catharine Beecher founded the Hartford Female Seminary in 1823.

Education for girls would, in Willard's words, "bring its subjects to the perfection of their moral, intellectual and physical nature in order that they may be of greatest possible use to themselves and others (Cott, 1977, p. 119). To do this, women would be exposed to a curriculum quite different from the "accomplishments" (map-drawing, painting, embroidery, sewing, and so forth) offered in other schools for young ladies. Rather, these schools broke through the barrier protecting the exclusivity of male knowledge by offering courses in the disciplines—rhetoric, logic, natural and moral philosophy, chemistry, history, and Latin (Cott, 1977, p. 115; Sklar, 1973, p. 62).

The founding of these schools and others like them signifies the attempt by women to disrupt the oppressive opposition between subject and object, or knower and known. By appropriating male knowledge, women sought to achieve the *status* of thinking, knowing subject, though their desire was not (at least at this point) to cross the boundary between man and woman, subject and object. The discourse never denied woman as mother, as womb, as Other. Instead, given *access* to the appropriate forms of knowledge, woman would *improve* her otherness, give it special value. She would be womb and more. She would be a *rational* mother by developing her mind. In Beecher's words, "The exercise of the mind makes [women] realize the high faculties and immortal destinies of our nature." Women would become "ministers" of the "family State" devoted to "the mission of self-denial" and the "self-sacrificing labor of training the ignorant and the weak" (Cross, 1965, p. 83; Sklar, 1973, p. 62).

Although introducing an important shift in the system of meaning producing male/female relations, this discourse did not challenge woman's social subjective position as servant to a male-dominated order. The desire for male knowledge as the key to women's *advancement* unconditionally accepted man as subject. Indeed, because the truth of woman was located in her reproductive body, it immediately excluded her from a capacity for reason by definition. Whereas it was "natural" for man to be rational, woman was other to rationality because of her reproductive "nature" and could only approach reason through a particular kind of education. This discourse thus reaffirms woman as man's inferior opposite by accepting him as the Absolute, the standard by which she should be measured.

Therefore, in participating in the discourse on knowledge, women did not seek to change their definition as other; rather, they sought to enhance that position, to give it value by introducing Reason (that which differentiated man and made him superior) into the definition.

Woman as Teacher

The discursive identification of woman as moral and rational guardian of children easily slid into a discussion of her qualifications as superior teacher in the public schools. With Beecher at the helm, a campaign to install women into teaching positions across the country was launched, allying the ideas of domestic reform and the discourse of motherlove with the rhetoric of the common school reformers.

The common school was envisioned by its founders as an institution to ensure a democratic and stable society. For writers like Beecher, struggling to assert women as having natural political influence, it was represented as the natural extension of the home where the nation would "receive its character and its destiny from her hands" (Beecher, 1846). Using the representation of woman produced within the discourse of domestic reform, these writers promoted her as best suited to the moral and democratic influence needed in the public schools. Based on her God-given moral superiority, women's childrearing labor could easily be transported into the public classroom.

> The educating of children, that is the true and noble profession of a woman—that is what is worthy of the noblest powers and affections, of the noblest minds . . . If our success equals our hopes, soon in all parts of our country, in each neglected village or new settlement, the Christian female will quietly take her station, collecting the ignorant children around her teaching them habits of neatness, order, thrift; opening the book of knowledge, inspiring principles of morality and awakening the hope of immortality. (Beecher, 1846, p. 51)

Promoting women's services as particularly crucial to the nation's future, these crusaders described the sufferings of working-class children, particularly those in the "uncivilized" West—ignorant, deprived, neglected—who would be transformed into examples of moral citizenry under the care of sensitive, educated women. Educated woman's self-sacrifice and mercy would lead the human race into salvation. The two places that this could be done were the home and the school. If the home was the church of woman's ministry, the school was only an extension of that, a means of bringing to the "vast multitude of neglected American children" a "proper education" and a "moral environment." By defining the other as in need, in this case children of other, ignorant women, this discourse produced the middle-class woman as superior, as leader and teacher of the degraded. Thus, she was defined and differentiated both as woman—man's opposite—and as part of a superior, more educated class.

The assertion of the middle-class woman as educator, grounded in her naturalized capacity for nurturance, produced her as a facilitator of knowledge. She was a reproducer of knowledge and of the knower, support for, yet opposite of the producer of knowledge (Walkerdine, 1985). ". . . If men have more knowledge, they have less talent at communicating it, nor have they the patience, the long suffering and gentleness necessary to superintend the formation of character," said Harriet Beecher Stowe (Woody, 1929, p. 463). Despite women's actual participation in producing a certain truth of womanhood, that truth presented woman as reproductive not productive. Women's discursive activity was practiced within relations of power and knowledge that repositioned them as servants in the reproduction of man, in particular, middle-class man.

In fact, the entire discourse on woman as educator revolved around her identification as reproducer. While women's maternal instincts would make them better teachers, teaching would make them better women. In Beecher's words:

> The greater purpose of a woman's life—the happy superintendence of a family—is accomplished all the better and easier by preliminary teaching in school. All the power she may develop here will come to use there. (Woody, 1929, p. 483)

Stated this way, woman does not threaten the male social symbolic order; rather, the hierarchical division between the sexes is preserved through this naturalized definition of their respective relations to knowledge. Just as subject is valued over object, productive knowledge is valued over reproductive knowledge. Man's superiority is maintained if veiled by the discursive projection of woman as teacher.

Furthermore, this differentiation between male and female relations to knowledge legitimated the employment of female teachers for less pay. As Horace Mann said,

> . . . a female will keep quite as good a school as a male at two thirds the expense, and will transfer into the minds of her pupils, purer elements, both of conduct and character, which will extend their refining and humanizing influence far outward into society and far onward into futurity. (Sugg, 1978, pp. 77–78)

In 1841, men teaching in rural schools were making an average of $4.15 per week while women were making only $2.51. The discrepancy was even greater in the urban schools where men and women had weekly salaries of $11.93 and $4.44 respectively. By 1864 the gap between salaries had further widened, making the average rural male teacher's salary $7.86 while women received only $4.92. It was apparently even more difficult to find men willing to teach in the cities, for those who did were paid $20.78, a generous salary compared to the $7.67 that women received that year (Elsbree, 1939, p. 274).

These gaps in salary signify the secondary position assigned women's relation to education and knowledge. Indeed, for many supporters of the common school movement, women's alleged superiority in the classroom was dubious, at best, indicating that the discourse on womanhood and education was not unified. Rather it was constituted of competing desires and knowledges which converged to inscribe the middle-class woman as educator. The grave need of public school teachers and the large pool of willing women, as opposed to the lack of men, forced some writers, like Thomas Galluadet, to admit to the possibility of women as a cheap source of labor:

> While we should encourage our young men to enter upon this patriotic field and . . . missionary field of duty and present much higher inducements to engage them to do so, I believe everyone must admit, that there is but little hope of attaining the full supply, or anything like it from that

sex. This will always be difficult, so long as there are so many other avenues open in our country to the accumulation of property, and in the attaining of distinction. We must, I am persuaded, look more to the other sex for aid in this emergency, and do all in our power to bring forward young women of necessary qualifications to be engaged in the business of Common School instruction. (Woody, 1929, p. 462)

Here, there is no shrouding of male superiority with assertions of woman's unique qualifications as in the rhetoric of domestic reform. This statement directly asserts man as master of the social order, as the Absolute with regard to knowledge and rationality in relation to which even "women of necessary qualifications," that is, women who had *attained* knowledge, remain the second choice, "the other sex."

Oppositional Discourses from the Association of Masters

Others argued most stridently against women's entrance into the once male-dominated arena of public education, producing what can be seen as counter-discourses in the production of woman as teacher. In 1844 an attack was mounted against Horace Mann and his plans to establish a network of normal schools for the preparation of (mostly female) teachers. The Association of Masters of the Boston Public Schools, a group of male educators whose pedagogy was based on the traditional principles derived from Calvinism, correctly perceived their positions as threatened by these plans. To fight what they saw as the installment of a "pedagogy of love" which directly criticized their own instructional philosophies, these men challenged Mann to battle.

The conflict was played out in a series of articles in which two opposing conceptions of education were expressed—a "preventative" conception versus a "curative" conception. These differing ideas sprang from the fundamental differences in the idea of human nature being expressed in traditional and liberal theological rhetoric. The Masters' arguments defended old pedagogical methods, which included the free use of the rod to correct undesirable flaws in children, while Mann and the common school supporters asserted a softer, more nurturant approach to the education of the child. Though they never directly attacked women as educators, the idea of the female NORMALITE was unquestionably unsettling for the Masters, who were struggling to hold on to a quickly eroding social position (Sugg, 1978). Ironically, their argument about educational method strengthened the definition of woman as gentle servant to society and thus affirmed woman's "natural" place as public school teachers.

In the end, the insistence on discipline and authoritative education was no match for motherlove. A new, less visible, and hence more powerful form of

---

NORMALITE: A term used for the young women who were training to become teachers in normal schools or institutions of teacher education.

Christian authority and regulation had been introduced. Public schools provided the space for new configurations of power and knowledge where social life could be closely monitored, organized, and controlled. With women settled in their places as guardians of the moral order, the middle class put into operation a system which would help insure its dominant future in a modern capitalist world.

Conclusion: The Educated Woman and the University

The educated woman as teacher was produced at the nexus of social transformation, of competing and contradictory desires, discourses, and practices. Within circulating relations of knowledge and power, a new truth re-presented woman. Her procreative body, once the source of exclusion, now became the means to her influence in a male-dominated social order.

In their passion to be someone and somewhere else, nineteenth-century middle-class women participated in the production of new knowledges about themselves that propelled them into new positions, both subjective and social. Part of the knowledge produced had to do specifically with their own relation to knowledge itself. That is, women began to insist on their need and ability to be educated, not in the traditional sense of women's education, but in schools modeled after the organization and presentation of knowledge for and by men. If women were to be educators of a rational and moral population, they needed "mental discipline," which could not be acquired in learning such "womanly accomplishments" as embroidery or cooking. The foundation of "normal schools," where women's "natural maternal instincts" could be organized, and disciplined, introduced women to a new set of knowledges, previously the exclusive domain of men. Beyond normal schools, women began to apply and to be accepted into universities, insisting upon the necessity of teachers to be "properly" educated. The opening of the West and the increasing need of teachers helped to justify their demands to doubtful administrators and trustees.

More importantly, however, the production of woman as educator introduced the very possibility of a relation between women and knowledge. Women's entrance into public education altered the space within which woman would now be defined; it changed the relational space of meaning within which women's lives were produced. This was the disruption needed by women in the last decades of the century to push themselves into the male-dominated realm of higher education and into the public sphere. Without it, without a shift in the way women thought of themselves, their demands for such access would not have been voiced at all. "Woman" as a social construction and subjective position would have remained completely external to a relation with the public sphere, with the sphere of market exchange and the exchange of knowledge.

Created within this burgeoning industrial capitalist system and supported by the interests and needs of a rising capitalist class, a new middle-class woman emerged, her function and identity as reproducer of man expanded to include man's knowledge. So defined, women's discursive struggles for the right to a place in higher education took place within specific boundaries, boundaries historically determined within a context of shifting POWER/KNOWLEDGE relations. An analysis of women's relation to knowledge and education must consider these conditions. The forms women's arguments took at the turn of the century were shaped by the subjective positions from which they spoke, positions created within the discursive context of the nineteenth century.

questions for discussion

1. Notice how the author uses the terms "woman" and "women." Why does she make this distinction? How does the distinction operate in this author's analysis?
2. In what ways do you see the intersection of class interests and the interests of patriarchy operating in these historical processes?
3. In what ways do you see the results of these historical processes of feminization still operating in schools and in the general conception of teaching today?
4. Can you identify any specific discourses or discursive practices that are currently contributing to the social construction of "woman" or of "man"? How do these constructions relate to our notions of what it means to be a teacher currently? Think about this in terms of your own day-to-day experiences.

teachers as researchers

Examine the ways in which the traces of "feminization" still exist in schools and shape the day-to-day lives of teachers and students. Find out who the main decision makers in your district are. How many men as compared to women? How is power distributed among men and women in your district, in your school? Interview teachers, administrators, and board members about their perceptions of what a teacher is. Devise questions that would begin to get at the ways gender plays a part in framing the lives of teachers and teaching. Are there differences in the ways that male and female teachers are perceived, or perceive each other? To what extent does the discourse of motherlove still function in today's schools?

suggested readings

Apple, M. (1989). *Teachers and texts.* New York: Routledge.
Cott, N. (1977). *The bonds of womanhood.* New Haven: Yale University Press.
Douglas, A. (1977). *The feminization of American culture.* New York: Avon Books.

POWER/KNOWLEDGE: This term is used by Foucault to describe the circular relation between power and knowledge. For a complete analysis of this relation see Jennifer Gore's essay in this book.

Hoffman, N. (1981). *Woman's "true profession": Voices from the history of teaching.* Boston: The Feminist Press.

Grumet, M. (1988). *Bitter milk: Women and teaching.* Amherst: University of Massachusetts Press.

Pagano, J. (1988). *Exiles and communities: Teaching in the patriarchal wilderness.* Albany: SUNY Press.

Tyack, D., & Hansot, E. (1982). *Managers of virtue: Public school leadership in America, 1820–1980.* New York: Basic Books.

r e f e r e n c e s

Beauvoir, S. de. (1953). *The second sex.* New York: Knopf.

Beecher, C. (1843). *Treatise on domestic economy for the use of young ladies at home and at school.* Boston: T. H. Webb.

Beecher, C. (1846). *The evils suffered by American women and American children: The causes and the remedy.* New York: Harper and Brothers.

Beecher, C., & Beecher Stowe, H. (1869). *The American woman's home, or principles of domestic science.* New York: J. B. Ford.

Child, L. M. (1835). *American frugal housewife.* Boston: Carter and Hendee and Co.

Cott, N. F. (1977). *The bonds of womanhood.* New Haven: Yale University Press.

Cross, B. M. (1965). *The educated woman in America.* New York: Teachers College Press.

Degler, C. N. (1980). *At odds: Women and the family in America from the revolution to the present.* New York: Oxford University Press.

Douglas, A. (1977). *The feminization of American culture.* New York: Knopf.

Elsbree, W. S. (1939). *The American teacher: Evolution of a profession in a democracy.* New York: American Book.

Foucault, M. (1989). An ethics of pleasure. In S. Lotringer (Ed.), J. Johnston (Trans.), *Foucault live: Interviews, 1966–84* (pp. 268–269). *Semiotext(e).*

Hale, S. (1868). *Manners.*

Kerber, L. K. (1980). *Women of the republic: Intellect and ideology in revolutionary America.* Chapel Hill: The University of North Carolina Press.

Kuhn, A. L. (1947). *The mother's role in childhood education: New England concepts, 1830–1860.* New Haven: Yale University Press.

Sklar, K. K. (1973). *Catharine Beecher: A study in American domesticity.* New Haven: Yale University Press.

Slater, P. G. (1977). *Children in the New England mind: in life and in death.* Hamden: Archon Books.

Sugg, R., Jr. (1978). *Motherteacher: The feminization of American education.* Charlottesville: University Press of Virginia.

Tyack, D., & Hansot, E. (1982). *Managers of virtue: Public school leadership in America, 1820–1980.* New York: Basic Books.

Walkerdine, V. (1985, April). Science and the female mind: The burden of proof. *PsychCritique, 1*(1), p. 10.

Willard, E. H. (1861). *Educational biographies, memoirs of teachers, educators and promoters and benefactors of education, literature and science, part one. Teachers and educators.* New York: F. C. Brownell.

Woody, T. (1929). *A history of women's education in the United States.* New York: The Science Press.

chapter 12

Margaret A. Haley, 1861–1939

A Timeless Mentor for Teachers as Leaders

Maureen McCormack

guiding questions

1. What is the author trying to say or teach?
2. What is the significance of what you read here for you personally and for you as a teacher?
3. What are the perspectives drawn on by the author to make the analysis?
4. How does this analysis help to inform our practice in classrooms?

It has been concluded by some that America's best and brightest do not choose to become public school educators. Further, it has been said that the few who do make this choice rarely remain in public education. We might speculate from the recent recruitment advertisements for teachers why this is so. Posters, magazine ads, and media recruitment in the eighties and early nineties sought to interest "the best and the brightest" by appealing to career desires for power and leadership and for making a difference. Simultaneous with this recruitment is that of a private foundation, Teach for America, which is seeking talented young people to make a two-year commitment to public school teaching in rural and urban America, basing its appeal for service on national security.

These events awaken us to an unpleasant reality—marketing of teaching careers needs to sell the idea that teaching has significant meaning. That young people have to be "sold" this idea is both sobering, depressing, and alarming to those within and without the profession who wish to raise the practice of education beyond the production of mediocrity and drop outs.

It appears that currently the profession of education has few stars and little inspirational leadership. I offer the following in the hope that this story can alert us to the kind of commitment and values America needs from her best and brightest. It is because of her dedicated, passionate, and intelligent leadership that Margaret A. Haley makes a timeless mentor for all educators who would like to make a difference.

> I have usually visioned myself as so integrally part of the teaching force that, although, I have not been in a schoolroom for almost forty years, I record myself, almost unconsciously, as a teacher. It is as a teacher . . . that I want to emphasize to other teachers, . . . what they must do to hold their heritage of freedom. (Haley, 1982, p. 270)

With these words Margaret A. Haley, 1861–1939, began the final chapter of her autobiography. Although Haley was and is best known as the dynamic leader of the Chicago Teachers Federation (CTF), her story, *Battleground, The Autobiography of Margaret A. Haley** (Haley, 1982) reveals that she pursued several other roles as well. Robert L. Reid, editor of Haley's autobiography, describes Haley's narrative as that of a "grade school teacher, a social reformer, and a labor advocate." I would add that a further look at her life work reveals other equally significant voices, that of a teacher leader and teacher educator, a democratic feminist, and a social philosopher. In this essay I argue that these latter dimensions of Haley, in particular her passionate commitment as a teacher leader, make her a natural mentor for those who would lead from both inside and outside the classroom.

Much has been said during the present wave of education reform about school principals assuming the mantle of instructional leader. Little has been said, however, about the instructional role of teacher union leaders. In this time of union bashing and calls for teacher union reform, Haley can teach us a lot about the need for teachers as leaders. In this sense, Haley has a significant contemporary role to play in the reform of teacher education.

---

*Unless otherwise cited, this work is the source for the references to Haley's thought.

Introduction

//

Many have written of Margaret A. Haley's efforts as a labor leader. In that role Haley appeared as a heroic figure, fighting against great odds as she took on entrenched educational, political, and economic bureaucracies. While most of her work was in Chicago and the state of Illinois, she also took on a national bureaucracy, the National Education Association, and campaigned for national women's suffrage. Numerous researchers have captured and assessed her many long struggles to combat oppressive and unfair legislation that in her words "placed the burden of taxation upon the little fellow, while allowing the big fellows to escape."

My own historiography has highlighted Haley's efforts to define an alternative meaning of education for women (McCormack, 1988). In this chapter I ask the reader to further consider her work, even that which falls within labor advocacy, as a leader for teachers. While I have argued elsewhere the significant role of Haley as a teacher educator (McCormack, 1988), I ask the reader here to consider the appropriateness of the dual nature of Haley's position as leader of the Chicago Teacher Federation and of teachers as citizen leaders. My belief that Haley should serve her teacher union as an instructional leader is not without precedent. Ella Flagg Young, a contemporary of Haley and the superintendent of the Chicago Schools, argued that Haley should handle the CTF "as an educational institution" (Haley, 1982).

I argue that Haley provides a timeless teacher education mentor as a teacher leader, union leader, and educator. This mentorship is especially significant for those committed to the social foundations of education. It is the purpose of social foundations to provide an interpretive focus for education as it seeks to unite theoretical perspectives with praxis. To this tapestry Haley provides a lived experience that can educate us to the spiritual and material dynamics that taken together give direction to the purpose for public school education. By example, she provides us with an alternative idea of women as educators, departing from the traditional perspective of teachers as martyrs and bringing a social philosophy to a democratic conception of feminism.

The following personal sketch will hopefully grant an understanding of those values that sustained Haley's long, challenging, and brilliant commitment as a teacher leader.

Haley's Personal Reality

//

Margaret A. Haley, 1861–1939, was born to a working-class family at the beginning of the Civil War and died as World War II was about to begin. Her life spanned a time of great change, from self-made entrepreneurs to corporate entities; from an agrarian-based economy to an urban industrial economy; from women who sought small increases in autonomy via deference to male prerogatives to certain women who claimed democratic equality; from the domination of rural schooling and local control of school to urban schooling and decreased local control; and, finally, from volunteer public schooling to compulsory schooling.

Haley's autobiography reveals that her family socialization resulted in her sensitivity to social injustice. She learned from her Irish immigrant parents how withholding a proper education to a group of people resulted in their inferiorization and discrimination. She learned also that schooling did not guarantee a proper education—her classroom teacher never taught her to read, but her mother did. Additionally, her father dramatically demonstrated his respect for those who fought for justice, in particular Susan B. Anthony. Thus, her home socialization paved the way for values that would dominate her adult life.

It was also in her childhood that she developed her interest in economics. Her awareness and education came from readings in economics, as well as from firsthand experience. Haley learned the destructive power of financial manipulation when her father lost his small business because he refused to accept a bribe. To help support her family, Haley, at sixteen, became a teacher. Thus, it is not surprising that she should place great emphasis on the necessity for teachers to awaken to the precarious nexus of labor, social well-being, and greed.

Haley's memorial tribute noted that her physical appearance could be disarming when preceded by her reputation as "lady labor slugger." Haley was an attractive and petite woman with a flashing smile and a love of fashionable clothes. Her penchant for fashion combined with a passionate commitment to academic freedom, social democracy, labor, and politics to give her a larger-than-life character. However, by her own admission, she was not always so committed. She admitted to being transformed, after nearly twenty years of teaching, from a naive and conforming woman to a steadfast fighter for social justice and democracy. She found her "battleground" in the affairs of public interest as they found expression in and with public education. Steinhart (1991) argues that her enemies opposed her because they recognized that her steadfast commitment and energy was meant to make democracy survive. Apparently true democracy had its enemies.

Turning to Haley's own description of her lifework captures the larger context in which she saw herself:

> I had gone forth from it [the Illinois prairie] to the village, the town, the city. I had fallen in with the surging cavalcade of my generation. I had joined the army of women laboring for daily bread. I had fought for what I felt was right on a gory battlefield. That is the sum of my story.
>
> To me—because it has always been [a] quest—life has been high romance. The circumstances of living may have been difficult at times, but life itself has been a great glowing adventure. Work has been more than compensation. It has been thrilling joy. Sadness has come to me often . . . deaths . . . I did not survive them. I lived through them. I have met, too, treacheries that leave a deeper sadness than does loss. Always, though, I have met the next day with the courage to take up the banner again.

> I have been, I realize, merely a scout from the ranks of the besieged. If my work has any value to any one but myself, it will be because, at one point of the battleground, I have given service to my comrade-in-arms. Now that my work must be nearly done, the one service I can still give is my plea that they [educators] hold the field. (Haley, 1982, pp. 275–276)

In these words Haley reveals her passion and her life project. Her "work" was not just work; it was her identity; it was her love. We should not lose sight of this personal commitment to a good beyond her own when we think of the factors that generate leadership. Haley had a cause, a noble one, and she knew it.

For forty years as the leader of a radical teachers union, the CTF, she represented the interests of Chicago teachers and children as she did battle with what she believed were the "foes of democracy." According to Haley, the foes of democracy were those who placed the industrial ideal, capitalism, above the democratic ideal. These two ideals were not synonymous; in fact, they represented two opposing poles of interests and values. It was not possible, stated Haley, for there to be two masters. American educators had to decide which master or value system should lead the schools and thus the nation. Repeatedly Haley challenged educators to confront the substance and consequence of these two oppositional interests.

Haley saw that, for the most part, the foes of an ideal democracy were big businessmen, who conspired with politicians and educators to make the public schools an instrument for their interests, as against the interests of the COMMONWEAL. However, big businesses were not the only foes. Other foes of democracy were those educators who remained naive to the machinations of power and greed as they found expression in matters of economics, taxation, property evaluation, and the control of knowledge and academic freedom both within and without public school education.

Haley as Teacher and Union Leader

Haley stated that she had no more preparation to become a union labor leader than she had to become a teacher, which was none. Like her entrance into teaching, her initiation into union work came about without much warning. Having completed nearly twenty years of grade school teaching, Haley found herself in the late 1890s embroiled with other Chicago grade school teachers in a fight to save their small pensions. With another teacher, Catherine Goggin, Haley represented the teachers successfully, stopping the takeover of their pension funds. Thus, it was to Haley and Goggin that the teachers turned for continuing leadership.

COMMONWEAL: The interests of the community or of the masses.

In 1897 the Chicago grade school teachers established what was to become one of the pioneer activist teacher unions of America, the Chicago Teachers Federation (CTF), a forerunner of the present American Federation of Teachers. Because Haley and Goggin had to leave their classrooms, the primary school teachers sacrificed part of their already meager salaries to pay them. The teachers asked for and supported Haley's and Goggin's leadership in response to two major events.

Principals and high school teachers historically received pay increases. However, many years of neglect and exploitation with no pay raises characterized the plight of the grade school teachers, who were about 96 percent female. Because the teachers lacked a proper academic and professional education they were unprepared for the most difficult teaching assignments. The poorest conditions for teaching and learning in America could be found in the Chicago public schools. Overcrowded classrooms lacking basic resources were further exacerbated by new compulsory school laws that forced many reluctant, poor, and non-English speaking immigrant children to leave their jobs and attend school. In addition, for several years an inadequate school budget forced the premature closing of schools for lack of funds. Thus, the attempted removal of the teacher pension served as the proverbial "last straw" and a first rallying point for the teachers.

The second came when Haley learned of a possible reason for the inadequate school funding. Haley brought to the teachers' attention a rumor that large business interests were not paying their fair share of taxes, because of a deliberate lack of assessment of all their property assets. Haley and Goggin were asked to investigate. The story that followed was one of high drama. Haley's foes frustrated her every effort to ferret out the truth. Because part of her challenge was to end the unfair deals between the school board and the newspapers, Haley became forever a villain in the eyes of several major Chicago newspapers. Prior to losing her partner to death in 1916, Haley and the CTF successfully won a suit demanding the proper valuation of most major businesses and public utilities and payment of the uncollected taxes. Although the courts returned to the school board over a half million dollars, legal measures were required to get the school board to give the teachers their long-awaited and promised raises (Haley, 1982, pp. 42–85).

While the battle against unfair property assessments continued throughout her career, Haley also did battle on yet another front. To understand this arena of struggle, it is helpful to see the larger social context of this era.

Progressive Educational Reform

Many diverse calls for social reform were made at the turn of the century. Reforms were conceived as some form of progress. Some movements for reform had working-class roots; others were driven by elites. One such elite group calling for the reform and restructuring of education was a partnership of businessmen, university presidents, and school superintendents. This group, now conceived as progressive administrators, aimed to reconstruct the American school to better serve the needs of a changing American workforce (Tyack, 1980). From the struggle to find a means to justify a more specialized curriculum for the workforce, a compromise resulted. A new high school idea won acceptance.

Called the comprehensive high school, this new high school initiated a three-track curriculum system, a marked departure from the traditional single curriculum offered in the past. This tracking system brought with it a drive for standardization of curriculum, testing, and methods that set in motion a complex process that would reduce the academic freedom of a classroom teacher. This mode of education became the common twentieth-century curriculum format for high school education (Spring, 1990).

Accompanying this tracking system was a reorganization of the school administrative structure. Designed for national implementation, this education reform required state initiatives. In Illinois the reorganization legislation emerged as the Harper Bill, named after the University of Chicago president who was the major educator involved in that state's initiative. The reorganization followed the bureaucratic design of the developing industrial organizations. Such a design called for the creation of an "expert" to head the new educational organization and the reduction in size and power of the local school boards. It also gave most authority to the expert manager, called the superintendent.

Margaret Haley objected to this design, arguing that it eroded local control of the schools and, thus, directly reduced the practice of democracy. This new school superintendent would direct through a chain of command a multileveled, top-down hierarchy characterized by specialized role functions. This structure was clearly not democratic (Haley, 1903; 1982). Parallels to state restructuring during the 1980s and 1990s are obvious.

Haley saw this new structure as further eroding teacher autonomy because it presumed, in her words, only the head of the school system to have any "grey matter," that is mental ability (Haley, 1903). She opposed this reorganization because it appeared to be fundamentally undemocratic and because it would reduce teacher initiative, thereby encouraging teachers to take less responsibility for their teaching.

Teachers were given no opportunity to provide input to this school reform. The reform was the collective brainchild of a group of university presidents and school administrators who came together through their membership and direction of the National Education Association, the NEA. Although teachers were the rank and file of NEA, they had no power and thus no say in the policies and actions advocated by this professional education association.

The Industrial Philosophy Brought to Education

Giving support to and filling out the new bureaucratic design was a new "theory" called efficiency or scientific management. Scientific efficiency held that workers could be better managed and more profitably educated if required to know only an isolated and specialized body of knowledge. Thus, each occupational role would require only a limited knowledge base. Seeing this new conception of teaching as an expression of authoritarianism, and not autonomy, Haley urged her fellow teachers to resist such a plan of organization and philosophy (Haley, 1903). Haley recognized the consequences to a democracy of the exploitation of teachers as factory laborers or technicians.

Within the progressive administrative group were several who advocated a dual school system. It was a success of the CTF and Haley's personal efforts that the Cooley Vocational Bill was defeated in 1913. Its passage would have created a dual school system in Illinois and would have separated cultural education from industrial. Such a state of affairs, argued Haley, was desired by those who understood that the less children knew about their historic and cultural values, the more easily they could be subordinated to factory service (Haley, 1982, p. 211). Unfortunately, the successes of the union were not to last.

In Illinois the Harper Bill, which contained the new reorganization plan, was repeatedly introduced into the legislature. Initially it was defeated by the efforts of the CTF. However, when it was reincarnated as the Otis Bill, it succeeded against CTF opposition under Haley.

The Death Knell of Teacher Power

Two events preceded the passage of the Otis Bill in 1917 that may well have lessened Haley's personal strength and/or resolve for another successful resistance of the school restructuring bill. Early in 1916, Haley lost to accidental death her CTF colleague and dearest friend, Catherine Goggin. Haley wrote of Goggin's death (and others), "that I did not survive them, I only lived through them." While Haley was in what we could expect was a state of shock over the death of her friend, the Chicago school board passed a bill that fired teachers affiliated with a labor organization. Because the CTF had affiliated with the American Federation of Labor to gain clout from the male voters (women could not vote), many teachers lost their position at this time. Haley was clearly devastated by the firings.

Curricular Reform

The epitome of the specialized curriculum, social efficiency, and school reorganization came with the creation of the platoon system. In 1924, Haley, writing for *The New Republic,* said schooling in America had come to resemble a factory. Like Ford cars, children were now seen first as products, something to be used as human capital. Hailed by many administrators and businessmen as a great cost saver, the platoon plan placed 10 to 70 percent more children in a school than there was room for. The extra children were kept in a holding area until it was their time to be passed to a teacher. Six-year-old children would have as many as six or seven teachers a day. Teachers would see as many as four hundred children a day and up to a thousand per week. As Haley said, "The lack of money was given as justification for the organization of the schools on a mechanical basis." However, most astounding and disturbing to Haley was that university professors gave their acceptance to such a plan (Haley, 1924).

The results of the platoon system pointed to the serious effects of the new doctrine of efficiency, which supported the reorganized American school. The doctrine appeared to give legitimation to inadequate educational funding. The lack of funding became an acceptable excuse for the implementation and production of a mechanical pedagogy. The platoon system was a natural consequence of the concern for efficiency that sought to do more with less, a perspective that dominated administrative direction. (This "more with less" doctrine has resurfaced in the reform movement of the 1990s.)

The Growth of Teacher Alienation

A second and more serious effect of the new ideology was its impact on the public mind (Haley, 1903). As Haley stated, even university educators appeared subject to vitiation by the industrial ideal. The seductiveness of the industrial ideal and its effect upon educators dominated Haley's thoughts during the 1920s, a decade in which she came to a new realization of the growing power of the industrial ideology. In fact, Haley's optimism for the survival of democracy grew dim.

In a series of articles published in the *Daily News,* Haley (1928) observed that the fighting spirit was gone from many teachers. She reckoned that the cause was one of two things: either the teachers' hopes had been dashed for too long, and thus their spirits had given way to a resocialization to the organization ideology, or the seductiveness of leisure and money promised by the industrial ideal had more appeal than the ideals of democracy. This latter reasoning by Haley reflects that other educators did not share her meaning of democracy as a social as well as a political philosophy.

Haley's Political Philosophy

Apparently, Haley found it hard to accept that others could equate the values of democracy with the values of commercialism. Haley's sense of democracy was not based in liberalism, but it appears that liberalism's conception of democracy did dominate the ranks of teachers. Dietz (1989) has argued that the pursuit of a good life under liberalism is not a "morally virtuous society" but equal access to pursuing "profit according to the rules of the market." Therefore what citizenship means to a liberal conception of democracy is more of an economic activity than collective and individual participation as citizens in and for the public good. Dietz has also argued that liberal political philosophy possesses real threats to feminist values. I believe Haley's meaning of democracy, and her feminism, was about commitment to the moral life of society. Such a feminism and commitment to democracy requires a political consciousness and participation that results in active citizenship. One major point of Haley's moral activism, of course, was her focus on the inequities in education. She believed such inequities were structured by, and resulted from, the pursuit and realization of the profit motive. Such inequities were found in method, curriculum, organization, and policy.

The correctness of Haley's insistence on focusing on school financing was borne out time and again, but never more so than with the adoption of the platoon system. The inequities in the platoon system certainly affirmed her commitment to challenging the status quo on unfair tax assessments and other monetary activities that made vulnerable the democratic freedom of the American school system. Thus, she continued until her death to demand fair enforcement of existing laws and to confront legislation and tax evasion that threatened the commonweal. The platoon system reflected the need for another ongoing battlefront, that is, the struggle for academic freedom.

Teachers as Decision Makers: Academic Freedom

Haley noted that under Superintendent Ella Flagg Young, 1909–1915, teacher councils had been initiated and a real effort had begun to effuse the system with a democratic structure. The teacher councils were a means, said Haley, to allow the teachers to develop a code of ethics that reflected their autonomy and commitment to democratic education (Haley, 1982, p. 285). While the councils were banished with Young's successor, they were reinstated in the next superintendency, only to be abolished again in 1924 by the school board under the direction of Superintendent McAndrews. Haley saw this removal as a serious blow to the professional esteem of the teachers. Haley wrote,

> In 1924, the Board passed an amendment . . . denying to members of voluntary organizations of teachers the right to freedom of communication on school grounds, outside of school hours, in regard to business of their organization. (Haley, 1982, p. 209)

Haley believed this rule was passed to penalize the teachers for voting against the platoon schools.

This punitive measure was directed by McAndrews, who, in his earlier years as an educator, appeared to support the democratic cause. Once established as an administrator, however, he supported the industrial ideal. While in previous years an expressed erosion of democracy came with the firing of excellent teachers who insisted upon the right to choose their own texts, the focus in the twenties became the manipulation of history texts. Thus it was that Haley wrote:

> Ever since the World War, the great forces of reaction have recognized the advisability of controlling the thought of the children who were passing through the public schools. They have known that, if these children learned the true answers to the true questions of our modern civilization, they, grown into manhood and womanhood, would change the system which continued special privilege for the few and injustice for the many (1982, p. 173).

While we see here expressed Haley's concern about the control of thought for students, her many addresses to teachers show a similar concern for the

American teacher. In fact, the CTF established from its beginning a plan to further formal teacher education ("Report," 1898). The purpose was to educate teachers in all areas not formally expected of teacher education. Thus, Haley's early years directing the CTF were marked by her role as a teacher educator (McCormack, 1988).

Haley as Teacher Transformation Leader

Haley wrote, "If teachers are to teach children of the nation how to think clearly and constructively on matters of national importance, they must first learn their own lessons" (1982, p. 272). What did Haley consider the teachers' own lessons? And how did Haley think the teachers were to become educated?

Although grade school teachers had little encouragement to secure an education beyond high school, Haley participated in a self-directed plan to further her own education. Thus, she expected and encouraged other women teachers to continue their education. To support this effort the union established a department of teacher education for the explicit purposes of making up for the neglect of general teacher education and finding out if the charges of incompetency against them were true and, if so, assisting in remediation. This department held regular after school and Saturday classes with noted speakers as well as local teachers. Summarized lectures appeared in the *Chicago Teachers Federation's Bulletin,* as did the calendar of lecturers and their topics. This emphasis indicates Haley's recognition of the significance of intellectual enlightenment to realizing the democratic ideal.

Haley resented the severe criticism of the grade school teachers by businessmen and certain school administrators. She reminded the teachers that they had not established the standards or the expectations for qualified teachers. While she managed to turn the finger of blame round to higher administration, she insisted that teachers needed to study "intensively and intensely" real issues, not just to take courses for credit. In keeping with the times, Haley urged scientific study both for academic ability and professional skills. Such an education was necessary for teachers to remove their "inferiority complex" and to make sure they stimulated the natural curiosity of their students. She told them it was necessary to place their teaching efforts within an informed scientific perspective. Though she has been accused of holding a naive perspective on the "goodness" of science (Morris, 1992), she was clearly more concerned that teachers develop a democratic perspective on teaching, learning, and administering.

Even the most cursory reading of Haley's addresses to teachers reveals her teacher leader focus. I submit that Haley's intent was for the American grade school teacher to transform this nation into an ideal democracy (Haley, 1903). However, Haley saw that such a transformation was unlikely when teachers did not know the meaning of being free. Therefore, she insisted that ". . . the teacher must be *made* to realize that she is a free human being" (Haley, 1982,

p. 273). In an apparent paradox, Haley, in her teacher educator role, revealed that while freedom is a right, what constitutes it must be learned. Once the teachers had learned "their lessons" about the nature of freedom and responsibility only then could they teach it. But of greater need was that teachers embrace an ethical commitment to give service to democratic freedom. Thus, teachers needed a diligent education on the vicissitudes that make for the power relations that govern any context of freedom.

Haley agreed with the conclusions of her mentor, Ella Flagg Young, that while many did not know the meaning of being free, women were especially unaware. This fact and how to overcome it remain a most fundamental challenge. Teachers for a social democracy must embrace personal autonomy, yet most are naive to their unfreedom. Haley also knew that while teacher leadership required autonomous assertion and activity, it meant living with greater anxiety. In her many after-school-hour addresses Haley modeled this challenge. Haley often used the term "awake" in her addresses to teachers, and reflecting upon her personal story, I submit that she meant to shatter their naivete to power relations. She did so by relating with graphic clarity and passion what she and others were learning about the obstacles to better teaching and learning. These obstacles ranged from the evasion of fair taxation and policies that favored the wealthy to educational decisions that removed the necessity for responsible teaching from the teachers. In an effort to woo teachers she drew for them pictures of teachers who acted for the betterment of all while framing it as the politics of democracy. She repeatedly told them how courageous they were to resist authoritarian school policies. It appears that she tried to make of their resistance a solidarity of pride in service to a democratic America.

In addition she shared with them the words of her mentors, one being Colonel Parker. "The ideal of education controls both method and means. A republic can logically hold but one ideal, and that is to make of each individual child all that he (she) possibly can be." "Citizenship, in the best sense of the word, cannot possibly be attained under any other striving but towards the highest goal." "Happiness is in ourselves, and is the outcome of devotion to something not ourselves" (CTF Bulletin, 1902). With such she hoped to help the teachers to see past the self-serving school/state funding rhetoric.

Haley detailed how inadequate school funding led to poor working conditions for teachers and students. What was good for the child, said Haley, was good for the teacher, and freedom was good for both. Inadequate funding encouraged large classroom size and encouraged efficiency oriented instruction that eliminated responsive teaching to individual interest, development, and needs. It led to shallow learning as teachers relied upon rote and drill. Such pedagogy was antithetical to the expressed needs for proper childhood learning. Children, Haley reminded teachers, needed activity for learning. Yet, the standardization of group instructional method worked against activity learning. Thus, teachers were to become "automatons" who could not possibly invest in the care of children as children.

Haley hoped that a bipartisan consensus might be possible if the various reformers could be brought together on a common concern, the welfare of the child. If a consensus could be obtained on what was best for the child, an approach or plan would then follow for the proper working conditions, curriculum, instruction, and teacher education. Such an effort was necessary in order to enlighten those reformers who insisted that the child was nothing but a resource for industry.

Haley considered controlling the thought of children, for whatever reason, as robbing the nation of many gifts. Such a robbery would have negative long-term effects on individuals as well as on the nation. "That's when the nation will blame, with reason, the American public school teacher . . .", said Haley. This control of thought represented an outright evil that stemmed from greed and ignorance (Haley, 1982, p. 274).

Thus, Haley called for the formal education of teachers to include the power relations of economics and politics. Haley wanted teachers to understand the workings of power within the social system, especially those essentials of property valuation and taxation. This meant that teachers must have more than a nodding acquaintance with the "methods and purposes" of those who would control, be they in or out of public office. In addition, teachers needed to know the fundamentals of democracy—that is, that freedom of choice meant a freed intelligence, not a controlled intelligence. Teachers also needed to know how to use the legal procedures of a democracy, such as the initiative, referendum, and recall procedures, as well as how to use parliamentary procedures, so they could correct public wrongdoing. Because legislation could work against the interest of democracy, teachers had to understand the social-political texts that constituted the production and reproduction of information. However, Haley recognized that teachers had no voice on an individual basis and she urged them to organize as had other laborers.

Unions as Transformative Organizations

I argue then that Haley thought it was possible to give teachers a grassroots experience of democracy through the collective life and work of the union. It was in her address in 1904 on "Why Teachers Should Organize" that she first confronted teachers with the need to overcome their authoritarian socialization. Haley reminded her audience that most Americans did not know the meaning of democracy, that few, if any, had ever experienced it. She also cautioned those who would organize teachers on the necessity to retain democratic practices. A nondemocratic organization would defeat the purpose of organizing, "for teacher organizations must be in harmony with the fundamental object of the public school in a democracy, to preserve and develop the democratic idea" (Haley, 1982, p. 280). Likewise, said Haley, a "false or incomplete educational ideal" will "fail to free the intelligence necessary for the work of constructing a democracy out of our monarchical inheritance" (Haley, 1982, p. 281).

One of her motivating questions seemed to ask how citizens were to embrace democracy when they had no way in which to learn it or to practice it. A partial answer to this question may well be reflected in the CTF union constitution. The first requirement was that members be taught how to use parliamentary procedure. In this union effort members were thus introduced to the use of democratic procedures for conducting their public business. But teacher organization needs more than technical ability.

Inspiration as a Necessity for Transformation

Haley found inspiration from several individuals, all lovers of democracy and moral leaders, and she attempted to carry forward the inspiration she had received. The emphasis on inspiration was meant to work as a form of consciousness-raising, and this spirit was present in the *Chicago Teachers Federation Bulletin* and later in the *Margaret Haley Bulletin*. These newsletters carried graphic accounts of her activities with dialogue, intrigue, frustration, anger, and joy. Included in these bulletins were inspirational addresses by others, including John Dewey, Ella Flagg Young, Jane Addams, and William James. A letter from Susan B. Anthony urging the teachers to act on behalf of women's rights was printed in full. Anthony reminded the women teachers that what teachers did in the past made it possible for them "to be ignored" in the present. Thus, to remedy their present working conditions, they would have to make a stand (Anthony, 1903). In addition, human interest stories captured the moral sense of democracy and high praise flowed for those teachers and others who stood up like soldiers for justice both within and outside education. Included also were the member names and agendas of various teacher councils and the dates and places of noteworthy public lectures.

Continuing in this same vein, Haley told the teachers that their work was the most noble. She argued forcefully that the salvation of the republic and of democracy remained with them, "for you alone teach one hundred percent of those who pass through public education." She did so knowing that many teachers needed to be removed from their classrooms. Yet, she insisted that it was the fellow teachers who needed to shape their profession with their own code of ethics and it was the teachers who needed to assume the dominant position relative to teaching and learning in the schools.

Unfortunately, all leadership was coming from outside education and such leadership did not have moral democratic aims. Fearing that the absence of teacher leadership resulted in part from the fear of speaking up, Haley hoped to encourage a moral vision of teaching that would empower women to politically astute leadership. Central to this was the creation and adoption of a teacher code of ethics that mandated academic freedom.

Transforming the NEA

Haley attempted to reform the leading educational policymaker, the National Education Association. Breaking the long tradition of women teachers being seen but not heard, Haley became in 1901 the first woman to speak from its public forum. She challenged the grand face being put upon public education by the then commissioner of education, William T. Harris, as well as his wish that wealthy industrialists contribute to the schools. To this latter wish, Haley responded that the public would no longer own their own schools if private industrialists paid for schooling. Although she invited Harris to talk with her and to see for himself the real conditions in the urban elementary schools, he dismissed her as one of many "hysterical" grade school teachers (Haley, 1982).

Haley was determined to transform the control of the organization and she did meet with some success. Under her leadership, the first woman president, Ella Flagg Young, was elected and alternate sex leadership commenced. In addition, Haley led the creation of a department that gave focus to the concerns of grade school teachers, theretofore ignored.

It was to this body of nationally assembled teachers that she delivered her now famous speech calling for collective, democratic activism by public school teachers. In "Why Teachers Should Organize" Haley stated it was the ethical responsibility of teachers to "challenge the existing conditions" of public education. She reminded the teachers that it was the responsibility of the public to create the schools their children deserved. In this plea Haley asked the teachers to assist the American public in seeing a vision and purpose of the American school that was larger than that of the industrial ideal. While urging teachers to see an education that was in harmony with the ideals of freedom, she also chastised educators for their lack of leadership in the development of the democratic ideal. Haley stated, "We teachers are responsible for existing conditions to the extent that the schools have not inspired true ideals of democracy . . ." (Haley, 1982, p. 281). In this address she stressed the role of the teacher as modeling democratic practices. The first aim of the American teacher should be to equip the nation with intelligent citizens able to think by using their own freed intellectual power and to effuse their activity with a "moral courage" when seeking solutions to the industrial questions of the nation. With these fundamental words she cautioned American educators:

> Two ideals are struggling for supremacy in American life today: one the industrial ideal, culminating through the supremacy of commercialism, which subordinates the worker to the product and the machine; the other, the ideal of democracy, the ideal of the educators, which places humanity above all machines, and demands that all activity shall be the expression of life. If this ideal of the educators cannot be carried over into the industrial field, then the ideal of industrialism will be carried over into the school. These two ideals can no more continue to exist in American life than our nation could have continued half slave and half free. If the school cannot bring joy to the work of the world, the joy must go out of its own life, and work in the school as in the factory will become drudgery. (1982, p. 286)

I believe these words reveal Haley's democratic feminism. Seeing that devotion to democracy had to preempt all other ideals, she placed her meaning of democracy within feminist values, that is, the elevation and nurturance of all life. Here she reminds us that we cannot separate politics from the quality of life. In weaving together the spiritual, the physical, the social, and the political, she offered an alternative vision of caring. In so doing, she also offered feminist teachers an alternative conception of politics.

Conclusion

I have argued that Margaret A. Haley was a teacher extraordinaire whose efforts make her a timeless mentor for teacher leaders and teacher educators, especially those teachers concerned with the social foundations of education. With passion for a participatory democracy, she brought to the field of education a focus on democracy; to women as teachers she showed that an alternative vision of the public school teacher was necessary and possible; to the grade school teacher, male or female, she gave a new vision of nobility and courage; to teachers and teacher educators she shifted the emphasis from following the leader to being a leader of social ethics. She cast democracy as a practice of social ethics as opposed to economic ethics, and, as a feminist, she made the politics of a participatory democracy her social philosophy.

In so doing, Haley never separated politics from caring. Thus, she presented to women teachers an alternative to the maternal teacher tradition with its ethics marked by docility and subordination. This uniting of politics and caring separated Haley from traditional public educators who made of politics something for charlatans only, and who cared only for those not involved in politics. In so doing, Haley changed the nature of caring from private politics to full public participation. Thus, she offers us an alternative to the singular and still dominant mode for teacher education. Haley offers to those who love a democracy and wish to embrace a commitment to it an appropriate gift, a noble teacher project. She placed her feminism within the credo of "the personal is political" as she made doing in the public realm an imperative to caring, and she offers contemporary teachers a model of the teacher as an active rather than a passive citizen.

Articulating her politics of democracy as standing in direct opposition to those of greed, Haley saw the foes of democracy as those who would make the purpose of education a servant of the industrial ideal or of unlimited exploitation. Thus, she called for a teacher education that would inform and awaken the teachers of America to the realities of power in the social system, of greed, with its various faces in policy, school organization, and instruction and curriculum that are channeled through the teacher. While alerting us to the many roadblocks to personal transformation that make our resocialization as democratic teachers most difficult, Haley saw the reform of schooling necessitating an end to political naivete and a teacher commitment to democratic citizenship.

Nearly a hundred years ago she prophesied only too well what has come to be. Again, her words say it all:

> Today, teachers of America, we stand at the parting of the ways. Democracy is not on trial, but America is. (1982, p. 287)

q u e s t i o n s   f o r   d i s c u s s i o n

1. What social value systems stood in opposition to each other? Describe the value differences.
2. What was lacking in the education of teachers? How does your education compare to that urged by Haley?
3. How do you think Haley would respond to the reforms that give direction of the schools to corporations and politicians?
4. Why did Haley believe unionizing was essential for teacher professionalization?
5. Why was freedom for teachers seen as essential to keeping a democracy?

t e a c h e r s   a s   r e s e a r c h e r s

Do a comparative analysis on the significance of teacher autonomy as found in the work of Margaret Haley and in contemporary writings on teacher leadership.

s u g g e s t e d   r e a d i n g s

Haley, M. (1982). *Battleground, the autobiography of Margaret Haley.* Chicago: University of Illinois Press.

Herbst, J. (1989). And sadly teach: Teacher education and professionalization in American culture. Madison: University of Wisconsin Press.

Hogan, D. J. (1985). *Class and reform: Schools and society in Chicago 1880–1930.* Philadelphia: University of Pennsylvania Press.

Tyack, D. (1980). *The one best system: A history of urban education.* Cambridge: Harvard University Press.

Urban, W. (1982). *Why teachers organized.* Detroit: Wayne State University Press.

Wrigley, J. (1982). *Class politics and public schools: Chicago 1900–1950.* New Brunswick, NJ: Rutgers University Press.

r e f e r e n c e s

Anthony, S. B. (1903). A letter to Margaret A. Haley. *Chicago Teachers Federation Bulletin, 1.*

Deitz, M. G. (1989). Context is all: Feminism and theories of citizenship. In J. K. Conway, S. C. Bourque, & J. W. Scott (Eds.), *Learning about women: Gender, politics and power* (pp. 1–24). Ann Arbor: University of Michigan Press.

Haley, M. A. (1902). *Chicago Teacher Federation Bulletin,* February 7 and March 14. Chicago Teachers Federation Files. Chicago: Chicago Historical Society.

Haley, M. A. (1903, Sept. 10). Democracy in action. [An address to Henry George Association of Chicago]. Chicago: Chicago Historical Society File.

Haley, M. A. (1924, November 12). The factory system. *The New Republic,* p. 18.

Haley, M. A. (1928, January 31). What's wrong with our schools? *The Daily News,*
    p. 107.
Haley, M. A. (1982). In R. L. Reid (Ed.), *Battleground, the autobiography of Margaret
    A. Haley.* Chicago: University of Illinois Press.
McCormack, M. E. (1988). *The female grade school teacher and equal rights for
    women: An alternative view on the meaning of education and the organization of
    the American school.* Unpublished doctoral dissertation, University of Cincinnati,
    Cincinnati.
Morris, S. (1992). *Response: Why teachers should organize.* Unpublished paper.
Report on the committee on education and information of the Teachers Federation.
    (1898, November 25). Chicago: Chicago Teachers Federation Files, Chicago His-
    torical Society.
Spring, J. (1990). *The American school, 1642–1990.* New York: Longman.
Steinhart, R. (1991). *America 2000: Only the names have changed.* Unpublished paper.
Tyack, D. (1980). *The one best system: A history of urban education.* Cambridge:
    Harvard University Press.

13

Solitary Spaces

Women, Teaching, and Curriculum

Janet L. Miller

> *I am alone in the house. But for me the world does not recede. . . . Quite the contrary. The world is given point by my solitude. For even as I sit alone in my room, I feel a pull on my attention that necessarily attaches me to the world. Our intellectual work ought to give point to and signify those attachments. Our attachments ought to give point to that work.*
>
> Jo Anne Pagano ("The Claim of Philia")

> *And when is there time to remember, to sift, to weigh, to estimate, to total? I will start and there will be an interruption and I will have to gather it all together again. Or I will become engulfed with all I did or did not do, with what should have been and what cannot be helped.*
>
> Tillie Olsen ("I Stand Here Ironing")

One of my mother's favorite Perry Como renditions is "In My Solitude . . . ," and I remember her humming that tune as she ironed, her swaying body keeping gentle time with the music drifting from the radio that was permanently anchored on a shelf above the kitchen sink. That particular form of solitude, a reverie laced with static from both the radio commercials and her two young daughters and embroidered with household and child care routines, could only have been fragmentary and fleeting. Yet, I think that my mother wove together those moments for her own thoughts from strands of music and from breezes that barely puffed the white curtains shading our kitchen window, knowing that she never would completely sever her musings from the bustle surrounding her.

So, as I remember this particular scene from my childhood, I think that my mother's humming could have signaled doubled spaces—spaces of both insulation and inclusion. The humming keyed us into her desire for time ". . . to remember, to sift," as well as enabled us to locate her within her own solitude. And, although I was busy playing with my sister, I know that I listened for her humming as she bent over the ironing board, creating those doubled spaces amidst our squabbles and the banging of screen doors and the squeals of neighborhood children playing on the swing set in the backyard.

As a young child, then, I learned to hum like my mother, trundling behind her as she swept through the daily household chores with Perry Como or Rosemary Clooney or Nat King Cole as her constant cleaning companions. At that point, replicating only her accompaniment, not her intentions, my hums most often melded into my sister's and my high-pitched inquiries and conversations. And, even though we had learned early that my mother's humming expressed, in part, her desire to be alone with her own thoughts, we often disrupted its melodic flow as we called for her to watch us play our games or, more often, to settle disputes over ownership rights of game pieces or a favorite toy.

Later, when my mother went to work outside our home in order to help with family finances, I took over the ironing and dishwashing duties, my adolescent alto replicating my mother's versions of "In My Solitude . . ." or "Mona Lisa" as well as Elvis' renditions of "Hound Dog" and "Blue Suede Shoes." And even as much as I loved those teenage moments when I could be alone in the house, vocalizing to my latest junior high school crush, I missed her as I hummed and ironed. I was waiting, in the midst of my industriousness, for her to come home from work so that we could talk about the latest incidents at my school or her office.

In the ensuing years, I too have had to learn to extract my own versions of solitude from the patterned inundations of daily work and responsibilities. Lately, my desire for solitude seems to increase in direct proportion to the amount of work and related stress that I am experiencing at any particular moment. That desire quite often demands that I literally separate myself from others and from a normally routine schedule that has jumbled itself into momentary chaos. During those moments, I often feel that isolation and separation are the only states of mind and being that can enable me to regain a sense of myself and what I want and need to do.

Sometimes, especially at the end of a semester, I long to spend days alone, puttering in my study or re-potting plants—doing anything, so long as it is not in any way attached to the required events of university life. The few times that I have been able to carve out such spaces, I have momentarily withdrawn from the world. I have unplugged the telephone—the answering machine was not a sufficient barrier, because I eventually had to return calls or, if I didn't, to confront the seemingly inevitable question, "Where have you been?" I have built a fortress around me of books and music and unopened mail and catalogues from every mail order business in the United States, I swear. Then, quite often, I have read, listened, or attended to none of these. Instead, I have waited and watched for myself to return and to enter into the spaces that I had been filling with the needs and desires and requests of others. And I think that, in those moments, I was protecting myself, not from the intrusion of others but rather against further alienation from myself.

What I want and am still learning how to do is to construct moments of both solitude and connectedness for myself—those doubled spaces—in which I am fully present, neither sifted into others' spaces nor drained from my own.

I think my desire for that particular scenario of solitude as isolation also reflected a certain desperation on my part. That desperate feeling kicked in, I think, especially when I saw myself in either/or positions. Either I was in the university, with all of its related committee meetings and journal article deadlines and student papers to read, or I could be in a world where none of those pressures existed. The second part of that either/or construction is the idealized academic dream that I've only lately begun to unravel.

For years, when I felt as though I needed to withdraw totally from my schedule and work commitments at the university, I truly believed that, if I could just finish my perpetual list of things to do, I would be able to successfully remove myself from every obligation that accompanied my daily life. And I could have a form of solitude that was unencumbered by the pressures and attachments and commitments that constituted a large part of my work at the university.

Of course, what I have begun to realize in recent years is that this version of solitude not only is impossible, but also is not what I really want. I cannot, nor do I wish to, disconnect myself from the students, colleagues, and friends with whom I work or from the ideas and theories and debates that we exchange. Instead, I want to spin and shape and spew out series of doubled spaces, overlapping and intersecting spaces that connect the many passions and commitments in my life and from which I can both replenish and share myself.

I am still working to construct possibilities of solitude as moments spun from webs of connectedness. But connectedness, I am still learning, is different from immersion in others' versions or demands of me. That immersion threatens a suppression or subversion of my own desires and needs to those of others. And that's when I lose myself, and have to concoct that isolated version of solitude as a way of connecting with myself before I can effect similar connections with others, with ideas, with actions in the world.

Connectedness and attachment, in ways that I want to construct them, entail spaces of shared as well as individual questions, challenges, interests, intentions, and actions. Those permeable spaces allow me both to enter into relationships with others and to maintain room for myself within those relationships. I watched my mother, seemingly alone with her thoughts as she embellished both her ironing and Perry Como, and she watched me, constantly aware of what my sister and I were doing at any given moment. Her particular versions of solitude, swirled together with music and children's prattle and the hiss of the iron as it flattened damp clothing, are not mine. But her versions continue to teach me that I need not construct only detached or isolated forms of solitude in order to replenish connections to myself or others.

I still might wish for those isolated forms on days when students and meetings and deadlines threaten to squeeze me out of myself and into others' versions of who and what I should be. I am sure that my mother also longed for those forms of solitude that could guarantee protection against children's interruptions and the constant juggling of demands from both her home and outside workplace. But, my mother's versions of solitude, shaped within the midst of those demands and interruptions, have taught me that I can replenish myself even as I acknowledge and participate in my attachments to others and to the work that connects us.

By extension, then, in my work at the university, I see ways in which those versions inform my interests in curriculum, teaching, and research as reciprocal and interactive, rather than as separate and discrete, constructions. My mother's versions of solitude, in which she watched and responded both to herself and to her family, have enabled me, in turn, to both claim and question constructions of myself and the communities in which I participate, to both honor and challenge boundaries that can enclose as well as exclude, to both thread together and unravel moments of solitude and relationship that inform my life as a woman academic.

Like my mother, I juggle demands and responsibilities. For me, those come in the forms of teaching, of preparing classes and advising students, of writing and researching. And like my mother, I now attempt to create solitary spaces as pauses, as shifting and momentary respites rather than as definitive and constricted separations between myself and others. As I work to create those doubled spaces, I now can see ways in which the tensions that erupted in me as I tried to construct an either/or version of my life in the university are reflected in the themes that have dominated my academic work. I have struggled to identify the fragmentation that I have felt in my life as a woman academic by looking at the separations of public and private, of authority and nurturer, of theory and practice, that historically have characterized not only the field of education but also of women's work within that field.

So, for example, I continue to explore these separations as representative of ways in which social constructions of women's work and voices, as situated within a private, domestic sphere, devalue teachers who wish to be both nurturing and facilitative in their work. I am interestd in ways that we might reshape the historically immovable boundaries between the public and the private into spaces that might include notions of communities and collaborations without consensus. Instead of promoting educational communities and identities that promise unity and sameness, where we all will become "reflective practitioners" or cheerful "teacher-researchers," for example, what might we do to shape communities and forms of collaboration in which we could struggle together to create versions of curriculum, teaching, and learning that do not posit particular voices and experiences as representative of us all?

I continue to struggle to create solitary spaces for myself that do not replicate or reify historically and culturally constructed boundaries between self and other or between particular selves and others. But I also am aware of the difficulties of constructing a doubled-spaced version of solitude that does not easily slide into silence or confinement or isolation or sameness.

Like my mother, ever watchful in her momentary solitude, I drive home from my evening's teaching, already casting an eye toward the next class discussion, mindful of a student's request for further reading, of the questions to which I want to attend in our next session, and of the students' papers that I must read before tomorrow's class. Like my mother, even as I savor the drive home as a small sliver of solitude, shaved from the day's schedule of endless meetings and teaching, I am watching and responding, aware of my connections to others whose varied and multiple interests and concerns inform, though often do not replicate, my own.

As I teach, research, and write as part of my university responsibilities, however, I continue to confront myriad versions of ways in which schooling structures perpetuate the separations and compartmentalizations that keep us from ourselves and others. Just as I want to create solitary spaces that both enclose and invite, that acknowledge my attachments both to the world and to myself, so do I also want to incorporate such doubled spaces into the ways in which I work as a woman academic. For me, the continuing challenge in all of this is to claim the connections and the differences created within such spaces while constantly questioning those boundaries against which I must push in order to claim myself.

For example, in my work with graduate students who are themselves teachers and administrators in the schools, we still must grapple with versions of teaching and curriculum that conceptualize pedagogy as a series of discrete skills and curriculum as content, as separate and autonomous disciplines, each with its testable facts and measurable knowledges. To create spaces in which to consider other possibilities for curriculum and teaching, then, we study conceptions of curriculum that extend traditional definitions of curriculum as content into analyses of social, historical, cultural, and economic forces that shape and influence the constructions of such content. We try to examine those forces as they are occurring in the experience of our particular situations, in the contexts of our daily lives.

But, as we do so, teachers bring to class stories of daily confrontations with their school districts' central office mandates about students' raised achievement scores as evidence of "rigorous curriculum" and "effective" teaching and learning. Or administrators tell of pressures to squeeze curriculum into testable areas, so that chunks of material are "integrated" into conveniently measurable segments of knowledge. Or I talk of my frustration in working with a school administrator who wants to see, in a multiple-choice test format, measurable differences in students' writing. This "evidence" will inform the school district's decision to continue or halt a writing process in-service program for teachers and students in which I have been participating for eight years.

These various vignettes that my graduate students and I share and analyze and deconstruct illustrate the separations and distillations of curriculum, teaching, and learning into neat packages of measured and predetermined knowledges. Such conceptions propose that teaching and curriculum are actually separable from my students' or my own musing drive home after class and from the relationships that spill from our classrooms and meetings into those momentary and moving solitary spaces. Those conceptual separations then threaten to become reified spaces that demarcate the public arenas of education as places filled with official words and actions of certain others who have been designated as "experts" or as representatives of us all.

Within such authoritative and restricted boundaries, my graduate students and I are officially separated from the interactions, relationships, and cultural forces that we know frame and influence our curriculum and teaching constructions. In those separated, autonomous, and reified conceptions of teaching and curriculum, my versions of solitary spaces, of curriculum, and of teaching as connected clearings in which to both watch and respond are shoved to the margins of educational practice. They are squeezed into distorted spaces of fragmentation and separation, of isolation and exclusion, or of totalizing discourses that certify only particular knowledges. Such reified constructions threaten my own as well as my students' attempts to clear solitary spaces in which we might reflect, question, replenish, and constantly transform our connections to our varied and multiple worlds.

In order to create the kinds of doubled versions of solitary spaces that I initially experienced as I listened to my mother's humming, I also have had to increase my tolerance for ambiguity. In order to work in the schools, I have to deal with school districts' versions of curriculum as content that teachers must "cover" before they can turn their attentions to me and to the writing processes that I think can enable students and teachers to create curriculum. And, in order to work in the university, I still must struggle with my internalizations of how I "should be" in the academy. I am attempting to create versions of myself as a woman professor who is able to claim both my own sense of authority as teacher and researcher and writer as well as my sense of connectedness to myself and others. At the same time, I still struggle with the "shoulds" that have been constructed from social, historical, and cultural framings of women in such positions. I still struggle with "either/or" versions of professor as "authority and expert" or as "nurturer and facilitator," for example. As I try to move into fluid conceptions of myself as possibly both/and, I remember my mother and her doubled versions of solitude that I still am working to create.

I continue to confront the silences and omissions as well as the possibilities within my emerging versions of solitude, for I still want to create solitary and communal spaces within teaching and curriculum that are overlapping and connected but that also acknowledge and claim differences. I know that my versions of solitude and of curriculum and teaching, constructed from my position as a white, middle-class woman academic, do not necessarily reflect the same ambiguities, conflicts, and exclusions felt by other women in similar positions. I also know that the luxury of even contemplating such versions may not be in the province of many women who have little, if any, time to "remember, to sift, to weigh, to estimate, to total. . . ."

Perhaps my early recollections of solitude, formed in the connected yet ambivalent spaces of my mother's work and reverie, can enable me to enlarge my understandings of my own privilege and of my particular constructions of myself as a woman academic. Perhaps my understandings of solitude as spaces forged in the midst of daily educational work and connected both to the relationships and the contents that are the focus of those activities also will enlarge. I want such enlarged understandings in order to work with others to forge educational communities and collaborations without consensus, without the pressure to merge into one position or one right answer or one identity.

I talked with my mother about this essay and about her versions of solitude. We hummed a few phrases of "In My Solitude . . ." to one another, and then we laughed. "How did you ever remember that?" she asked, just as I voiced the same question to her, knowing that her remembrances and versions would not be mine. We talked for a few more minutes, as she recalled returning to work full-time outside our home when my sister and I were in elementary school and really enjoying new forms of solitude in her daily bus ride into downtown Pittsburgh and in the work that awaited her there.

My mother recently had moved into a new apartment, and she was unpacking a box of photographs even as we were speaking on the telephone. I could hear her humming a bit between the lines of our conversation, especially as she debated the best placement of the pictures of my father and my sister and me. She was both with me and not, both watching and responding, and that slight solitary space in the midst of our conversation hung in the air for a few moments after I hung up the phone, connecting us still across our separations and differences.

q u e s t i o n s   f o r   d i s c u s s i o n

1. What versions of solitude characterize your relationships to yourself as student, to your particular disciplines of study, to your teachers and fellow students, and to the processes and conceptions of curriculum, teaching, and learning?
2. What might your versions of solitude indicate about structures and processes within education both as an institution and as a field of study?
3. What foundational concepts within education in the United States might inform your particular notions of solitude and its relations to your educational experience? How do your versions of those relationships differ from others? How might gender, race, class, age, sexual preference, and other differences among individuals affect those versions?

t e a c h e r s   a s   r e s e a r c h e r s

In this essay, expectations for oneself as teacher turn on social and cultural constructions of gender and of relationships among and between identities, curriculum, teaching, and research. Thinking about these constructions, create an educational timeline for your own life. Note especially those persons, events, and situations that have influenced your present understandings of such constructions for versions of yourself as teacher. Extract from your timeline a series of autobiographical sketches in which you explore these various relationships and constructions. Looking for the shifts and changes in your thinking over time, note how the process of writing and reflecting on these sketches informs your teaching.

s u g g e s t e d   r e a d i n g s

Gannett, C. (1992). *Gender and the journal: Diaries and academic discourse.* Albany: SUNY Press.

Graham, R. J. (1991). *Reading and writing the self: Autobiography in education and the curriculum.* New York: Teachers College Press.

Knopp Bilken, S., & Pollard, D. (1993). *Gender and education.* Chicago: University of Chicago Press.

Luke, C., & Gore, J. (Eds.). (1992). *Feminisms and critical pedagogy.* New York: Routledge.

Schubert, W. H., & Ayers, W. C. (Eds.). (1992). *Teacher lore: Learning from our own experience.* New York: Longman.

The Personal Narratives Group. (Eds.). (1989). *Interpreting women's lives: Feminist theory and personal narratives.* Bloomington: Indiana University Press.

Wear, D. (Ed.). (1993). *The center of the web: Women and solitude.* Albany: SUNY Press.

chapter 14

Curriculum as Making Do

William M. Reynolds & Alan A. Block

guiding questions

1. What are the authors trying to say or teach?
2. What is the significance of what you read here for you personally and for you as a teacher?
3. What are the perspectives drawn on by the authors to make the analysis?
4. How does this analysis help to inform our practice in classrooms?

Inside/Out: Contemporary Critical Perspectives in Education

> *I can't dance and I can't talk only thing about me is the way I walk.*
> Genesis (1992)

Phil Collins and Genesis discuss the cultural image and its uses in the song "I Can't Dance." This objectification of popular culture is the central issue that this essay discusses. The use of the objectified popular cultural artifact in classrooms and their curriculum is a serious historical and theoretical dilemma for curriculum scholars to address as we struggle to find a meaningful curriculum for the students in our public schools.

Popular culture, such as rock and roll music, television, and popular film has largely been condemned by both the political left and right, but for different reasons. In the left's critique of popular culture, "two positions have held center stage in different instances of Marxist theory" (Giroux & Simon, 1989, p. 4). In the first view, "popular culture simply represents a view of ideology and cultural forms imposed by the culture industry on the masses in order to integrate them into the existing social order" (p. 4). In other words people are produced in the image of the culture industry's own logic, "a logic characterized by standardization, uniformity, and passivity" (p. 4).

The second view of popular culture from the left is:

> . . . popular culture becomes a version of folk culture and its contemporary variant, that is the object of historical analysis, working class culture is excavated as an unsullied expression of popular resistance. Within this form of analysis the political and the pedagogical emerge as an attempt to reconstruct a "radical and . . . popular tradition in order that 'the people' might learn from and take heart from the struggles of their forebearers," or it appears as an attempt to construct "the people" as the supports of [a] 'great culture' so that they might eventually be led to appropriate that culture as their own. (Bennett in Giroux & Simon, 1989, p. 6)

In the conservative view of popular culture there is a tendency to treat culture as an "artifact," which students are required merely to absorb. "Culture is treated as a warehouse filled with the goods of antiquity, waiting patiently to be distributed anew to each generation" (Giroux & Simon, 1989, p. 7). We can witness the specter of this view in the works produced lately referring to the struggle over the canon—for example, *Cultural Literacy* (Hirsch, 1987) and *The Closing of the American Mind* (Bloom, 1987). It is the classical works of Western civilization that deserve our sole attention; the works of the "mass culture" are pabulum that simply stupefy the young. In both cases, perhaps more so in the conservative mentality, popular culture becomes a reified object and is not seen as a site of struggle for meaning.

What have been the consequences of these views of popular culture and its uses in the public schools in the last twenty years? This is one of the questions that this essay attempts to address by placing the uses of popular culture in the schools into a historical perspective. The historical analysis may lead us to question the very notions of the radical and conservative analyses of popular culture, particularly the notion held in common by the left and the right that popular culture is an object.

John Lennon, in "Working Class Hero" (1970), describes education as a process of interpellation: one is named to be discovered either as part of the dominant culture (the folks on the hill) or to be observed as a part of the dominated (working-class heroes).

> As soon as you're born they make you feel small
> By giving you no time instead of it all
> Soon the pain is so big you feel nothing at all.
>
> They hurt you at home and they hit you at school
> They hate you if you are clever and they despise the fool
> 'Til you're so fucking crazy you can't follow their rules.
>
> When they have tortured and scared you for twenty odd years
> Then they expect you to pick a career
> When you can't really function you're so full of fear.
>
> There is room at the top they are telling you still
> But, first you must learn to smile as you kill
> If you want to be like the folks on the hill.
>
> A working class hero is something to be
> If you want to be a hero then just follow me.

Education is, says Lennon, learning to follow a path to home so that we can be like the "folks on the hill." Lennon indicates that home is the snare and that schools serve, by defining and carving the path, to ensure our various locations and arrivals. Schools and the curriculum serve as a panopticon.[1] Curriculum in the schools can serve as a denial in and of the everyday lives of students and teachers. We are defined and, paradoxically, denied. Foucault, in an interview with Pierre Boncenne, discusses this notion of fixing and locating people, constricting them to a number of "gestures and habits," which is the practice of the educational system. The process is about defining and denying.

> What developed then was a whole technique of human dressage by location, confinement, surveillance, the perpetual supervision of behavior and tasks, in short a whole technique of "management" of which prison was merely one manifestation of its transposition in the penal domain. (Kritzman, 1988, p. 105)

Schools are another manifestation of this panopticonal mechanism. Of course, students, and teachers, do not need to be apprised of this fact—they always already are aware of their experience—but the panopticonal mechanism in its curriculum fixes the student and teacher, denies the efficacy of action. Paul Willis (1981) recounts how in resistance, working-class students actually reproduce the very social structure that their resistance was meant to deny. As heroic as their struggle is conceived, their efforts doom them. The work of the panopticonal school prescribes the direction these working-class heroes must take even in their resistance, indeed, as a result of it.

Lennon's response seems more appropriate; his role as working-class hero is predicated on his use of the dominant culture to continue his resistance, reaping the rewards of the dominant culture while speaking out as one of its more vocal critics. Since the late 1960s the curriculum field, too, has attempted to define, to explain, and to intervene in the appearance of—the creation of—working-class heroes as a product of the educational system. Curriculum theorists and scholars in other academic disciplines have studied the phenomenon of reproduction in education—the process by which education reproduces not only the folks on the hill, but also those who are denied access and who are made to serve them. The resulting literature spoke of the curriculum as designed to reproduce societal structures and was referred to as reproduction theory. Reproduction theory created working-class students as heroes by revealing the oppression experienced by them—and others—in schools and described the means by which they were denied access to the hill except as its servants. Reproduction theory was valuable as an opening wedge in the tight hegemonic hold that kept the educational system free from criticism except from an idealized—reified—educational philosophical standpoint. But, reproduction theory was soon critiqued for being overly simplistic and deterministic.[2] Men and women are not simply made and determined: they resist. With this understanding there followed a literature on resistance.

Work in resistance theory started as a refinement of the reproduction emphasis in political curriculum scholarship, and then moved to a discussion of resistance/reproduction as a dialectical process. In the mid-1980s, it began to focus upon the daily educational practice, especially the pedagogical and political issues of race, class, and gender. The focus on race, gender, and class, begun in earnest in the late 1980s, continues into the 1990s, but there has recently appeared a new center of interest on the role of popular culture in the educational process.

Recently, Giroux and Simon have argued that the old model of reproduction/resistance is a limited and limiting notion when applied to the process of being schooled. Being schooled, they argue, must be "analyzed as part of a complex and often contradictory set of ideological and material processes through which the transformation of experience takes place" (1989, p. 1) and leads, as well, into a language of possibility as we reconceptualize the work of education in these transformative experiences. Giroux and Simon contend that one of the more effective methods of "teaching resistance" is to deal with the popular culture as a vehicle to enable that transformation of experience. In the work of popular culture, students may be taught to discover the creation of their subjectivities by the dominant cultures and may then learn how to intervene in that process. Giroux and Simon view educational practice as both a "site and form of cultural politics" (1989, p. 11). In *Border Crossings: Cultural Workers and the Politics of Education,* Giroux discusses not only of the work, but calls those involved in educational situations "cultural workers" (1992, p. 5). In a theme reminiscent of earlier work, the project for critical pedagogy continues to be radical interventional practice. This type of educational practice, Giroux and Simon feel, would allow individuals

> to intervene in the formation of their own subjectivities and to be able to exercise power in the interest of transforming the ideological and material conditions of domination into social empowerment and demonstrate possibilities. (1989, p. 11)

Resistance becomes the process of learning of the existence of the already constructed subject and the interventional process anticipating the possible construction of new subjectivities. "For radical teachers, it is imperative that strategies be developed that take as their starting point an understanding of how knowledge and patterns of social relations steeped in domination come into being in schools, how they are maintained, how students, teachers, and others relate to them, and how they can be exposed, modified, and overcome, if possible" (Giroux & Aronowitz, 1985, p. 132). Resistance theory, in this manner, begins to account for the complexities of race, class, and gender in the construction of subjects. Giroux and Simon discuss the notion of critical pedagogy, resistance, and possibility. They suggest that teachers who are "committed" to the project of critical pedagogy must now "read the ground of the popular for investments that distort or constrict human potentialities" (1989, p. 25). To read the popular is to understand the construction of subjectivities by the dominant ideas of the dominant culture. Resistance is here the end product of education, and popular culture a monolithic and repressive structure. This reading, Giroux and Simon argue, will allow teachers, students, and education to realize and "give voice to unrealized possibilities" (1989, p. 25). Here popular culture becomes the site for resistance; and the attainment of unrealized possibilities, the goal of critical pedagogy.

However, its inability to deal with the often contradictory daily practices that take place in school has necessitated a reevaluation and development of resistance theory. Leslie Roman, in an essay that addresses these very contradictions, points out some of the limitations of resistance theory. In her essay, "Intimacy, Labor and Class: Ideologies of Feminine Sexuality in the Punk Slam Dance" (1988), Roman defines what she notes as some weaknesses in cultural studies of youth, particularly in the area of resistance. First, citing Walker (1988), she alludes to the fact that indiscriminate use of the concept of resistance romanticizes the "potential of specific instances of working class practices to create emancipatory social transformation" (Roman & Christian-Smith, 1988, p. 143). Second, there is the possibility of over-formalizing the "intentions" and behaviors of social subjects into a single structuralist typology or "grammar of challenge" (contestation and resistance). There is, she asserts, the "risk of creating a new problem for cultural studies, namely class essentialism" (p. 143). The third problem is that there is a tendency in these studies to

> pay homage to a productivist logic in Marxism, a logic which treats the domination of women by men as either secondary to or as a consequence

of the exploitation of workers (usually presumed male) in the sphere of commodity production and waged work. (pp. 143–144)

Roman argues that merely defining behavior as antisocial and then calling it resistance is to misrepresent actual human motives and consequences of action and, therefore, to negate the possibility for radical intervention.

Stanley Aronowitz, acknowledging these shortcomings in resistance theory in "Working-Class Identity and Celluloid Fantasies," elucidates the development of identity (particularly of the working class) and its connections with popular culture and schooling. Aronowitz suggests that the major purpose of schooling, "conscious or not," is the denial of identity:

to strip away what belongs to the student, to reconstitute his/her formation in terms of the boundaries imposed by the hegemonic intellectuals acting for the prevailing social order. (In Giroux & Simon, 1989, p. 200)

Aronowitz emphasizes further that those students who succeed are first stripped of their ethnicity, race, and sex. For working-class students, Aronowitz believes, this "submission to the curriculum" already would signify social mobility (in Giroux & Simon, 1989). In this formulation, he captures the process of interpellation within the panopticon of the school. Aronowitz suggests that we move toward a curriculum in popular cultural studies and that, within that curriculum, production become the central focus. Rather than a curriculum of popular cultural criticism, he suggests a curriculum of popular culture production that would prove radically interventionist. This would be a curriculum in which students write, produce, and perform their own ideas. This concept appears to move us in a positive direction—away from being consumers to being writers, performers, and producers—but it does not, as yet, confront the construction of the already constructed identities that are contradictorily present in schools. These issues with regard to popular culture have yet to be addressed.

In their essay, "Schooling Popular Culture and a Pedagogy of Possibility," Giroux and Simon discuss the central issues of popular culture, the curriculum, and critical pedagogy.

How does one make popular culture an object of pedagogical analysis without undermining its privileged appropriation as a form of resistance? How can popular culture become part of a critical pedagogy that does not ultimately function to police its content and form? (1989, p. 229)

These questions for and about popular culture and the curriculum that Giroux and Simon conceive as central may not, indeed, be central, particularly if definitions of popular culture are examined. These notions of bringing popular culture into the curriculum—to promote and intervene in the formation of students' own subjectivities, to acknowledge the everyday influences of popular culture on students' lives, to have students produce their own ideas as popular culture, or to make popular culture an object of pedagogical analysis—are important considerations. But we do not wish to return to the conservative New Critical analysis of the lyrics of Simon and Garfunkel or Bob Dylan as poetry. Students easily recognized this as an educational wolf in sheep's clothing and quickly rejected it as yet another hegemonic ploy and co-optation of the culture of youth by the dominant powers. Instead, contemporary investigations into popular culture must first call into question the very concept of popular culture itself. A focus on the nature of popular culture and its relationship to curriculum should be a significant new direction in the study of curriculum. We have to ask ourselves, however, two fundamental questions: What is popular culture? How does our understanding of popular culture relate to the political analysis of the curriculum and to reproduction/resistance theory? It is these questions that I will briefly address. The issues are complex and I mean, at this time, simply to begin this curricular discussion.[3]

We can explore some possible responses if we examine popular culture not as a *product* but as a *process*. Indeed, if we are to ensure agency, we must believe that popular culture is only a process rather than an object, that it is an activity which is engaged in, not a commodity that may be purchased. Rather, popular culture ought to be viewed as the uses to which the products offered by society are put. These cannot ever be determined. "Popular culture," as deCerteau (1984) notes, "is the art of making do with what the system provides" (p. 29).

> The fact that the system provides only commodities, whether cultural or material, does not mean that the process of consuming those commodities can be adequately described as one that commodifies the people into a homogenized mass at the mercy of the barons of industry. (Fiske, 1989a, pp. 25–26)

This idea emphasizes the need to reconceptualize both reproduction and resistance theory, because, as Marx has shown, consumption completes production, and we must, therefore, examine that consumption if we are to understand the production at all. This study of consumption is the study of popular culture. Reconceptualized, popular culture can be explored, then, as the relations between containment and resistance (see Stuart Hall, 1981) or the struggle within relations of power. Popular culture is a site *and* practice that, within a set of power relations, describes the contestation between the dominant powers attempting to exercise their control over the everyday lives of people whose will cannot be so easily controlled.

> The opposition can also be thought of as one between **homogeneity** as the power bloc attempts to control, structure and minimize social differences so they serve its interests, and **heterogeneity,** as the formations of the people intransigently maintain their sense of social difference that is also a difference of interest. (Fiske, 1989b, p. 8)

In education, this struggle can be represented in the power relations of the panopticonal school, which tries to create and control the everyday lives of teachers and students, attempting to exert its surveillance by what has been called the uninterrupted stream of writing. Popular culture can be conceived of as the inherently oppositional process to the power bloc, to the panopticon.

But, popular culture is not necessarily a vehicle for the overt, oppositional, radical, interventionalist type of resistance described in much of the popular culture/resistance/critical pedagogy literature that has been discussed. The working(s) of popular culture may be too fluid for that.

> One person may, at different times, form cultural allegiances, with different, not to say contradictory, social groups as he or she moves through the social formation. I may forge for myself quite different cultural allegiances to cope with and make sense of different areas of my everyday life. (Fiske, 1989a, p. 30)

Resistance is never constant, and similar behaviors cannot always be conceptualized as resistance. Our locus of resistance within the process of popular culture is fluid or changing. In other words, one day we (you or I) may make do with what the system provides based on our age. At still other times, our making do may result from allegiances based on gender, race, class, or sexual orientation. Popular culture is a struggle over the meaning of social experience, "of one's personhood and its relation to the social order and of the texts and commodities of that order" (Fiske, 1989a, p. 28).

Again, popular culture is a process not a thing. Fiske elucidates that popular culture is making do with what we have, and everyday life is always a making do. I suggest that everyday life in schools is also a making do with what we have or are given: the curriculum. As contemporary critical curricular theory has demonstrated, the characteristic tactics of that everyday life of making do in schools are "adaptation, manipulation and trickery" (Fiske, 1989a, p. 34). Tricks and ruses (making do) are the "art of the weak" that enables them to exploit their understanding of the rules of the system, and turn it to their advantage. They are a "refusal to be subjugated" (Fiske, 1989b, p. 17). In Penelope Spheeris' film *Suburbia*, the extended family of outcast teenagers, who have taken up residence in an abandoned house in the midst of suburbia, carry strips of lawn sod from the local nursery into the shopping mall, install the grass on the hard concrete in front of the home appliance store, and watch the TVs all alight in the window in what must be seen as both a parody of the typical American evening experience and as a touching image of the work of popular culture. Fiske, too, discusses this notion of making do in his discussion of shopping malls.

> The youths consumed images and space instead of commodities, a kind of sensuous consumption that did not create profits, the positive pleasure of parading up and down, of offending 'real' consumers and the agents of the law and order, of asserting their difference within, and different use of, the cathedral of consumerism became oppositional cultural practice. (Fiske, 1989b, p. 17)

This trickery in the shopping malls is the expression of an "ethics of tenacity"—countless ways of refusing to accord the established order the status of law, a meaning, or a fatality (deCerteau, 1984, p. 26). This ethics of tenacity—and it must be emphasized that its manifestations are infinite—should be conceptualized as what we will refer to as paths of least resistance. Resistance here need not be carved out or marked; it is already part of the daily practices by which identities are formed. Shopping malls, in this instance, just happen to be places where the strategy of the powerful is vulnerable to the tactical raids of the weak.

There are already paths of least resistance present in schools as students and teachers make do much the same way teenagers make do in the shopping malls. In fact, high schools were equated to shopping malls in a recent study (Powell, Farrar, & Cohen, 1985). In their depiction of the American high school, Powell, Farrar, and Cohen demonstrate similarities between schools and malls:

> If Americans want to understand their high schools at work they should imagine them as shopping malls. Secondary education is another consumption experience in an abundant society . . . Both institutions bring hopeful purveyors and potential purchasers together. The former hope to maximize sales but can take nothing for granted. Shoppers have a wide discretion not only about what to buy but also about whether to buy. (p. 8)

What we are suggesting is that the decision "to buy or not to buy" is not so easily recognized by the test scores, college entrances, dropout rates, or any of the traditional (and nontraditional) methods for adjudging the efficacy of education. Indeed, the formulation is erroneous. The question is not one of purchase, but of use. Students are always already making do in the schools in much the same way that they are employing an ethics of tenacity in shopping malls. Take an example from popular film. In *Fast Times at Ridgemont High* (1982), Spicoli, the surfer, orders a pizza and has it delivered at the beginning of his history class. His teacher, Mr. Hand, amazed and appalled, confronts Spicoli.

> "Just what are you doing, Mr. Spicoli?" asks Mr. Hand.
> "Learning about Cuba and having some food."

Spicoli is making do with what the school offers him. He is prepared to learn about Cuba and to have some food. We need not speculate on his motives for having pizza delivered—our culture has made this an accepted practice. It is the school which denies this practice. When Hand appropriates Spicoli's pizza, the student loses the opportunity both for food and learning about Cuba. Spicoli's original act is the path of least resistance: It is making do with what the system provides. It is popular culture. The school, in the person of Mr. Hand, attempts to appropriate making do and thus inspires overt resistance in a process that leads to the serious condition in today's schools where education is lost in the struggle over *control*. Or, as Mr. Hand says, a condition where we will blindness and ignorance, where, he says, "the teachers pretend they don't see you and you pretend you don't ditch." All of this pretense denies subjectivity by denying what actually exists.

Freire and Shor, in *Pedagogy for Liberation* (1987), state, "We do not have to view our task as walking all over the world as Peregrines of the revolution, not discussing 'truth,' simply putting it inside as many heads as possible." That way of discussing or enabling resistance is not empowering. Elizabeth Ellsworth, in her essay "Why Doesn't This Feel Empowering? Working Through the Repressive Myths of Critical Pedagogy" (1989), discusses the notion of students and resistant or oppositional voices.

> The literature on critical pedagogy also recognizes the possibility that each student will be capable of identifying a multiplicity of authentic voices in her/himself. But it does not confront the ways in which any individual student's voice is already a "teeth gritting" and often contradictory intersection of voices constituted by gender, race, class, ability, ethnicity, sexual orientation or ideology. (p. 298)

As Spicoli shows us, and as we have always known, the students are always already making do—gritting their teeth within the panopticon. It is here that education must intervene.

Having discussed the work on popular culture and curriculum, we would like to suggest that the importance of popular culture cannot be denied. The approach to and analysis of popular culture and the curriculum, however, needs to be closely examined. Perhaps a shift in our conceptualizations needs to be addressed. Curriculum scholars should begin to move away from analyzing popular culture for the curriculum and begin to look at curriculum as popular culture. What popular culture do we bring into the classroom to analyze? Is Tracey Chapman better than Metallica? Do we watch *Dirty Dancing* or *The Bicycle Thief*? These types of questions would become less important if our conceptualizations moved toward notions of curriculum as popular culture. Indeed, it doesn't matter at all what film we show, what music we listen to, what books we read. If popular culture is the process of making do with what we are given, then the students will also make do with any popular culture that is part of the curriculum. Just as those young, unemployed Australian "proletarian shoppers" turned the place of the mall into their space to enact oppositional culture, to maintain and assert their social difference and their subordinated but hostile social identities (Fiske, 1989a, p. 380), students will likewise treat the culture imported into the classroom as part of the uninterrupted stream of writing of the panopticonal curriculum. The issue is not to substitute popular cultural criticism for the analysis of canonical texts. The one type of analysis can be as disempowering as the other. The issue is to illuminate the already existing paths of least resistance and to explore their intricacies.

We could begin to illuminate with students this "making do." We do not want to advocate telling students how to make do; they do not need this redundant instruction. We need to articulate with students the process that is popular culture. In this manner, the process of interpellation or identity formation can be exposed and elaborated. To think of the curriculum as popular culture is to reveal the power that already exists and that is already responsible for the creation of identity, despite what is given out as curricula. Even though interpellation has already attempted to establish relations from which identity should derive, this new emphasis on curriculum as popular culture reinvests power in what is already occurring. That consciousness might deny the panopticon.

To treat curriculum as popular culture becomes the path of least resistance. To offer ourselves and our students, not what we feel are the most significant items of popular culture for the curriculum, but strategies for understanding original interpellations, identity relations, power relations that are part of identity, and the process of making do is to begin to offer real strategies for change in curriculum and education. The point is to have students recognize the paths of least resistance and the power they have within the relations of power that characterize the panopticon.

> The actual order of things is precisely what "popular" tactics turn to their own ends, without any illusion that it will change any time soon though elsewhere it is exploited by the dominant power . . . here order is tricked by art. (deCerteau in Fiske, 1989b, p. 17)

Students can begin to discover and recognize the power they always already have. Students can begin a process to discover that it is always already present within them and to understand that power as relations of power and as a component of identity. Part of the process of curriculum as popular culture is having students understand their historically situated resistance, which is always already present within the power relations that are the panopticonal school. In an essay entitled, "The Subject and the Power," Foucault discusses the analysis of the economy of power relations.

> It consists of taking the forms of resistance against different forms of power as a starting point. To use another metaphor, it consists of using this resistance as a chemical catalyst so as to bring to light power relations, locate their position, find their point of application and methods used . . . it consists of analyzing power relations through the antagonisms of strategies. (Foucault in Dreyfus & Rabinow, 1983, p. 211)

Students, by articulating making do, can begin to change those relations and, consequently, the panopticon without the illusion that it will change soon, but with the realization that it can change. Perhaps this is a "language of possibility"?

What are the specific pedagogical and curricular implications of these suggestions? Those become a different and central issue for further work with the curriculum as popular culture and the paths of least resistance. But, Bob Dylan, in 1965, may have provided the most sagacious advice for the work on curriculum and the paths of least resistance:

> Don't follow leaders
> Watch the parkin' meters.

q u e s t i o n s   f o r   d i s c u s s i o n

1. What would the notion of curriculum as popular culture mean for your individual classroom teaching?
2. What would determine exactly what you taught in a classroom?

3. According to this essay, what is the purpose of education and the curriculum?
4. Describe the ways students and teachers "make do" within the schools.

teachers   as   researchers

Select some examples of popular culture (films, television shows, or music) that your students find interesting or exciting. After watching or listening to the examples, explore with them through their journals or discussions the notion of how these cultural artifacts affect the development of their identities.

Discuss with students this whole notion of "making do." How do they make do in schools? How does the culture affect them? Are they simply puppets of the offerings of our culture or do they, as the essay suggests, make do?

suggested   readings

Fiske, J. (1989). *Reading the popular.* London: Unwin Hyman.
Fiske, J. (1989). *Understanding popular culture.* London: Unwin Hyman.
Giroux, H. A., & Simon, R. (1989). *Popular culture, schooling and everyday life.* Boston: Bergin & Garvey.

notes

[1]Bentham's panopticon is a design for a prison so constructed that the prisoner can be seen but will not be aware of being observed or of observing others also incarcerated. The panopticon "reverses the principle of the dungeon; or rather, of its three functions—to enclose, to deprive of light and to hide—it reserves only the first and eliminates the other two." Full lighting and the eye of a supervisor capture better than darkness, which ultimately protected. Visibility is a trap.

[2]For incisive critiques of reproduction theory see, for example, Henery Giroux, *Theory and Resistance in Education: Pedagogy for the Opposition* (1983); Michael Apple, ed., *Cultural and Economic Reproduction in Education: Essays on Class, Ideology and the State* (1982); *Ideology and Curriculum,* 2nd ed. (1991); and Samuel Bowles and Herbert Gintis, "Contradiction and Reproduction in Educational Theory," in *Schooling, Ideology and the Curriculum,* ed. L. Barton, R. Meighan, and S. Walker (1980).

[3]For a complete history of the literature of reproduction and resistance, see William F. Pinar, William M. Reynolds, Patrick Slattery, and Peter Taubman, *Understanding Curriculum* (forthcoming).

references

Althuseer, L. (1971). *Lenin and philosophy* (B. Brewster, Trans.). New York: Monthly Review Press.

Bloom, A. (1987). *The closing of the American mind: How higher education has failed democracy and impoverished the souls of today's students.* New York: Simon and Schuster.

deCerteau, M. (1984). *The practice of everyday life.* Berkeley: University of California Press.

Dreyfus, H. L., & Rabinow, P. (1983). *Michel Foucault: Beyond structuralism and hermeneutics.* Chicago: University of Chicago Press.

Dylan, B. (1965). "Subterranean homesick blues." New York: Warner Brothers Inc.

Ellsworth, E. (1989). Why doesn't this feel empowering? Working through the repressive myths of critical pedagogy. *Harvard Educational Review, 59,* 297–324.

Fiske, J. (1989a). *Understanding popular culture.* London: Unwin Hyman.

Fiske, J. (1989b). *Reading the popular.* London: Unwin Hyman.

Foucault, M. (1979). *Discipline and punish.* (A. Sheridan, Trans.). New York: Vintage Books.

Freire, P., & Shor, I. (1987). *Pedagogy for liberation: Dialogues on transforming education.* South Hadley, MA: Bergin & Garvey.

Giroux, H. A. (1992). *Border crossings: Cultural workers and the politics of education.* New York: Routledge.

Giroux, H. A., & Aronowitz, S. (1985). *Education under siege: The conservative, liberal and radical debate over schooling.* Boston: Bergin & Garvey.

Giroux, H., & Simon, R. (1989). *Popular culture, schooling and everyday life.* Boston: Bergin & Garvey.

Hall, S. (1981). In R. Samuel (Ed.), *People's history and socialist theory.* London: Routledge & Kegan Paul.

Hirsch, E. D. (1987). *Cultural literacy: What every American needs to know.* Boston: Houghton Mifflin.

Kritzman, L. D. (Ed.). (1988). *Michel Foucault: Politics, philosophy, culture: Interviews and other writings, 1977–1984.* New York: Routledge Chapman Hall.

Lennon, J. (1970). "Working class hero." *John Lennon and the Plastic Ono Band.* London: Apple Music.

Ollman, B. (1988). *Alienation.* Cambridge: Cambridge University Press.

Powell, A., Farrar, E., & Cohen, D. K. (1985). *The shopping mall high school: Winners and losers in the educational marketplace.* Boston: Houghton Mifflin.

Roman, L., & Christian-Smith, L. (Eds.). (1988). *Becoming feminine: The politics of popular culture.* London: The Falmer Press.

Walker, J. (1986). Romanticizing resistance; romanticizing culture: Problems in Willis's theory of cultural production. *British Journal of Sociology in Education, 7,* 59–80.

Willis, P. (1981). *Learning to labour: How working class kids get working class jobs.* Hampshire, England: Gower Publishing.

chapter 15

The Practice of Freedom

A Historical Analysis of Critical Perspectives in the Social Foundations

WILLIAM M. Reynolds &
Rebecca A. Martusewicz

guiding questions

1. What are the authors trying to say or teach?

2. What is the significance of what you read here for you personally and for you as a teacher?

3. What are the perspectives drawn on by the authors to make the analysis?

4. How does this analysis help to inform our practice in classrooms?

> *We are free not because of what we statically are, but in so far as we are becoming different from what we have been.*
>
> John Dewey[1]
>
> *The liberty of men is never assured by the institution and laws that are intended to guarantee them . . . liberty is what must be exercised.*
>
> Michel Foucault[2]

These thoughts on freedom by Dewey and Foucault provide excellent starting points for a discussion of the social foundations of education, particularly as it is being shaped by current critical scholars in various fields of educational study. That we must constantly be engaged in thought about the world and our involvement in it is basic to their understanding. Freedom is not something given or guaranteed. It is an active lived process, in which we are willing to look at and alter not only the thought of others but our own as well.

Accepting these arguments, we must also agree that educators of all levels have an enormous responsibility in the practice of freedom. Teachers can either encourage or discourage their students to think about the world in which they live. We all can think of those teachers who challenged our commonsense understanding of the world, prodding us to see and think differently, as we can those who did not. Educational institutions themselves, although often seen as the panacea, the cure-all for most any social problem, cannot guarantee freedom any more than institutions of government, religion, or family. It is rather what people choose to do within those institutions that will make a difference (or not) in the way we live our lives. This includes what happens between teachers and students.

The social foundations of education teaches teachers to consider the complex social, political, and historical forces that affect what they do with students in schools. It is a cross-disciplinary field of study within teacher education traditionally comprised of philosophical, historical, sociological, and comparative analyses of education. More recently the field has expanded to include disciplines such as economics and anthropology. Although this field has had a varied history in terms of its aims in teacher education,[3] in general the goals have been to study the broad problems and trends in modern society as they are related to education. Importantly, this field of study contrasts with other, more technically oriented, methods courses in teacher education in its view of the need to ground the study of education in the sociopolitical context within which it is practiced.

This orientation often gets interpreted by those outside of the field as the obsession with theory over practice within social foundations. This view may be the result, in part, of the historical organization of curriculum within institutions of teacher education.[4] Material covered within courses in social foundations is often presented as separate or distinct from pedagogical concerns associated with methods courses. Such organizational separations often set up a false dichotomy. Theory and practice exist in an inseparable and interdependent relationship. Indeed, what we do is always guided, whether consciously or not, by someone's ideas and explanations of the world and our positions in it. How we teach, the orientation that we take to the teaching-learning process, is always situated in a particular set of social, political, and historical relations. Pedagogy is affected by varying ideas of what it means to be a learner, what it means to be human in relation to knowledge, and these ideas are always enacted within a social and political context. It is only within this matrix of ideas and social relations that freedom is effectively practiced.

Historical Overview

Obviously, the study of the history, philosophy, or sociology of education does not guarantee that teachers will be engaged in the practice of freedom. These fields of study can just as easily be used to prevent students from asking questions about the context of their lives. Tozer and Mcaninch have shown that the early approaches to the social foundations of education were in fact more concerned with education's role in the maintenance of existing relations of power than in the critical examination of those relations. Drawing on the work of Harold Rugg, they point out that courses in teacher education in general from the 1880s to World War I were developed around a "concern for adaptation and adjustment to the emerging industrial social order."[5] Such an approach was assured by the financial support that the major teacher education institutions got from the owners of capital. Himself a student of education during these years, Rugg points out that curriculum and policy decisions in teacher education were often controlled by captains of industry, who "claimed the right to determine the kind of education the masses got."[6] Institutions such as Teachers College, University of Wisconsin, University of Illinois, Stanford, and others developing foundations courses in the early part of the century were influenced in large part by the ideological interests of "practical men" concerned with educating workers and citizens to fit the needs of a developing social, economic, and political order dominated by scholarship as well as texts and curriculum within the foundations.[7]

As will be discussed later in this essay, the influence on teacher education, curricular reform, and educational policy by economic interests is still with us as part of the political context of teacher education. Though this influence on the foundations dominated during the first part of this century, there were others in teacher education who preferred a more creative, critical approach. The work of John Dewey, William Heard Kilpatrick, Francis Wayland Parker, Boyd Henry Bode, and others helped prepare the ground for a more critical approach wherein teachers would understand the social and political processes shaping the nation's schools and be prepared to ask questions about those processes. As stated by Tozer and Mcaninch, men like Bode and Kilpatrick:

> sought to apply Deweyian principles of democratic problem solving to the general education of teachers. Each influenced others to conceive of

teachers not as technicians who were to simply pass on knowledge to the next generation, but as potentially critical and independent thinkers who could induct their pupils into processes of "scientific" and democratic processes themselves.[8]

A critical perspective is a view of the world with an interest in understanding the complex processes and meanings that operate to produce the ways we live. It is a view concerned with promoting more democratic, equitable social relations even if that means challenging the existing order of things. It means that "the way things are" may be questioned, denaturalized in the process of seeking different ways of living. The commonsense view of the world that is promoted to keep things "in place" may be shaken up, shifted by questions that seek to uncover the connections between institutions, knowledge, and power. Maxine Greene has referred to this process of questioning as uncovering "the processes of mystification" necessary to the maintenance of the status quo, a task assigned to the social foundations and historically grounded there.[9]

From the mid-thirties through the fifties, studies in the social foundations of education were influenced by what was referred to as a social reconstructionist perspective on education. Influenced by and initially one with the progressive educators that had gone before them, social reconstructionists implemented a decidedly cross-disciplinary approach to introduce students to critiques of educational ideas and institutions in relation to broad social, political, and economic structures. History and philosophy were taught as necessary to an understanding of present social conditions. The proponents of this shift in teacher education curriculum believed that teachers should have a broad understanding of the workings of society through the integrated study of fields such as sociology, economics, philosophy, and history. Such study would promote democratic action in schools, shaping students into independent thinkers and citizens.

Social reconstructionists promoted teachers as agents of social change through rigorous examination of the interests and ideals dominating the institutions of American society. Influenced by Dewey's understanding of freedom as grounded in action leading to social and personal transformation, these educational scholars did not hesitate to challenge the social and political order in which they lived. As exemplified by the 1932 text, *Dare the Schools Build a New Social Order?*, George S. Counts believed such thought was to be the foundation of teacher education, and he hoped, practiced in the public schools. Teachers, Counts argued, must be willing to take responsibility for the "courageous and intelligent reconstruction of economic institutions." "The times," he argued, "are literally crying for a new vision of American destiny. The teaching profession, or at least its progressive elements, should eagerly grasp the opportunity which the fates have placed in their hands."[10] As Tozer et al. point out, Teachers College at Columbia provided a model program in preparing teachers to become active agents of educational and social reform.

> The Teachers College program envisioned teachers as potentially important decision makers in educational institutions—"educational statesmen," they said who would apply theory to their practice and who would

help formulate educational policy at the local and state levels in a rapidly urbanizing, industrializing society with new educational needs . . ."[11]

The relative influence that any theoretical perspective or social practice may have is directly affected by intersecting social, cultural, and political forces and events at any historical moment. Although the reconstructionist points of view remained influential into the fifties, their ideas did not go without challenge. Nor did the theorists themselves remain unchanged by historical events. By the end of World War II, the general popular fear of communism and totalitarianism resulting from major shifts in international power relations began to affect the positions, both in terms of tenure and theory, of many American intellectuals. Right-wing attacks (foreshadowing the 1970s, 1980s, and 1990s) were waged against the critical attitudes of intellectuals in academia as subversive of "American ideals." Public schools and school personnel began to be scrutinized by citizen's groups for their perceived roles in instilling communist tendencies into the hearts and minds of the nation. Demands were made that curriculum, texts, and personnel be purged of any "un-American" influence.[12] The work of men like Harold Rugg, whose series of texts in the elementary social studies[13] had revolutionized study in that area, fell under heavy attack. The center of concern for these texts was the "problems, issues and characteristics of our times."[14] The series was a great success and was widely used. In fact, "between 1929 and 1939, 1,317,960 copies in the series were sold along with an additional 2,687,000 workbooks."[15] Rugg's textbook series was the greatest success of the social reconstructionists. In the late 1930s, however, the series came under heavy attack as un-American and subversive. There was concerted defense of Rugg's texts, including an articulate self-defense.[16] "Some of the most damaging charges were eventually wrested from Rugg's accusers, but the series was never completely revised and, after 1940, it diminished rapidly in popularity."[17] Texts in teacher education at this time were valued for their eclectic and ameliorative focus, allowing school administrators a certain zone of comfort and removing them from such controversy.[18] Even among major reconstructionist thinkers in social foundations of education the theoretical focus began to change from a critique of the economic structure and domestic policies to an emphasis on the threat to democracy from totalitarian regimes abroad. "Fear of totalitarianism replaced fear of capitalist exploitation for many liberals . . . They believed that the foreign threat made it even more imperative that Americans critically examine their understandings and expectations of the American democratic outlook."[19]

It is not surprising under these conditions that the critical approach to the study of social foundations of education would be replaced by a more conservative apolitical view of the relation of schooling to society. The Cold War between the Soviet Union and the United States was based upon more than ideological differences. It was also a matter of economics. In 1957, the Soviets launched Sputnik, and the schools were once again launched into the middle of public criticism and debate. Much emphasis began to be placed on the reform of math and science curriculums in the wake of charges that schools were failing to prepare students for the technological needs of the nation. Influencing the development of education in the late fifties was the National Defense Act (1958). Because of the multitude of charges generated by critics of American education,[20] the tendency was to keep teachers out of curriculum development and various other aspects of schooling. Money from the National Defense Act was funneled primarily into the National Science Foundation (NSF), whose premise was that experts (university physicists, biologists, and mathematicians) should create the curriculum of schools, not the teachers. This trend would return again in both the 1970s and 1980s. Of course, this directly and indirectly affected the education of teachers and the curriculums of social foundations.

From the late 1950s into the 1960s and 1970s, the dominant tendency in many social foundations texts and programs was to represent education as the primary vehicle to upward social mobility, opportunity, and equality in American society. The major texts used in undergraduate and graduate programs presented uncritical, apolitical, and ahistorical views of the relation between education and the broader social context. They replaced the integrated, cross-disciplinary study with a traditional, functionalist view of schooling, which was dominating the sociology of education. Tozer and Mcaninch argue that the popularity of such texts as *Society and Education* by Robert Havinghurst and Bernice Neugarten "may have helped to obscure and interrupt—perhaps permanently—the distinctive social foundations tradition that had developed for over two decades."[21]

Though this may be true, these early scholars laid important groundwork for future critical work in the social foundations of education. Interestingly, current critical perspectives in educational scholarship are sometimes characterized as belonging to a social reconstructionist view. While inaccurate, this view is testimony to the important influence of these early thinkers. Unfortunately, however, it disregards important differences between work being done currently and that of the early part of the century. Obviously, such a view misses the importance of a particular historical moment and its intersecting social conditions to the production of knowledge about education—a problem not surprising given the decline of history and philosophy in the study of education and the preparation of teachers. The current critical analysis of social, political, and economic relations, the very interest in doing such analysis in relation to education, and the theories used are certainly different from those of the 1930s and 1940s. Such an oversimplified conception of critical points of view offers important evidence of a crucial lack of historical, political, and cultural understanding among many in the business of preparing teachers for our schools. Unfortunately, as we move toward the twenty-first century, the influence of a technocratic approach to curriculum and teacher preparation seems to be dominant. Once again, trends in the economic sphere and the interest of corporate America continue to have an important influence in how the preparation of teachers is constituted. Corporations like Exxon and IBM, for example, have vested interests and considerable influence in the determination of outcomes and objectives in teacher education as well as curriculum reform in the public schools.

Critical Perspectives in the Current Context
//

In order to understand the current situation in broad historical context, we must analyze the developments in the United States and its educational system from 1969–1991. These dates are not arbitrary but coincide with particular historical, political, and social contexts that have helped to shape teacher education and schooling in this country.

Conservative Restoration

The period between 1969 and 1984 has been called the "conservative restoration."[22] The conservative restoration was and is a reaction to the sociopolitical crisis of the 1960s. In education, it has had profound effects. The period of the 1960s and early 1970s (until approximately 1972) in education could be called an era of experimentation and questioning. It was a time when many innovations were attempted in teacher education and, consequently, in the schools. Humanistic education was developed, which encouraged teachers to examine the affective aspects of learning as well as the cognitive.[23] There were experimental orientations such as open schools, open classrooms, values clarification programs, modular scheduling, and a plethora of electives. In order to prepare teachers for this experimental orientation, teacher education programs geared their curriculum to a more creatively oriented and less technical point of view. In spite of this approach, however, programs during this period still missed a well-defined, researched, and historically grounded critical social foundations component.

With the reelection of Richard Nixon in 1972, the experimental, reform orientation began to be eliminated.

> In schooling, the Nixon program included a vast national plan called "career education." Curriculum was tilted in the direction of work discipline and job-training. Perhaps that would cool the ardor of youth. If not, careerism was followed in the mid-1970's by a "Literacy Crisis" and a "back to basics" movement. Perhaps those programs would put some noses to the grindstone.[24]

This careerism orientation was, of course, not new as we have discussed. It had been the historically dominant orientation in education, with the only other exception found in the writing of the progressives and, in particular, the social reconstructionists. Careerism helped return teacher education from its concern with student-centeredness and affective education to its former conservative orientations. In fact, much of the literature of the 1970s and 1980s bemoaned the 1960s as a period that set the country's educational system backward. In fact, in a speech given in 1982 to the American Federation of Teachers, Albert Shanker, president of the American Federation of Teachers, said, "The 1960s brought a widespread loosening of standards and a bias against teaching a specific set of values."[25] Even the leader of the second largest teacher organization in the country was bashing the 1960s. What was missing in the schools, according to the Nixon administrative agenda, was rigorous discipline and attention to the basics (reading, writing, and arithmetic). It blamed the period of electives and open schools for the lack of student achievement and discipline.

This resulted in many schools returning to basic programs, not only at the elementary and secondary levels, but also in teacher education programs and teacher materials. The 1970s saw the development of competency-based teacher education, which made a preservice teacher's graduation and certification dependent upon the successful fulfillment of a long list of skills/competencies that were checked off by both teacher education professors and sponsor teachers. A preservice teacher's success became the basic accomplishment of demonstrating the competencies. Very seldom, if ever, were philosophical questions or critical perspectives discussed. Teacher training emphasized "basic skills" and the technocratic development of teachers. It concerned itself with providing techniques and left out most philosophical, theoretical, and political questions. These questions were the type asked in the 1960s and were not appropriate to the discussion of the career of teaching or, as some foundations texts have labelled it, the professionalization of teaching. Social foundations as a component of teacher education began to direct its attention almost exclusively to discussions of the day-to-day activities of teachers within a job-focused orientation. Replaced by the technocratic, the critical perspective was, for the most part, diminished or lost entirely. The critical and questioning attitude was seen as inappropriate to the development of good teachers. Hence, the long process of deskilling teachers continued. The process separated conception from execution. Teachers would no longer have to concern themselves with the conceptual aspects of teaching, just the mechanical techniques. Accordingly, teacher education programs and their foundations components shifted to discussions of management strategies and discussions of job specifications and satisfactions.[26]

This back-to-basics instructional orientation led not only to competency-based teacher education but, in the schools themselves, to competency testing. As a direct result of the "literacy crisis" and the graduation of secondary school students who were later found to be illiterate, basic competency tests—aimed at testing minimum proficiencies in reading, writing, and mathematics—emerged in school districts across the country. As of 1990, about forty states had developed some type of competency-testing program and other states were contemplating or developing them.[27] Associated with competency testing was the need for a standardized curriculum.

This emphasis on skills and standardized curriculum was instrumental in leading to the development of "teacher-proofed" materials in the 1970s. With the decline in standardized test scores and the perceived lack of rigor and discipline in the schools, many in education thought it necessary to develop materials that were errorproof. In other words, no matter how competent or incompetent the teacher who used them was, the materials themselves would prove effective. These "teacher-proofed" materials were basically scripted lessons with all quizzes and tests prepared by the textbook companies. The teacher simply had to read the script and give out the prepackaged materials.[28] This was clearly a different conception of the development and role of teachers than the reconstructionists, or anyone sharing a critical perspective, would have in mind. However, the tendency in teacher education and our society has been to prepare and treat teachers as "clerks of the empire"[29] rather than as critically aware and awake human beings.

One other component of the conservative restoration in teacher education was the establishment of teacher testing, which requires teachers to pass not only the particular required training courses but also some standardized measure of competency. It is another method of maintaining a less critical, more career oriented program in teacher education. The National Teacher Exam and the Pre-Professional Skills Test (PPST) are the major examinations given. The National Teacher Exam is available in all fifty states; in thirteen states, the PPST is required. The trend seems to be toward the establishment of some type of test for preservice teachers. Most recently, the inclination toward standardization is evidenced by the National Board for Professional Teaching Standards and the National Council on Education Standards and Testing. With the publication of the *Initial Policies and Perspectives of the National Board for Professional Teaching Standards* (1989), a national agenda for the improvement of education in the United States into the twenty-first century was introduced. The issuance of the document was the first part of a five-year plan that intends to transform the practice of education by determining the exact skills and competencies required of teachers and by constructing assessment instruments to measure the degree of competency attained.[30] This will allow for the eventual national certification of teachers, which may someday necessitate a national curriculum in teacher education.

"A Nation at Risk": The Reagan Years

In the late 1970s and early 1980s the United States was suffering economically. There was double-digit inflation and other nations began to effectively compete with the United States for larger and larger shares of the world market. Just as they had in the Sputnik era, and critics sought a scapegoat for the problems the nation was facing, and they turned with vengeance upon the public schools. The criticism of both schooling and the quality of teachers was sparked by the fear that failure of the public schools would contribute to the erosion of America's position in international trade. The 1980's crisis was not sparked by a single event but by a number of socioeconomic problems for which education was deemed responsible. With the election of Ronald Reagan in 1980, the continuation of the conservative restoration was assured. Now the "silent majority" of the Nixon administration became the "moral majority." Not only were attacks on liberal reforms based on political differences, but now also on the interests of the religious right. It became a moral mandate to reform the schools. President Reagan asked Secretary of Education T. H. Bell to submit a report on the state of education in the United States, and Bell created The National Commission on Excellence in Education in 1981. The resulting report was *A Nation At Risk*.[31] The report stated that our nation was at risk particularly in the areas of commerce, industry, and the military, and it denounced the decline in SAT scores. With regard to teaching, the report recommended that people entering teacher training programs should be required to meet high educational standards, salaries should be increased, teacher contracts should be for eleven months instead of ten, career ladders or master teacher plans should be developed, and various other job incentives should be generated. We see in these recommendations the economic interests that have historically driven reform in education. There was a profusion of reports issued during the 1980s, the decade of reports. The composition of the committees responsible for the various reports is indicative of the perceived role of teachers as clerks:

> The commissions, their reports and memberships were as follows: National Commission on Excellence in Education (*A Nation At Risk*)—18 members, 1 teacher; Twentieth Century Fund (*Making the Grade*)—11 members, no teachers; National Science Foundation (*Educating Americans for the 21st Century*)—20 members, 1 teacher; Education Commission of the States (*Action for Excellence*)—41 members, 1 teacher; The Paideia Group (*The Paideia Proposal*)—22 members, no teachers.[32]

Teachers, clearly, did not have a role in educational agenda making and reform. Business and political leaders constructed the agenda; teachers' ideas were not encouraged or promoted either by the report process or in the reports' respective recommendations for reform. Excellence, efficiency, and economy became the educational buzzwords of the decade. To be "excellent" meant for teachers to be "effective." This prompted an entire literature on effective teaching, focusing attention not only on teachers' performance but also on the achievement of students on standardized exams as a means of evaluating that performance. High achievement by students on standardized exams indicated excellence in teaching. Moveover, the resultant literature developed for preservice teachers promoted more of the industrial and business ideology and brought it to the study of teaching. Subjects such as time management, time on task, allocated time, classroom organization, and classroom management were and are emphasized in many teacher education courses, including the social foundations.[33]

Excellence in teacher education came to mean producing teachers who could implement instructional packages, manage and organize their classrooms, and have their students achieve high scores on standardized examinations. This, of course, is far from the conception of teacher that the social reconstructionists were discussing or, for that matter, the type of educator the humanistic educators of the 1960s and 1970s attempted to create. But in the period of conservative restoration, the effective and efficient educator was/is the type of teacher desired by the corporate order. Teachers will function as transmitters of cultural heritage and the status quo and not as transformative agents of either.

Education in the Year 2000: Bush and Clinton

With the election of George Bush to the presidency, the conservative restoration continued. Bush promised on the campaign trail to be the "education president," and soon after his election he called for an "Education Summit." At this meeting, held in 1989, he met with governors of the states (including then

Arkansas Governor Bill Clinton) to determine the educational goals for the year 2000. The administration and the National Governors Association agreed on the following six goals: 1) all children will start school ready to learn; 2) high school graduation rate will increase to 90 percent; 3) students will demonstrate competence in critical subjects; 4) U.S. students will be the first in the world in mathematics and science; 5) every adult will be literate and have skills to compete in the economy; 6) schools will be free of drugs and violence. Two years later, on April 18, 1991, Bush presented plans for achieving national goals for education, emphasizing the necessity of improving corporate competition in international markets. His plan consisted of four main components. Echoing previous reform agendas, Bush announced plans for the creation of model schools, national standards, voluntary national achievement tests, and incentives for parental choice. It is interesting to note the inconsistencies between his plan and the goals set by the "Education Summit." As Joel Spring indicates, "missing from the plan were the goals of improving preschool preparation, lowering the dropout rate, and banishing illegal drugs from schools."[34]

While Bush's agenda emphasized his alliance with corporate interests, Bill Clinton's initial plans for educational reform reinstated the Governors Association's original commitment to some social issues. While Clinton's "Goals 2000: Educate America Act" includes an emphasis on improving math and science skills, setting national standards for competency, and enhancing workforce skills in order to boost economic competition in the world market, there is also strong emphasis on equality of educational opportunity and educating "all children." As stated in his "Goals 2000" bill:

> As used in this bill, the term "all students" means students from the broad range of backgrounds and circumstances, including disadvantaged students, students with diverse racial, ethnic, and cultural backgrounds, students with disabilities . . .

Clinton's strong commitment to Headstart and children's preparedness for school is another sign of his administration's emphasis on the relation between educational reform and concerns for the improvement of social life.

Both Bush and Clinton fall in line behind the concerns expressed by *A Nation at Risk* that our schools are failing the economic interests of the country. Making our educational system number one in math and science through adoption of specific curriculum reforms and American achievement tests continues the corporate link with schools and a national agenda for the standardization of education. In spite of our Constitution's reservation of power over education to the states and our founders' fears of a national curriculum, the goals for education in the year 2000 indicate a growing nationalization of education. The establishment by Bush and support by Clinton of the National Board for Professional Teaching Standards demonstrates another dimension of the phenomenon of standardization and nationalization through teacher education. This movement toward a "de facto" national curriculum is a direct move toward the control of thought of the American citizenry, precisely what the creators of the Constitution hoped to avoid.

Diversity and the Debate over the "Canon"
//

The struggle over the course of study for teachers enters into yet another dimension in the 1990s and will be of immense importance as our society enters the twenty-first century. This struggle has been called the debate of the "canon." The debate centers around the old curriculum question with a new twist. Instead of asking "what knowledge is of most worth?", we ask "whose knowledge is of most worth?" The proponents of the conservative restoration claim that one of the problems with the process of education in the United States has been the continual movement away from tradition and the "essential knowledge" of the great books of Western civilization.[35] Current radical educational critics argue that the tradition being supported is a "selective tradition," which excludes or marginalizes certain groups such as women and ethnic or racial minorities (see Ellsworth's essay in this text). What is necessary, they argue, is diversity and a plurality of voices and perspectives.[36]

Critical Voices: Social Foundations and Curriculum Theory

The conservative restoration both in the society and its concomitant development in education have not progressed unchallenged. There have been voices of opposition in the educational arena. The critical voices that were emerging in the 1970s, despite the Nixon agenda for a career-based, basic skills orientation, had their antecedents in the work of Rugg, Counts, and others as we have previously discussed.[37] The reconceptualization of curriculum study, which included the study of curriculum and education contextualized socially, politically, and economically, emerged in the early 1970s as a dissident voice within the technocratic development of teacher education. The reconceptualization of the curriculum field was initiated by William F. Pinar, who developed a conference in 1973 at the University of Rochester entitled, "Heightened Consciousness, Cultural Revolution and Curriculum Theory."[38] Pinar says that he invited Dwayne Huebner, James Macdonald, and Maxine Greene to the conference:

> . . . in hope that these dissidents might find common cause. I linked the conference to the notions of "cultural revolution" and "heightened consciousness" dated terms that make one wince today. Yet, it was an effort to link the ideas of curriculum theorists to developments in the political and cultural spheres, and those efforts continued, indeed became one of the themes of the reconceptualist movement.[39]

This placing of curriculum, and consequently education, in its broader social context was the critical perspective in the 1970s. Termed variously as "new sociology of education," "radical educational theory," and "politically oriented educational theory," this body of work has become (during the last twenty years) the most voluminous and influential in the curriculum field in particular.[40] The critical study of education has, indeed, become interdisciplinary and cross-disciplinary.

It is difficult to distinguish between critical perspectives in the curriculum field and in the social foundations of education primarily because of the cross-disciplinary nature of the topic and concepts developed. Indeed, much of the study of education with a social, political, economic, and cultural context crosses academic boundaries. Although the social foundations field is separate from the curriculum field in many institutions, the ideas and concepts freely float between at least these two areas.

The area of social foundations is identified with the American Education Studies Association, which holds an annual conference. At this conference the paper presentations demonstrate the interconnectedness of both foundational and curriculum studies. In fact, many of the professors teaching foundations courses came from institutions where their major area of study was in departments of curriculum and foundations, or curriculum and instruction. Many of the authors of this present volume, including the editors, were graduates of curriculum programs and are presently teaching courses in the foundations area. The social foundations area also includes revisionist historians, who take a look at history as it has been written, try to analyze historical developments with a broader social context, and present new analyses of historical developments.[41] The authors included in this present volume were instrumental in the development of the critical voices in the 1970s and 1980s. Many are students of the initiators. They are continuing the development of the critical perspectives in American education.

Those of us who share in the chorus of critical voices believe that teachers ought to be able to take informed theoretical, philosophical, and political positions in the debates that ensue about curriculum, about teaching and learning, about the nature of truth, about what it means to be human, about "good" and "bad" values. The ideas that swirl around these questions make policy in schools and affect what gets made as "pedagogical knowledge." To be critical means to be able to open up those ideas, to expose the relations of power in which they are enmeshed, and to articulate a response to those relations. Returning to Dewey and Foucault, to be critical means to be actively engaged in the creation of freedom. In the words of Maxine Greene:

> The challenge is to engage as many young people as possible in the thought that is freedom . . .
> . . . In the classroom open to possibility and at once concerned with inquiry, critiques must be developed that uncover what masquerades as neutral frameworks . . . Teachers, like their students, have to learn to love the questions, as they come to realize there can be no final agreement, or answers, no final commensurability.[42]

We invite you, as students of social foundations and as educators, to take up this challenge, to engage with us and with your own students in the practice of freedom.

q u e s t i o n s   f o r   d i s c u s s i o n

1. How have outside forces such as business, politics, and economic conditions affected the development of education in the United States?
2. What are the connections between past educational reforms and the changes that have taken place in education in the '780s, '80s, and '90s?
3. What does it mean to be critical? How does being critical influence the practice of teaching? How are freedom and a critical perspective connected?
4. What has changed in education in the last 40 years? What have been the consequences of those changes?
5. What has been the role of teachers in educational reform?

t e a c h e r s   a s   r e s e a r c h e r s

Construct a list of the similarities and differences between Bush's educational agenda and the educational agenda of the Clinton administration. Discuss with fellow teachers the implications of these agendas.

Discuss with fellow teachers the growing trend toward nationalization and standardization in education. How would these trends affect daily classroom practice?

s u g g e s t e d   r e a d i n g s

Dewey, J. (1966). *Democracy and education.* New York: The Free Press.
Kliebard, H. (1986). *The struggle for the American curriculum 1893–1958.* New York: Routledge & Kegan Paul.
McLaren, P. (1988). *Life in schools: An introduction to critical pedagogy in the foundations of education.* New York: Longman.
Spring, J. (1989). *The sorting machine revisited: National educational policy since 1945.* New York: Longman.
Spring, J. (1991). *American education: An introduction to social and political aspects.* New York: Longman.

n o t e s

[1] John Dewey, "Philosophies of Freedom," in *On Experience, Nature and Freedom,* ed. R. Bernstein (New York: Minton, Balch and Co., 1960), 280.
[2] Michel Foucault, "An Ethics of Pleasure," in *Foucault Live* (New York: *Semiotexte,* 1989), 264, 265.
[3] See for example, Steve Tozer and Stuart Mcaninch, "Social Foundations of Education in Historical Perspective," *Educational Foundations,* 1 (fall 1986).
[4] See Lee S. Shulman, "Reconnecting Foundations to the Substance of Teacher Education," *Foundational Studies in Teacher Education: A Reexamination, Teachers College Record* 91, 3 (spring 1990).

[5] Tozer and Mcaninch, "Social Foundations in Historical Perspective," 7.

[6] Tozer and Mcaninch, 7.

[7] Historian Ellwood Cubberly's work is a good example of the particular benign conformist view of schools and schooling that characterized this era. See Joel Spring, *American School* (New York: Longman, 1990), for an excellent analysis of Cubberly's historical interpretation in comparison to other historians.

[8] Tozer and Mcaninch, 8.

[9] Maxine Greene, "Challenging Mystification: Educational Foundations in Dark Times," *Educational Studies* 7, 1 (spring 1976).

[10] George S. Counts, *Dare the Schools Build a New Social Order?* (Carbondale, Ill.: Southern Illinois University Press, 1978).

[11] Steven Tozer, Thomas Anderson, and Bonnie B. Armbruster, "Psychological and Social Foundations in Teacher Education: A Thematic Introduction." In *Foundational Studies in Teacher Education: A Reexamination, Teachers College Record* 91, 3 (spring 1990).

[12] See Joel Spring, *The Sorting Machine Revisited: National Educational Policy Since 1945* (New York: Longman, 1989), 3–4.

[13] Harold O. Rugg, *Man and His Changing Society, The Rugg Social Science Series of the Elementary School Course*, 6 vols. (Boston: Ginn, 1929–1932).

[14] Herbert M. Kliebard, *The Struggle for the American Curriculum: 1893–1958* (Boston: Routledge & Kegan Paul, 1986).

[15] E. A. Winters, "Harold Rugg and Education for Social Reconstruction" (unpublished doctoral dissertation, University of Wisconsin-Madison, 1968).

[16] Harold O. Rugg, *That Men May Understand: An American in the Long Armistice* (New York: Doubleday, Duran, 1941).

[17] Kliebard, 207.

[18] This was particularly true in methods texts as well as curriculum texts. See William F. Pinar and William M. Reynolds, *Understanding Curriculum: A Comprehensive Introduction to Curriculum Study* (New York: Peter Lang, forthcoming).

[19] Tozer and Mcaninch, 15.

[20] There were many texts written criticizing American education. Probably the most famous would include: Arthur Bestor, *Educational Wastelands: The Retreat from Learning in Our Public Schools* (Urbana: University of Illinois Press, 1953); Hyman G. Rickover, *Education and Freedom* (New York: E. P. Dutton, 1959); and Hyman G. Rickover, *American Education—A National Failure: The Problem of Our Schools and What We Can Learn from England* (New York: E. P. Dutton).

[21] Tozer and Mcaninch, 23.

[22] For an excellent study of this period, see Ira Shor, *Culture Wars: School and Society in the Conservative Restoration 1969–1984* (Boston: Routledge & Kegan Paul, 1986).

[23] Pinar and Reynolds, Chapters 3 and 4.

[24] Shor, 4.

[25] Albert Shanker, "American Schools Are Envy of the World," speech reported in the United Federation of Teachers' newspaper, the *New York Teacher*, 24 January 1982, 16, quoted in Ira Shor, 13.

[26] See Michael W. Apple, *Teachers and Texts: A Political Economy of Class and Gender Relations in Education* (New York: Routledge & Kegan Paul, 1986).

[27] See William M. Reynolds, "Comprehensiveness and Multidimensionality in Synoptic Curriculum Texts," *Journal of Curriculum and Supervision* 5, 2 (winter 1990): 189–193.

[28] For an extended discussion and analysis of these texts, see William M. Reynolds, "Freedom from Control: Toward an Abolition of Teacher Materials and Minimum Competency Tests," *The Journal of Curriculum Theorizing* 7, 4 (winter 1988): 65–87, and Michael Apple, *Ideology and Curriculum,* 2nd ed. (Boston: Routledge, 1990).

[29] See Henry A. Giroux, *Teachers as Intellectuals: Toward A Critical Pedagogy of Learning* (Granby, MA: Bergin & Garvey, 1988), and Peter McLaren, *Life in Schools: An Introduction to Critical Pedagogy in the Foundations of Education* (New York: Longman, 1989).

[30] See Alan A. Block and William M. Reynolds, "I Once Was Lost, But Now Am Found: Curriculum As Grace" (paper presented at the 12th Annual Bergamo Conference on Curriculum Theory and Practice, October 1990).

[31] The National Commission on Excellence in Education, *A Nation at Risk: The Imperative for Educational Reform* (Washington, DC: U.S. Government Printing Office, April 1983).

[32] George Wood, "Democracy in Education," in *The Curriculum: Problems, Politics and Possibilities,* ed. Landon Beyer and Michael W. Apple (New York: SUNY Press, 1988).

[33] For an excellent survey of this research agenda, see Penelope L. Peterson and Herbert J. Walberg, eds., *Research on Teaching: Concepts, Findings and Implications* (Berkeley: McCutchan, 1979).

[34] Joel Spring, "Annual Update for *American Education: An Introduction to Social and Political Aspects* (New York: Longman, 1991), 2.

[35] For texts supporting the maintenance of Western tradition see, E. D. Hirsch Jr., *Cultural Literacy: What Every American Needs to Know* (Boston: Houghton Mifflin, 1987), and Allan Bloom, *The Closing of The American Mind: How Higher Education has Failed Democracy and Impoverished the Souls of Today's Students* (New York: Simon and Schuster, 1987).

[36] See Stanley Aronowitz and Henry A. Giroux, *Postmodern Education: Politics, Culture and Social Criticism* (Minneapolis: The University of Minnesota Press, 1991), and Michael W. Apple, "The Text and Cultural Politics," *The Journal of Educational Thought* 24, 3A, 17–33.

[37] For a detailed study of both the antecedents and the current state of critical work, especially in the curriculum field, see Pinar and Reynolds, Chapters 2, 3, 4, and 5.

[38] The proceedings and papers from this conference were later collected and published by William F. Pinar, ed., *Heightened Consciousness, Cultural Revolution, and Curriculum Theory* (Berkeley: McCutchan, 1974).

[39] William F. Pinar, ed., *Contemporary Curriculum Discourses* (Scottsdale, AZ: Gorsuch Scarisbrick, 1988).

[40] For excellent studies of this work, see Philip Wexler, *Social Analysis of Education: After The New Sociology* (New York: Routledge & Kegan Paul, 1987), and Michael W. Apple, ed., *Cultural and Economic Reproduction in Education: Essays on Class, Ideology and the State* (Boston: Routledge & Kegan Paul, 1982).

[41] For examples see Joel Spring, *Education and the Rise of The Corporate State* (Boston: Beacon Press, 1972); Michael B. Katz, *Class, Bureaucracy and Schools,* Expanded ed. (New York: Praeger Publishers, 1975); and Michael B. Katz, *Reconstructing American Education* (Cambridge: Harvard University Press, 1987).

[42] Maxine Greene, *The Dialectic of Freedom* (New York: Teachers College Press, 1988), 125, 134.

Resisting Racial Awareness

How Teachers Understand the Social Order from Their Racial, Gender, and Social Class Locations

Christine E. Sleeter

guiding questions

1. What is the author trying to say or teach?
2. What is the significance of what you read here for you personally and for you as a teacher?
3. What are the perspectives drawn on by the author to make the analysis?
4. How does this analysis help to inform our practice in classrooms?

As student populations become more radically and culturally diverse and the teaching force becomes increasingly white, interest in training teachers in multicultural education is growing. Many educators conceptualize this task as helping them "unlearn" negative attitudes about race, and develop positive attitudes and a knowledge base about race, various racial groups, and classroom applications. I will argue that the task is more complex than that. White women teachers, many of whom have worked themselves up from working-class origins, already have considerable knowledge about social stratification in America, and it tends to be fairly conservative. They are more likely to integrate the information about race provided in multicultural teacher education programs into the knowledge they already have than they are to reconstruct that knowledge.[1]

Various theorists have examined teachers as upwardly mobile members of the working class,[2] as women,[3] and as working-class women,[4] focusing on how they construct their understanding of reality from these social class and gender locations. Teacher race has been examined primarily by comparing how white teachers and teachers of color interact with and teach children of color.[5] Teacher race is seen as an issue mainly when teachers display overt prejudice toward children of color, expect less of them than they do of white children, or fail to understand them. In this essay, I will use data from a two-year ethnographic study of thirty teachers (twenty-six of whom are white) who participated in a staff development program in multicultural education, to illustrate how social class and gender life experiences inform white teachers' understanding of the social order that they use to construct an understanding of race.

Theoretical Perspectives about Social Inequality

I will examine the teachers' perspectives about social inequality and multicultural education in relation to three theoretical views: CONSERVATISM, LIBERALISM, and RADICAL STRUCTURALISM. How one interprets the basis of social inequality informs one's interpretation of multicultural education and what one chooses to attend to, remember, perceive as important, and attempt to use.

From a conservative perspective, the good society places as few restrictions as necessary on individuals, allowing them to strive for whatever they want. All

CONSERVATISM: Political perspective that advocates allowing individuals to strive with minimal regulation, values privatization over public regulation, and holds that society should be regulated by natural aristocracy of talent and breeding.

LIBERALISM: Political perspective that values individual competition, but with state regulation to protect "disadvantaged" groups, rejects notion of natural aristocracy, values public institutions as much as private institutions.

RADICAL STRUCTURALISM: Political perspective that focuses on groups rather than individual mobility, views dominant groups as structuring social institutions in ways that maintain their dominance and subordinate groups as attempting to change the "rules" or balance of power in their favor.

individuals except those who are believed to be unfit, such as lawbreakers or the mentally ill, should have an equal opportunity to compete with each other. Government should restrict individual competition minimally, but private institutions such as the family and the church should "instill a sense of personal discipline, courage, and motivation" into people and curb or control immoral temptations—"the mistakes that people make."[6] Those institutions that regulate society should seek to preserve the best of historic tradition and should be controlled by "good people, by the natural aristocracy of talent, breeding, and very likely, wealth."[7]

Inequality is viewed as natural, resulting mainly from individual differences in natural endowment and effort, Cornell West summarized conservative explanations for oppression of African Americans and, by extension, other groups. The SOCIOBIOLOGY explanation for inequality holds that racial minority groups (and other low status groups such as women) are genetically inferior or different. The culturalist explanation holds that "the character and contents of Afro-American culture inhibit Black people from competing with other people in American society"[8] and this problem can be corrected by replacing the culture of a "disadvantaged" group with one more suited to successful competition in public institutions. The market explanation holds that employers and other members of dominant groups discriminate against individuals on the basis of tastes (preferences or prejudices), such as aversion to black people; this could be corrected by modifying people's tastes to make them more inclusive.

Liberalism shares conservatism's orientation toward competition among individuals for mobility. However, it rejects the sociobiologist explanations for inequality and the idea of a "natural aristocracy." Reform liberals have some sympathy with claims by "disadvantaged" groups that many social institutions restrict their opportunities.[9] For example, Alison Jaggar explained,

> Liberal feminists believe that the treatment of women in contemporary society violates, in one way or another, all of liberalism's political values, the values of equality, liberty, and justice. Their most frequent complaint is that women in contemporary society suffer discrimination on the basis of sex. By this, they mean that certain restrictions are placed on women as a group, without regard to their individual wishes, interests, abilities, or merits.[10]

Reform liberals support state interventions that try to ensure that people will be treated as individuals regardless of group membership. Liberals also support state interventions, such as affirmative action, that attempt to redress effects of past discrimination in the belief that one day they will no longer be needed and individuals will be able to compete as equals. Ultimately, liberals believe that cultural, attitudinal, and institutional dysfunctions that block the strivings of individuals can be corrected.

SOCIOBIOLOGY: Theory that ties much of human social behavior to underlying biological characteristics of humans, particularly biological differences among groups (such as the sexes, the races).

Radical structuralists reject the individual as the main unit of analysis and focus on competition among and inequality across groups. They characterize society as involving continuous struggle among competing groups: "There is no ultimately good society, only a continual struggle to overcome specific obstacles to human fulfillment as these become apparent."[11] Inequality across groups is more significant than inequality among individuals and results from group conflict much more than natural endowment or individualistic factors. As Martin Carnoy explained,

> The struggle of dominated groups to change the conditions that oppress them and the attempts of dominant groups to reproduce the conditions of their dominance are the key to understanding changes in the economy, in social relations, and in the culture. These changes, in turn, are reflected in state policies and in public schooling, both prime targets of conflict.[12]

Most social organizations, including the state, are structured primarily by groups with the most power and operate to their benefit. Therefore, inequality cannot be addressed effectively through solutions that alter changes for individuals. In addition, the state cannot be relied upon to serve the interests of OPPRESSED GROUPS; oppressed groups themselves must mobilize to challenge and restructure specific institutions that thwart their own interests. Many radical structuralists view education as crucial to the process of social change, because through education young people can learn to examine social relations and learn to act collectively to create a more just social system.

Multicultural education rejects conservatism, particularly biological and cultural deprivation explanations for inequality. But it is neither clearly liberal nor radical structural. In England, multiculturalists, who hold a liberal position, debate with antiracists, who hold a radical structural position.[13] In the United States, the debate is not so clearly demarcated, and the field has been criticized as growing out of liberalism.[14] While the field of multicultural education generally has used the language of liberalism, as I have argued elsewhere I see it more closely linked to radical structuralism because of the concerns it addresses, the historical context from which it emerged, and the assumptions of its main advocates, a large proportion of whom are educators of color.[15]

Multicultural education in the United States originated in the racial debates and protest of the 1960s.[16] In its inception, multicultural education was connected with a broad social and political racial struggle that was rooted in a radical structuralist understanding of oppression. Multicultural education addressed school practices with the understanding that reform of schools was linked with other movements outside education. Most of the language and conceptual work in multicultural education is drawn from ethnicity theory (which is based on analysis of the experience of European immigrant groups), however, rather than a theory of racial oppression (such as internal colonialism

OPPRESSED GROUPS: Categories of people in a society that share certain identifying characteristics (usually physiological characteristics), and that lack sufficient power to attain the material resources necessary to control their own lives, under the domination of a more powerful group.

or a class-racial theory), mainly because of the wide use and mainstream acceptability of ethnicity theory. Discussion often revolves around pluralism versus assimilation, ethnic identity, and prejudice, which are themes in the ETHNICITY PARADIGM. To teachers, the language of ethnicity theory may make multicultural education seem less threatening than more radical language would, but it also deflects attention away from structural inequalities in the distribution of power and wealth.

Background of the Study

This essay probes teachers' understanding of multicultural education and society in general. Data are drawn from a two-year study of thirty teachers who voluntarily participated in a staff development program in multicultural education.[17] The teachers were from two contiguous school districts, taught preschool through high school (most taught grades 1–6), and were from eighteen schools in which at least one-third of the students were of color (mostly African-American or Latino) or from low income families. They had taught between four and twenty-nine years; the average was fourteen years. Twenty-six were white, three were African-American, and one was Chicano; twenty-four were women and six were men. Seven taught special education, two taught English as a second language, and the rest taught in the general education program.

During school year 1987–1988, the teachers were released to attend nine all-day sessions held at a staff development center located between the two school districts. They also attended three after-school sessions and a dinner meeting. During school year 1988–1989, eighteen teachers continued to participate and attended five all-day sessions at the staff development center. A list of session topics is included in Table 1. The topics were selected, partly on the basis of interests teachers expressed in the first session, by a steering group composed of African-American, Latino, and white educators from the local community and university. The sessions were led mainly by consultants with expertise in particular topics. Although the sessions differed considerably from one another, most used a combination of lecture, discussion, and practical application.

For example, session number three began with a two-hour multimedia presentation by a local district administrator, describing changing demographics in the United States and the local region and suggesting implications of these changes for how Americans define ourselves. After a short break, a university professor contrasted European-American and African-American struggles for assimilation and success in the United States, addressing the question: If white

ETHNICITY PARADIGM: Perspective about cultural diversity that derives from the study of ethnic groups (groups that share a common culture and history) rather than racial groups (groups that share visibly identifiable physiological characteristics). In the U.S. the ethnicity paradigm is usually based on the experiences of European immigrant groups.

table 1 / Schedule of Sessions

First Year
    Full-Day Session #1: Introduction, Assessments of Interests
    Full-Day Session #2: Building Home-School Partnerships
    After-School Session #1: Star Power Simulation
    Full-Day Session #3: Race, Ethnicity, Social Class, and Gender in Society
    Full-Day Session #4: Ethnic Learning Styles and Racism Awareness
    Full-Day Session #5: Community Resources
    After-School Session #2: Discussion
    Full-Day Session #6: Working with Curriculum and Instruction
    After-School Session #3: Teachers as Leaders
    Full-Day Session #7: Cooperative Learning
    Full-Day Session #8: Library Resources for Multicultural Education
    Full-Day Session #9: Drop-Out Prevention Programs, Motivation and
       Self-Esteem, and Sharing

Second Year
    Full-Day Session #1: Action Research and School-Based Change
    Full-Day Session #2–4: Teachers selected three from among the following:
       Working with Your Staff, Making Curriculum Multicultural, Cooper-
       ative Learning, Building Self-Esteem, Parent Involvement
    Full-Day Session #5: Wrapping Up and Organizing for Change

ethnic groups were successful, why are Americans of color and particularly African Americans not following the same pattern? After lunch, another university professor discussed gender differences in how people attribute their successes and research on how teacher-student interaction patterns in the classroom reinforce these gender differences. An hour was provided for open discussion, and the teachers talked mainly about sexism. During the last half hour of the session, teachers viewed a videotape on bilingual education, which related directly to the morning presentations.

Session four was not as crowded with information. In the morning, a university professor discussed the creation of culturally compatible classrooms. She began with a lecture on achievement and learning and how culture affects information-processing strategies. She then involved teachers in an activity in which they drew their ideal classroom using crayons and newsprint. The facilitator had teachers share their drawings, then used them to discuss cognitive styles among children from racial minority groups, especially African Americans, and how their styles conflict with most classrooms. She included in her talk many specific recommendations for teachers. After lunch, a panel of three professional women of color discussed their own personal experiences with racism as they grew up. The panel was followed by a discussion in which the teachers reacted and asked questions.

The sessions drew most heavily on the language of liberalism, but some facilitators also drew on conservative ideas about social class and some drew lightly on radical structuralism. Although in the third session the European ethnic experience was contrasted with that of African Americans, many concepts used in other sessions reflected those of the ethnicity paradigm.

Research was conducted using a variety of methods, but mainly classroom observation and interview. Three one-hour observations were conducted in teachers' classrooms during the first year and two during the second year for a total of 121 hours. In the classroom observations, data were recorded on time use and instructional strategies, curriculum in use, teacher-student interaction patterns, student seating patterns, classroom decor, instructional materials, and decision-making patterns. Most of the staff development sessions were also observed. Each classroom observation was accompanied by an interview; a total of 125 interviews were conducted.

Over the two-year period, observable changes in classroom teaching were fairly limited. I will describe them here briefly to provide a context for examining how teachers defined multicultural education. At the start of the program, the curriculum and room decor in most classrooms was about as multicultural as published textbooks are.[18] About half of the teachers tried using or developing some multicultural curriculum on a sporadic basis, mainly incorporating "little things" into existing lessons. Eight wrote and taught one new unit or some lessons, usually in elective subject areas such as art, music, and home economics or in special education. Four used a multicultural calendar they had received in the program, and six taught one or two lessons from books they acquired in the program. The quantity and quality of classroom decorations representing human diversity stayed much the same over the two years, although about half reported preparing displays with diversity in mind, to which they drew my attention during observations.

To respond to student learning styles, half of the teachers gradually increased their use of cooperative learning and cut back on individual seat work and whole-class recitation, which dominated their teaching. While at the beginning of the program they spent an average of 11 percent of observed time using small group work, by the end this proportion had doubled. They reported that students found cooperative learning much more interesting than individual seat work and seemed to learn better when it was used. Five teachers reported supplementing print, such as using more oral reading.

Most of the teachers interacted with students in a very warm and friendly manner throughout the study period, but there were some changes in their distribution of attention to students. Over the two years, with the exception of one observation following a session on gender patterns in teacher-student interaction, boys received a disproportionate share of questions and praise (e.g., in the first observation, boys comprised 54 percent of the students but received 61 percent of the questions and 68 percent of the praise). At the beginning of the study, teachers distributed questions and praise in proportion to racial representation in the classroom. Over the first year, they gave a growing proportion to African-American students and particularly African-American boys. But by the second year, patterns were about the same as they had been at the beginning of the study.

One-third of the teachers reported trying new strategies to improve home-school communication, primarily sending or phoning home positive messages, getting parents to help more with homework, and looking for ways to make parents feel welcome in the building. Five teachers worked on long-range plans to strengthen home-school relationships. Their work was inspired by other involvements in their buildings, but they used ideas they had gained in the program.

Although some observable changes occurred, the program's impact on classroom teaching was fairly limited. This was not because most of the teachers found it useless. Teachers frequently commented on how "excellent" the consultants were and how much they enjoyed the sessions. Although some felt they were getting few ideas they could use in their classroom, several said they found the sessions to be practical and "solution-oriented," and many described the program with unqualified enthusiasm.

During one of the interviews, twenty-six teachers were asked to discuss their goals for teaching and how they saw multicultural education contributing to those goals. In other interviews, teachers were asked to discuss their own personal and professional backgrounds and their reactions to the staff development sessions. Data for the discussion below are drawn from these interviews. I first discuss how the teachers defined multicultural education in relationship to their goals for teaching. I then examine teachers' life experiences as whites, women, and upwardly mobile members of the working class to show how these experiences informed their understanding of multicultural education.

How the Teachers Saw Multicultural Education

I categorized their perspectives on multicultural education into four groups: those who saw it as irrelevant, those who saw it as human relations, those who saw it as building self-esteem among out-groups, and those whose perspectives defied classification.

Conservatism: Multicultural Education as Irrelevant

Seven teachers saw multicultural education as irrelevant to their work. They described their main goals as promoting academic achievement and individual development; two flatly stated that their main goal was to get students to perform at grade level. Those who also discussed individual development defined it within the parameters of grade level achievement. For example:[19]

> We have the district goal that they must attain certain things before they're promoted, but each individual then besides that would be getting some goals. Like, if they have reversals, I know one little boy, oh, really a lot of reversals and that was my goal, to make sure that by the end of the year, hopefully, that he would be improving a lot. (5-16-88)

They wanted their students to think, solve problems, and feel confident in their ability to achieve.

> I would like the students to understand that . . . I am teaching them problem solving through the content approach and processes approach and thinking on their feet, to know what you should do if in fact you encounter a problem. (5-10-88)

> I try to accomplish the goal of having every child leave my class with a spirit of self-confidence, knowing that they can believe in themselves and do whatever they set out to do if they have enough determination and self-confidence. (5-10-88)

For the most part, they believed that everyone who works hard can achieve their goals; they felt optimistic about society. Those at the primary level believed that if they made learning fun and gave plenty of reinforcement, the students would achieve. Secondary level teachers admitted perplexity about some of their students; they believed many were failing because they came from families that simply did not encourage and support achievement and learning.

Conservatives view inequality as natural, resulting mainly from individual differences in natural endowment and effort. These teachers who saw multicultural education as irrelevant drew on the culturalist and market explanations for inequality that West described.[20] They spoke of students' homes like the following teacher did:

> Where are they coming from? What's going on in their brains, you know? Because sometimes I realize how irrelevant it is to stand up here and talk, and I have a very close family, . . . [my husband and I] have been very strong disciplinarians and we encourage the work ethic . . . I realize how foolish and presumptuous [it is] to think all these kids are coming from the same thing. Just to have a totally helter-skelter house where there is nothing regular and the people who are your parent figures come and go and—you don't know, you know what I mean, just what is going on in their brains and where they are coming from. (5-16-88)

They used the market explanation when trying to be colorblind, wanting *not* to be among those who discriminate unfairly. All seven, who were white, did not find multicultural education useful primarily because of its stress on color, believing that acknowledging color or other ascribed characteristics would either reinforce limiting stereotypes or excuse people from performing. They emphasized paying attention to individual needs, not group membership.

> You know, this has been a constant, boring—I have never really thought about Asian Americans or blacks until I got into a multicultural course. I just treat them as children. (5-18-88)

As long as they saw their own expectations as appropriately high and their treatment of children as caring and unbiased, they did not see themselves as interfering with children's progress, and thus saw no need to change what they were doing. The only use they saw in multicultural education was its insights into culturally different students that might help them teach more effectively, such as information on learning styles or parent involvement.

Liberalism: Multicultural Education as Human Relations

Six teachers saw multicultural education as human relations. They described two main goals for teaching: promoting academic achievement and helping students get along with and appreciate each other. For example:

> Academics, I want them to be as near grade level as possible, which for some kids isn't a problem, but for a lot of other kids it is a very big problem . . . with behavior, it's important for me that they learn to work together, so that's some of the reason I'm doing the cooperative learning. (5-6-88)

They saw multicultural education as relevant to the extent that it gave them strategies for addressing both achievement and interpersonal relations in the classroom. Like the teacher above, they were quite interested in cooperative learning because it can address both goals.

They also expressed some interest in infusing multicultural content into lessons to help students understand each other better, to the extent time would permit without compromising academics. This infusion usually took the form of adding little things "when it comes up." For example:

> We try to talk about different cultures when it comes up . . . The English curriculum, with literature especially, like Ann Frank . . . Grammar, not nearly as much. But the calendar idea, putting different days on the board and the holidays, we do things for Women's History and Black History Month. (5-2-88)

In addition, some taught lessons on individual differences to help foster good relationships among students.

These six teachers were all white. But unlike those who saw multicultural education as irrelevant, they were comfortable thinking in terms of race and color and attached positive feelings and images to racial diversity. They also recognized a connection between race, student self-image, and student-student relationships. As one teacher said,

> You've had these groups going to school together and still have a lack of understanding. (5-27-88)

Therefore, they sought strategies and content to add into their daily lessons that would address these concerns. Their orientation toward children seemed to be very humanistic; personal fulfillment, inner peace, and harmony seemed to be of greater value than mobility or material gain. For example, one described multicultural education as an "atmosphere . . . of openness and acceptance" (2-23-88). Another had served in the Peace Corps and emphasized the tragedy of war in her teaching; another was active in a peace organization in her personal life.

I categorized these teachers as having a liberal orientation because their discussions of students' home cultures focused on positive as often as negative characteristics, and they did not describe themselves as colorblind. This suggested that they acknowledged worthwhile meaning in racial group membership. In addition, they occasionally criticized conservative national policies like the military build-up and political leaders like President Reagan.

Multicultural Education as Helping Members of Out-Groups to Cope

Eight teachers were interested mainly in developing self-esteem among their students and preparing them to survive and cope in a somewhat hostile society, and they saw multicultural education as fostering empathy for the personal struggles of society's out-group members. The main feature that distinguished them from those above was that they taught in special programs: English as a second language, special education, alternative education, art, and "at-risk" students. With the exception of the art teacher, all of their students were "behind" in one or more areas and were struggling in school. Their goals for students focused on their struggles for success:

> I work a lot on improving their self-image and their self-esteem. And I think that's probably my main goal, and I think that if I accomplish that, the other things will come along, the academics will come along and the social skills will come along. (5-27-88)

> The one goal is to help them to identify where they need to work, and help them to be successful, helping them to realize a little success and then to build on that success. (5-19-88)

The eight teachers (seven white and one African-American) saw multicultural education as helping children cope, particularly those who had encountered many difficulties in life.

> There are a number of us who really try to fight all the negative things and so forth, but the negatives have been so many, so powerful. (5-16-88)

They discussed sensitivity to individual needs and feelings, optimism about the worth of those whom others have rejected, and having flexibility for students.

They differed among themselves in their attributions of students' academic difficulties and their theoretical perspectives about social inequality. Their views ranged from conservatism to glimmerings of radical structuralism. For example, an elementary special education teacher saw lower-class students' homes as the main source of their difficulties, commenting that

> I don't know how much love goes on in most of the families, or how much attention they get at home. (5-23-88)

The teachers of English as a second language saw their students' difficulties as stemming from the fact that they were having to learn a new culture; once they learned it, they would be able to compete successfully. Several teachers saw their students as encountering negative experiences in many areas of their lives, including school, due to inflexible attitudes and institutional procedures. A special education teacher saw the whole of society as stacked against her students.

> Our society is basically built on not being able to handle differences. And that's why these kids can't get through school. That's why we have these little red-necked teachers who will not see anything but their own little box. (5-19-88)

On the basis of her experience in special education, she was beginning to develop a radical structuralist critique of social institutions.

More Complex Perspectives

Five teachers (three white, two African-American) discussed multicultural education in ways that were more complex and harder to categorize than the other teachers. These were some of the teachers who had showed the most interest in multicultural education; their own insights came in fits and jumps. They were in the process of active growth, and their discussions were less systematic than those of other teachers. In my interviews with them, which tended to be long, they often responded to questions by discussing in detail a new idea or insight without necessarily integrating it with other comments they had made. At times, some of them espoused conservative perspectives; at times, all five took liberal perspectives; and occasionally some expressed radical structuralist insights.

For example, an African-American teacher's main goals were to teach students what is morally right and to help them become strong enough to overcome life's inevitable barriers.

> My attitude is right now that in America we are raising a generation of wimps and followers. That's generally the way I feel. Because if we were not, . . . the drug problem would not be as prevalent as it is. Kids are not strong enough to resist their peers or resist other people who talk them into it. (5-13-88)

Multicultural education meant not sheltering students from the tough realities they would face. It also meant believing in the capabilities of children from low-income and minority backgrounds, and helping them develop the moral strength to succeed and do the right thing. His discussions mixed together culturalist explanations of poverty with institutional explanations of racism.

A white home economics teacher described multicultural education as "something that has to be incorporated into everything" (5-13-88). To think through how to do that, she developed a very creative unit about culture and clothing, which examined the relationship between climate, local cultures, and clothing design. She saw a relationship between multicultural education and, not only achievement and intergroup relationships, but also issues such as world hunger, which she was in the process of thinking through how to teach about.

Summary

Most of the teachers' conceptions of multicultural education emphasized individuality and success within the existing social system. They differed from each other mainly in the extent to which they saw race and culture as helpful factors to consider in preparing children to compete successfully. They also differed in their assessments of their own students' chances for success and their estimates of the kinds of support and help their students needed. Their debates were primarily between conservatism and liberalism. Several had adopted the conservative "children-at-risk" discourse in that they focused on characteristics of students that hinder their success (culturalist explanations of inequality) rather than characteristics of institutions that block attempts to advance.

> I took a course back last fall, I believe, which was basically understanding at-risk kids and not really multicultural, but you know, they would be included in both of those scenarios. They are at risk, many of them, because of either their background, the level of acceptance they receive from school, or just basic lack of understanding. (11-23-87)

With few exceptions, most of the teachers did not link multicultural education with a collective social movement aimed at redistributing resources across groups. For them, it was a tool for addressing problems they saw in their classrooms: tensions among groups of students, boredom, and failure.

Teachers as White Upwardly Mobile Women

Most of the teachers were enthusiastic about the program because they were acquiring much new information. What I came to realize, however, was that they were adding that information into conceptions they already had about the workings of the social system, rather than reconstructing those conceptions. Their interpretations of what they were hearing minimized institutional racism and racially-based conflict in society's reward structure.

As Martyn Denscombe and others have argued, teachers' perspectives stem partly from the structure of their work as teachers,[21] and I examine their work in detail elsewhere.[22] But in spite of the structure of their work, teachers have some autonomy in their classrooms. They decide what to do with that autonomy based on how they frame problems and issues. How they frame diversity and inequality results from their own experiences within particular racial, gender, and class locations. Although most of the teachers in the study had been insulated from perspectives and experiences of oppressed racial groups, they had constructed a fairly well-developed conception of the social order based on their experiences as white women and upwardly mobile members of the working class.

Teachers as White

Teachers bring to their work a worldview that is constructed within unequal racial relationships, but they usually do not recognize it as such. Kathleen Weiler, based on a study of white teachers, observed:

> [A]s whites they are in a position of dominance and thus do not identify themselves by race, since white privilege is so much a defined part of U.S. society that whites are not even conscious of their relationship to power and privilege. In U.S. society, white is the norm, people of color are defined as deviating from the norm and therefore their race becomes an issue.[23]

White Americans and Americans of color grow up in different locations in the racial structure. According to David Wellman,

> Given the racial and class organization of American Society, there is only so much people can "see." The positions they occupy in these structures limit the range of their thinking. The situation places barriers on their imaginations and restricts the possibilities of their vision.[24]

Most whites live in racially homogeneous neighborhoods, families, social groups, and churches and consume media that are dominated by whites. Most whites spend little or no extended time on nonwhite "turf," although they may incorporate a few people of color into their own worlds.

The worldviews of whites tend to support white privilege, but do so in ways that whites interpret as natural or as fair. Wellman argued that a contradiction whites face is how to interpret racial inequality in a way that defends white interests in publicly acceptable terms. Generally, sociobiological explanations for inequality are not acceptable today, so whites construct alternative explanations. They "resolve the contradiction by minimizing racism. They neutralize it."[25] Working-class whites, particularly, have a vested interest in protecting their own privileges by adopting strategies of racial exclusion that appear fair.[26]

Most of the white teachers in this study had fairly little exposure to the life experiences and worldviews of Americans of color. All but one had grown up in white neighborhoods. Eighteen had virtually no life experience with Americans of color outside teaching and, in some cases, having participated in formal instruction about racial diversity. They acquired firsthand experience with Americans of color mainly by having children of color in class.

The other eight white teachers had somewhat more substantial life experiences with racial diversity, which they had acquired through travel, outside interests, or involvement in school-related projects. For example, one had served two years in the Peace Corps in Thailand and had traveled in the Middle East and Europe; another had been an exchange student in Mexico City one summer, living with a wealthy family but witnessing much dire poverty. Travel can expose teachers to other people's perspectives and ways of life, but it does not substitute for experience with American racial minority groups. Two white teachers had attended multiracial schools, one had grown up near a black neighborhood, and one participated in a summer program for students of color that required extensive home visits.

Travel and contact experiences can sometimes help whites realize how much they do not understand about race relations and sensitize them to injustices and to perspectives and experiences of other groups. One white teacher described her first teaching experience in a university town:

> I taught in the highest minority school I've ever been in, it was 95 percent black. And to my surprise, that's when my commitment began. I didn't like the fact that the university community didn't know there was a black school there. And they didn't. And I knew there was something wrong. (3-10-88)

However, such experiences can also help whites get past the discomfort they feel around other racial groups without opening them to alternative perspectives. A few of the white teachers commented that they were raised "to be open to anybody" and "without any prejudice" yet their discussions revealed a limited understanding of racism.

Over half of the white teachers had taken a course or a workshop in multicultural education. Four had taken a required course as part of their preservice education, three from African-American professors. Each said the course had raised his or her awareness, but one commented that the professor had been "really big into black culture" (11-20-87), and another described the course as a "hostile experience" (3-24-88). Eight had participated in workshops when their school district was desegregated. What seemed to have stuck with them from the workshops was awareness that curriculum materials should include diverse people, some background information about minority groups in the community, and familiarity with multicultural education terminology. One emphasized having learned that

> I didn't feel that there was the prejudice that I had been led to believe, especially in the elementary teachers. I know I've heard many people say, I don't like when you say you're colorblind, because you shouldn't be colorblind, but I really believe that elementary teachers feel that kids are kids, . . . 'cause people would say, well, what's your minority breakdown? And teachers would really have a rough time saying, you know. It was like asking how many of your kids are wearing glasses. And so really, I'm not denying that there's prejudice but I just don't think it's as strong in the school system as people really assume. (12-15-87)

A few other teachers had attended courses or workshops on other topics, such as Southeast Asians. Some found such courses interesting and signed up voluntarily for more. At the same time, most were uncomfortable with what they perceived as racial anger; they sought similarities among groups and concrete classroom applications they could add to what they already did. Many did not see a need to radically change what they did, and were offended by strong suggestions that they should.

As the staff development program progressed, several white teachers tried to minimize race by negating it altogether. The seven who advocated a colorblind perspective clearly tried to negate race. Five tried to show interest in race by criticizing the project's emphasis on some racial groups—African Americans and Latinos—to the exclusion of others, such as native Americans, Arabs, or Japanese. Most white teachers had an unresolved dilemma: how to accept all children, regardless of race, while explaining their difficulties in school without seeming racist. Some directly used culturalist explanations that blame the "culture of poverty," asserting that race was not the issue. Several tried to ignore culturalist explanations but unconsciously used them anyway for lack of another explanation for children's classroom behavior and achievement. They first mentioned the racial or socioeconomic composition of their students, then immediately described their problems.

> Well, we have quite a mixture [of students]. We have two Vietnamese children. I have a mulatto. I haven't counted the Blacks. I have a few Spanish, a couple Spanish. And the majority of them do come from a low socioeconomic class. But then I do have a couple of them, about four, from the higher middle class, you know. So it is quite a motley crew of kids, and you've got your middle straight down. There's 27 and they aren't the brightest group that I've had. It's basically an average, low average class. (12-9-88)

For the most part, teachers did not have a convincing alternative framework for thinking about racial inequality.

The teachers of color, on the other hand, held different perspectives. All four had moved north from southern states, where they had grown up in segregated neighborhoods and attended segregated schools. All four had experienced racial discrimination while growing up, and had learned about family experiences with it. They did not have to be convinced that racism exists. For example, one described discrimination his ancestors had experienced in Texas, as well as what he had experienced as a child.

> I remember my third grade teacher telling that we were animals because we didn't know how to eat with a knife and a fork like white children, because we ate with tortillas. I wanted to take German in high school, and they . . . would not let me take German, I had to take, as a foreign language I had to take Spanish. Jesus Christ, it doesn't make sense, I could read, write, and speak Spanish because we did it at home! (12-11-87)

All four had been angry but learned to keep going.

> There are roadblocks, there are obstacles, there are some people who will throw obstacles in front of you or try to keep you from achieving. OK, you don't have to hate them to get back at them, you just have to do what you need to do, . . . Go on and achieve what you want to achieve. (1-6-88)

Their parents' education levels ranged from not having completed elementary school to having earned a college degree; but their parents had stressed the importance of education, and the teachers of color understood that most families of color value education. They identified with the minority community and tried to serve it through their work.

The main difference between the white teachers and the teachers of color is that the latter flatly rejected conservative explanations of racial inequality. Further, although they recognized racism as it is expressed through personal attitudes, they did not reduce it to attitudes. Neither did they accept culturalist explanations for racial inequality, although two articulated culturalist explanations for school class inequality. None of the teachers of color offered a radical structuralist interpretation of race relations, but they had insights that would support that perspective, such as a recognition that whites consistently erect barriers against people of color. Further, they had been involved in social protests during the Civil Rights movement, understood that many of the battles being fought then were still not won, and could see a relationship between multicultural education and social movements for racial equality.

In their investigation of how Americans view inequality, James Kluegel and Eliot Smith found most Americans to believe that opportunity for economic advancement is widely available and that inequalities are due mainly to unequal efforts and talents. But they also found that

> The largest and most consistent group disparities in expressed doubt about the workings of the American stratification order are those between blacks and whites. [N]either the disparity by status nor by sex is so large or so consistent across beliefs as that by race. . . . [B]lacks are the group of Americans that come closest to being "class conscious" in the Marxian sense.[27]

White Americans generally are not victims of racial discrimination. They do not experience as barriers the institutional rules and processes that oppress other groups. Further, whites usually do not experience the strength and resilience of racial minority communities and families. Spending their lives on white-dominated turf, most whites develop an experience base that allows them to deny or minimize racism.

Women in a Gendered Profession

Two white women teachers discussed their interest in feminism, which might suggest that a feminist analysis of society would cause them to question the ideology of individualism and equal opportunity. Although the program focused much less on sexual than racial discrimination, because most of the teachers were women, it is worth wondering to what extent their experiences with sex discrimination sensitized them to other forms of discrimination. Contrary to what may seem obvious, the data suggest that women's *unexamined* experience with sexism limits their understanding of social stratification by encouraging them to believe they understand discrimination. I can only speculate on this, because the idea did not occur to me until after I had finished collecting data, but my speculation fits patterns in the data.

In the first session of the program, teachers discussed and rank-ordered topics of interest to them. Very few indicated an interest in studying gender equity, although it was one of several topics suggested to them. Their relative lack of interest seems to have stemmed from a perception that they already understood it. The most lively exchanges among the teachers occurred when men made sex stereotypic statements or accepted instances of obvious sexism and the women challenged them. For example, in a session on cooperative learning, a technical education teacher mentioned having only one girl in class. Two women immediately asked what he would do next year to change that. He replied, "I have no idea," and he went on to say that he uses four different rooms, so students can hide and do things other than work. He was teased heartily, but some women grumbled about sexism in the distribution of students to vocational courses.

An attitude assessment that was administered at the beginning and end of the first year provides some insight into this.[28] It asked teachers to respond on a Likert-type scale to 100 items, which I analyzed by categorizing items by race, language, social class, and gender, then computing mean scores (1=low, 5=high) for each category for pre- and post-assessments. Since the interview data proved much richer than data from this assessment, I did not test the scores for statistical significance. However, I was struck by the high mean scores for items about gender. On the pre-assessment, average scores for items on race, language, and social class were 3.54, 3.32, and 3.70, respectively; on the post-assessment, they rose to 4.05, 3.83, and 3.96, respectively. The average score for items on gender on the pre-assessment was 4.44, and on the post-assessment, 4.49. These scores suggest that the teachers entered the project already much more sensitized to gender than to issues of race, language, and social class.

But the women's understanding of sex discrimination was probably a liberal understanding, locating sexism mainly in biased attitudes of individuals who limit the opportunities of other individuals by treating them stereotypically. A speaker on gender equity reinforced this view as she discussed how patterns in teacher-student interaction encourage boys and discourage girls. The main solution to sexism from a liberal perspective is to try to eliminate sex stereotyping and sexist practices in social institutions, so that all may strive for their dreams as individuals, without regard to sex. From a radical structuralist perspective, liberalism leaves several problems unexamined and contains some contradictions. For example, by stressing the value of careers that men of wealth have dominated, liberal feminism tacitly accepts disdain for manual labor and work involving care of the body. Liberal feminism does not offer a critique of the economic structure or the relationship between the economy and the state, which leads to naive assumptions about the neutrality of the state and blindness to the role of capitalism in women's oppression.[29] From a radical structuralist perspective, reform liberal solutions to discrimination would end neither sexism, racism, nor class oppression.

However, the very having of a theory of sexism can suggest to its holders that they do, indeed, understand one form of discrimination and need only learn how that theory applies to other forms. Thus, to the extent that women are consciously aware of sex stereotypes that other people articulate and that have limited their own choices, they feel they understand sex discrimination and do not need to analyze it further. Transferring their understanding of sexism to racism leads them to focus mainly on stereotyping and on persevering, in spite of the hurt other people's stereotypes may cause a person. In this way, women's unexamined experiences with sexism, in the context of discourse rooted in liberalism, strengthens their own adherence to liberalism as a generalized perspective for understanding social inequality and gives them a framework for thinking about how discrimination works.

The lives of the women teachers, however, had been structured by gender in ways they took for granted. Historically, teaching has been one of the few socially acceptable routes many women have had into public life and paid work. Madeline Grumet argues that women enter teaching in an effort to move out of the domestic sphere and develop their own potentials and identities as individuals.

> Bonded, interminably, it would seem to her mother and then to her child, the woman who survives the demands of these relationships to work in the world as a curriculum theorist, school administrator, or teacher is often engaged in the project of her own belated individuation and expression.[30]

As teachers, women experience the contradiction of being controlled by a male bureaucracy that has hired them to bring children under control, while they themselves are seeking growth, achievement, and productivity.

All of the women in this study were married and most had children of their own. Fifteen were asked about their mothers' work. The mothers of six had been full-time homemakers (one had taught school before she was married, then quit); the mothers of seven had been homemakers and had also held clerical jobs; and the mothers of two had been farmers. Unlike their mothers, the teachers had taken on full-time work in the public sphere. In a sense, they had rejected gendered limitations on their lives that their mothers had accepted.

However, the women teachers with children all described a pattern of balancing their careers with, and usually deferring them to, the demands of childbearing and mothering. In this sense their lives had reproduced traditional gendered patterns. Some were consciously aware that they had initially chosen a different career. For example,

> My dad was a pharmacist, and my mother had been a teacher, but she taught for maybe three years and then they were married and it was not acceptable for a pharmacist's wife to work, so she was at home . . . I really wanted to go into pharmacy, but my mother told me that I should leave that for my brother, that it would be a good idea for me to go into nursing and teaching. Being an obedient child, I did. My brother tried to go to school and he did not like anything that had to do with pharmacy, not the math or chemistry that I enjoyed, and so he never did go into pharmacy. (12-1-87)

Many described career patterns that were checkered by moves necessitated by their husbands' work or by the stops and starts surrounding childbirth. The following story was typical:

> I taught kindergarten, went back to school, worked in a child develop-
> ment lab while I was in semigraduate school. My husband . . . [was] do-
> ing some graduate work, but then I taught so he could finish. That's why
> I didn't finish my program . . . I taught there three years and that was the
> extent of my teaching at that time because I started a family and chose to
> be at home for 12 years. And just a fluke, I turned in a sub application
> the day before Thanksgiving, and on the following Monday I had a call
> saying, We have a kindergarten opening quite unexpected. Your sub ap-
> plication is here, would you like to apply for a job? (12-17-87)

At the same time, most of the teachers showed an active interest in continuing to learn, grow, and create within the bounds of their gendered lives.

For example, one teacher developed an interest in Indian art that she pursued with determination.

> I got very interested in Indian art. My poor ex-husband had to crawl out
> of and into every settlement that the Indians inhabited, whatever the
> height of Indians had ever been, and he had to go hiking in there because
> Shari was interested in it. And this last summer, my husband and I were
> in Arizona, because I'm very interested in this group of Indians. (1-7-88)

But, like most of the women teachers, her teaching career was interrupted peri-
odically by family demands. Even the fact that she was a teacher, rather than another professional, was due mainly to following her husband and taking what job she could get in the town in which his job was located.

The teachers seemed to accept their gendered family responsibilities and career choices. Many of them were very bright and capable, and within a con-
text that was shaped and limited by their gender, they had sought opportunities for growth and achievement. As Weiler discussed, we see in the career choices and patterns of women teachers "a logic of existing social structures and ideology" that subordinates women's lives to men's careers.[31] A critical examina-
tion of their own lives could form the basis for a radical structural analysis of gender oppression, but this becomes personally very threatening.

Mobility through the Class Structure

Liberalism values individualism and hard work; the image of pulling oneself up by one's own bootstraps is taught to American citizens from their early years. Patricia Ashton and Rodman Webb noted that

> The life experiences of most teachers demonstrate their allegiance to the
> ethic of vertical mobility, self-improvement, hard work, deferred gratifi-
> cation, self-discipline, and personal achievement. These individualistic

values rest on the assumption that the social system . . . works well, is essentially fair, and moves society slowly but inevitably toward progress.[32]

Several teachers described life experiences that had taught them that one can work one's way up the class structure through persistence and hard work. Twenty-three discussed their parents' occupations. Four of their fathers had held jobs that normally require college education—pharmacist, engineer, manager of a company, and minister—and two fathers had owned small businesses. The fathers of the other seventeen had worked as laborers of various sorts, such as factory worker, railroad laborer, welder, farmer, and firefighter. Most of the teachers had raised their own social class standing by earning college degrees. Further, at least twelve had completed a master's degree when the study began, and three more were in the process of doing so. Their volunteering to participate in this project was part of a broader pattern of bettering themselves through education.

Most who were white believed that anyone else who worked and struggled could also achieve success. For example, one had grown up in a poor family in Chicago. He had joined the Navy at age seventeen "for a place to sleep and a place to eat" (1-25-89). Of nine siblings, he was the only one to work his way out of poverty; he was driven by "the inner feeling of wanting to be successful" (1-25-89). He did not know why so many other people did not have that same drive; it had worked for him so presumably it could work for others.

Several teachers talked about their own (or their spouses') European ethnic backgrounds and about their grandparents' and parents' work ethic. For example, a daughter of Italian immigrants commented,

> One of my pet peeves, that I know if you want to work, you can work. . . . I know what my father did when he was in need, and we didn't have free lunches and we didn't have the clothes that other kids wore. (12-15-87)

She went on to describe her father working two jobs and the family pitching in to do agricultural work. As a result, without government help, she had been able to attend college and establish a fairly comfortable life. Opportunity is there, if people will only work.

Many Americans regard their own social standing as higher than that of their parents. While most social mobility has been due to an expansion of middle-class jobs and widespread improvement of the living standard of Americans in general, people tend to attribute their own improved status to their own individual efforts. As Kluegel and Smith point out,

> while the most common pattern is stability of class position from one generation to the next, upward mobility has also been common and outweighs downward mobility by roughly two to one. . . . Even those who have not been mobile have benefited, on the whole, from the aggregate improvement in living standards that has taken place since World War II.[33]

Attributing their own family's improved life to individual effort, many people then blame those whose lot has not improved as greatly.

None of the teachers who had been born into the working class identified with it or discussed strategies to raise the class as a whole. One's social class of origin, unlike one's race or gender (usually), can be left behind. The teachers who did so successfully saw, in their own example, the best strategy for confronting social class inequality: working one's way up into another social class. By extension, group membership should not matter, at least in considering life choices. How group membership may affect individual mobility is a subject of debate between liberals and conservatives, but both agree that individual mobility is desirable. Radical structuralists, on the other hand, focus more on group relations, and ask, not how to leave behind one's group of origin, but how to strengthen the position of the group as a whole.

Conclusion

Anthony Giddens advanced his analysis of social theory on the premise that "every social actor knows a great deal about the conditions of reproduction of the society of which he or she is a member."[34] Regardless of how little experience with racial or cultural diversity teachers have had, they enter the classroom with a considerably rich body of knowledge about social stratification, social mobility, and human differences based on their life experiences. The analogies the white teachers in this study drew between racism and what they knew about sexism, class mobility, and the white ethnic experience tended to minimize or neutralize racism and multicultural education's implications for action. However, from the teachers' perspectives, they were accounting for racial discrimination, not ignoring it. The teachers participated in as many as fourteen all-day sessions of multicultural education. Classroom observations and interviews suggested that they took from the staff development sessions information and teaching strategies to add into their thinking and their work, but that few of the teachers (if any) substantively restructured their perspectives about racial inequality or classroom teaching.

Of the twenty-six teachers in this study who discussed the relationship between their goals for teaching and multicultural education, seven saw it as irrelevant, basing their arguments on a conservative understanding of society that all Americans have fairly equal opportunity to achieve upward mobility and that those who do not progress well are hindered mainly by their own efforts or deficient home backgrounds. Two more, who were concerned with the struggles of out-groups, also articulated mostly conservative perspectives. They probably rejected the sociobiological explanation for racial inequality and, in so doing, regarded themselves as relatively progressive. All nine were white, but their sex and social class backgrounds were diverse. The women acknowledged their own experiences with sex stereotyping, one doing so at some length, but they saw this as inescapable and too easily used as an excuse for not trying. Those who had grown up in socioeconomically poor homes had pulled themselves up and, as a result, believed anyone else could do the same. They maintained that life is not easy; advancement requires work and at times a tough skin; but, in general, opportunity is open to everyone.

The remaining seventeen teachers interpreted multicultural education broadly within a liberal understanding of society. Ten—all women—focused on personal and interpersonal connection. The six who defined multicultural education as human relations showed interest in interpersonal relations more than in how social mobility works, and they willingly addressed the social and personal ambiance within their classrooms. Four of the eight teachers who focused on the struggles of out-groups were also interested mainly in nourishing students' self-esteem and interpersonal relationships. When asked about social processes outside the classroom, they acknowledged discrimination and, at times, showed anger about unfairnesses, but they were concerned more with helping children to cope with the world than to change it. Their interpretation of multicultural education was feminine in their emphasis on connection, community, and feeling,[35] but it was not yet politicized. Like the feminist teachers Kathleen Weiler studied, they valued "the creation of a classroom where 'it's okay to be human' in terms of relationships," but unlike them, had not "developed a commitment to raising issues and questioning accepted social values and ideology."[36]

The rest, whom I have classified broadly within liberalism, brought some degree of political criticism to their understanding of multicultural education. The teachers of color brought their awareness of institutional racism; two special education teachers brought awareness of how schools institutionalize failure. The other white teachers brought life experiences they began to connect with political criticism for reasons the data do not suggest.

For the most part, the teachers took as given the social context of the individual and asked how to prepare the individual to live within that context. Most further assumed that, with some variations, society's rules apply similarly to everyone, the rules may not always be fair but they are acceptable, and processes for setting them are fair.

It is important to note that the teachers in this study were a self-selected group. They volunteered to participate because they believed multicultural education might be useful to them. The proportions advocating conservative and liberal perspectives (as well as radical structuralist glimmerings) are probably rather different from those of the teaching profession at large, where it is likely that a much higher proportion subscribe to conservatism.

Teacher educators who work with teachers in multicultural education need to confront teachers' political perspectives, doing so in a way that accounts for, rather than dismisses, the experiential basis of those perspectives. For example, I have required preservice students to read Lois Stalvey's *The Education of a WASP,* which traces a white middle-class woman as she relearns how race in America works for African Americans.[37] Such a book can help white teachers rethink their beliefs about race while acknowledging both the validity and limitations of their own life experience. Other teacher educators begin with teachers' experiences as women, working to politicize their interpretation of gender. This does not lead automatically to a politicized understanding of race and social class, but it can provide a basis for doing so by reconceptualizing sterotyping and unfairness as collective and structural rather than just individual and attitudinal phenomena.

questions for discussion

1. How would an education program that assumes that people have no knowledge about cultural diversity be different from one that assumes that people have considerable knowledge based on their life experience?
2. What difference does it make in one's thinking about multicultural education, whether one holds a conservative, liberal, or radical structuralist explanation for inequality?
3. What does it mean that women's *unexamined* experience with sexism limits their understanding of social stratification?
4. What has been your own family's experience with social mobility? What has that experience taught you to believe about the opportunity structure in society? To what extent do you believe your family's experience transfers to that of families of another race?

teachers as researchers

Analyze the mission statement in your school for its commitment to multiculturalism. (Every school has a mission statement. Ask the administrator of your school for a copy.)

• Does the mission statement address equal opportunity, diversity, or multiculturalism?
• If it does not, inquire from the administrator the reason for omitting it.
• If it does contain such a commitment, how strongly is it expressed?
• Investigate how the school supports that mission statement.

How is it put into practice by the teachers? By the students? What other policies are affected by the mission statement? In general, how is life in the school affected by this statement? Investigate the history of the writing of the mission statement. Who was responsible for its creation? What was the historical and political context under which this mission statement got produced?

suggested readings

Lightfoot, S. L. (1973, May). Politics and reasoning: Through the eyes of teachers and children. *Harvard Educational Review, 43.*

Lortie, D. C. (1975). *Schoolteacher.* Chicago: Chicago University Press.

Lynch, J. (1987). *Prejudice reduction in the schools.* New York: Nichols Publishing.
McCarthy, C. (1991). *Race and curriculum.* London: Falmer Press.
Sennett, R., & Cobb, J. (1972). *The hidden injuries of class.* New York: Vintage Books.
Weiler, K. (1989). *Women teaching for change.* South Hadley, MA: Bergin & Garvey.
Weis, L. (1988). *Class, race and gender in American education.* Albany, NY: SUNY
   Press.

notes

[1] This work was supported by the Joyce Foundation of Chicago. I would like to thank
   Susan Gould and Tom LoGuidice for their partnership in the project, Margaret
   Oliver for her help collecting the data, and William McKersie and Angel Zapata for
   their encouragement. I am also grateful to two anonymous reviewers for their
   suggestions on an earlier draft of this article.

[2] See, for example, Dan C. Lortie, *Schoolteacher* (Chicago: University of Chicago Press,
   1975); and Patricia T. Ashton and Rodman B. Webb, *Making a Difference: Teachers'
   Sense of Efficacy and Student Achievement* (New York: Longman, 1986).

[3] See, for example, Madeline R. Grumet, *Bitter Milk* (Amherst: University of Massachusetts Press, 1988); and Jo Anne Pagano, *Exiles and Communities* (Albany, NY:
   SUNY Press, 1990).

[4] See, for example, Michael W. Apple, "Gendered Teaching, Gendered Labor," in *Critical Studies in Teacher Education,* ed. Thomas S. Popkewitz (Basingstoke, England:
   Falmer Press, 1987), 57–84.

[5] See, for example, Jacqueline J. Irvine, "An Analysis of the Problem of Disappearing
   Black Educators," *Elementary School Journal* 88 (1988): 503–513; and A. W. Simp-
   son and Marilyn T. Erickson, "Teachers' Verbal and Nonverbal Communication
   Patterns as a Function of Teacher Race, Student Gender, and Student Race,"
   American Educational Research Journal 20 (1983): 183–198.

[6] Kenneth R. Hoover, *Ideology and Political Life* (Monterey, Calif.: Brooks/Cole, 1987),
   33.

[7] Hoover, *Ideology and Political Life,* 34.

[8] Cornell West, "Race and Social Theory: Towards a Genealogical Materialist Analysis," in *The Year Left 2: An American Socialist Yearbook,* ed. M. Davis, M. Marable,
   F. Pfeil, and M. Sprinker (London: Verso, 1987), 76.

[9] See Hoover, *Ideology and Political Life,* for a discussion of the difference between
   classical and reform liberalism.

[10] Alison M. Jaggar, *Feminist Politics and Human Nature* (Totowa, NJ: Rowan &
   Allanheld, 1983), 175–76.

[11] Jaggar, *Feminist Politics and Human Nature,* 208.

[12] Martin Carnoy, "Education, State, and Culture in American Society," in *Critical
   Pedagogy, the State, and Cultural Struggle,* ed. Henry A. Giroux and Peter McLaren
   (Albany, NY: SUNY Press, 1989), 6–7.

[13] Barry Troyna and Jenny Williams, *Racism, Education and the State* (Beckenham,
   England: Croom Helm, 1986), 46.

[14] See Cameron McCarthy, "Rethinking Liberal and Radical Perspectives on Racial
   Inequality in Schooling: Making the Case for Nonsynchrony," *Harvard Educational
   Review* 58 (1988): 265–279; and Michael Olneck, "The Recurring Dream: Symbol-
   ism and Ideology in Intercultural and Multicultural Education, *American Journal of
   Education* 98 (1990): 147–174.

[15] I have developed these arguments in more detail elsewhere. See Christine E. Sleeter, "Multicultural Education as a Form of Resistance to Oppression," *Journal of Education* 171 (1989): 51–71.

[16] See Geneva Gay, "Multiethnic Education: Historical Developments and Future Prospects," *Phi Delta Kappan* 64 (1983): 560–563.

[17] The entire study is reported in Christine E. Sleeter, *Keepers of the American Dream* (London: The Falmer Press, 1992).

[18] See Christine E. Sleeter and Carla A. Grant, "Race, Class, Gender, and Disability in Current Textbooks," in *The Politics of the Textbook,* ed. Michael W. Apple and Linda K. Christian-Smith (New York: Routledge, 1991), 78–110.

[19] All names are fictitious; dates following quotations refer to the dates of interviews.

[20] West, "Race and Social Theory."

[21] Martyn Denscombe, "The Work Context of Teaching: An Analytic Framework for the Study of Teachers in the Classrooms," *British Journal of Sociology of Education* 1 (1980): 279–292. See also Kathleen Densmore, "Professionalism, Proletarianization and Teacher Work," in *Critical Studies in Teacher Education,* ed. Thomas S. Popkewitz (Basingstoke, England: The Falmer Press, 1987), 130–161; and Andrew Gitlin, "School Structure and Teachers' Work," in *Ideology and Practice in Schooling,* ed. Michael W. Apple and Lois Weis (Philadelphia: Temple University Press, 1983), 192–212.

[22] Sleeter, *Keepers of the American Dream,* Chapter 7.

[23] Kathleen Weiler, *Women Teaching for Change* (South Hadley, Mass.: Bergin & Garvey, 1988), 75–76.

[24] David T. Wellman, *Portraits of White Racism* (Cambridge: Cambridge University Press, 1977), 235.

[25] Wellman, *Portraits of White Racism,* 219.

[26] Bernard R. Boxill, "Is Civil Rights Legislation Irrelevant to Black Progress?" in *Race: Twentieth Century Dilemmas, Twentieth Century Prognosis,* ed. Winston A. Van Horne (Milwaukee: The University of Wisconsin System Institute on Race and Ethnicity, 1989), 12–48.

[27] James R. Kluegel and Eliot R. Smith, *Beliefs about Inequality: Americans' Views of What Is and What Ought to Be* (New York: Aldine de Gruyter, 1986), 289.

[28] See Carla A. Grant and Christine E. Sleeter, *After the School Bell Rings* (Basingstoke, England: The Falmer Press, 1986), 270.

[29] Limitations to liberal feminism are discussed in detail in Jaggar, *Feminist Politics and Human Nature,* 186–203.

[30] Grumet, *Bitter Milk,* 28.

[31] Weiler, *Women Teaching for Change,* 89.

[32] Ashton and Webb, *Making a Difference,* 29–30.

[33] Kluegel and Smith, *Beliefs about Inequality,* 24.

[34] Anthony Giddens, *Central Problems in Social Theory* (Berkeley: University of California Press, 1979), 5.

[35] Carol Gilligan, *In a Different Voice* (Cambridge: Harvard University Press, 1980).

[36] Weiler, *Women Teaching for Change,* 113–114.

[37] Lois Marks Stalvey, *The Education of a WASP* (Madison: University of Wisconsin Press, 1989).

chapter 17

The Foundations of Social Education in Historical Context

William B. Stanley & Jack L. Nelson

guiding questions

1. What are the authors trying to say or teach?
2. What is the significance of what you read here for you personally and for you as a teacher?
3. What are the perspectives drawn on by the authors to make the analysis?
4. How does this analysis help to inform our practice in classrooms?

Paraphrasing the opening lines of the classic Dickens story, *A Tale of Two Cities,* social studies incorporates the best of times and the worst of times. This seeming paradox is suitable as an introduction to the historical contradictions and conflicts in social studies in the schools.

Social education is the most inclusive of subjects, the study of all human enterprise over time and space. This comprehensiveness is humbling to an educator, but challenging. Because of the magnitude of potential content of social education, we use the term social studies to represent the more limited body of knowledge which is selected for teaching in schools. The determination of limits for social studies requires decisions about which social knowledge is most important, what skills and behaviors are most valuable, what values are most significant, and what sequence of content best fits the subject and students. As you can suspect, these battles about purpose, content, and pedagogy are among the difficult battles over social studies in the school curriculum.

Social studies includes the oldest of human knowledge as well as the most recent. It involves the study of individuals and the study of the totality of humankind. It promotes both traditional stability and progressive change, and it considers radical ideas too. It suggests not only obedience but also resistance to authority. And it represents the least and the most controversial topics. Although these contradictions and conflicts make social studies difficult to understand, they also contribute to its dynamic status and make it intellectually stimulating. Where social studies is dull is where there is no conflict. Social studies includes the study of conflict and is itself the subject of conflicting views—the best and worst of subjects.

Social studies has been the focus of continuing debate and conflict throughout much of our nation's history.[1] These debates over the purpose, content, and methods of social studies education contribute to periodic shifts in emphasis, as well as curriculum fragmentation. The resulting lack of consensus about social studies is blamed, by some critics, for the general erosion of our core social values, the rise of relativism, and poor student test performance.[2] Others argue that such lack of consensus is a natural outgrowth of our pluralistic society and its diverse elements, appropriate for realistic social study, and any attempt to force a national consensus on the social studies curriculum would be counterproductive.[3] The most recent attempt to establish national curriculum guidelines and standards is a topic certain to fuel more debate.[4]

Understanding the development of social studies as a school subject entails recognition of both the internal conflicts that are an integral part of social studies and the comprehensiveness that is social studies. Debates over such issues as what content should be included and how it should be taught are the product of basic differences over conflict study in social studies and the extent of comprehensiveness of the field.

There is even current debate about the origins of social studies in the schools. The traditional view, expressed in standard teacher methods textbooks, is that it originated from an NEA committee, which officially endorsed the term *social studies* in 1916, with its content coming primarily from history and historians exerting the most influence. More recent scholarship, however, indicates that the term was common in the literature well before the 1916 NEA committee, that it was originally drawn from ideas about social welfare and social improvement rather than from history, and was more problems and issues oriented than traditional views suggest.[5] Social studies, then, has at least two main arteries of origin—history and social improvement. This may explain some internal conflict evident in contemporary social studies. History tends to look backward and to stress stability and conservatism, while social welfare tends to focus on current issues, SOCIAL CRITICISM, and CIVIC RESPONSIBILITY for change.

We suggest that the American tradition of social education, those social purposes of schooling that include the curriculum topic of social studies, predates by two centuries the use of the term *social studies*. Before discussing this history, a brief examination of current major disputes provides a context for understanding the impact of historical conflicts and contradictions.

Cultural Transmission vs. Critical Thinking

A long-standing major dispute in social studies involves the relative emphasis given to CULTURAL TRANSMISSION or to critical or reflective thinking as the primary purpose of social studies.

Cultural transmission intends to impart traditional core knowledge, skills, and values to students. The emphasis is on teaching that content, sets of behaviors, and attitudes that reflect standard and socially accepted views. This content is the traditional CANON of the field, and this approach is the most widely practiced social studies in schools. It offers stability and common standards of behavior and thought.

Critical thinking intends to impart to students the means and attitudes of independent judgment and the processes for developing and using critical thought. The emphasis is on teaching the content, behaviors, and attitudes that question and critique standard and socially accepted views. This is the more progressive view and, although widely advocated, is less commonly practiced in schools. It offers diversity and the potential of social action.

Within this context—the relative emphasis on transmission of the cultural heritage or the development of critical thought—the social studies curriculum

SOCIAL CRITICISM: An emphasis on the need to be reflective critics of our culture and society. The purpose is to enable students to reorganize when social change might be necessary and how to act to achieve it. This was a perspective taken by social reconstructionists.

CIVIC RESPONSIBILITY OR COMPETENCE: The ability and responsibility to interpret, understand, and act effectively as a member of one's culture and society. Also the ability to act, when necessary, to bring about social change.

CULTURAL TRANSMISSION: The focus of cultural transmission is on transmitting what is seen as the "best" social knowledge to our students and using schools to help maintain the present social order. It is similar to nationalistic education, which is discussed later in this essay.

CANON: A body of principles, rules.

has had a mixed history. There are many variations of curriculum and pedagogy, but the basic orientations fall into three broad categories: subject-based, civics-related, and issues-focused.

Subject-Centered Social Studies

This position argues that social studies derives its purpose and content from those subject fields commonly taught in higher education. Some advocates perceive social studies as limited to only the study of history. Some consider it a subject that draws not only on the knowledge and methods of history but also on the traditional social sciences (e.g., geography, political science, anthropology, sociology, psychology, and economics). Still others want to define social studies as not simply including history and the traditional social sciences but also the emerging social sciences (e.g., law, women's studies, Holocaust studies, ethnic studies, etc.) and relevant aspects of other disciplines (e.g., the arts, humanities, natural sciences, etc.). Each of these views is based on the common assumption that discipline knowledge from higher education should be the organizing framework for social studies and the criteria for evaluation of students. Some subject-centered advocates argue for cultural transmission from a narrow perspective, without multiculturalism, while others argue for using the disciplines as a means for stimulating critical thinking and diversity; but both see subject knowledge as paramount.

Civics-Centered Social Studies

This approach is concerned with individual and social attitudes and behaviors more than with subject-field information. Educators who favor it argue that social studies is essentially concerned with good character, citizenship education, or CIVIC COMPETENCE. As in subject-centered social studies, there is a spectrum of views from inculcating cultural traditions to promoting social action to correcting social ills. They differ on the relative emphasis that should be given to uncritical loyalty, to socially approved behaviors, and to social criticism and improvement, but they share a view that social studies is more than just the study of disciplines and must be tied to good citizenship or civic competence.

Issues-Centered Social Studies

A third camp proposes that social studies is really the examination of issues. This group argues that personal and social problems and controversies are the main content of social studies. The variety of views here range from personal development to social problem solving as the social studies' purpose. Some in this group believe in examining only historic social issues that have stood the

---

CIVIC RESPONSIBILITY OR COMPETENCE: The ability and responsibility to interpret, understand, and act effectively as a member of one's culture and society. Also the ability to act, when necessary, to bring about social change.

test of time, but others emphasize issues that are current or personal, like moral dilemmas. And while some in this group view the study of issues primarily as a way to help students adapt to society (transmission), others see social criticism or activism as the main reason for studying issues.

The three social studies approaches (subject-centered, civics-centered, and issues-centered) are not necessarily separate or opposing. Knowledge from the disciplinary subjects is used in each; none disagrees that one purpose of social studies is civic development; and each accepts social issues as a valuable construct. The main differences are in primary purposes, emphases, and expected results—another way of suggesting the continuing dispute between cultural transmission and critical thinking. That is, each of the approaches has at least one strand that advocates social studies as the transmission of socially approved ideas and another strand that advocates independent critical thinking or action. The three orientations differ in how each would approach either transmission or criticism: one primarily uses subject knowledge; one uses character development; and one uses issues. These are, of course, important differences and account for much of the debate over social studies during this past century. In a given school curriculum, it is likely that a mix of these would be represented as emphases and individual teachers change over time.

The Development of Social Studies Knowledge

In its broadest sense, social education can be understood as that knowledge of society deemed important enough for the education of youth. In that sense, one can trace the roots of social studies in American education to our earliest colonial schools. The main purpose of education in colonial America was the inculcation of religious views; the content was the dogma of the dominant religion in each colony and the pedagogy was mainly indoctrination. The earliest laws establishing schools, the Massachusetts School Laws, specify the need for religious instruction. Teaching material was dominated by religious views, and teachers were employed by virtue of their religious beliefs. In the Latin Grammar School of New England in the colonial period, catechism and Bible composed a significant subject, a social study, while geography and moral philosophy were other social subjects taught.

Following the American Revolution came a second main purpose for social education, one that continues to exert considerable influence on the social studies today: NATIONALISTIC EDUCATION. Nationalistic education, intended to develop strong patriots, replaced religion as the main purpose of social education. From 1797, when Webster inserted nationalistic material about America in his geography books, through the twentieth century, nationalistic education has permeated the social studies. By the Civil War, social instruction in the schools

NATIONALISTIC EDUCATION: The study of our nation's history and institutions with a focus on patriotism and student acceptance of the core values and structures of our society.

included U.S. history and U.S. government as well as moral philosophy, geography, ancient history, and political economy. By the middle of the twentieth century, virtually every state had requirements for patriotic exercises in schools and mandatory coursework in U.S. history and U.S. government. Several states now require free enterprise rather than more general economics education.[6]

There is a close link between social forces and the social studies curriculum. Throughout history significant concerns of the society have influenced the social studies curriculum—for example, immigration provided interest in Americanization programs, the Cold War sparked anti-communism and patriotic teaching, and drug and crime problems prompted their inclusion in current social studies.

The Social Studies 1890–1915

By the last decade of the nineteenth century, historians emerged with the greatest influence on the social studies curriculum.[7] This impact is evident in the work of several National Education Association (NEA) committees that made curriculum recommendations between 1890 and 1910. These committees were often formed with the active involvement of the American Historical Association (AHA), and most committee members were historians. They made specific recommendations for the social studies curriculum, and by 1910 a general curriculum pattern had emerged. Historical myths and national holidays were the focus of grades one to three. Grade four was the study of state history and grade five was community civics. Grades six through twelve all focused on historical studies: European and American history in grades six through eight, ancient history in grade nine, medieval and modern European history in grade ten, English history in grade eleven, and American history and civil government in grade twelve.

History is obviously dominant in this curriculum; it was considered essential for citizenship and patriotism, but it was also to be studied for its own sake. Usually, history was taught as a set of factual information to be memorized. It was not viewed as practical knowledge for day-to-day living, but as part of the essential knowledge for any educated person.

Committee recommendations influenced the curriculum in the schools, but the response was not uniform. Great variations existed, especially among the noncollege track programs that contained almost ninety percent of all students as late as 1915. Still, the success of the various committees reflects the early and dominant influence of historians on the conception of social studies education as cultural transmission.

The Social Studies 1916–1945

The 1916 NEA Commission on the Reorganization of Secondary Education included a Committee on Social Studies, which issued a report that marked an important turning point in social studies education.[8] The official endorsement of the term *social studies,* still the most widely used label for this area of the curriculum, represented a gradual movement away from history as the singular core discipline and framework for social education to an expanded emphasis on civics and social problems. Nevertheless, history continued as the premier discipline in the commission's curriculum proposal—providing the primary focus in grades seven, eight, ten, and eleven—and the historical component for grades one through six remained.

Still, the proposed changes were significant in the reduction of recommended time spent on history in high school from three and one-half to two years and in a shift away from ancient and medieval history to modern European history. The proposed ninth-grade civic course had an interdisciplinary focus, combining elements of government, recent economic history, and sociology. And, the recommended twelfth-grade "Problems in Democracy" course marked the first national proposal for a course centered on social issues.

There were several reasons for the changes recommended in the 1916 report. The influence of historians, while dominant from 1890 to 1915, had not gone unchallenged. Rising new social science professional organizations led to claims for greater emphasis on political science, sociology, and economics in the curriculum, although most representatives of these various fields did not seem to question that history should retain a central role as the organizing discipline of social studies.[9]

Another source of change was the emergence of the revisionist "new history" movement led by several prominent historians. These revisionist historians questioned the value of teaching history for its own sake.[10] Instead, they described history as a functional discipline, contributing to the improvement of society. Students were to learn more than the mere content of history; they should acquire historical mindedness and learn how to apply the methods and content of history to the study of contemporary problems.

Another possible reason for the 1916 commission changes was the increasing support for a scientific approach to curriculum to promote social efficiency. Social efficiency educators rejected as elitist many of the earlier, traditional academic arguments of the NEA and AHA Commissions. They wanted the schools to help students fit into the current social order by preparing them to perform existing jobs and to function in various social roles. Social efficiency educators supported one cultural transmission approach to social education; but the emphasis was on basic skills and knowledge, as opposed to the earlier emphasis on high culture and the disciplines proposed by various curriculum committees from 1890 to 1915.[11]

John Dewey and the Progressive Education Movement

The gradual development of the progressive movement in education also influenced the recommendations of the 1916 commission report and the subsequent development of the social studies curriculum. Progressivism is a term subject to various and, at times, conflicting interpretations.[12] Nevertheless, progressivism represents a political and educational reform movement that emerged at the start of the twentieth century, and elements of this movement influenced social studies education. Progressivism was based on the assumption that the quality of human existence could be improved by the application of scientific reasoning to social problems. Consequently, education, as a major social institution, could play a key role in developing competent citizens, who would be better prepared to deal with the new challenges facing our modern industrial society.

John Dewey was the single most powerful influence on educational theory within the progressive tradition. Dewey's contributions to social studies education and the curriculum in general have been paradoxical. He is one of the most widely known United States educators, cited throughout this century by both supporters and critics, as a major influence on the development of "progressive" education. Yet, Dewey spent much of his career distancing himself from the Progressive Education Association and criticizing progressive educators who he felt misrepresented his ideas. He was particularly concerned with the association of his ideas with more extreme child-centered approaches to curriculum, but Dewey's ideas were often in conflict with prevailing educational norms. Other educational theories, particularly the social efficiency movement described above, gained wider public support, and, despite his popularity, Dewey's complex approach to education was never widely implemented in classroom practice.[13]

Dewey had a major impact on the philosophy of social studies, and his intellectual legacy remains alive in the work of numerous social educators who locate themselves in the reflective inquiry tradition. What Dewey helped construct is an important challenge to history or the social sciences as adequate to form the framework for the social studies.[14] Dewey built his conception of curriculum around what he called *occupations,* an awkward term to which he attached special meaning.[15] Occupations refer to fundamental social activities required for the realization of human survival and development. Thus, occupations also determine the standards against which human actions are judged. In short, they are the activities fundamental to human life. As basic human activities, the occupations link individual and social interests and avoid the false distinction between the individual and society that undermines so many approaches to educational theory.

History, along with manual training, literature, and science, was one of the major components of the elementary curriculum proposed by Dewey. He wanted the student to engage in activities that approximated the basic social activities of his or her community.[16] Such activities would help cultivate the attitudes and competencies required to participate in society and to help improve society when necessary. These activities would also form vehicles for learning the more abstract knowledge of the SCHOLARLY DISCIPLINES, including history and the social sciences.

SCHOLARLY DISCIPLINES: In the social studies, this term refers to history and the social sciences (primarily anthropology, economics, geography, political science, psychology, and sociology). Some scholars argue that each discipline is defined by its emphasis on particular concepts, special knowledge (generalization, theories), methods of study, and areas of interest. Others see the disciplines as social constructs that change constantly and have no clear boundaries or definitions.

In other words, while Dewey wanted students to learn about the scholarly disciplines, he thought it best to do this through initiation into the fundamental social activities from which these disciplines had evolved. Dewey's views on geography help illustrate this point. "Geography is not only a set of facts and principles, which may be classified and discussed by themselves; it is also a way in which some individual feels and thinks the world."[17] And the human ways of feeling and thinking the world were more important than any set of facts and principles. Furthermore, there can be no body of knowledge that is set apart once and for all as a discipline (e.g., history, geography). It is the perspective of the individual, a perspective formed in social interaction, that shapes understanding of any particular social environment, not the abstractions of geography, geometry, or geology. Put another way, organized subject matter is always a reflection of how we think in order to function competently in our culture.[18] What schools must do is help develop each child's perspective to its fullest potential so that it comes to resemble the systematic structure of an informed adult consciousness.[19]

In the case of history, Dewey believed our purpose should not be to have students memorize historical information but to develop a historical mindedness. History was the account of "how man [sic] learned to think to some effect, to transform the conditions of life so that life itself became a different thing."[20] Thus the social dimension of history was the most important. The traditional chronological study of history was neither a significant nor an essential approach, and the child's interests and experiences might be a better guide when selecting which historical periods to study. It was also important to relate the study of history to the basic occupations or activities that shape our social existence. Consequently, it was never sufficient to appeal merely to the child's interests as a guide to curriculum construction. In Dewey's laboratory school at the University of Chicago, the study of traditional chronological history was not introduced until about the fifth grade. And even at this grade level, the specific chronological periods chosen were subject to change in terms of how well they related to the students' needs.

To summarize, Dewey did not accept that any social science discipline, including history, could ever serve as the unifying framework for the social studies. Instead, such a framework would be derived from the occupations, although history might serve as a particularly useful discipline to provide examples of fundamental social activities to be learned. The purpose of schooling for Dewey (unlike those advocating cultural transmission) was not to fit students into the present social order, but to instill a method of intelligent reflection, which would give students both command of their environment and the capacity for action to make it better.[21]

Social Criticism/Social Meliorism

For some social educators the Great Depression provided evidence for the need to change our approach to the social studies. The most significant theoretical development in the depression years was social reconstructionism, an approach rooted in the SOCIAL MELIORIST tradition in curriculum. Social meliorists took a critical stance toward our society and argued that we can (and should) use education to improve the social order. In 1932, George Counts issued a reconstructionist manifesto for educators.[22] Counts claimed that schools were being used to maintain an unfair socioeconomic system that served the interests of certain powerful social groups at the expense of others and that this arrangement posed a threat to our democratic culture.

For Counts, and other reconstructionists like Harold Rugg and Theodore Brameld, education should be used to critique and expose the injustices in the present society and to pose alternative conceptions of a new social order. Counts provoked considerable controversy by arguing that indoctrination was an inevitable feature of any educational program and that a critical program requires counterindoctrination to help create a better society.

The reconstructionists were criticized by both conservatives and liberals. Conservative educators saw reconstructionism as a dangerous threat to our traditional way of life, while some liberal educators were concerned that the reconstructionists had gone too far. Dewey, for example, believed it was not appropriate to counter the effects of conservative indoctrination with counterindoctrination from a leftist perspective.[23] Dewey argued that education was capable of developing informed, competent citizens who could criticize our social institutions and make recommendations for change. In contrast, by indoctrinating students, however noble our intentions, we would in effect deny them the development of competence for critical judgment.

Reconstructionists helped define how education often serves to reproduce the current social order and its inequities, and they presented an argument for the importance of taking a critical stance in our educational programs. The use of indoctrination in education posed a problem, but, as reconstructionists made clear, educators were never neutral when planning a curriculum, selecting materials, and designing methods of instruction. These were not random acts but deliberate choices in accordance with a conception of social betterment. Dewey agreed with such arguments, but insisted that the schools be limited to the imposition of a method of intelligent reflection. It would be up to the students, acting as citizens in the future, to determine how to go about creating a better society.

World War II's impact on social studies education included the diversion of public attention from educational reform. In addition, patriotic feelings aroused by the war prompted conservative educators and others to question various progressive approaches, particularly reflective inquiry and social criticism.[24]

Social Studies 1945–1975

From the end of World War II to 1960, conservative approaches to social studies gradually became dominant and focused on cultural transmission. The onset of the Cold War and fear of communism stimulated hostility to social

SOCIAL MELIORISM: A perspective held by social educators who believed that schools (and social education in particular) should be used to help improve society.

studies programs that emphasized reflective inquiry or social criticism. Progressive education was attacked, and conservative reformers called for a return to basics, a core curriculum, and a focus on the disciplines.[25] The 1945 Harvard report *General Education in a Free Society* marked the resurgence of an academic tradition traceable to the NEA/AHA committees formed between 1890 and 1910.[26] The Harvard report emphasized return to a core curriculum with a focus on disciplinary areas—the humanities, social sciences, natural and physical sciences, and mathematics—that were defended as necessary to the survival of a democratic society. Emphasis on civics was reduced and history was recommended as the central discipline for social studies. Historical reasoning was emphasized and the value of studying current social problems was questioned.

The decline of one form of progressive education was signaled by the end of the Progressive Education Association in 1955. Two years later, the successful launching of the U.S.S.R.'s Sputnik satellite led to intensified attacks on the schools and social studies. Social studies was even seen as too "socialistic." The 1950s attacks on schooling were similar to more recent attacks in the 1980s and 1990s.

One reaction to the conservative critique was the emergence of the NEW SOCIAL STUDIES in the early 1960s. *New social studies* is a vague label that was applied to a variety of programs that were subject-centered and used "discovery" or "inquiry" pedagogy.[27] Discovery or inquiry techniques cause students to use content derived from history and the social sciences to find the concepts, generalizations, and methods of study in those disciplines. Proponents of the new social studies never recommended a particular national curriculum scope and sequence.

A key influence in new social studies was Bruner's *The Process of Education,* which, although it did not focus specifically on social studies, provided a framework for curriculum based mainly on recent developments in cognitive psychology.[28] The book made several key arguments. Each discipline was assumed to have a unique structure defined by key concepts, generalizations, theories, and modes of inquiry. Bruner also asserted that "any subject can be taught effectively in some intellectually honest form to any child at any stage of development."[29] Bruner's curriculum would have students study the structures of the disciplines in successive grades and at increasingly difficult levels of complexity. A few social studies educators (e.g., Lawrence Senesh at Purdue and Edwin Fenton at the Carnegie Institute of Technology) had worked on related programs since the 1950s, but Bruner's book provided a popular framework and stimulus for all such social studies programs during the 1960s.

The federal government, concerned with a perceived decline in educational quality, provided a lot of funding for projects inspired by Bruner's curriculum

NEW SOCIAL STUDIES: A general term that refers to the range of social studies curriculum reforms and projects developed during the 1960s and early 1970s. Among the major elements of this period were an emphasis on the structure of the discipline, discovery learning, reflective inquiry, and values education.

framework. In these various projects, students were given subject-centered material (either actual or simulated data) and asked to analyze it and draw conclusions. The focus was on developing intellectual processes to discover the fundamental structure and content of the disciplines. This approach attempted to avoid or resolve the old debate over teaching students how to think (process) versus teaching them what to think (content) by providing a way for doing both.

New social studies stimulated discussion as well as the production of many curriculum materials. However, the actual impact on the curriculum was relatively limited.[30] There are several possible explanations for this lack of effect. Producing materials took several years and the focus of social studies reform had already shifted by the late 1960s. The growing concern with civil rights, cultural diversity, the counterculture, and the antiwar movement all led to an increased emphasis on relevance, student interests, values education, and study of social problems. By the early 1970s, Bruner himself had begun to reconsider the value of studying the structures of the disciplines without adequate attention to the study of pressing social problems.[31]

In addition, a major controversy over one of the new social studies projects, Man: A Course of Study (MACOS), undermined public support. MACOS was criticized by conservative religious and other groups for "promotion cultural relativism and secular humanism" and as a direct threat to the core values of our culture.[32] This controversy revived earlier arguments raised in the 1920s and 1930s against the new revisionist historians, social reconstructionists, and proponents of reflective inquiry.

There were also some serious intellectual problems with the new social studies focus on the structure of the disciplines. From the start, some social educators questioned the assumption that knowledge of the disciplines should be the central focus of social studies. Again, this was a new instance of an old argument. For these critics, the central purpose of public education was not to train future social scientists but competent citizens and thinkers. Others raised serious doubts concerning the very existence of unique disciplinary structures.[33] As Dewey argued many years before, the disciplines only represented various perspectives by which we tried to understand social reality. A human society itself is not divided into discrete spheres that coincided with the disciplines. No aspect of social life was ever merely economic, historical, sociological, etc. Even the academic effort to draw distinct boundaries between the disciplines has not worked very well.

Finally, like all attempts to reform the social studies curriculum, the new social studies had great difficulty changing the traditional ways social studies was actually taught in schools. After more than seventy years of social studies development, it was not easy for any reform movement to effect significant changes in current courses of study or teaching practices. This resistance to change was exacerbated by the general failure to provide adequate training for teachers to use the new curriculum materials. In addition, some of the materials were mediocre at best, difficult to evaluate, and unlikely to provoke student interests. The new social studies movement provided new support for both the history/social science and the reflective inquiry/social issues approaches, but it also contributed to the continuing fragmentation of and debate over the social studies curriculum.

Impact of the 1960s Reforms: The 1980s

As the reform efforts of the 1960s and early 1970s faded into the 1980s, we entered a period of conservative restoration involving renewed attacks on schooling reminiscent of the 1950s.[34] In the early 1980s, numerous reports and books critical of education gained wide public attention. These contributed to the current emphasis on teacher accountability, instructional objectives, core curriculum, basic education in the disciplines, and standardized test scores. One major objective was to outperform German and Japanese students.[35]

Recent criticism and conservative reforms have had an impact on social studies. Conservative critics argue that student work in social studies has deteriorated and is significantly worse now than in earlier periods. Among the major reasons given for the decline of social studies knowledge are the influence of Dewey's progressive education legacy, the reforms of the 1960s, and the lack of coherence in the social studies curriculum.

Conservative critics believe progressivism promotes cultural relativism, diversity, and thinking processes at the expense of learning basic content and traditional American information, and the 1960s reforms are seen as Dewey-inspired. The lack of consensus on social studies (coherence) is blamed on special interest groups like advocates of ethnic, environmental, law-related, and global education, which now demand social studies time.

There are several things wrong with this line of argument. First, the reforms of the sixties represented more than one approach to curriculum. The new social studies movements, described above, dominated social studies reform for more than half of the 1960s, but the social science discipline emphasis on which it was based had relatively little in common with Dewey's ideas. Only during the last years of the sixties was there a significant revival of a reflective inquiry approach with some similarity to Dewey's ideas.

Second, while the reforms of the sixties did result in new materials, the expansion of electives and minicourses, and a renewed emphasis on the "process" of education, there is little evidence that these progressive reforms ever penetrated much of the curriculum or classroom practice. Studies over the past two decades indicate that a traditional cultural transmission approach to social studies continued to dominate the field, even during the height of the 1960s' reforms.[36] Teachers generally relied on textbooks and lecture-discussion methods, and there is little evidence of a shift to discovery or inquiry approaches to instruction. The extensive Project SPAN study also reported that the prevailing social studies curriculum scope and sequence in 1980 was remarkably similar to the one proposed in the 1916 NEA commission report. However, as in 1916, there was variation around the typical curriculum pattern. Whether or not one sees this sort of continuity as a problem, it certainly does not support the view that the impact of the sixties' reforms was a major cause of the perceived decline in our educational system.

Third, the current "crisis" in social studies education is frequently contrasted with what we might call a "golden era" from which we have witnessed a decline or fall since the 1960s. Again, the evidence simply does not support this interpretation. Throughout our history different groups have lamented what they saw as the poor performance of our schools. As early as 1905 an American Political Science Association (APSA) study of students entering ten different universities concluded that they had a very poor understanding of government.[37] In the same report the APSA recommended mandating the teaching of government in grades five through twelve. In 1905 less than 15 percent of all students graduated from high school. Thus, it is likely that the sample studied represented better than average students. Similar results of poor performance were reported in other studies through the next decades. In 1943 the *New York Times* tested 7,000 college freshmen on history. The results were disappointing. Twenty-five percent did not identify Lincoln as president during the Civil War or Wilson as president during World War I.[38] Historian Allan Nevins blamed the poor results on chaotic history requirements and too much emphasis on social studies (or what he termed "social slush"), which watered down the historical content.[39]

After the *New York Times* study, a committee of the American Historical Association and the Mississippi Valley Historical Association designed a new test of historical information. Groups of high school students and adults were tested to make comparisons. Even relatively well-informed adults performed poorly, although better than the students. Ironically, students who had taken history courses did no better than those who had not. But the committee attributed some of the blame to the social studies influence on the curriculum and urged a return to more history courses and an emphasis on historical facts.[40]

Almost twenty-three years later there was a second *New York Times* test of historical information. The 1976 test was not a direct replication of the 1943 test (there were important structural and methodological differences between them), but the results were similar as most students performed poorly. This 1976 test, however, did not support claims that the students of the 1970s had less knowledge of history than those tested in 1943.[41]

National tests of social studies knowledge have been conducted by the National Assessment of Educational Progress (NAEP) since 1969. The scores declined by 1976 and increased slightly in 1982 and 1988, the most recent scores available. There is no clear evidence that the changes in student scores can be attributed to social studies curriculum reforms. A more likely explanation is that the student populations changed over the past two decades.[42]

Diane Ravitch and Chester Finn argued, based on NAEP multiple-choice test scores, that seventeen-year-olds had a poor understanding of history.[43] They partly blamed the social studies curriculum. But in a comparative analysis of all the major national history tests, Whittington concluded that Ravitch and Finn's study is flawed and inconclusive.[44] The Ravitch/Finn data do not reveal if today's seventeen-year-olds know less than today's adult groups or if they are less knowledgeable than any other seventeen-year-olds from the past. Furthermore, Whittington demonstrated that it is not possible to make any clear comparisons of the different history tests results throughout this century. The test structure and items differ so significantly from decade to decade that direct statistical comparisons are not feasible.

The point is we do not have *any* reliable test data to suggest students in past generations performed significantly better than students today. Consequently, there is no clear evidence of a golden era of social studies education to which we might return. In fact, given that more students attend and graduate from high school now than in the past, our present school age population might even be better educated than their predecessors. Certainly there is evidence that our teachers are generally better trained than those who taught in the 1920s through the 1950s. This is not to argue that present practice in social studies education is satisfactory; it is not. The evidence does suggest that students have scored poorly on tests of history and social studies throughout this century. This may be reason to be concerned that our students might not develop their competence for critical analysis and decision making, because such competencies require an adequate understanding of our culture and institutions.

Concluding Thoughts

Conservative criticism of social studies over the past two decades has revitalized the cultural transmission approach using history and a few social science subjects to replace social studies. This is evident in many recent social studies curriculum proposals.[45] *Charting a Course* illustrates this trend.[46] It argues for history as the core discipline and places some emphasis on a few of the social science disciplines, particularly geography. *Charting a Course* rhetorically endorses critical thinking in its rationale but gives little attention to it in the proposed curriculum. Significantly, the interdisciplinary, twelfth-grade "Problems in Democracy" course first proposed by the 1916 commission has been relegated to an elective in this recent proposal. And contemporary social issues are not considered suitable to study until after eleven years of the history/geography program.

The National Standards Board for National Assessments in each school subject represents another major component of the conservative reforms of social studies. This board is only designing tests in history, geography, and political science knowledge and this amounts to a narrow conception of social studies consistent with the thinking in the 1989 *Charting a Course* proposal.

During the past decade, we have also seen a new backlash against multicultural education. This recent development has revived earlier dissatisfaction with including more emphasis on women and minorities in the curriculum and prompted calls for a renewed focus on nationalism and the dominant culture. In sum, the last two decades have not been encouraging for proponents of the more "progressive" versions of social studies reform, such as reflective inquiry and social criticism.

There have been some exceptions to this conservative trend. Strong critical reaction to *Charting a Course* has been thoughtful and widespread.[47] In addition, a number of social educators have generated curriculum proposals or commentary supportive of the reflective inquiry or social criticism approaches.[48] While these other proposals have not attracted as much public attention, they indicate the persistence of other, more critical approaches to social studies. But this new work is more than the mere survival of alternatives. Reflective inquiry and social criticism are being reinterpreted and enriched in ways that should enlarge their potential for the future of social studies education.

questions for discussion

1. Describe the major approaches to social studies in this century. In what ways are they similar and different? What are the possible strengths and weaknesses of these approaches?
2. What has been the dominant or most influential approach to social studies over the past century? What evidence would you use to support your claim? Why does this approach to social studies seem to be the most influential?
3. If you were to follow John Dewey's approach to social education, what sort of social studies curriculum reform proposals would you recommend for today's social studies educators? How would these changes affect current practice?
4. Conservative critics of social studies education have argued that our schools once did a much better job of teaching history and the social sciences. These critics claim that a combination of factors, including the influence of Dewey's ideas and the reforms of the 1960s have contributed to the present poor performance of social studies students. How would you analyze and respond to these claims?

teachers as researchers

These activities would be best suited to small groups.

Examine any social studies curriculum document (e.g., a course of study or a national, state, or local curriculum guide) for evidence of the approach to social studies the document recommends. Identify the strengths and weakness of the approach supported and how this curriculum guide might be improved.

Try to construct your own social studies curriculum framework for grades K–12. What do you think the primary purpose should be? What specific goals would you emphasize? What content should be taught at each grade level? What sort of knowledge about students and society do you need to answer such questions?

Examine a recent national or state curriculum proposal for literacy, math, or science education. How is this proposal similar to or different from current approaches to social studies education? What other educational conclusions can you draw from this comparison?

suggested readings

Barr, R. D., Barth, J. L., & Shermis, S. S. (1977). *Defining the social studies.* (Bulletin 51). Arlington, VA: National Council for the Social Studies.

Giroux, H. (1988). *Schooling and the struggle for public life: Critical pedagogy in the modern age.* Minneapolis: University of Minnesota Press.

Hunt, M. (1968). *Teaching high school social studies* (2nd ed.). New York: Harper & Row.

Jenness, D. (1990). *Making sense of the social studies.* New York: Macmillan.

Leming, J. S. (1992). Ideological perspectives within the social studies profession: An empirical examination of the two cultures thesis. *Theory and Research in Social Education, 20*(3), 293–312.

Morrissett, I., & Haas, J. D. (1982). Rationales, goals, and objectives in social studies. In Project SPAN Staff and Consultants (Ed.), *The current state of the social studies: A report of Project SPAN.* Boulder, CO: Social Science Education Consortium.

Newmann, F. M. (1975). *Education for citizen action: Challenge for secondary curriculum.* Berkeley: McCutchen.

Newmann, F. M., & Oliver, D. W. (1970). *Clarifying public controversy: An approach to teaching social studies.* Boston: Little, Brown and Company.

Shaver, J. P., Davis, O. L., Jr., & Helburn, S. W. (1979). *An interpretive report on the status of pre-collegiate social studies education based on three NSF-funded studies.* Washington, DC: National Science Foundation.

Stanley, W. B. (1992). *Education for utopia: Social reconstructionism and critical pedagogy in the postmodern era.* New York: State University of New York Press.

notes

[1] For summaries representing different interpretations of these debates, the reader should consult Robert D. Barr, James L. Barth, and S. Samuel Shermis, *Defining the Social Studies,* Bulletin 51 (Washington, D.C.: National Council for the Social Studies, 1977); O. L. Davis, Jr., "Understanding the History of the Social Studies," in *The Social Studies: 80th Yearbook of the National Society for the Study of Education,* ed. Howard D. Mehlinger and O. L. Davis, Jr. (Chicago: National Society for the Study of Education, 1981); Hazel W. Hertzberg, *Social Studies Reform, 1880–1989,* a Project SPAN Report (Boulder, Colo.: Social Science Education Consortium, 1981); David Jenness, *Making Sense of the Social Studies* (New York: Macmillan, 1990); Thomas S. Peet, "A Selective History of Social Studies Scope and Sequence Patterns, 1916 to 1984" (Ph.D. diss., Ohio State University, 1984).

[2] The following represent some of the recent kinds of criticism of the social studies curriculum: William J. Bennett, *First Lessons: A Report on Elementary Education in*

America (Washington, D.C.: U.S. Department of Education, 1986); "The Bradley Report 1987" in *Building a History Curriculum* (Washington, D.C.: Education Excellence Network, 1988); Lynne V. Cheney, *American Memory: A Report on the Humanities in the Nation's Public Schools* (Washington, D.C.: National Endowment for the Humanities, 1987); E. D. Hirsch, *Cultural Literacy: What Every American Needs to Know* (Boston: Houghton Mifflin, 1987); National Commission on Excellence in Education, *A Nation at Risk: The Imperative for Educational Reform* (Washington, D.C.: U.S. Government Printing Office, 1983); Diane Ravitch and Chester E. Finn, Jr., *What Do Our 17-Year-Olds Know?* (New York: Harper & Row, 1989); David Jenness, *Making Sense of Social Studies* (New York: Macmillan, 1990).

[3] See, for example, Shirley H. Engle, "Comments of Shirley H. Engle," in *Defining the Social Studies,* ed. Robert D. Barr et al. (Arlington, VA: National Council for the Social Studies, 1977); Shirley H. Engle, "The Commission Report and Citizenship Education," *Social Education,* 54, 7: 431–434; William B. Stanley, "Recent Research in the Foundations of Social Education: 1976–1983," in *Review of Research in Social Education: 1976–1983,* ed. William B. Stanley (Washington, D.C.: National Council for the Social Studies), 309–399.

[4] National Commission on Social Studies in the Schools, *Charting a Course: Social Studies for the 21st Century* (Washington, D.C.: National Commission on Social Studies in the Schools, 1989).

[5] David W. Saxe, "Framing a Theory for Social Studies Foundation," *Review of Educational Research,* 62, 3 (fall 1992): 259–277.

[6] Jack L. Nelson and Kenneth Carlson, "Ideology and Economic Education," in *Economics Education,* ed. S. Symes (Washington, D.C.: National Council for the Social Studies, 1981).

[7] Jenness, *Making Sense;* Hertzberg, *Social Studies Reform.*

[8] National Education Association, *The Social Studies in Secondary Education,* a report on the committee on social studies on the Reorganization of Secondary Education of the National Education Association, Bulletin 28 (Washington, D.C.: Bureau of Education, 1916).

[9] The American Political Science Association was founded in 1903 and American Sociological Association in 1907.

[10] Some prominent works by "new historians" include James Harvey Robinson, *The New History* (New York: Macmillan, 1912); H. Elmer Barnes, *The New History and the Social Studies* (New York: Century, 1925); Charles A. Beard, "Written History as an Act of Faith," *American Review* 39 (1934); Charles A. Beard, *Charter for the Social Sciences,* Part I, report of the Commission on the Social Studies (New York: Charles Scribner's Sons, 1932).

[11] See Herbert M. Kliebard, *The Struggle for the American Curriculum: 1893–1958* (New York: Routledge and Kegan Paul, 1986), Chapter 4, for an excellent discussion of scientific curriculum making and social efficiency.

[12] Kliebard, *The Struggle,* p. xi, has argued that progressivism is a term with so many conflicting (and contradictory) definitions as to be of little practical value in historical analysis.

[13] Kliebard, Chapter 3.

[14] Barr, Barth, and Shermis, *Defining the Social Studies;* see Jenness, *Making Sense,* for a different interpretation of Dewey's influence than the one presented here.

[15] John Dewey, "The Psychological Aspect of the School Curriculum," *Educational Review,* 13 (1897a): 356–369; John Dewey, "The University Elementary School: History and Character," *University [of Chicago] Record,* 2 (1897b): 72–75.

[16] Dewey, 1897b, 72.

[17] Dewey, 1897a, 361.

[18] Ibid., 359.

[19] Ibid., 364.

[20] John Dewey, "The Aim of History in Elementary Education," *Elementary School Record,* 1 (1900): 199–203.

[21] John Dewey, "The Theory of the Chicago Experiment," in K. C. Mayhew and A. C. Edwards, *The Dewey School: The Laboratory School of the University of Chicago, 1896–1903* (New York: D. Appleton-Century, 1936), 463–477.

[22] George Counts, *Dare the Schools Build a New Social Order?* (New York: John Day, 1932).

[23] John Dewey, "Education and Social Change," *The Social Frontier,* 3, 26 (May 1937): 238.

[24] Kliebard, Chapters 7, 8, and 9.

[25] For sense of this period see Kliebard, *The Struggle;* Lawrence Cremin, *The Transformation of the School* (New York: Knopf, 1961); Arthur E. Bestor, *Educational Wastelands: The Retreat from Learning in Our Public Schools* (Urbana: University of Illinois Press, 1953); Hyman Rickover, *Education and Freedom* (New York: Houds, Noble, & Eldridge, 1959).

[26] Harvard University Committee on the Objective of General Education in a Free Society, *General Education in a Free Society* (Cambridge: Harvard University Press, 1945).

[27] John D. Haas, *The Era of the New Social Studies* (Boulder, Colo.: ERIC Clearinghouse for the Social Studies and School Science Education Consortium, 1977).

[28] Jerome Bruner, *The Process of Education* (Cambridge: Harvard University Press, 1960).

[29] Ibid., 12.

[30] Haas, *The Era.*

[31] Jerome Bruner, "The Process of Education Revisited," *Phi Delta Kappan,* 53 (September 1971).

[32] Buckeley Barnes, William Stallings, and Roberta Rivner, "Are the Critics Right about MACOS?" *Theory and Research in Social Education,* 9, 1 (spring 1981): 35–44.

[33] Fred M. Newmann, "Questioning the Place of the Social Science Disciplines in Education," *Social Education,* 32, 7 (1967): 593–596.

[34] For example, see, Stanley Aronowitz and Henry Giroux, *Education under Siege: The Conservative, Liberal and Radical Debate over Schooling* (Granby, Mass.: Bergin & Garvey, 1983); Barbara Presseisen, *Unlearned Lessons* (Philadelphia: Falmer Press, 1985); Ann Bastian et al., *Choosing Equality: The Case for Democratic Schooling* (San Francisco: New World Publishing, 1985); Ira Shor, *Culture Wars* (Boston: Routledge & Kegan Paul, 1986); Jack L. Nelson, Kenneth Carlson, and Stuart Palonsky, *Critical Issues in Education* (New York: McGraw-Hill, 1993).

[35] Among the most widely known books and reports are Alan Bloom, *The Closing of the American Mind* (New York: Simon & Schuster, 1987); E. D. Hirsch, *Cultural Literacy: What Every American Needs to Know* (Boston: Houghton Mifflin, 1987); National Commission on Excellence in Education, *A Nation at Risk: The Imperative Ten Educational Reforms* (Washington, D.C.: U.S. Government Printing Office, 1983); Lynne V. Cheney, *American Memory: A Report of the Humanities in the Nation's Public Schools.* (Washington, D.C.: National Endowment for the Humanities, 1987).

[36] Stanley, *Recent Research.*

[37] W. A. Schater, "What Do Students Know about American Government before Taking College Courses in Political Science?" *Proceedings of the American Political Science Association* 2, 207ff.

[38] Benjamine Fine, "Ignorance of American History Shown by College Freshmen," *New York Times,* April 1943, sec. 1:1, 32–33.

[39] Allan Nevins, "American History for Americans," *New York Times Magazine,* 3 May 1942, 6; Allan Nevins, "More American History?" a letter, *Social Education* 6 (December 1942): 345.

[40] Edgar B. Wesley, *American History in School and Colleges* (New York: Macmillan, 1944).

[41] Jenness, *Making Sense,* 332–335.

[42] Ibid., 338–341.

[43] Diane Ravitch and Chester E. Finn, Jr., *What Do Our 17-Year-Olds Know?* (New York: Harper & Row, 1989).

[44] Dale Whittington, What Have 17-Year-Olds Known in the Past? *American Educational Research Journal* 28, 4 (1991): 759–782.

[45] For example, see the following: Bradley Commission on History in the Schools, *Building a History Curriculum: Guidelines for Teaching History in Schools* (Washington, D.C.: Educational Excellence Network, 1988); *History—Social Science Framework for California Public Schools* (Sacramento: California State Department of Education, 1988); Joint Committee on Geographic Education of the National Council of Geographic Education and Association of American Geographers, *Guidelines for Geographic Education: Elementary and Secondary Schools* (Washington, D.C.: AAG, 1984). National Commission on Social Studies in the Schools, *Charting a Course.*

[46] *Charting a Course.*

[47] See such criticism as Jack L. Nelson, "Charting a Course Backwards"; Cleo Cherryholmes, "Social Studies for Which Century?"; Linda Levstik, "The Research Base for Curriculum Choice: A Response"; and Jesus Garcia, "Does Charting a Course Include a Multiethnic Perspective?", all in *Social Education* 54, 7 (1990). Also, William Goetz, "Charting a Course and Beyond," *Social Education* 55, 4; *Social Education* 51, 1 (1991); Jack L. Nelson, "Social Studies and History: A Response to Whelan" *Theory and Research in Social Education* 20, 3 (1992).

[48] For example, see the following: Shirley H. Engle and Anna S. Ochoa, *Education for Democratic Citizenship: Decision-Making in the Social Studies* (New York: Teachers College Press, 1988); Walter C. Parker, *Renewing the Social Studies Curriculum* (Alexandria, Va.: Association for Supervision and Curriculum Development, 1990); and William B. Stanley, *Education for Utopia: Social Reconstructionism and Critical Pedagogy in the Postmodern Era* (Albany: State University of New York Press, 1992).

Epilogue

Toward Horizons of Hope

Rebecca A. Martusewicz & William M. Reynolds

RM: Well, we are talking about how critical perspectives have influenced our class-room teaching. You began last night by telling me how you came to be influenced by critical perspectives. Can you just reiterate that?

WR: I have been teaching about 18 years. The first five years I taught, I taught fairly traditionally. It was banking education, like Freire said, it was top down and I even had a podium to lecture from. I had students memorize things.

RM: Lines from Shakespeare.

WR: Lines from Shakespeare, Yes. But the whole time I was doing that, I felt there was something missing in the teaching. It is very hard to describe that, maybe it was an intuitive sense or something, but I knew something was missing. So, I went back to get a master's degree at a state college in New York and I was taught more "how to"—more technical approaches to teaching. I learned how to teach expository writing, how to teach the novel, how to teach poetry, that whole thing.

RM: What was the "how to"?

WR: The "how to" was how to do lesson plans and tricks and gimmicks on how to teach various parts of the English curriculum. And then I started working at the U of R as a graduate student in the doctoral program and I was immediately confronted with a whole new set of perspectives, which were critical. And I remember Philip Wexler recommending a book to me by Richard Ohmann called *English Teaching in America.* You know how every once in a while you have books that change your life?

RM: Yes, I sure do.

WR: That was certainly one book that changed my life because it critiqued the whole area of English teaching in the United States.

RM: From what point of view? What was its premise?

WR: The thesis was that the structure of English teaching in America was reproductive of the status quo. It was written from a neo-marxist perspective and basically it said that even the forms of writing that we use that are accepted at the university in many freshman composition courses are not necessarily the only way to write. It was kind of interesting, because it contradicted all that I had been taught about composition in all those "how to" courses.

RM: I understand.

WR: Remember that feeling that I had that something wasn't right? I began to be able to articulate questions about why it wasn't right.

RM: So can you give me an example of a question you might ask?

WR: Yes. A good one would be this: whose interest does it serve to have compositions formulated in the way they are with a thesis statement and a body of evidence and then a concluding statement. Why is that the only way you can write a composition? Before, I just accepted that was the form and taught that form and said, well this is what it is. Then, I began to ask different kinds of questions. And then, of course, it came back eventually after much more reading than just Richard Ohmann's book, to influence my day-to-day classroom teaching. Because I was teaching at the same time I was doing the doctoral program.

RM: Teaching high school?

WR: Teaching high school, right, and so I began to change my classroom around from this very traditional top-down, banking system.

RM: Can you talk more about what that is?

WR: Yes, it is Freire's notion of a banking system, where he says there are several assumptions that we make when we teach, that the teacher knows everything and the students know nothing. That the students are like an empty bank and the teacher's job is to fill it with as many deposits as he or she can and so that education in the United States becomes accumulation for accreditation.

RM: Exactly.

WR: We try to get as many A's as we can, as many courses as we can, as many degrees as we can, to fill up our empty vessels and I began to think, well, wait a minute, people aren't empty vessels. They know something and so I began to change that attitude of being a traditional teacher to trying to create what I have called a critical caring conversational classroom. Caring is very important. Listening to students and what they have to say is very important, and, of course, the banking notion would say you don't need to listen to students because they don't know anything so why would you need to listen to them in the first place? But I think it is important to listen to students, to give them that care. They are human beings. Since they are human beings, it is important to have students develop their critical abilities.

RM: Can you define what you mean when you use the word critical?

WR: Yes, I think it is just like my experience and that is that they need to ask the hard questions, the why questions. They are so used to asking how to. In fact, I think the school teaches them through the years to come to expect to be told what to do. Then they see being told what to do as a natural thing and they don't question it, they just accept it. So, they have to ask the why questions, to begin to disrupt that taken for granted attitude.

RM: As I listen to you tell your story about going to graduate school, I think about my own story. I guess, for me, as an undergraduate and a high school student, and all through my schooling until I was about a junior in college, there was always a kind of nagging discontent and boredom really with the way I was learning and with what I was learning. It always seemed to me that I wasn't getting at it, whatever "it" was. I wasn't inspired to think. What made me interested and joyous wasn't being tapped until one year I took a course called introduction to sociology with Frank Hearn at Cortland State University. I hope he is still there. I was on the edge of my seat for the rest of my college career. It was because Frank taught about life in society from a critical theory perspective and began to challenge us to ask questions about social justice and about political life basically. He taught about how it is that inequality and unjust social relations come to be reproduced, and he introduced us to new ways of thinking about social life. It seemed to be like that course expressed or articulated all the questions that had been swirling around inside of me since I think I was a child, actually. I have done a little work about my own critical life and I think as a child, even as a four-year-old, I was asking critical questions about the world. I mean questions like: why does it work this way, how come we have to do it this way, who decides that, and well, why? Pretty soon, by the time I was an adolescent, the why questions were all but silenced. They were silenced either by my peers or by just not being responded to and not taken seriously. I think children with their "why" questions get silenced a lot because those questions raise very difficult problematic issues. They raise ethic and political issues that people don't like to face. They expose a lot. I mean I think kids' "why" questions expose incredible problems in the world that we tend to ignore unless we encourage those questions and encourage kids to pursue the answers to them. Anyway, by the time I was a senior in my undergraduate work, I realized that I was just on the edge of my education and that there was something about education itself that was critical to improving social life. And somehow schools were failing. I was very acutely aware that somehow my schooling had failed me. Not only my schooling but my education. I mean my family education and my education in the larger world had failed to encourage me to ask the questions that could actually lead to making the world better. I was very concerned about racism. I was concerned about class inequalities, and I began to be able to articulate an understanding about gender inequalities which I had been experiencing all my life but had never really had a way to express legitimately. I had never been encouraged to articulate or formulate any kind of theoretical basis for my gut feelings. I guess Frank Hearn is the person who sort of opened the door for me. I guess the door of my soul had already been opened but no one had encouraged me to walk through and actually begin to live my life according to those gut feelings. I think the process of beginning to live our lives in ways that are sensitive and responsive to injustices is the process of becoming critical.

WR: I think it is a question of integration because you can intellectually accept what we are talking about, but it is also essential that you live it.

RM: That's right. So, what does that mean for you?

WR: Well, it means that it is not enough to talk about critical perspectives in the classroom. It has to carry over into your activities in daily life.

RM: I think a first step, however, is that we begin to articulate and encourage our students, or maybe challenge them first with questions and then listen to their questions. Then, allow them the space for questioning themselves, questioning us, questioning the world, thinking about how different structural relations, how different cultural practices, how our everyday beliefs about ourselves and the world affect what we can or can't do or will and won't do in the world. We need to challenge each other—students and teachers together—to consider how we treat other people. I mean, for me, if it hadn't been for Frank Hearn, this wonderful teacher, who knows how long it would have taken me to find the courage to really step out in the world. To ask questions and to do something. It took a long time and I'm quite positive that if it hadn't been for Frank Hearn and also John Alt at Cortland, I may never have gone to graduate school. I probably wouldn't have gone into education the way I am.

WR: Yes, I think there are always significant teachers that have affected that. I think of Bill Pinar and Philip Wexler and Madeleine Grumet, who were my dissertation committee. But those people, in the way they approached their work and the way they taught in the classroom, encouraged and rewarded you for asking those kinds of questions rather than punishing you for asking those kinds of questions.

RM: Yes, those people, Philip especially, were important to me, too. Philip really encouraged me to ask my questions. When you say "those kinds of questions," what kinds of questions do you remember?

WR: I guess I can use a story or an anecdote. When those people would talk in class, a responsive chord was struck in me. It was like "Oh yeah, that's exactly what I've been thinking and I thought I was just odd or crazy. But other people think that way so it is not wrong. It's not bad—it's good."

RM: In fact, it is the key to making the world a better place. That sounds so corny I guess but . . .

WR: Yes, it does. But, it's true.

RM: Well, I guess there is no easy way of challenging injustices. No easy way of trying to live more ethically, since it means a willingness, as Michel Foucault says, to change our own thought and ways of living as well as the thought of our students. There is no way of trying to care about other people and care about ourselves and to care about the earth and the creatures on the earth without allowing the questions to circulate and to come forth. To make openings toward different ways of thinking.

WR: Yes, as Maxine Greene discusses, both teachers and students must learn to love the questions. It is the questions that disrupt the taken-for-granted views of the world.

RM: We talk about critical thinking and we talk about making critical responses, making new ways of thinking but those responses, those ways of thinking, those new methods, those breakthroughs always bring with them the potential for new questions. The questions are always there in the spaces. I think being critical or any critical perspective is basically formulated through the allowance of this circulation of questions about our relations to each other and to the world. For teachers who are committed to improving their lives and improving children's lives, thinking about the world must be about loving the questions. I think education has to be that. Maybe that is what education is. We think about education all too often in very narrow terms. In terms of schooling, but I think education needs to be considered as that broad process through which growth, human growth and social growth, are nurtured. Allowing for differences, different ways of living, different ways of thinking, and different possibilities for living well is a part of this. I'm saying that education has to be the process through which differences and questions can constantly circulate.

WR: I guess what I've discovered about the present time is how filled with contradictions it is.

RM: Yes.

WR: Just an example. We were talking about critical thinking and there is a whole literature about critical thinking. It is so ironic and crazy because people want students to think and so what has come out is a literature on critical thinking which tells you how to critically think. Which is not critical thinking. You understand? Here is step one, step two, step three.

RM: Bloom's taxonomy.

WR: Right. So they have missed the point. But there is, I think, in our society probably a small element (I don't know how big the element is) that realizes that it is important for students to think. But only in certain ways and not to ask certain questions. That is absurd. It certainly doesn't lead to an opening of possibilities. Here we are and we need students to think, so now we are going to tell them "how to," which doesn't produce thinking at all.

RM: Yes, it produces a limited, kind of categorical thinking.

WR: Right. So, it doesn't move us very far. I'm also concerned about the schools and I think our notion of critical thinking addresses this problem. We were talking about this last night. About Pinar's notion of the destruction of the self in students. The schools do a very good job of destroying students' self-concept and self-esteem. Students emerge from school not knowing who they are. I know we could get into a long discussion about whether there is a self or not, but maybe that is for another day and another book. But I think that the critical perspectives reflected in this book begin to address that problem. Students begin to know who they are and I think knowing who you are helps you have agency in the world and, of course, critical thinking helps you have a focused agency.

RM: Can you explain what you mean by agency?

WR: Yes, agency means that we can take action in the world. We can take action in a self-directed and responsible way. We can act in accordance with internalized norms and principles. But I'm afraid if the banking notion of education continues in the public schools and I see that is happening. Agency becomes difficult to promote. Again, another contradiction is just as teachers are feeling a little power and feeling that their voices should be heard, in fact moving toward some agency, we have a whole new onslaught of standards and accountability and national curriculum and all of those things which we talk about in the Practice of Freedom chapter. It is becoming harder and harder, I think, to do this kind of teaching. The kind of teaching in a caring, critical environment that circulates around questions. The circumstances are mediating against it. Our times are not good for this perspective, although I don't want to be totally pessimistic. Maybe the times make even more necessary the ability and courage to ask challenging questions and make ethical judgments. As Henry Giroux makes clear, we can't just dwell on this discourse of despair. I think that critical perspectives do give this language of possibility. That, indeed, there is hope. I mean I have to live with that hope, or there is no reason to do this.

RM: Well, I think the hope lies in recognizing that with every effort to articulate new possibilities in this world, there are always new questions to be asked even of those new possibilities. So, for me, it is a kind of indefinite, almost infinite, opening up upon possibilities simply because as human beings we have the capacity to make meaning in the world, and we do it because we use language, because we represent through symbolic systems, because we make culture. We have the capacity to ask questions. Questions pop to the surface all the time. Who knows where they come from; they come from nowhere. They come from the spaces between thought or the spaces between words or the spaces between statements. I think the hope really comes from the fact that we have the capacity to ask questions, which can be generated through our desire to live. Not to sound too corny, but it comes from our need to love and our need to be loved and our need to be cared about and to live well and to feel happy and to be joyous. No doubt, there is sadness in the world, and there are people who seem to feed on sadness and violence. But there is also an incredible power and creative force that comes out of this generation of possible ways of thinking. For me, being critical is about searching for joy. It's about searching for openings and being touched by them, really touched, deeply touched by concern for the world on the part of my students or on the part of my friends or on the part of whomever. It comes from being touched by something beautiful, as though watching a beautiful dance. I think being in the classroom with students is as moving to me personally as hearing a beautiful piece of music or watching a beautiful dance. The hope is in the joy for life teaching brings.

WR: Yes, looking back, I think this book is filled with hope.

RM: Oh, it is exactly about hope.

WR: And I just want to define what I mean by hope. That is that hope is not the kind of thing that comes and goes with the passing of time; that it is not just like, "Gee, I hope I will do well tomorrow." That is one kind of hope. But the kind of hope that this book is filled with is the kind that you live with every day. It is the simple avowal, as Max van Manen said, that I will not give up on you. I know that you can make a meaningful life for yourself and that is what I think I have to live with. That hope day-to-day and I care that students are filled with that kind of hope because it doesn't matter to me, to be honest with you, if the things that I would like to see in schools and in the world happen in my lifetime. It really doesn't matter—it would be nice—but I will work as hard as I can, nonetheless, to make those things happen. So, I think the critical perspective fills you with hope, fills you with the joy that you are talking about.

RM: Well, at least it opens the possibility of finding the joy.

WR: It is interesting that as we epilogue this book, that we are talking about hope. Because sometimes I think students can look at the critical perspective and say you are so. . . .

RM: Negative.

WR: Yes, negative but actually to be critical is not to be cynical. It is to be filled with hope.

RM: Well, I guess we understand students' discomfort. There are perspectives that seem to describe the world in a hopeless way, even critical perspectives. We could point to some that feel, really feel, more hopeless than others.

WR: Yes, it is necessary to even question any perspective for the limits it imposes on possibility.

RM: Yes, Foucault and other post-structuralist philosophers have taught us that there is nothing inherently liberating in any particular discourse or world view. At the same time that some critical perspectives have dampening effects, the intention and the motivation is for the world to be a more just, happy, beautiful place and for people to be able to live well. Everyone should be able to live well, not just a privileged few. The responsibility, then, is to try to find ways of defining what living well might mean. Not just in one total sort of monolithic way, but maybe in many ways. Maybe diversity is precisely about finding as many ways as possible to live well.

WR: I teach multiple critical perspectives because one perspective may speak to one person and one perspective may speak to another, but I'm willing to make students aware of many perspectives. It takes many perspectives to get to that point where people are not afraid to ask the important questions, their questions.

RM: Isn't it interesting that you and I were in graduate school together? You studying under Bill Pinar, who we could describe as having had a huge influence bringing phenomenology and autobiographical method to the study of education, and with Madeleine Grumet as well. Madeleine brought a more sharply defined feminist point of view. Then, me studying under Philip Wexler, who clearly is coming out of critical theory and influenced by post-structuralism and certainly introducing me to post-structuralism. Of course, if we are talking about who our teachers were, probably the biggest influence on me has been Jacques Daignault, one of the most important post-structuralist thinkers in education, at least in North America. And yet those are very different points of view—critical theory, post-structuralism, and phenomenology—as we try to show in this book. And here we are, having this conversation about what is important about education and what is important for us about being teachers and teaching teachers and about getting teachers to think about it. We are talking about coming out of very different theoretical views and yet sharing a conversation about the relationship among joy, education, and social life.

WR: But there is a shared vision.

RM: Exactly.

WR: I think it is a good way to end this book. To say those things. That if people coming out of various critical perspectives, who may begin from different questions, can sit and have a conversation about hope for the world, then, this demonstrates the possibilities of these multiple points of view. I like the idea of ending this book on the note of hope. I think that is just great.

RM: Yes, I think I want to say one last thing and that is about friendship. We haven't really mentioned this, but without friendship much of the work collected in this book would not be possible. And I am talking about friendship between the authors, between the editors, between all of us and our students, which creates a kind of loving, caring community. And that is what makes it possible to struggle around problems that are often painful.

WR: Friendship opens horizons of hope.

r e f e r e n c e s

Giroux, H. A. (1988). *Teachers as intellectuals: Toward a critical pedagogy of learning.* Granby, MA: Bergin & Garvey.

Greene, M. (1988). *The dialectic of freedom.* New York: Teachers College Press.

Lotringer, S. (Ed.). (1989). *Foucault live: Interviews 1966–1984.* (J. Johnston, Trans.). Columbia: Semiotext.

Ohmann, R. (1976). *English in America: A radical view of the profession.* New York: Oxford University Press.

Pinar, W. F. (1976). *Sanity, madness and the school.* Meerut, India: Sadhna Prakashan.

van Manen, M. (1985). Hope means commitment. *The History and Social Science Teacher,* 42–44.

294

(Acknowledgments Continued)

Christine E. Sleeter, "Resisting Racial Awareness: How Teachers Understand the Social Order from Their Racial, Gender, and Social Class Locations," *Educational Foundations,* Volume 6, Number 2, Spring 1992, pp.7–32. Reprinted with permission of Christine Sleeter and Caddo Gap Press, publisher of *Educational Foundations.*

Janet Miller, "Solitary Spaces: Women, Teaching and Curriculum." Reprinted with permission of the publisher from Delese Wear, ed., THE CENTER OF THE WEB: WOMEN AND SOLITUDE, Published by the State University of New York Press © 1993 State University of New York. All Rights reserved.

index

Social relations, patriarchal
mind-set on, 161–162
Social sciences, blurring of
genres, 5
Social studies, 153
attempts to reform, 276
civics-centered, 268
conservative criticism of,
279
cultural transmission
versus critical thinking
as to purpose of,
267–269
debates over, 266
impact of World War II
on, 274
issues-centered, 268–269
link between social
forces and, 270
new, 275–277
origins of, in the schools,
266–267
subject-centered, 268
Social studies knowledge
development of, 269–279
national tests of, 278
Sociobiology
defined, 241n
on social inequality, 241,
252
Solitude, 202–208
Spelman, E., 50, 54, 56,
58n, 59n
Spender, Dale, 153,
159–160, 163, 164
Sports, power and team,
156–157
Spring, Joel, 6, 149n, 189,
233, 237n, 238
Stalvey, Lois Marks, 261,
264n
Standardized test scores,
decline in, 230
Stanford University, 225
Stanley, William B., 266–
284, 282n, 283n, 284n
Stanworth, M., 160
State
critical theory on, 6
defined, 6n
Statuses, conflicts between,
51–52

Steindam, S., 160
Steinhart, R., 186
Stowe, Harriet Beecher,
174, 177
Strain, Charles, 34n
Structural exclusion,
marginality as,
153–160
Subject-centered social
studies, 268
Subjective
defined, 168n
in poststructural theory,
168
Sugg, R., Jr., 178, 179
Superstructure
defined, 66n
relationship between
base and, in Marxism,
66–71
Sutherland, Margaret, 155
Sykes, G., 87
Symbolic order, 12
Systematic inquiry, 126
defined, 126n

Taoism, 23
Tarule, J., 53
Taubman, Peter, 220n
Taylor, C., 117
Teacher(s)
educated woman as,
180–181
perspectives of, on social
inequality, 240–243
as researcher, 127–128
view of, in problem
solving infusion
project, 82, 83–86
voice of, 128–131
as white upwardly mobile
women, 251–260
woman as, 176–179
Teacher behaviors
grousing, 82, 88–90
shop talk, 82, 87–88
work sheet practice, 82,
87
Teacher education
conservative restoration
in, 229–231
excellence in, 232

and multicultural
education, 240–264
role of Margaret Haley
in, 184
Teacher-proofed materials,
development of, 230
Teacher-researcher
movement, effects of,
126
Teachers College at
Columbia, 225,
226–227
Teach for America, 184
Teenage pregnancy,
140–148, 143
and changing social
demographics, 144
costs of, for taxpayers,
142–143
dominant images of, 141
and emotional disability,
142–143
and the family, 147
and gender relations,
144–146
prediction of mothering
skills, 142
rhetoric of, 141
and sexual
irresponsibility,
141–142
Temperance movement,
analysis of, 143
Texts, 24, 30
defined, 24n
organization of
traditional foundation,
4–5
from traditional societies,
25
Textuality, 29
Theory, 5–6
Three-track curriculum
system, 189
Tobias, L. K., 155, 156
Tobias, Sheila, 153
Totalizing, 25
defined, 25n
Tozer, Steve, 225–227, 228,
236n, 237n
Trace, 29
defined, 29n

the contributors

///

Edward K. Berggren currently teaches comparative world civilization at DePaul University in Chicago, and is concerned about improving the status, pay, and benefits of part-time academic workers. When not teaching he is running, swimming, biking, writing poetry, or playing the flute.

Ann Berlak has been perplexed about pedagogy since she was in third grade. She teaches humanities, social science, and teacher education courses in San Francisco.

Alan A. Block is associate professor and chair of the Department of Education at the University of Wisconsin-Stout. He taught for seventeen years in the public schools in the suburbs of New York City, working in the last five of those years in alternative public education. He is the author of *Anonymous Toil: A Reevaluation of the American Radical Novel in the Twentieth Century,* and is currently completing a book on the ecological theory of reading.

Charles E. Bruckerhoff is assistant professor in the School of Education at the University of Connecticut. His research interests include curriculum theory, philosophy of education, and the effects of policy and organization on the classroom teacher. He is the author of *Classes: Faculty Life at Truman High* and articles on issues and problems of disadvantaged youth, curriculum restructuring, and professional development of teachers.

Elizabeth Ellsworth is associate professor in the Department of Curriculum and Instruction at the University of Wisconsin-Madison. She teaches courses on the intersections and collisions of media, cultural studies, and education. Her current research and writings focus on the values of cultural studies and postmodernism for educators, and the constructing of situated educational practices.

Jennifer M. Gore is senior lecturer in education at the University of Newcastle, New South Wales, Australia. She is the author of *The Struggle for Pedagogies: Critical and Feminist Discourses as Regimes of Truth* and coeditor (with Carmen Luke) of *Feminisms and Critical Pedagogy.* Her current research is an empirical investigation of the function of power in a range of pedagogical sites.

Jaime Geraldo A. Grinberg was born and educated in Argentina. He attended The Hebrew University of Jerusalem and the Facultad Latino Americana de Ciencias Sociales in Argentina. He is a doctoral candidate at Michigan State University, and assistant professor of curriculum and social foundations at Eastern

Michigan University, teaching courses in curriculum and educational policy. Currently he is exploring the connection and tensions between cultural capital, personal knowledge, and the history of institutions of teacher education. His interests also include democratic pedagogy, school knowledge, social change, and the role of the community in shaping the self. His most powerful commitments are to his two daughters, Hannah and Mihal, who inspire his passion for teaching. His wife, Katia Goldfarb, is also a source of constant intellectual challenge.

Nancy Lesko teaches in the Departments of Curriculum and Instruction and Women's Studies at Indiana University-Bloomington. She is currently working on historical sociology of science, theories of youth, and the politics of reigning conceptions for girls and youth of color.

Angéline Martel is professor of linguistics and head of the Culture and Societies Department at Teleuniversite, University of Quebec. Her research interests lie in such varied fields as minority-education rights, minority-majority relations, pedagogy, language, and gender issues. She has published numerous articles and books, including *Minority Education Rights for Official Language Minorities in Canada* (1992).

Rebecca A. Martusewicz has found great joy and hope as a teacher educator at Eastern Michigan University. She teaches courses in social foundations and curriculum theory. Her writing and research interests include the history of women in higher education, the social construction of identity within schools, and, most recently, the use of post-structural philosophies to think about the connections between autobiography, pedagogy, and curriculum.

Maureen McCormack teaches social foundations at Eastern Michigan University. Her research interests include self-identity, the politics of women educators, and teacher prejudice reduction. Log cabins, deep-water sailing, big sky cross-country skiing, gardens, passionate music, and conversations are a few of her personal interests.

Janet L. Miller is professor at National-Louis University. Since 1978, she has served as managing editor of *JCT: An Interdisciplinary Journal of Curriculum Studies*. She is the author of *Creating Spaces and Finding Voices: Teachers Collaborating for Empowerment* (1990), and articles focusing on feminist and curriculum theorizing, teacher research, and forms of educational collaboration.

Jack L. Nelson received his undergraduate degree from the University of Denver, his masters degree from California State University, Los Angeles, and his doctorate from the University of Southern California. He served on faculties of California State University, Los Angeles and the State University of New York, Buffalo before joining the faculty at Rutgers University in 1968. He also served as visiting scholar at Cambridge University, Curtin University in Australia, University of California, Berkeley, University of Colorado, University of Washington, and Stanford University. His publications include sixteen books, the most recent of which is *Critical Issues in Education* (1993), and over 150 book chapters and articles in journals.

Linda Peterat was born in Portage la Prairie, Manitoba. She has lived in Edmonton, Alberta; Fredericton, New Brunswick; Champaign, Illinois; and Vancouver, British Columbia, where she now resides. She holds a Ph.D. (curriculum studies) and a M.Ed. from the University of Alberta, Edmonton. She is currently associate professor in the Faculty of Education, University of British Columbia. Her research interests include global education, teacher education, and gender equity. Recent publications have appeared in the *Canadian Home Economics Journal* and *The Journal of Vocational Home Economics Education.*

William M. Reynolds is associate professor of curriculum studies in the Department of Curriculum and Instruction at Oklahoma State University. He is the author of *Reading Curriculum Theory* (1989) and coeditor (with William F. Pinar) of *Understanding Curriculum as Phenomenological and Deconstructed Text* (1992). He is also editor of *JCT: An Interdisciplinary Journal of Curriculum Studies* and editorial advisor to *The Journal of Curriculum Discourse and Dialogue.*

Christine E. Sleeter is professor of teacher education at the University of Wisconsin-Parkside. Her research interests include multicultural education, school ethnography, teacher education, and sociology of special education. She has published articles in *Teaching and Teacher Education, Harvard Educational Review, Teachers College Record,* and *Review of Educational Research.* She is co-author (with Carl Grant) of *After the Schoolbell Rings* (1986), *Making Choices for Multicultural Education* (1988), and *Turning On Learning* (1989), and she is the editor of *Empowerment Through Multicultural Education* (1991).

William B. Stanley is chair of the Department of Educational Development at the University of Delaware, and professor of social studies and curriculum theory. His research interests include foundations of social education, curriculum theory, and concept formation. His publications have appeared in numerous journals, including *The Journal of Experimental Psychology; The Quarterly Journal of Experimental Psychology; Educational Theory; Theory and Research in Social Education;* and *The Journal of Thought.* His other publications include *Research in the Social Studies 1976–1983,* which he edited, and *Education and Utopia: Social Reconstruction and Critical Pedagogy in the Postmodern Era* (1992).